Stats Means Business

Stats Means Business

Business

A guide to business statistics

John Buglear

ELSEVIER
BUTTERWORTH
HEINEMANN

AMSTERDAM • BOSTON • HEIDELBERG • LONDON • NEW YORK • OXFORD
PARIS • SAN DIEGO • SAN FRANCISCO • SINGAPORE • SYDNEY • TOKYO

Elsevier Butterworth-Heinemann
Linacre House, Jordan Hill, Oxford OX2 8DP
200 Wheeler Road, Burlington, MA 01803

First published 2001
Reprinted 2003 (three times)

Permissions may be sought directly from Elsevier's Science and
Technology Rights Department in Oxford, UK: phone: (+44) (0) 1865 843830;
fax: (+44) (0) 1865 853333; e-mail: permissions@el.sevier.co.uk . You may also
complete you request on-line via the Elsevier homepage
(http://www.elsevier.com), by selecting 'Customer Support' and then
'Obtaining Permissions'.

British Library Cataloguing in Publication Data
Buglear, John
    Stats means business: a guide to business statistics
    1. Commercial statistics
    I. Title
    519.5'02465

Library of Congress Cataloguing in Publication Data
Buglear, John.
    Stats means business: a guide to business statistics/John Buglear.
    p. cm.
    Includes bibliographical references and index.
    ISBN 0 7506 5364 7
    1. Commercial statistics.   2. Statistics.   I. Title.
    HF1017.B84 2001
    519.5–dc21   2001044094

ISBN 0 7506 5364 7

For information on all Butterworth-Heinemann publications
visit our website at www.bh.com

Composition by Genesis Typesetting, Rochester, Kent
Printed and bound in Great Britain

Contents

Preface

Stats Means Business is designed to provide an understanding of the subject of Statistics for students of Business. As the sub-title, *A Guide to Business Statistics* suggests, it is a guide to using Statistics rather than a specialist Statistics textbook.

This book offers an accessible insight into the use of a wide variety of statistical techniques that have important Business applications. These techniques are discussed and demonstrated using worked examples set in Business contexts.

Stats Means Business aims to encourage readers to use computer software to carry out statistical work. It provides guidance on the use of MINITAB™* and the statistical tools in EXCEL.

Answers to all review questions, including some fully worked solutions, are included. These are intended to help students monitor their own progress and make the book an effective basis for independent learning.

*MINITAB is a trademark of Minitab Inc. in the United States and other countries and is used herein with the owner's permission. www.minitab.com

Acknowledgements

I would like to thank Allison for her creative contributions and critical assessment, Tom and Max for their patience, and my colleague Jan Lincoln for her assistance. I would also like to thank Maggie Smith and her colleagues at Butterworth-Heinemann.

CHAPTER   1

Starting up

Chapter Objectives

This chapter will help you:

- To understand why the ability to deal with numbers is important.
- To see how this book can help you develop that ability.
- To prepare effectively to study Statistics.

In this chapter you will find:

- A discussion of the importance of numbers to the business world.
- A description of the approach and style used in this book.
- An introduction to key words.
- Guidance on basic numerical skills you will need to use.
- Advice on technological support.

1.1 Numbers in business

This book is about analysing numbers. But why should analysing numbers matter to someone studying business? How relevant can it be for someone planning to build a business career?

To understand this, and to appreciate why the study of numbers is built into your course, think about the world of business. It is a world of rapidly evolving organizations producing and selling a huge range of products and services in a fluctuating environment.

How do organizations cope with this degree of change? The answer, in some cases, is that they don't. Many prominent companies that dominated their sectors a generation ago no longer exist. They became history because they failed to respond to changing markets. Others survived and some small operations thrived, becoming market-leaders within the lifetimes of their founders.

Although luck and the good fortune of happening to be in the right marketplace with the right product may have played a part, to succeed in a changing environment an organization needs to recognize the changes and anticipate the consequences for its operations. How can it do that? By constantly studying its markets and monitoring its operations. This means counting and measuring key factors, in other words gathering numerical facts, or statistics.

In every organization there is a flow of numbers which are either deliberately collected or arise from the regular interactions with customers, suppliers and other significant organizations. These figures alone cannot tell the organization what is going on in the market or how it is performing. One of the responsibilities of management is to ensure that such figures are used, which means they have to be processed and analysed. The patterns that emerge from this analysis provide information that enables managers to understand the situation they face and base their decisions on that understanding.

The ability to analyse figures and interpret the results is therefore considered a key management skill. Look at recruitment advertisements for management posts and you will see that employers attach great importance to 'numerical skills' and 'problem solving'.

If you want to build a successful management career these are skills that you have to acquire sooner or later. Your course will provide you with the opportunity of developing them. Make the most of that opportunity and you will have a cutting-edge skill that will pay dividends for you in the future.

1.2 How this book is organized

This book will help you deal with the numerical parts of your course. How you use it depends on how you approach the study of numbers you are about to start. It can be a crutch to help you limp through what may seem like an unwelcome revisit to the sums of schooldays, although it is better to think of it as a springboard that will help you to accumulate a key investment for your future – the skill of numeracy.

This book cannot decide your attitude to studying numbers, but it can influence it. The attitude you take is something for you to develop, but whether this book is to be a crutch or a springboard for you, it is intended to be a guide which will provide support for the numerical work you will undertake throughout your course.

The first five chapters of the book (including this one) deal with topics that you are likely to meet during the first stage of your course. They deal largely with *descriptive* techniques, methods that will enable you to arrange or analyse data in a way that helps to *describe* the situation being studied.

Chapters 6 to 9 cover topics that you may meet at a later stage of your course. They deal with *inferential* techniques, methods that enable you to make *inferences* or draw conclusions about an issue in general based on the study of a comparatively modest amount of data.

The final chapter is designed to help you to tackle numerical aspects of the final-year project or dissertation you will probably be asked to write.

The book will introduce you to a variety of analytical techniques that together constitute a 'tool-kit' of methods that can be used to investigate situations and help solve problems. Like any other tool-kit, the key to using it properly is to know not only what each tool does, but to know how and when to use it. The book will help you develop this ability by illustrating the application of the methods described using business contexts.

Each technique will be explained and demonstrated. Any calculations will be explained in words before symbols are used to represent the process.

Being able to apply a technique, to produce the correct result from a calculation, is important, especially if you find 'learning by doing' useful, but it is by no means the end of the story. It is even more important to be able to interpret the results that the technique has enabled you to produce and to communicate the meaning of those results. In your future career you may be asked to apply techniques of analysis but you are much more likely to need to be able to explain results, perhaps to judge whether appropriate techniques have been used to produce them. The book therefore provides you with not only a description of each technique and an illustration of its use, but also a discussion of the types of results you could get, and what each of them would mean.

At the end of Chapters 1 to 9 there are review questions that you can use to confirm your understanding of the methods and ideas featured in the chapter. You will find answers, including some fully worked solutions to these questions in Appendix 2 on pages 338–358.

1.3 Taking the first steps

There are two key preliminary tasks that are worth investing a little time and effort on getting to grips with from the very beginning. The first is to understand a few key words which may be completely new to you, or whose meanings in the context of this subject are unfamiliar to you. The second is to review a set of basic arithmetical operations, which are involved in the use of some of the methods demonstrated further on in the book. Being clear about these basics from the start will mean you avoid unnecessary confusion later on.

You will find that the terms explained below are used many times in this book. They are the first words in a technical vocabulary that will become familiar to you as you proceed. As with other subjects you study or interests that you have outside college, there are specialist words and phrases to comprehend, but once you have grasped their meaning you will get used to using them as a matter of course.

1.3.1 The key words you need to know

- *Data* A plural noun (the singular form is *datum*) which means a set of known or given things, facts. Note that data can be numerical (e.g. age of people) or non-numerical (e.g. gender of people).

- *statistics* Without a capital letter, i.e. in its lower-case form, this means a set of numerical data or figures that have been collected systematically.

- *Statistics* With a capital letter this is a proper noun that means the set of methods and theories that can be used to arrange, analyse and interpret statistics.

- *A variable* A quantity that varies, the opposite of a constant. For example, the number of mobile phones sold per day in a shop is a variable, whereas the number of hours in a day is a constant. In the expressions that we will use to summarize methods a capital letter, usually X or Y, will be used to represent a variable.

- *Value* A specific amount that it is possible for a variable to be. For example, the number of mobile phones sold per day could be 25 or 43 or 51. These are all possible values of the variable 'number of phones sold'.

- *Observation* or *observed value*   A value of a variable that has actually occurred, i.e. been counted or measured. For example, if 38 phones are sold on a particular day that is an observation or observed value of the variable 'number of phones sold'.

  An observation is represented by the lower case of the letter used to represent the variable; for instance 'x' represents a single observed value of the variable 'X'. A small numerical suffix is added to distinguish particular observations in a set; x_1 would represent the first observed value, x_2 the second and so on.

- *Random*   This adjective refers to something that occurs in an unplanned way. A *random* variable is a variable whose observed values arise by chance. The number of new accounts a bank opens during a month is a variable that is random, whereas the number of days in a month is a variable that is not random, i.e. its observed values are pre-determined.

- *Distribution*   The pattern exhibited by the observed values of a variable when they are arranged in order of magnitude. A *theoretical* distribution is one that has been deduced, rather than compiled from observed values.

- *Population*   Generally this means the total number of persons residing in a defined area at a given time. In Statistics a *population* is the complete set of things we want to investigate. These may be human such as all the people who have visited a supermarket, or inanimate such as all the policies issued by an insurance company.

- *Sample*   A subset of the population, that is, a smaller number of items picked from the population. A *random sample* is a sample whose components have been chosen in a random way, that is, on the basis that any single item in the population has no more or less chance than any other to be included in the sample.

1.3.2 The basic numerical skills you need

Addition and subtraction ● ● ●

Addition, represented by the plus sign '+', is the process of putting two or more numbers together to make a sum or total. As long as the numbers being added together are positive, i.e. more than zero, the resulting total grows as more numbers are added.

Example 1.1

To withdraw money from a cash machine a customer must insert a card, key in a PIN number, specify the amount, and wait for the money to be issued. If these tasks take 10, 12, 7 and 8 seconds, what is the total time that will elapse between the time a customer arrives at the machine and the time their cash is ready?

You can get the answer by adding together the times taken for the four operations.

Total time = 10 + 12 + 7 + 8 = 37 seconds

Because Statistics often involves combining observations, the arithmetical process of addition is a process you will come across in the context of several techniques dealt with later in the book.

Although you are probably already familiar with addition, you may not have encountered the symbol called 'sigma', which is used in Statistics to represent it. Sigma is the capital letter S from the Greek alphabet, written as 'Σ'. It is the letter s because s is the first letter of the word 'sum'. It is a Greek letter because at the time that much of the theory that makes up the subject of Statistics as we know it today was developed, the so-called 'classical' languages of the ancient world were taught in schools and universities. The Greek language, with its specific alphabet, therefore provided the pioneers of Statistics, and other fledgling disciplines, with a ready source of distinctive symbols.

The symbol Σ (sigma) stands for 'the sum of' when it is used in Statistical expressions, for example,

$$\Sigma x$$ means 'the sum of a set of observed values of the variable X'.

Sometimes it is necessary to specify precisely which observed values of X are to be added together. To show this, the letter 'i' is used to count the observations, for example,

$$\sum_{i=1}^{4} x_i$$ means 'the sum of the first to the fourth observations of the variable X'

The expression '$i = 1$' below the sigma tells us to start the addition with the first observed value of x and the '4' above the sigma sign tells us to finish the addition with the fourth observed value.

Example 1.2

In the situation described in Example 1.1, we could show that the total time taken for a customer arriving at a cash machine to get their cash (which we could represent by 'T') is the sum of the time taken for the four tasks (represented by t_1, t_2, etc.) to be performed by using the expression:

$$T = \sum_{i=1}^{4} t_i = t_1 + t_2 + t_3 + t_4 = 10 + 12 + 7 + 8 = 37$$

If it is necessary to indicate that all of a set of observations should be added together and the exact number of observations is not known, we use the letter 'n' to represent the last observation in the set, so:

$$\sum_{i=1}^{n} X_i$$ means 'the sum of the first to the last observations of the variable X'

As you proceed with your study of the subject, you will find that the letter 'n' is used throughout Statistics to represent the number of observations in a set.

At first these types of symbol may appear strange to you, but it is worth learning to recognize and use them, they can become very useful shorthand forms which will save you space and time in future work.

Subtraction, represented by the minus sign '–', is the process of subtracting or 'taking away' one or more numbers from another. As long as the numbers being subtracted are positive, i.e. more than zero, the result reduces as more numbers are subtracted.

Example 1.3

The gross weekly pay of a shop worker is £200. If her stoppages are £28 tax, £9 National Insurance, and £12 pension contribution, what is her weekly take-home pay?

You can get the answer by subtracting the stoppages from the gross wage:

Take-home pay = £200 – £28 – £9 – £12 = £151

An alternative approach to this operation is to add the stoppages first and then subtract the total stoppages from the gross pay. This would be represented in the following way:

Take home pay = £200 – (£28 + £9 + £12) = £151

The round brackets dictate that the operation shown within them must be carried out first. They are used to indicate priority.

You may well find addition and subtraction fairly easy, but there are cases where they are not so straightforward; first, when negative numbers are involved, and second, when the operation involves numbers measured in awkward units, e.g. minutes and hours.

Addition and subtraction may give you some difficulty if negative numbers are involved. If a negative number is added to a total, it reduces the total.

Example 1.4

A customer visits a store and buys 4 CDs that cost £13, £16, £8, and £11. He also claims a £5 discount for using a promotional voucher. What is the total amount that he should be charged?

The answer can be shown as:

Total amount = £13 + £16 + £8 + £11 + (−£5) = £43

You can see that round brackets have been used, both to highlight the fact that there is a negative number in the sequence and to indicate that it must be dealt with first. This means deciding how to tackle the apparently contradictory '+ −' sequence of symbols. In fact the minus sign overrides the plus sign, so adding a negative number is therefore the same as subtracting a number. The arithmetical expression used to find the total amount in Example 1.4 has exactly the same result as the following expression, which combines addition and subtraction:

Total amount = £13 + £16 + £8 + £11 − £5 = £43

But what do you do if you have to subtract a negative number? In fact subtracting a negative number produces the same result as adding a positive number.

Example 1.5

The sharp-eyed manager of the store in Example 1.4 spots that the voucher is out of date. What effect will this have on the total amount the customer should be charged?

The discount would have to be subtracted from the previous total, so now:

Total amount = £43 − (−£5) = £48

You get exactly the same result if you simply add the amount concerned, £5.

You may find it helpful to imagine the two minus signs 'cancelling each other out' to leave you with an addition. Alternatively it may help to think that taking away a negative is always positive.

Addition and subtraction involving time is something many people find difficult because time is measured in hours made up of 60 minutes, and minutes made up of 60 seconds, rather than nice, neat numerical parcels of ten. The use of the 24-hour clock on top of all this seems to faze many people completely.

Example 1.6

A business traveller drives for 12 minutes to reach her local railway station where she boards a train that takes 33 minutes to reach the London terminus. It takes her 24 minutes by tube to reach another London terminus, where she boards another train. After a journey that takes 1 hour 5 minutes to reach her station, she takes a 10-minute taxi ride to her destination. What is the total journey time?

To get the answer we can express all the times mentioned, including the figure for the second train journey, in minutes.

Total journey time = 12 + 33 + 24 + 65 + 10 = 144

The answer may not be satisfactory in this form. To convert it into hours and minutes we need to find how many units of 60 minutes there are in 144 minutes. The answer is two, so the total journey time is 2 hours (120 of the total number of minutes) and 24 minutes (the number of minutes left over when 120 is subtracted from 144).

Example 1.7

If the traveller described in Example 1.6 begins her journey at 11am, what time will she arrive at her destination, and how would this time be expressed using the 24-hour clock?

To get the answer, work in hours first, then minutes:

Arrival time = 11 + 2 hours = 1 pm

+ 24 minutes = 1.24 pm

To express this using the 24-hour clock, add 12 to the number of hours, because the arrival time is after midday:

Arrival time = 1.24 + 12 = 13.24

But what if the traveller started her journey later than expected, at 11.45 am, what time would she arrive? This is a little more complicated because the departure time and total journey time are measured in both hours and minutes. To find the answer we can start by adding the hours:

$$11 + 2 = 13$$

Then add the minutes together:

$$45 + 24 = 69$$

Since this amount of minutes is longer than an hour, we have to express it in hours and minutes, and add the result to the sum of the hours:

$$69 \text{ minutes} = 1 \text{ hour and } 9 \text{ minutes}$$

$$13 + 1 = 14 \text{ hours}$$

$$+ 9 \text{ minutes} = 14.09, \text{ or } 2.09 \text{ pm}$$

Multiplication and division • • •

Multiplication, or 'times-ing', represented either by the 'times' sign '×' or the asterisk '*', is the process of multiplying two or more numbers together. The result is called the *product*. If a number is multiplied by another number greater than one, the product will be greater than the original number.

Example 1.8

A property company receives an inquiry about a property from a US client. The rent is £2400 per month. If the exchange rate is $1.60 to the pound, what is the rent in US dollars?

You can get the answer by multiplying the total number of pounds by the exchange rate:

Rent in dollars = £2400 × 1.60 = $3840

In this case the number of dollars is greater than the number of pounds, the product represents a numerical increase. But if you multiply a number by another number that is less than one, you will get a product that is lower than your first number.

Example 1.9

A business traveller returning from Oslo has 3200 Norwegian krone that she wishes to change into pounds. If the rate available at a bureau de change is £0.08 per krone, how many pounds will she get for her krone?

To get the answer, multiply the total number of krone by the exchange rate:

Pounds she can buy = Kr3200 × 0.08 = £256

If you have to multiply a positive number by a negative number, the product will be negative. However if you multiply two negative numbers together, the product will be positive:

$$3 \times (-2) = -6 \quad \text{but} \quad (-3) \times (-2) = 6$$

Division, or finding how many times one amount 'goes into' another, is the process of dividing one number by another. It is represented either by the forward slash '/' or the sign '÷'. If you divide a number by another number that is greater than one, the result will be smaller than the original number.

Example 1.10

Eight residents sharing a house receive a gas bill for £361. If they agree to share the cost equally, how much will each resident need to contribute?

We can obtain the answer by dividing the amount of the bill by the number of residents.

Contribution from each resident = £361/8 = £45.125

Something to note in Example 1.10 is that although we can get a very precise result, in this case specified to three places of numbers after the decimal point, in the situation described the figure would be rounded up to the nearest whole number of pence, £45.13.

If you divide a number by another number that is less than one, the result will be larger than the original number.

Example 1.11

A visitor to Britain sees a sign saying 'City Centre 7 miles'. She asks you how far that is in kilometres.

A kilometre is equivalent to 0.6214 of a mile, so to reply to her question you need to find how many times 0.6214 will 'go' into 7, that is you must divide 7 by 0.6214:

Kilometres to the city centre = 7/0.6214 = 11.2649

Squaring and square rooting • • •

Squaring, or taking the square of a number, is the process of multiplying a number by itself. The process is represented by the number with a superscript showing the number two, for example the square of three, or three squared would be written 3^2, which tells us to multiply three by three.

If the number you want to square is more than one, the result will be larger than the number itself, for instance the square of three is nine. However, if the number you want to square is less than one, the result will be smaller than the number itself, for example the square of a half is a quarter.

Example 1.12

The floor covering of the dance space in a live music venue has to be replaced. If the dance floor is 4.2 metres long by 4.2 metres wide, how much new floor covering will be needed?

To find an area multiply the length by the width. In this case because the area is a square, that is, the length and width are the same, we need only take the square of 4.2:

Floor area = 4.2^2 = 17.64 square metres

Squaring a positive number will always give you a positive result. But because multiplying one negative number by another always gives you a positive product, squaring a negative number will always give you a positive result as well.

So: $3^2 = 9$ and $(-3)^2 = 9$

The fact that we always get a positive result when we square a negative number is worth remembering because it plays a vital role in several statistical techniques that you will meet.

Square rooting, or taking the square root of a number, is the process of working out what number squared would produce a particular number. It is represented by the radical or 'tick' sign, $\sqrt{\ }$, so the square root of 9 would be shown as $\sqrt{9}$. The result of $\sqrt{9}$ is 3 because the number 3 multiplied by itself gives you 9. You should bear in mind that the result of $\sqrt{9}$ could be –3, as the square of –3 is also 9. You will find that in most business contexts the positive root is the important one.

Example 1.13

A new ornamental garden featuring a square lawn area is to be laid out at a corporate headquarters complex. If there are 170 square metres of turf available, what will the dimensions of the lawn be?

You can find the answer by taking the square root of 170:

Lawn length/width $= \sqrt{170} = 13.0384$

The lawn would be approximately 13 metres long by 13 metres wide.

A note about precedence

Often you will find that the arithmetical operations we have looked at so far are combined. An expression may, for instance, involve addition, multiplication and squaring. If this is the case it is important that you conduct the operations in a specific order, with some operations preceding others. This order of precedence can be summarized as:

- First carry out any operations in brackets
- Then do any squaring and square rooting
- Then multiplication and division
- Finally, addition and subtraction

Example 1.14

A contractor wants to put in an estimate for laying a lawn area 13 metres by 13 metres at the corporate headquarters in Example 1.13. The cost of turf is £4.20 per square metre. He estimates the job will take 2 days. Labour costs will be £100 per day and equipment hire will cost £60 per day. He adds a margin of 15% to the total cost to cover overheads and profit. Work out his estimate.

The total cost is $\quad 13^2 \times 4.20 + 2 \times 100 + 2 \times 60$

Applying the margin $\quad 1.15 \times (13^2 \times 4.20 + 2 \times 100 + 2 \times 60)$

Start inside the brackets, squaring:

$\quad$ Estimate $= 1.15 \times (169 \times 4.20 + 2 \times 100 + 2 \times 60)$

Then multiplying:

$\quad$ Estimate $= 1.15 \times (709.80 + 200 + 120)$

Then adding:

$\quad$ Estimate $= 1.15 \times (1029.80)$

Finally the multiplication outside the brackets:

$\quad$ Estimate $= £1184.27$

Fractions, proportions and percentages ● ● ●

Fractions, proportions and percentages sound very different, but they are only different ways of doing the same thing: expressing a part of something in relation to the whole. If, for example, printing costs amount to £0.50 out of the total cost of a £2.50 magazine, this could be explained as either:

$\qquad$ printing costs constitute one-fifth of the total cost

Or $\quad$ printing costs constitute 0.2 of the total cost

Or $\quad$ printing costs constitute 20 per cent of the total cost.

One-fifth is the fraction, 0.2 is the proportion, and 20 per cent is the percentage. They are different ways of saying the same thing because there are five fifths in one, five lots of 0.2 in one, and five lots of 20 per cent in 100 per cent. You should bear in mind that each of them is a number less than one, including the percentage, which doesn't look as if it is less than one.

It is easier to use percentages if you understand that the literal meaning of 'per cent' is per hundred. (The word 'cent' originally meant one hundred; a Roman centurion was an officer in the

Roman army in charge of one hundred men.) This will help especially when you have to perform arithmetical operations using percentages.

Example 1.15

A car dealer promises a new member of the sales team commission of 5 per cent of the profits made on the cars she sells. If the profit margin on the cars sold is 40 per cent and the new member of the team sells cars to the value of £37 000 in her first month, how much commission will she receive?

The dealer receives a profit of 40% of £37 000, and the new saleswoman should receive 5 per cent of the 40 per cent of £37 000, so:

$$\text{Commission} = 5/100 \times 40/100 \times £37\,000 = £740$$

Note that the percentages appear in the expression as amounts per hundred.

Rounding and approximation ● ● ●

You may find it easy to manipulate figures in your head, or you may find such a skill impossible and marvel at those who possess it. The truth is that anyone can learn how to carry out mental arithmetic, the tricks are to round the numbers involved so that they are easier to deal with, and to use approximation to get a ballpark result which can be refined with a little more effort.

People who find it easy to work out numerical problems in their head often use rounding and approximation intuitively, that is without thinking about it. In fact you may already round certain numbers as a matter of course. If someone asks how old you are, you would say '18' or '21' as appropriate, you wouldn't say '18 years, 3 months and 10 days' or '21.63 years'. Automatically you round down to the nearest completed year of your age. If you want to check how much money you have you probably look at the notes and large denomination coins in your purse or pocket and make an approximation. Only if you are particularly concerned about how much there is, or have time on your hands, are you likely to count every penny.

Rounding and approximation are therefore not entirely new concepts to you. If you can apply them systematically in your numerical work you will develop a skill which will give you a better 'feel' for numbers, enable you to spot mistakes and think numerically 'on your feet'.

Example 1.16

You walk into a fast food restaurant which is so empty that there is a member of staff waiting to take your order. You know what you want but you don't know how much it will cost. As you give your order your eyes take in the prices of the items you want: one burger £1.49, another burger £1.69, one portion of fries £0.89, one cold drink £0.79, one hot drink £0.59. You want to work out roughly how much it will be so you can decide whether to count up your change or get out a note.

If you want a really quick answer, round up each item to the nearest pound:

Approximate total cost = £2 + £2 + £1 + £1 + £1 = £7

Because we have rounded every figure up, this result will be an overestimate, so we can be certain that the total cost will be no more than this, but it is a rather crude estimate.

You could get a more accurate approximation if you rounded each figure to the nearest ten pence:

Approximate total cost = £1.50 + £1.70 + £0.90 + £0.80 + £0.60 = £5.50

Each of the five figures used here is rounded up by one penny, so you can get the exact total by taking five pence away from £5.50, which comes to £5.45.

Significant figures and decimal places • • •

Generally rounding is used to produce informative figures when complete accuracy is unnecessary. The convention is that figures under 5 are rounded down and figures of 5 and over are rounded up. The extent of rounding is described as the number of *significant figures*.

Example 1.17

A record company sold 367 527 copies of an album. Round this figure so that it is expressed to:

(a) five significant figures

(b) four significant figures

(c) three significant figures

(a) 367 530   the 7 is rounded up, so 27 becomes 30

(b) 367 500   the 3 is rounded down, so 530 becomes 500

(c) 368 000   the 5 is rounded up, so 7500 becomes 8000

If rounding is applied to numbers with figures after the decimal point, the degree of rounding is described as the number of *decimal places*.

Example 1.18

A bank pays interest of 4.1358 per cent on savings accounts. Express this figure to:

(a) three decimal places

(b) two decimal places

(c) one decimal place

(a) 4.136 per cent

(b) 4.14 per cent

(c) 4.1 per cent

Note that in Example 1.18 zeros have not been written to the right of the last specific or *significant* figure, whereas zeros were included in the answers to Example 1.17. The reason is that in Example 1.17 the zeros preserve the magnitude of the figures.

1.4 Technological support

Although the subject of Statistics is about numbers, the amount of time you will spend actually performing calculations during your study of the subject can be minimized by using readily available technology, specifically a suitable calculator and appropriate computer software.

If you do not already have a calculator you really need to get one. It is an essential tool for the numerical aspects of your course, and probably some of the not so numerical parts of it as well. To be of use to you in statistical work the calculator you have must have a square root function, and it really is worth spending a little more money to get one with statistical functions. Sometimes such calculators are described as having a 'statistical mode' or an 'SD' (Standard Deviation) mode. Whatever it is called by the manufacturer, if you have a calculator that can perform statistical operations it will assist you immensely.

When you have your calculator the first thing that you should do is to make sure you don't lose the instructions. Your calculator is a sophisticated scientific instrument that can do much more for you than you might imagine, but you can only find out how if you have the instructions. As a safeguard it is a good idea to keep a photocopy of them in a safe place.

You will most likely have access to a computer, perhaps at home but almost certainly at your place of study. Because today computers are used so widely to send messages and to access Internet facilities, it is easy to forget that computers were originally developed as machines to process data.

The computers we have today still possess that capability. With the right software the machine you use should become an invaluable aid to you in carrying out statistical work. It will do most of the laborious calculations for you, leaving you free to concentrate on learning how to understand and interpret the results.

This reflects how you are likely to be involved in using Statistics later in your career; it is your perception and interpretation of results that will be important, rather than whether you can compete with a computer to do the calculations. Of course, it is important to be able to understand how the computer has arrived at the results, but let the machine do the hard work for you.

So, what is the right software? There are two types of software that can help you with statistical tasks: statistical packages and spreadsheet packages.

Statistical packages such as MINITAB (which has been used to produce the diagrams and results for this book), Splus, and SPSS offer a full range of statistical functions and can carry out just about all the techniques you are likely to meet during your studies. The authors of packages of this type are usually qualified in Statistics.

Spreadsheet packages such as Excel are intended primarily for accounting work and offer a more limited range of statistical functions, but nonetheless can perform the majority of methods you will probably need to use.

Although these two types of package offer different ranges of functions and different styles of output, they have become increasingly similar in some respects. The data storage layouts in statistical packages have become more like spreadsheets; numbers are usually stored in the rows and columns of a 'spreadsheet' in Excel, and in the rows and columns of a 'worksheet' in MINITAB. The statistical output generated by Spreadsheet packages looks more like that produced using a statistical package.

Example 1.19

What are the relevant commands to use in a Spreadsheet package and/or a statistical package to store the costs of the items listed in Example 1.16, and to produce the total cost of the order?

Using EXCEL:

- Enter the first value in cell A1 then press **Enter**.

- Enter the next value in cell A2, press **Enter**, and repeat until all the values are stored in Cells A1 to A5 and the cursor is resting in cell A6.

- Click on the **Autosum** button (labelled Σ) that is located among the toolbars at the top of the screen. The message '=SUM(A1:A5)' will appear in cell A6.

- Press the **Enter** key. The figure that now appears in cell A6 should be 5.45, the total cost of the items.

Using MINITAB:

- Enter the first value in row 1 of column 1 (C1) of the worksheet that occupies the lower half of the screen, and then press **Enter**.

- Enter the next value in row 2 of C1, press **Enter**, and repeat until all the values are stored in rows 1 to 5 of C1.

- Click on **Calc** (Calculations) in the menu at the top of the screen.

- Click on **Column Statistics** in the **Calc** pull-down menu.

- In the Command Window that appears select **Sum**, click on the box beside **Input variable**, type C1 in the box and click the **OK** button. A message telling you that the sum of C1 is 5.45 appears in the Session window that occupies the upper half of the screen.

If you have a choice, learn how to use the statistical package at your disposal. If you have time, learn to use both the statistical package and the statistical functions of the spreadsheet package. After all, in the course of your career the software you use will evolve and you will need to adapt to it, so why not get used to learning how to use a variety of software while you are studying?

If you have to choose between a spreadsheet and a statistical package, it may help to consider some of the pros and cons of each.

The advantages of a spreadsheet are:

- They are fairly straightforward to use.

- Basic calculations and diagrams can be produced quickly and easily.

- They are useful for more than statistical work, e.g. for accounting or manpower planning.

The disadvantages of a spreadsheet are:

- They can perform only a limited range of statistical tasks.

- The control you have over the composition of some output, particularly diagrams, is limited and tricky to manage.

The advantages of a statistical package are:

- They can carry out a comprehensive range of statistical operations.

- The methods they use and the output they produce are statistically meticulous.

The disadvantages of a statistical package are:

- They can be more difficult to learn to use.

- Transferring output into other software may not be straightforward.

Because computer software is continually being upgraded and improved the disadvantages are being reduced and the advantages extended so check the latest available versions before making your decision.

Whatever package you use for your statistical work, don't expect to know how to use all its functions straight away. It is worth investing some time in learning how to get the best out of the software you use.

Any package should have a help facility; use it to search for advice. It is really an on-line user manual available at your fingertips! You will find that what you regard as awesome when you begin will very soon become familiar.

Review questions

Answers to these questions, including fully worked solutions to those questions marked with an asterisk (*), are on pages 338–339.

1.1 Match the definitions listed below on the right to the words listed on the left.

(a) statistics	(i) something that occurs by chance
(b) Statistics	(ii) a subset of a population
(c) random	(iii) a complete set of things to study
(d) sample	(iv) a value of a variable that has occurred
(e) population	(v) a set of numerical data
(f) observation	(vi) the study of statistics

1.2 Match each of the symbols on the left to the definitions listed on the right.

(a) X	(i) the number of observed values
(b) Σ	(ii) the third in a set of observed values of the variable X
(c) x	(iii) a variable
(d) n	(iv) a single observed value of the variable X
(e) x_3	(v) the sum of

1.3 A till-roll from a cash register in a chemist's shop shows the following transactions:

Medicines	£4.85
Cosmetics	£2.65
Cosmetics	£8.54
Cosmetics	£7.20
Medicines	£2.36

If the variable X is defined as the money taken per transaction,

(a) Calculate $\sum_{i=1}^{n} x_i$, the total amount taken through the till.

(b) Calculate $\sum_{i=2}^{4} x_i$, and explain what the answer means.

1.4 You have to fly from London to Tashkent. The plane is due to depart at 21.30 and the airline insists that you check in two hours before take off. You estimate that it will take an hour and a half to drive to the airport and a further 20 minutes to make your way from the car park to the check-in desk.

(a) What time should you start your journey to the airport?
(b) The flight is scheduled to take 6 hours 45 minutes. Going through passport control and collecting your baggage should take an hour. If local time is five hours ahead of UK time, by what time should the person who is meeting you aim to be at the airport in Tashkent?

1.5 A motoring journalist is studying the technical specification of a new car not yet available in the UK. The fuel economy is expressed in continental European style; according to the document the vehicle uses 7.3 litres of fuel per 100 kilometres travelled. What is the fuel economy of the car in miles per gallon? (There are 4.546 litres in a gallon and 1.609 kilometres in a mile, both to three decimal places.)

1.6 The central feature of a new shopping centre is a square platform composed of one-metre square marble tiles.

(a) If the designer wants the platform to measure 14 metres by 14 metres, how many one-metre tiles will be required?
(b) If the budget is sufficient for only 175 of these tiles and the tiles cannot be cut, what are the dimensions of the largest square platform that can be assembled?

1.7* An electricity supplier charges domestic consumers a fixed quarterly fee of £8.50 for maintaining the supply and 6.08 pence for each unit of electricity consumed. The total amount is then taxed at 5 per cent. A household uses 829 units of electricity in a quarter, how much will it be charged, including tax?

1.8 A visitor to Britain from Bahrain wants to buy some articles of clothing in a department store in London. He selects a man's jumper costing £29.99, a lady's cardigan that costs £34.99, and a pair of men's shoes for £49.99. A large sign in the store says that visitors from abroad can buy goods 'VAT-free'. The prevailing rate of VAT is 17.5 per cent. How much will he be charged for these goods?

1.9 The promotional brochure produced by a Health Club informs us that '75 per cent of our members are under 30, and 60 per cent of our members who are under 30 are female'. If the Club has 900 members, how many of them are women under 30?

1.10* A single graduate is offered a job at a salary of £18 000 per annum. She would like to know how much pay she will receive per month after tax and National Insurance. She has obtained the following advice from her local tax office:

(a) A single person is entitled to a tax allowance of £4600. This must be subtracted from total pay to give the taxable pay.
(b) The first £4200 of taxable pay is taxed at 15 per cent.
(c) Any remaining taxable pay is taxed at 23 per cent.
(d) The National Insurance is 10 per cent of total pay, but is subtracted from the amount of pay after tax.

Work out how much her take-home will be per month.

1.11 A credit card company charges interest of 2.15 per cent per month on outstanding balances. A customer has no out-standing balance at the beginning of September. During September he spends £279 using his card and pays off £150 within the payment deadline. In October he spends £94 using his card.

(a) What is the amount he owes at the end of October?
(b) What is the minimum amount he will have to pay at the end of October if the company insists that 5 per cent of the balance must be cleared?

1.12* A UK businessman working in a former Soviet republic discovers that he can buy a new car from a local factory for 500 000 units of local currency, soom. The official exchange rate is 120 soom to one US dollar, but in the bazaars he can get 180 to the dollar. What is the cost of the car in pounds sterling if one dollar is worth 65 pence

(a) if he changes money at the official rate?
(b) if he changes money in a bazaar?

1.13 Ray Vonman wants to make 5 litres of punch for a party. The recipe he intends to use requires 3 parts vodka to 1 part vermouth to 1 part lime cordial to 3 parts orange juice to 2 parts lemonade. He already has; a half-full 75 cl bottle of vodka, a full 75 cl bottle of vermouth, a three-quarters full litre bottle of lime cordial, two unopened one-litre cartons of orange juice, and a half-full one-litre bottle of lemonade. What, if any, further supplies will he need to obtain?

1.14 A regulatory authority assesses the performance of railway operators on the proportion of trains that arrive late at their destinations. If more than one in twenty trains are late the operator receives a public warning. If more than one in five trains are late the operator is fined. The performance of the operators over the most recent review period is set out below:

Operator	Total train journeys	Number of late arrivals
Ingenue	8 497	521
Low Commotion	12 038	580
Midlands Trainline	4 277	862
Rock Island	10 355	512
Union Specific	15 273	928

Work out the percentage of each operator's trains that are late and identify those that will be warned and those that will be fined.

1.15 In one month consumers purchased 58 749 517 litres of bottled still mineral water. Of this total, sales of the three largest suppliers, in litres, were:

Vodder	6 602 362
Aquaria	5 191 584
Lake	4 051 948

(a) Specify the total sales and the sales of each of the suppliers to (i) four significant figures (ii) two significant figures
(b) Specify the market share of each of the suppliers to two decimal places.

'A picture is worth a thousand words . . .'

Presenting data

This chapter will help you:

- To recognize different types of data.
- To produce a variety of statistical diagrams.
- To interpret basic statistical diagrams.
- To know which diagrams are suitable for which types of data.

In this chapter you will find:

- A description of different data types.
- Diagrams to use for qualitative data.
- Diagrams to use for quantitative data.
- Diagrams to use for bivariate and time series analysis.
- Guidance on producing diagrams using computer software.

This chapter is about using diagrams and charts to present or display data. The pictorial techniques you will meet are widely used in business documents and being able to understand what they mean is an important skill.

When you apply these techniques you will be presenting data in visual forms that will reveal patterns and sequences. You will be taking the first steps in transforming data (sometimes people talk of data as 'meaningless') into *information*, which is something that *informs*. You will be bringing meaning to the apparently meaningless.

There are many different diagrams and charts that can be used to do this, so it is important to know when to use them. Deciding which type of diagram to use from such a wide selection is not always straightforward, but picking the right one depends on the type of data you have. In the same way that a fork is an invaluable tool if you are eating spaghetti, but completely useless for consuming soup, a particular statistical diagram may be appropriate for some types of data and entirely inappropriate for others.

2.1 Types of data

The word *data* means a set of known facts. There are different types of data because there are different ways in which facts are gathered. Some data may exist because specific things have characteristics that been categorized whereas other data may exist as a result of things being counted, or measured on some sort of scale.

Example 2.1

Holders of a certain type of credit card are described as 'wealthy'.

To verify this we could use socio-economic definitions of class to *categorize* each cardholder, or we could *count* the number of homes owned by each cardholder, or we could *measure* the income of each cardholder.

The first important distinction to make is between *qualitative* data and *quantitative* data. Qualitative data consists of categories or types of a characteristic or attribute. These categories form the basis of the analysis of qualitative data. In Example 2.1 the socio-economic definitions, social class A, B, C1 and so on, would be qualitative data, whereas the numbers of houses or amount of income would be quantitative data. Quantitative data is based on counting or measuring. The numerical scale used to produce the figures forms the basis of the analysis of quantitative data.

The second important distinction to make is between the two different types of quantitative data: *discrete* and *continuous*. Discrete data is quantitative data that can take only a limited number of values because it is produced by counting in distinct or 'discrete' steps, or measuring against a scale made up of distinct steps.

There are three types of discrete data that you may have to deal with,

1 Data that can only take certain values because other values simply cannot occur, for example the number of t-shirts sold by a clothing retailer in a day. There could be 12 sold one day and 7 on another, but selling 9.3 t-shirts in a day is not possible because there is no such thing as 0.3 of a t-shirt.

2 Data that take only certain values because those are the ones that have been established by long-standing custom and practice, for example public houses in the UK sell draught beer in whole and half pints. You could try asking for three-quarters of a pint, but the bar staff would no doubt insist that you purchase the smaller or larger quantity.

3 Data that only takes certain values because the people who have provided the data or the analysis have decided, for convenience, to round values that don't have to be discrete. This is what you are doing when you give your age to the last full year. Similarly, the temperatures given in weather reports are rounded to the nearest degree, and the distances on road signs are usually rounded to the nearest mile. Such data is discrete by convention rather than by definition. It is really *continuous* data.

Discrete data often but not always consists of whole number values. The number of visitors to a website will always be a whole number, but shoe sizes include half sizes. In other cases, like the sizes of women's clothing, only some whole numbers occur.

The important thing to remember about discrete data is that there are gaps between the values that can occur, that is why it is sometimes referred to as *discontinuous* data. In contrast, continuous data consists of numerical values that are not restricted to specific numbers. Such data is called continuous because there are no gaps between feasible values. This is because measuring on a continuous scale such as distance or temperature yields continuous data.

The precision of continuous data is limited only by how precisely the quantities are measured. For instance, we measure both the length of bus journeys and athletic performances using the scale of time. In the first case a clock or a wristwatch is sufficiently accurate, but in the second case we would use a stopwatch or an even more sophisticated timing device.

Further on you will find the terms *discrete variable* and *continuous variable*. A discrete variable has discrete values whereas a continuous variable has continuous values.

Example 2.2

A motor magazine provides descriptions of cars that contain the following data:

Type of car – hatchback/estate/MPV/off-road/performance;
Number of doors;
Fuel type – petrol/diesel;
CO_2 emission rate – grams per kilometre.

Which data will be qualitative and which will be quantitative?

The type of car and fuel type are qualitative; the number of doors and the CO_2 emission rate are quantitative.

Which quantitative data will be discrete and which will be continuous?

The number of doors is discrete; the CO_2 emission rate is continuous.

In most of your early statistical work you will probably be analysing data that consists of observed values of a single variable. However, you may need to analyse data that consists of observed values of two variables in order to find out if there is a connection between them. For instance, we might want to ascertain whether taxi fares are related to distance travelled.

In dealing with a single variable we apply *univariate* analysis, whereas in dealing with two variables we apply *bivariate* analysis. The prefixes uni- and bi- in these words convey the same meaning as they do in other words like unilateral and bilateral.

2.2 Displaying qualitative data

Arranging and displaying qualitative data is quite straightforward as long as the number of categories of the characteristic being studied is relatively small. Even if there are a large number of categories, the task can be made easier by merging categories.

The easiest way you can present a set of qualitative data is to *tabulate* it, to arrange it in the form of a summary table. As well as being a useful way of displaying qualitative data, compiling such a table is an essential preliminary task if you want to draw a diagram to portray the data.

A summary table consists of two parts, a list of categories of the characteristic, and the number of things that fall into each category, known as the *frequency* of the category.

Example 2.3

Suppose we want to find out how many retail outlets in a city sell trainers.

We might survey the streets or consult a telephone directory in order to compile a list of outlets, but the list itself may be too crude a form in which to present our results.

By listing the types of outlet and the number of each type of outlet we find we can construct a summary table:

The number of outlets selling trainers by type of outlet

Type of outlet	Frequency	Relative frequency (%)
Shoe shops	15	38.5
Sports shops	8	20.5
Department stores	6	15.4
Other	10	25.6
Total number of outlets	39	100.0

In Example 2.3 the outlet types are qualitative data. The 'Other' category, which might contain several different types of outlet, such as hypermarkets and market stalls, has been created in order to keep the summary table to manageable proportions.

Notice that for each category, the number of outlets as a percentage of the total, the *relative frequency* of the category, is listed on the right-hand side. This is to make it easier to communicate the contents; saying 38.5 per cent of the outlets were shoe shops is more effective than saying 15/39ths of them were shoe shops, although they are two different ways of saying the same thing.

You may want to use a summary table to present more than one attribute. Such a two-way tabulation is also known as a *contingency table* because it enables us to look for connections between the attributes, in other words to find out whether one attribute is *contingent* upon another.

Example 2.4

Four large retailers each operate their own loyalty scheme. Customers can apply for loyalty cards and receive points when they present them whilst making purchases. These points are accumulated and can subsequently be used to obtain gifts or discounts.

A survey of usage levels of loyalty cards provided the information in the following table:

Number of transactions by loyalty card use

	Transactions		
Retailer	With card	Without card	Total
Alimental	236	705	941
Brogues	294	439	733
Comestible	145	759	904
Dinewell	191	436	627
Total	866	2339	3205

Whilst summary tables are perfectly adequate means of presenting qualitative data, it is possible to show qualitative data in a visually more dramatic way using a diagram.

A diagram is usually a much more effective way of communicating data because it is easier for the eye to digest than a table. This will be important when you have to include data in a report or presentation because you want your audience to focus their attention on what you are saying. They can do that more easily if they don't have to work too hard to understand the form in which you have presented your data.

There are three types of diagram that you can use to show qualitative data: *pictographs*, *pie charts* and *bar charts*. They are listed here in order of increasing sophistication.

Pictographs

A pictograph is no more than a simple adjustment of a summary table. The categories of the attribute are listed as they are in a summary table, but we use symbols to represent the number of things in each category. The symbols used are thematically linked to the nature of the data.

Example 2.5

The table below shows the number of medals in different sporting categories that competitors from a particular country won in an international games event.

Number of medals won by type of sport

Type of sport	Medals won
Track and field	6
Swimming	3
Team games	2

Show this set of data in the form of a pictograph.

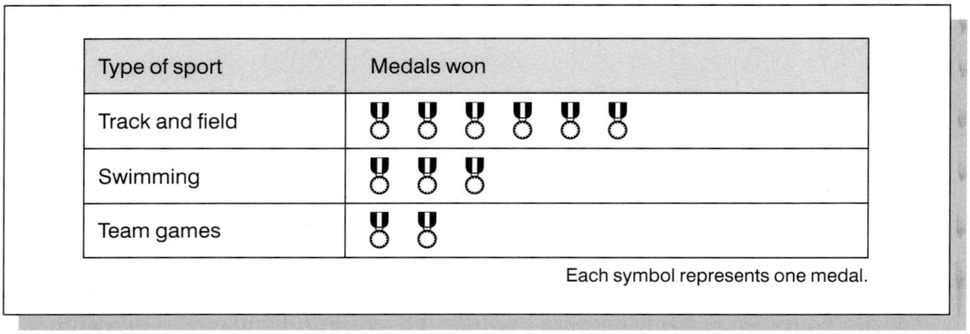

Type of sport	Medals won
Track and field	🏅 🏅 🏅 🏅 🏅 🏅
Swimming	🏅 🏅 🏅
Team games	🏅 🏅

Each symbol represents one medal.

Figure 2.1
Pictograph of the number of medals won by type of sport

A pictograph like Figure 2.1 can be an effective way of presenting a simple set of qualitative data. The symbols are a straightforward way of representing the number of things in each category and have the extra advantage of emphasizing the context of the data.

Unfortunately pictographs have several drawbacks that are likely to deter you from using them. Unless you are artistically gifted and can create appropriate images by hand, you will probably have to rely on computer software to produce them for you. Creating a pictograph by computer can be a laborious process. Spreadsheet and statistical packages cannot produce a pictograph for you directly from data, so symbols have to be grafted alongside text in a word-processing package.

You need to choose the symbol you use carefully. It should be easy to associate with the context of the data and not so elaborate that the symbols themselves become the centre of attention rather than the data they are supposed to represent.

You may occasionally spot a pictograph used in academic and business documents; you are more likely to see them used on television and in newspapers. Sadly, the computer graphics software at the disposal of reporters and editors is much more sophisticated than any that you are likely to have access to during your studies!

Pie charts ● ● ●

The second way of displaying qualitative data is much more commonly used than the pictograph, the pie chart.

A pie chart, like a pictograph is designed to show how many things belong to each category of an attribute. It does this by representing the entire set of data as a circle or 'pie' and dividing the circle into segments or 'slices'. Each segment represents a category, and the size of the segment reflects the number of things in the category.

Example 2.6

Present the data from Example 2.3 in the form of a pie chart.

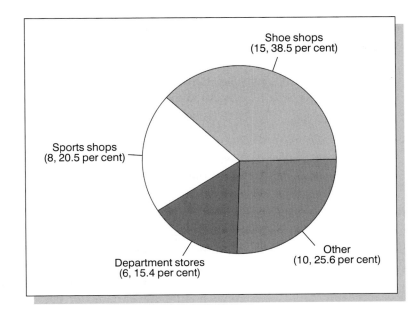

Figure 2.2
Number of outlets selling trainers by type of outlet

You can produce a pie chart like Figure 2.2 using MINITAB. Put the categories in one column of the worksheet and their frequencies in another. Select **Pie Chart** from the **Graph** menu.

When the **Pie Chart** command window appears, select **Chart table** and specify the columns in which the categories and frequencies are stored. Click the **OK** button and the graphic will appear.

Alternatively you could store the categories and frequencies in an EXCEL spreadsheet then select **Chart** from the **Insert** menu. In the sequence of windows called **Chart Wizard** that appears, choose **Pie** as the type of chart and the default sub-type.

Just about every spreadsheet or statistical package can produce a pie chart for you, either from the original data or from a summary table. They will probably offer you a number of ways of embellishing the pie chart: colour and shading patterns, three-dimensional effects, and exploded slices to emphasize a particular segment.

With practice you will be able to use these options in creating pie charts, but don't overdo it. Remember that the pattern of the data is what you want to convey not your ability to use every possible gimmick the software offers.

Pie charts are so widely used and understood that it is very tempting to regard them as an almost universal means of displaying qualitative data. In many cases they are appropriate and effective, but in some situations they are not.

Because the role of a pie chart is to show how different components make up a whole, using one when we cannot or do not want to show the whole is inappropriate. In Example 2.6 it may be tempting to present the chart without the 'Other' category, but if we left it out we would not be presenting the whole.

One reason that people find pie charts easy to grasp is that the analogy of cutting up a pie is quite an obvious one. As long as the pie chart looks like a pie it works. However, if we construct a pie chart that has too many categories it can look more like a bicycle wheel than a pie, and confuses rather than clarifies the situation. If you have a lot of categories to present, say more than ten, either merge some of the categories in order to reduce the number of segments in the pie chart or consider another way of presenting your data.

Bar charts

A third way of presenting qualitative data is to display it in the form of a bar chart. Like pie charts, bar charts are widely used, straightforward to interpret, and can be constructed using a spreadsheet or statistical package. However, because there are several different varieties of bar charts, they are more flexible tools. By using a bar chart we can portray a two- (or even three-) way tabulation in a single diagram.

The basic function of a bar chart is the same as the function of a pie chart, and for that matter a pictograph: to show the number or frequency of things in each of a succession of categories of an attribute. It does this by representing the frequencies as a series of bars. The height of each bar is in direct proportion to the frequency of the category: the taller the bar that represents a category, the more things there are in that category.

Example 2.7

Produce a bar chart to show the data from Example 2.3.

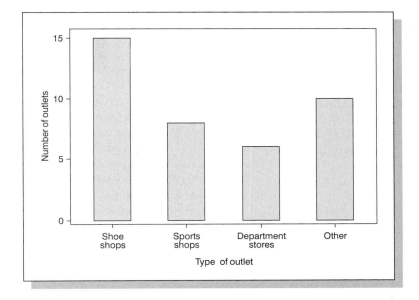

Figure 2.3
Number of outlets selling trainers by type of outlet

You can produce a bar chart like Figure 2.3 using EXCEL. Store the summary table in a spreadsheet, then select **Chart** from the **Insert** menu. In the **Chart Wizard** window, choose **Column** as the type of chart (or **Bar** if you prefer a chart with horizontal bars).

To use MINITAB to produce your bar chart, store the summary table in two columns in the worksheet then select **Chart** from the **Graph** menu. You will need to put the column location of the number of outlets in the **Y** (**Measurement**) box and the location of the types of outlets in the **X** (**Categories**) box then click on the **OK** button.

The type of bar chart shown in Figure 2.3 is called a *simple* bar chart because it represents only one attribute. If we had two attributes to display we might use a more sophisticated type of bar chart, either a *component* bar chart or a *stack* bar chart.

Example 2.8

Produce a component bar chart to portray the data from Example 2.4

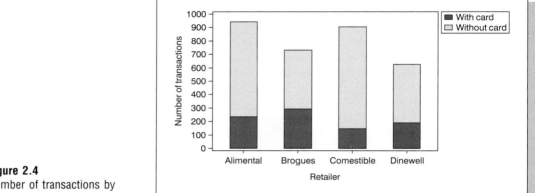

Figure 2.4
Number of transactions by
loyalty card use

You can produce a component bar chart using MINITAB by following the same procedure, as you would in order to produce a simple bar chart, but with some amendments. To begin with, put the data in three columns: one for the retailer, a second for the number of transactions, and a third for the card usage.

The worksheet might look like this:

Retailer	Number of transactions	Card usage
Alimental	236	Without card
Brogues	294	Without card
Comestible	145	Without card
Dinewell	191	Without card
Alimental	705	With card
Brogues	439	With card
Comestible	759	With card
Dinewell	436	With card

Because a retailer has *two* numbers associated with it, every retailer must appear *twice*. Because each card usage category has *four* numbers associated with it, card usage categories appear *four times*.

To obtain the bar chart, choose **Chart** from the **Graph** menu. Type the column location of the number of transactions in the **Y (measurement)** box and the column location of the retailers in the **X (category)** box. Click the ▼ button by **For each** and choose

Group. Put the column location of the card usage categories below **Group variables** then click the **Options** button. Select **Stack** in the **Options** window and specify the column where the card usage categories are stored in the box alongside **Stack**. Click the **OK** buttons on first the **Options** window then the **Chart** window.

To get this sort of diagram from EXCEL, put the retailer categories in one column of a spreadsheet, the number of transactions with cards in a second and the number of transaction without cards in a third. Select **Chart** from the **Insert** menu then **Column** from **Chart Wizard**. Pick the **Stacked Column** chart sub-type and specify the location of your data in the **Data range:** window that appears at the next stage in the **Chart Wizard** sequence.

This type of bar chart is known as a component bar chart because each bar is divided into parts or components. The alternative name for it, a stacked bar chart, reflects the process of stacking the components of each bar on top of one another.

A component bar chart is particularly useful if you want to emphasize the relative proportions of each category, in other words to show the balance within the categories of one attribute (in the case of Example 2.8 the retailer) between the categories of another attribute (card usage). If you want to emphasize the absolute differences between the categories of one attribute within the categories of another you may prefer to use an alternative form of bar chart that is designed to portray a two-way tabulation, the *cluster* bar chart.

Example 2.9

Produce a cluster bar chart to show the data from Example 2.4.

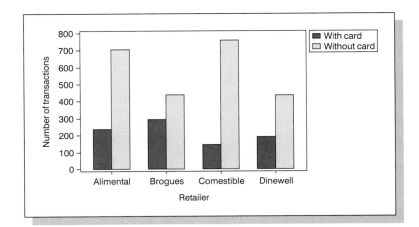

Figure 2.5
Number of transactions by loyalty card use

EXCEL will give you this type of bar chart if you put the summary table in a spreadsheet then select the **Clustered Column** chart sub-type from the **Chart Wizard** sequence.

To get the same sort of chart from MINITAB, follow the same procedure as you would for obtaining a component bar chart, but select **Cluster** instead of **Stack** in the **Options** window. Put the column location of the card usage categories in the box alongside **Cluster**.

This type of bar chart is called a cluster bar chart because it uses a group or cluster of bars to show the composition of each category of one characteristic by categories of a second characteristic. For instance in Figure 2.5 the bars for Alimental show how transactions in Alimental are composed of purchases made with and purchases made without loyalty cards.

2.3 Displaying quantitative data

The nature of quantitative data is different from qualitative data and therefore the methods used to present quantitative data are rather different. However, the most appropriate ways of presenting some types of quantitative data are the same ones used to present qualitative data.

This applies to the analysis of a discrete quantitative variable that has a very few feasible values. You simply treat the values as you would the categories of a characteristic. As a first step, tabulate the data to show how often each value occurs. When quantitative data is tabulated the resulting table is called a *frequency distribution* because it demonstrates how frequently each value in the distribution occurs. Once you have compiled the frequency distribution you can use it to construct a bar chart or pie chart.

Example 2.10

The 'Accommodation to Let' column in the classified advertisements pages of a local newspaper contains details of 20 houses available to rent. The number of bedrooms in these properties are:

2 3 5 2 4 2 4 4 4 3 2 5 3 2 3 4 4 3 2 4

These figures could be first tabulated and then presented in the form of a simple bar chart.

Number of bedrooms	Number of houses
2	6
3	5
4	7
5	2

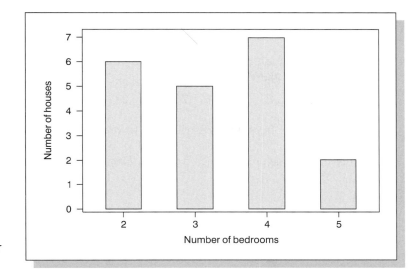

Figure 2.6
Number of houses by number
of bedrooms

You can produce this type of chart in EXCEL by selecting **Insert/Chart/Chart Wizard** and **Column** as the type of chart. Alternatively you could select **Graph/Chart** in MINITAB then specify the column location of the number of houses in the **Y (measurement)** box and the column location of the number of bedrooms in the **X (category)** box.

2.3.1 Grouped frequency distributions

We can present the data in Example 2.10 in the form of a bar chart or a pie chart purely because there are only a very limited number of values so a bar can represent each value. Unfortunately this is not always the case, even with discrete quantitative data.

For instance, if Example 2.10 included properties from small studio flats to huge mansions then the number of bedrooms might go from one to 20 or so. If you try to use a simple bar chart to represent such a wide range, the bar chart would contain far too many bars to be of much use in communicating the data.

To get around this problem we can *group* the data into fewer categories or *classes* by compiling a *grouped* frequency distribution, which shows the frequency of observations in each class. Once the data is arranged in this way we can use a relatively simple diagram to portray it.

Example 2.11

The numbers of e-mail messages sent by 22 office workers are:

50	14	25	8	10	33	52	12	45	15	7
5	98	13	31	52	6	75	17	22	12	64

Produce a grouped frequency distribution to present this set of data.

Number of messages sent	Frequency
0–19	11
20–39	4
40–59	4
60–79	2
80–99	1

In order to compile a grouped frequency distribution you will need to exercise a little judgement because there are many sets of classes that could be used for a specific set of data. To help you, there are three rules:

1 Don't use classes that overlap.

2 Don't leave gaps between classes.

3 The first class must begin low enough to include the lowest observation and the last class must finish high enough to include the highest observation.

In Example 2.11 it would be wrong to use the classes 0–20, 20–40, 40–60 and so on because values on the very edge of the classes like 20 and 40, which may very well occur, could be put into either one, or even both, of two classes. Although there are numerical gaps between the classes that have been used in Example 2.11, they are not real gaps because no feasible value could fall into them. The first class finishes on 19 and the second begins on 20, but since the number of messages sent is a discrete variable a value like 19.6, which would fall into the gap, simply will not occur. Since there are no observed values lower than zero or higher than 99, the third rule is satisfied.

We could sum up these rules by saying that anyone looking at a grouped frequency distribution should be in no doubt where each feasible value belongs. Every piece of data must have one and only one place for it to be. To avoid any ambiguity whatsoever, you may like to use the phrase 'and under' between the beginning and end of each class. The classes in Example 2.11 could be rewritten as:

0 and under 20
20 and under 40   and so on.

It is especially important to apply these rules when you are dealing with continuous quantitative data. Unless you decide to use 'and under' or a similar style of words, it is vital that the beginning and end of each class is specified to at least the same degree of precision as the data.

Example 2.12

Spot-checks of the amount of nail varnish in bottles labelled as containing 10 millilitres have produced the following figures (in millilitres):

10.30	10.05	10.06	9.82	10.09	9.85	9.98	9.97	10.28	10.01	9.92	10.03
10.17	9.95	10.23	9.92	10.05	10.11	10.02	10.06	10.21	10.04	10.12	9.99
10.19	9.89	10.05	10.11	10.00	9.92						

Arrange these figures in a grouped frequency distribution:

Nail varnish (ml)	Frequency
9.80–9.89	3
9.90–9.99	7
10.00–10.09	11
10.10–10.19	5
10.20–10.29	3
10.30–10.39	1

When you construct a grouped frequency distribution you will also need to decide how many classes to use and how wide they are. These are related issues: the fewer the number of classes, the wider each one needs to be. It is a question of balance. You should avoid having a very few very wide classes because they will only convey a crude impression of the distribution. On the other hand, if you have very many narrow classes you will be conveying too much detail. So, what is too few and what is too many? As a starting point, take the square root of the number of observations in the set of data. In Example 2.12 there are 30 observations. The square root of 30 is 5.48, which we round up to 6 or down to 5 because we can only have whole numbers of classes.

Once you have some idea of the number of classes, the width of the classes has to be decided. When you come to producing a diagram to represent a grouped frequency distribution you will find it helpful (but not essential) if all the classes have the same width.

The set of classes you use must cover all the observations from lowest to highest, so to help you decide the width of classes, subtract the lowest observation from the highest observation to give you the difference between the two, known as the *range* of values. Divide this by the number of classes you want to have and the result will be the minimum class width you must use. In Example 2.11 the range is 93 (98 minus 5) which, when divided by 5 gives 18.6. So if we want a set of five classes of equal width to cover the range from 5 to 98, each class must be at least 18.6 wide.

This number, 18.6, is not particularly 'neat', so to make our grouped frequency distribution easier to digest we can round it up. The most obvious number to take is 20, so 5 classes 20 units wide will be sufficient to cover the range. In fact because these classes will combine to cover a range of 100, whereas the range of our data is 93 we have some flexibility when it comes to deciding where the first class should start.

The first class must begin at or below the lowest observation in the set, in Example 2.11 this means it must start at 5 or below. Because 5 is a fairly 'neat' round number it would make a perfectly acceptable start for our first class, which would then be '5–24', the second class would be 25–44' and so on. But what if the first observed value was 3 or 7? Starting a set of classes with such a value would result in a grouped frequency distribution that would look rather ungainly. If we start the classes at a round number lower than the lowest value in the distribution, zero in Example 2.11, we can guarantee that the resulting set of classes will have 'neat' beginnings and ends.

2.3.2 Histograms

The best-known way of displaying a grouped frequency distribution is the *histogram*. This is a special type of bar chart where each bar or *block* represents the frequency of a class of values rather than the frequency of a single value.

Example 2.13

Construct a histogram to display the grouped frequency distribution in Example 2.11. See Figure 2.7.

You can use MINITAB to produce a histogram like Figure 2.7 by putting the raw data into one of the columns of the worksheet and selecting **Histogram** from the **Graph** menu. Specify the column location of the data in the command window that appears and click **OK**. Clicking on the **Options** button in the command window will allow you to choose how to arrange your

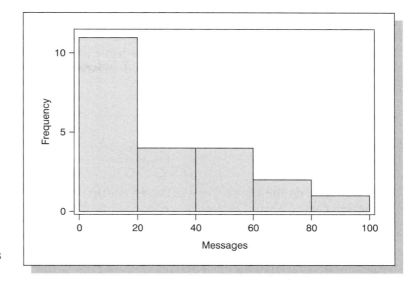

Figure 2.7
Histogram of e-mail messages
sent by 22 office workers

classes if you are not satisfied with the diagram the package produces for you.

To plot a histogram using EXCEL, put the data into a column of the spreadsheet and select **Data Analysis** from the **Tools** menu. (If you cannot find **Data Analysis** click **Add-Ins** in the **Tools** menu to check that it is available in your package.) Click on **Histogram** in the list of techniques that appears in the command window. Specify the location of the data in **Input Range** and click on **Chart Output** to obtain your diagram. If you are not satisfied with the classes the package has used you can alter them by putting your choice of classes in a column of the spreadsheet and putting the column location in the **Bin Ranges** box in the command window. The word 'bin' is used as a synonym for class because putting observations into classes is the same sort of thing as sorting objects into different bins.

Producing an effective histogram is often a matter of trial and error so experiment to try to find the balance which best enables you to present the data.

A histogram is a visual tool that displays the pattern or distribution of observed values of a variable. The larger the size of the block that represents a class, the greater the number of values that has occurred in that class. Because the connection between the size of the blocks and the frequencies of the classes is the key feature of the diagram the scale along the vertical or 'Y' axis must start at zero.

As long as the classes are of the same width it is simply the height of the block that reflects the frequency of observed values in the class. If the classes have different widths it is important to ensure that the areas of the blocks are proportional to the frequencies of the classes.

Example 2.14

The ages of savers opening accounts at a bank are given in the grouped frequency distribution below. Produce a histogram to depict this distribution.

Age range	Frequency
Under 15	0
15 to 24	5
25 to 44	22
45 to 64	19
Over 64	7

Here not only do the classes have different widths, but the first and last do not have a numerical beginning and end, they are 'open-ended'. Before we can plot a histogram we must 'close' them. For the first class this is straightforward, we can express it as '0 to 14'. The last class is problematic: if we knew the age of the oldest saver that could be the upper limit of the class, but as we don't we must select an arbitrary yet plausible class end. To reflect the style of other classes we could use '65 to 84'.

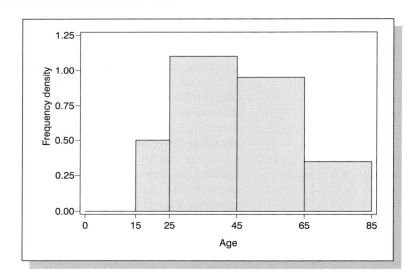

Figure 2.8
Histogram of ages savers opening accounts

To ensure that the areas of the histogram blocks are proportional to the class frequencies when the class widths are unequal, we must plot *frequency density* along the vertical axis. The frequency density of a class is its frequency divided by its width. The frequency of the '15 to 24' class in Example 2.14 is 5 and the width is 10, so its frequency density is 5/10, 0.5. The frequency density of the '25 to 44' class is 22/20, 1.1, and so on. In Figure 2.8 the effect of this is to increase the height of the block representing the '15 to 24' class, as it is narrower. The class is *half* the width of the classes to its right, so the height of the block is *doubled*.

The pattern of the distribution shown in Figure 2.8 is broadly balanced or *symmetrical*. There are two large blocks in the middle and smaller blocks to the left and right of the 'bulge'. From this we would conclude that the majority of observed values occur towards the middle of the age range, with only a few relatively young and old customers.

In contrast, if you look back at Figure 2.7, the histogram showing the numbers of e-mail messages sent, you will see an asymmetrical or *skewed* pattern. The block on the left-hand side is the largest and the size of the blocks gets smaller to the right of it. It could be more accurately described as *right* or *positively* skewed. From Figure 2.7 we would conclude that the majority of office workers send a relatively small number of e-mail messages and only a few office workers send a large number of e-mail messages.

2.3.3 Cumulative frequency graphs

Another method of presenting data arranged in a grouped frequency distribution is the cumulative frequency graph. This diagram portrays the way in which the data accumulates through the distribution from the first to the last class in the grouped frequency distribution. It uses the same horizontal axis as you would employ to produce a histogram to present the same data, but the vertical axis begins at zero and must go far enough to cover the total frequency of the distribution.

To plot a cumulative frequency graph you must begin by finding the cumulative frequency of each class in the grouped frequency distribution. The cumulative frequency of a class is the frequency of the class itself added to the cumulative, or combined frequency of all the preceding classes. The cumulative frequency of the first class is simply the frequency of the first class because it has no preceding classes. The cumulative frequency of the second class is the frequency of the second class added to the frequency of the first class. The cumulative frequency of the third class is the frequency of the third class added to the cumulative frequency of the second class, and so on.

Example 2.15

Find the cumulative frequencies of each class in the grouped frequency distribution in Example 2.11.

Number of messages sent	Frequency	Cumulative frequency
0–19	11	11
20–39	4	15
40–59	4	19
60–79	2	21
80–99	1	22

Notice that the cumulative frequency of the last class is 22, the total frequency of values in the distribution. This should always be the case. Once we have included the values in the final class in the cumulative total we should have included every value.

The cumulative frequency figures represent the number of values that have been accumulated by the end of a class. A cumulative frequency graph is a series of single points that represent the cumulative frequency of each class plotted above the end of the class. The final step is to connect the points with straight lines.

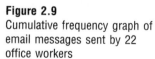

Example 2.16

Produce a cumulative frequency graph using the cumulative frequencies from Example 2.15.

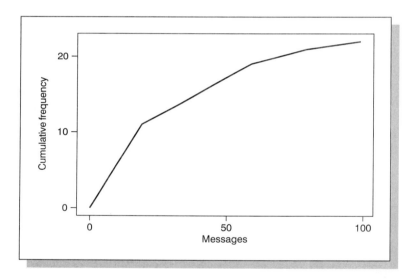

Figure 2.9
Cumulative frequency graph of email messages sent by 22 office workers

If you look carefully at Figure 2.9 you will see that the line begins at zero on the horizontal axis, which is the beginning of the first class, and zero on the vertical axis. This is a logical starting point. It signifies that no values have been accumulated before the beginning of the first class.

The line in Figure 2.9 climbs steeply at the beginning then flattens off. The steep climb represents the concentration of values in the first class, which contains half of the values in the distribution. The flatter sections to the right represent the very few values in the later classes.

Example 2.17

Plot a cumulative frequency graph for the data in Example 2.12.

Nail varnish (ml)	Frequency	Cumulative frequency
9.80–9.89	3	3
9.90–9.99	7	10
10.00–10.09	11	21
10.10–10.19	5	26
10.20–10.29	3	29
10.30–10.39	1	30

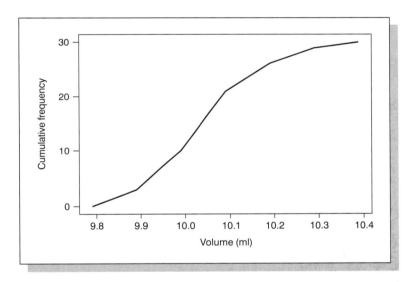

Figure 2.10
Cumulative frequency graph of contents of nail varnish bottles

The line in Figure 2.10 starts with a gentle slope then rises more steeply before finishing with a gentle slope. This signifies that the first classes contain few values, the middle classes contain many values, and the final classes contain few values. This is a symmetrical distribution, whereas the distribution depicted in Figure 2.9 is a skewed distribution.

It may be more convenient to plot a cumulative *relative* frequency graph, in which the points represent the proportions of the total number of values that occur in and prior to each class. Figure 2.11, based on the data in Example 2.18, illustrates this type of graph. It is particularly useful if the total number of values in the distribution is an awkward number or if you want to compare cumulative frequencies of two or more distributions.

Example 2.18

The size of cash payments made by 119 customers at a petrol station are summarized in the following grouped frequency distribution. Plot a cumulative relative frequency graph.

Payment (£)	Frequency	Relative frequency	Cumulative relative frequency
5.00–9.99	15	15/119 = 0.126	0.126
10.00–14.99	37	37/119 = 0.311	0.437
15.00–19.99	41	41/119 = 0.344	0.781
20.00–24.99	22	22/119 = 0.185	0.966
25.00–29.99	4	4/119 = 0.034	1.000

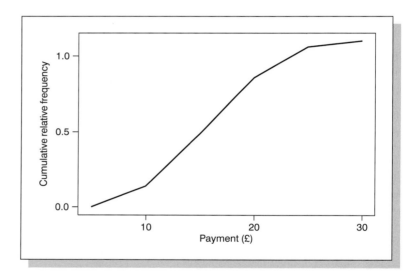

Figure 2.11
Cumulative relative frequency graph of cash payments at a petrol station

You will find further discussion of cumulative frequency graphs in the next chapter because they offer an easy way of finding the approximate values of medians, quartiles and other order statistics.

2.3.4 Stem and leaf displays

Histograms are effective and widely used diagrammatic means of presenting quantitative data. Until fairly recently they could be described as unrivalled. However, there is an alternative way of presenting quantitative data in visual form, the *stem and leaf display*. This is one of a number of newer techniques known collectively as *Exploratory Data Analysis (EDA)*. If you want to know more about the field of EDA, the books by Tukey (1977) and Velleman and Hoaglin (1981) provide a thorough introduction.

The role of a stem and leaf display is the same as the role of a histogram, namely to show the pattern of a distribution. But unlike a histogram a stem and leaf display is constructed using the data itself as building blocks, so as well as showing the pattern of a distribution it is also a list of the observations that make up that distribution. It is a very useful tool for making an initial investigation of a set of data as it portrays the shape of the distribution, identifies unusual observations and provides the basis for judging the suitability of different types of average.

The basis of a stem and leaf display is the structure of numbers, the fact that a number is made up of units, tens, hundreds and so on. For instance, the number 45 is composed of two digits, the 4 tens and the 5 units. Using the analogy of a plant, the stem of the number 45 is the number on the left-hand side, 4 (the number of tens) and the leaf is the number on the right-hand side, 5 (the number of units). A stem on a plant can have different leaves; in the same way the numerical stem 4 can have different numerical leaves. The number 48 has the same stem as the number 45, but a different leaf, 8.

To produce a stem and leaf display for a set of data we have to list the set of stem digits that appear in the data and then record each observation by putting its leaf digit alongside its stem digit. When we have done this for every observed value in the set of data the result is a series of 'stem lines' each of which consists of a stem digit and the leaf digits of all the observations sharing that particular stem. The final stage in the process is to arrange the leaf digits on each stem line in order of magnitude.

Example 2.19

The audience figures for the 26 programmes in a TV series (in millions) are:

4.0 3.8 4.2 2.9 2.5 3.5 2.6 3.6 5.0 3.5 4.9 2.9 3.3
4.8 1.0 3.2 5.1 2.4 3.7 4.2 3.5 3.8 3.6 2.3 3.9 2.1

Produce a stem and leaf display for this set of data.

Every number consists of two digits: millions and tenths of millions. The millions are the stem digits and the tenths of millions are the leaf digits. The lowest value is 1.0 and the highest is 5.1 so the first stem line will be for the stem digit 1, and the last one for the stem digit 5. The first stem line will have one leaf digit, the 0 from 1.0. The second stem line, for the stem digit 2, will have six leaf digits, the 9 from 2.9, the 5 from 2.5, and so on.

Stem	Leaves
1	0
2	9 5 6 9 4 3 1
3	8 5 6 5 3 2 7 5 8 6 9
4	0 2 9 8 2
5	0 1

This is a stem and leaf display, but it is not yet finished. We need to rearrange the leaf digits so they are listed from the smallest to the largest.

Stem	Leaves
1	0
2	1 3 4 5 6 9 9
3	2 3 4 5 5 6 6 7 8 8 9
4	0 2 2 8 9
5	0 1

Leaf unit = 0.1 million

The message 'leaf unit = 0.1 million' that has been added to the final version of the stem and leaf display in Example 2.19 has the same role as the scale on the horizontal or 'X' axis of a histogram, it specifies the order of magnitude of the data. Without the message you might look at the display, see that the highest value in the distribution has the stem digit 5 and the leaf digit 1, but the number could be 0.51, 5.1, 51, 510, 5100, or any other number that consists of a 5 followed by a 1. It is only when you know that the leaf digits are tenths of millions in this display that you can be sure the stem digit 5 and the leaf digit 1 represents the number 5.1 million.

You can produce a stem and leaf display using MINITAB. Select **Stem-and-Leaf** from the **Graph** menu and specify in the command window the column location of your data.

Although the stem and leaf display may look a little odd at first it is a tool that is well worth learning to use because of two clear advantages that it enjoys over a histogram: particular values can be highlighted and two distributions can be shown in one display. A histogram can't do the former because it consists of blocks rather than data. It is possible to plot a histogram showing two distributions but the result is cumbersome and you would do better to plot two separate histograms.

Example 2.20

The scheduled time of transmission of five of the programmes whose audiences are listed in Example 2.19 was changed at short notice. The sizes of the audiences for these five programmes are shown in bold type.

4.0   3.8   4.2   2.9   **2.5**   3.5   **2.6**   3.6   5.0   3.5   4.9   2.9   **3.3**
4.8   **1.0**   3.2   5.1   2.4   3.7   4.2   3.5   3.8   3.6   **2.3**   3.9   2.1

The same means of distinguishing the audiences of the programmes that were rescheduled can be incorporated into the stem and leaf display by putting the leaf digits representing the audiences of those programmes in bold type.

Stem	Leaves
1	**0**
2	1 **3** 4 **5 6** 9 9
3	2 **3** 4 5 5 6 6 7 8 8 9
4	0 2 2 8 9
5	0 1

Leaf unit = 0.1 million

You can see from the display in Example 2.20 that the rescheduled programmes tended to attract lower audiences.

To show two distributions in one stem and leaf display you simply list the leaf digits for one distribution to the left of the list of stem digits and the leaf digits for the other distribution to the right of the stem digits.

Example 2.21

The audiences (in millions) for the 26 programmes in the second series of the TV show in Example 2.19 are:

3.6 4.4 2.8 4.5 3.5 3.7 5.7 3.8 4.4 5.8 3.4 2.8 3.6
4.1 3.8 2.9 5.7 2.5 3.6 5.1 5.5 3.6 5.2 3.3 4.2 3.8

Produce a stem and leaf display to show this set of data and the data in Example 2.19.

First series	Stem	Second series
0	1	
9 9 6 5 4 3 1	2	5 8 8 9
9 8 8 7 6 6 5 5 4 3 2	3	3 4 5 6 6 6 6 7 8 8 8
9 8 2 2 0	4	1 2 4 4 5
1 0	5	1 2 5 7 7 8

Leaf unit = 0.1 million

By looking at the display in Example 2.21 you can see that the programmes in the second series appear to be attracting higher audiences than the programmes in the first series.

You can modify stem and leaf displays to reduce long rows of leaf digits by stretching the stems. It is like using smaller classes in a grouped frequency distribution.

Example 2.22

Produce a stem and leaf display for the audience figures for the second TV series in Example 2.21.

Stem	Leaves
2	5 8 8 9
3	3 4
3	5 6 6 6 6 7 8 8 8
4	1 2 4 4
4	5
5	1 2
5	5 7 7 8

Leaf unit = 0.1 million

In Example 2.22 the stem and leaf display contains two stem lines for each stem digit, except 2. The first stem line for a stem digit contains leaf units 0 to 4 inclusive. The second stem line contains leaf units 5 to 9 inclusive. There is only one stem line for stem digit 2 because the stem digit 2 has no leaf digits less than 5.

The data we have used so far to construct stem and leaf displays has consisted of two-digit numbers which makes it fairly easy, the left-hand digit is the stem and the right-hand digit is the leaf. But what if we are dealing with more complex figures? In the same way as we can experiment with different classes to produce a suitable histogram, we can try rounding, dividing stem lines, having longer stems or longer leaves to produce a suitable stem and leaf display. Just as we can have too many or too few classes in a histogram, we can have too many or too few stem lines in a stem and leaf display. We need to construct the display so that it is an effective way of presenting the data we have.

Example 2.23

The prices in £s of 16 different mountain bikes are:

| 448 | 423 | 284 | 377 | 502 | 459 | 278 | 268 |
| 374 | 344 | 256 | 228 | 380 | 286 | 219 | 352 |

Produce a stem and leaf display to show this set of data.

There are a number of ways to approach this task. You could try longer, two-digit stems and one-digit leaves, so 448 will have a stem of 44 and a leaf of 8. This implies that your list of stem lines will begin with 21 (the stem of 219, the lowest value) and end with 50 (the stem of 502, the highest value). You would end up with a very long list of stem lines (30) with only 16 leaf digits scattered among them.

Alternatively you might try one-digit stems and longer, two-digit leaves, so 448 will have a stem of 4 and a leaf of 48. This is much more promising.

Stem	Leaves
2	19 28 56 68 78 84 86
3	44 52 74 77 80
4	23 48 59
5	02

Leaf unit = £1.0

You can see by looking at the stem and leaf display in Example 2.23 that there are many cheaper but few expensive bikes. This is another example of a positively skewed distribution.

Although a stem and leaf display is essentially an alternative to a histogram, it can be used instead of a grouped frequency distribution as a way of sorting the data before plotting a histogram.

Example 2.24

Produce a histogram to portray the data in Example 2.23.

To do this we can use each stem line in the stem and leaf display as a class, which will be represented as a block in the histogram. The first stem line could be expressed as the class '200 and under 300' and so on.

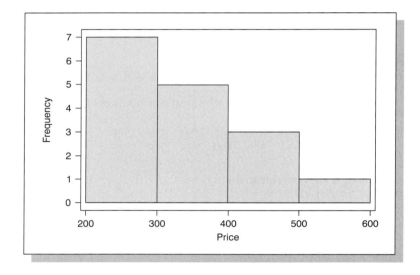

Figure 2.12
Histogram of prices of
mountain bikes

2.3.5 Presenting two variables

The techniques for presenting quantitative data that you have met so far in this chapter have one thing in common; they are all designed to portray the observed values of one variable. They are sometimes described as tools of *univariate analysis*.

But what if we want to present the observed values of two variables in one diagram in order to illustrate a connection (or maybe a lack of connection) between them? In that case we need to use another type of graph, the *scatter diagram*, which is a tool of *bivariate*, that is, two-variable, analysis. The word scatter is used because the intention of the diagram is to show how the observed values of one variable are distributed or *scattered* in relation to the observed values of another variable.

A set of bivariate data consists of two sets of observed values, a pair of values for each item or thing or person that has been studied. A scatter diagram is constructed by plotting a point for every pair of observed values in the set of data. The first value in the pair is plotted against one axis, the second value against the other axis. The result is a *scatter* of points that will form some pattern if there is a connection between the variables.

Typically when we plot a scatter diagram we do so because we have a specific theory about the possible connection between the two variables. We may believe that one variable depends in some way on the other variable. If this is the case we refer to one of the variables as the *dependent* variable whose values we think depend on the values of the other, which is called the *independent* variable. The dependent variable is known as the *Y* variable and its observed values are plotted against the Y, or vertical, axis. The independent variable is known as the *X* variable and its values are plotted against the X, or horizontal, axis.

Example 2.25

The midday temperature (in degrees Celsius) and the amount of barbecue fuel (in kg) sold at a convenience store on 13 days are:

Temperature (°C)	15	17	18	18	19	20	21	22	24	25	27	27	28
Fuel sold (kg)	10	15	25	20	45	50	40	85	130	135	170	195	180

Produce a scatter diagram to portray this set of data.

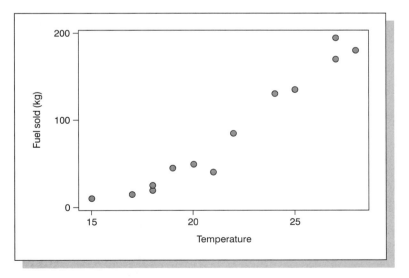

Figure 2.13
A scatter diagram of temperature and barbecue fuel sold

You can use MINITAB to produce a scatter diagram by selecting **Plot** from the **Graph** menu and then specifying the column locations of the observed values of the *Y* and *X* variables in the appropriate boxes in the command window. In EXCEL select

Chart from the Insert menu, XY(Scatter) from the Chart Wizard menu and specify the cell locations of your data.

In Figure 2.13 you can see 13 points in the diagram, one for each of the 13 days in the set of data. Each point represents both the temperature and the amount of barbecue fuel sold for a particular day. The position of the point along the vertical or Y axis tells you the sales level for the day and the position of the point along the horizontal or X axis tells you the temperature on that day. So, for instance, the point on the bottom-left of the diagram represents the day when the temperature was 15 degrees Celsius and the sales level was 10 kg.

The diagram shows us that there appears to be a clear connection between the temperature and the barbecue fuel sold. The sales level seems to be higher on days when the temperature is higher. This type of relationship, in which the values of one variable increase as the values of the other variable increase, is a *direct* relationship. A relationship in which the values of one variable decrease as the values of the other increase is an *inverse* relationship.

2.3.6 Presenting time series data

Sometimes we go about presenting two variables in a rather different way. This is when we need to present a *time series*, which is a set of bivariate data in which one of the variables is time. A time series is a set of data that consists of observations collected over a period, usually at regular intervals. Businesses of all kinds collect this sort of data as a matter of course, for instance weekly sales, monthly output, annual profit, so presenting time series data is important.

The type of graph used to portray time series data is a *time series plot*. It is similar in style to a scatter diagram in that each point represents a pair of observed values of two variables plotted against a pair of axes.

However, there are some key differences. In a time series plot the time variable is always plotted on the horizontal, or X, axis which represents the passage of time from left (the first observation) to right (the last observation). The points that represent the data are usually joined up to emphasize the flow of time, whereas in a scatter diagram they are never joined up. The scale of the vertical, or Y, axis should begin at zero so that the fluctuations over time are not over-emphasized, whereas the scales on the axes of a scatter diagram do not need to start at zero.

Example 2.26

The number of employees of a computer games company over nine years were:

Year	1992	1993	1994	1995	1996	1997	1998	1999	2000
Employees	7	15	38	112	149	371	371	508	422

Produce a time series chart to show this set of data.

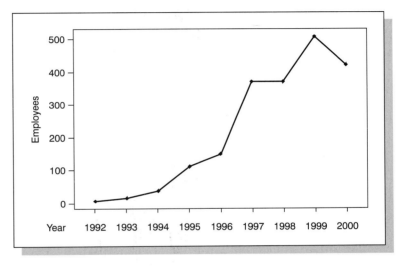

Figure 2.14
Employees of a computer games company

You can produce a time series chart by selecting **Time Series Plot** from the **Graph** menu in MINITAB and then specifying the column location of the time series in the command window. The time scale along the axis will be plotted for you, but you need to specify the intervals of time under **Time Scale** and then click **Options** and enter the first time period, for the data in Example 2.26 these are 'year' and '1992' respectively. In EXCEL you can obtain a simple plot by selecting **Chart** from the **Insert** menu then **Line** chart from the **Chart Wizard** sequence.

You can see from Figure 2.14 that in general this company has undergone a dramatic growth in its number of employees over this period. In other words there has been a strong upward *trend*, or basic movement. Plots of other time series might show a more fluctuating pattern, perhaps with *seasonal* variations, that is, a recurrent pattern within each year, or *cyclical* variations, that is, recurrent variations over periods of years.

Example 2.27

The sales (in £s) of cold and flu remedies in a pharmacy over two years were:

Year	Quarter			
	1	2	3	4
1	6375	2791	2964	8283
2	6941	2309	3128	8537

Produce a time series plot to show this set of data.

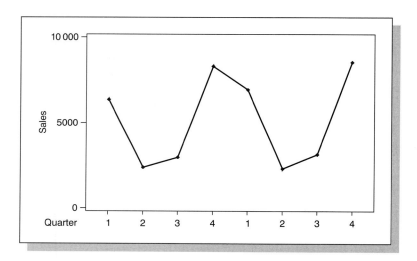

Figure 2.15
Sales of cold and flu remedies

You can tell by looking at Figure 2.15 that this pharmacy sells far more cold and flu remedies in the autumn and winter months (quarters 1 and 4) than it does in the spring and summer months (quarters 2 and 3), and that this pattern occurs in both years.

Review questions

Answers to these questions, including fully worked solutions to those questions marked with an asterisk (*), are on pages 339–341.

2.1 Which of the variables below are:

(i) Qualitative
(ii) Discrete quantitative
(iii) Continuous quantitative?

(a) Duration of telephone calls
(b) Mode of travel to work
(c) The alcohol content of beers
(d) Size of theatre audiences
(e) Place of birth of passport applicants
(f) Number of websites found in a search

2.2* A bus company operates services to and from the East, North, South, and West of a city. A recent report from the Chief Executive contains the following summary of their operations. All figures have been rounded to the nearest thousand.

> 'The total number of passenger journeys made on our services was 430 000. Of these, 124 000 were to and from the North, 63 000 to and from the South, and 78 000 to and from the East. Passengers used bus passes to pay for 158 000 of the total number of journeys: 43 000 on northern services, 51 000 on western services, and 35 000 on eastern services. Passengers who did not use a bus pass paid for their journeys in cash.

(a) Construct a two-way tabulation with rows for the city areas and columns for the method of payment. Work out the figures that are not quoted in the summary by using the information provided.

(b) Plot a component bar chart, with bars for each city area, to represent the data.

2.3 A machine vending company operates three hot drinks machines, one at a bus station, another at a train station, and the third at a leisure centre. The number of coffee, tea, and chocolate drinks dispensed from each in a single day is given in the following table.

Location of machine	Number of drinks		
	Coffee	Tea	Chocolate
Bus station	68	91	23
Train station	105	74	47
Leisure centre	49	67	89

(a) Plot a cluster bar chart to represent these figures.
(b) Plot a component bar chart to represent these figures.

2.4 The number of people in 35 passenger cars travelling along a road during the morning rush hour were:

```
1 1 2 1 2     1 3 5 1 1     2 1 1 1 4     1 2 1 1 1
4 1 2 1 1     4 1 1 2 3     2 3 1 4 1
```

(a) Compile a frequency distribution for this set of data.
(b) Construct a bar chart to represent your frequency distribution.

2.5 The ages of 28 applicants for a graduate management trainee post are:

```
21 23 21 21 23     21 24 22 21 24     21 26 23 22 21
22 23 21 22 21     22 25 21 22 21     22 21 24
```

(a) Produce a frequency distribution for these figures.
(b) Plot a bar chart to represent the frequency distribution.

2.6* The speeds (in miles per hour) of 24 vehicles travelling along a road that has a 30 mph speed limit were:

```
31   35   35   27   26   30   36   23   36   33   27   31
32   38   26   40   21   39   33   24   28   23   28   35
```

(a) Construct a grouped frequency distribution for this set of data.
(b) Plot a histogram to represent the data.

2.7 The number of a particular brand of PC sold during a week in each of the 37 outlets of a chain of computer dealers were:

```
 6   14   22   17   15   12   18   11   23   10   13   17   8
25   13    0   13   20   18   13   16   15    0   15   14
15    9    7   14   17   13    3   15    7   23   10   15
```

(a) Present this set of data in the form of a grouped frequency distribution.
(b) Plot a histogram of the distribution.

2.8 The rates of growth in revenue (%) of 25 leading companies over a year were:

```
4.22   3.85   10.23   5.11   7.91     4.60   8.16   5.28    3.98
2.51   9.95    6.98   6.06   9.24     3.29   9.75   0.11   11.38
1.41   4.05    1.93   5.16   1.99    12.41   7.73
```

(a) Compile a grouped frequency distribution for these figures.
(b) Construct a histogram to portray the distribution.

2.9 The rent per person (to the nearest £) for 83 flats and houses advertised on the notice boards at a university was recorded and the following grouped frequency distribution produced:

Rent per person (£)	Frequency
30–34	13
35–39	29
40–44	22
45–49	10
50–54	7
55–59	2

(a) Plot a histogram to display this distribution.
(b) Find the cumulative frequencies for each class.
(c) Plot a cumulative frequency graph of the distribution.

2.10 A video rental shop has 312 different feature films that are available for hire overnight. The number of times these videos were rented out during a month is presented in the following grouped frequency distribution:

Number of rentals	Number of videos
0–4	169
5–9	71
10–14	39
15–19	18
20–24	11
25–29	4

(a) Construct a histogram for this distribution.
(b) Calculate the cumulative relative frequency for each class.
(c) Plot a cumulative relative frequency graph of the distribution.

2.11 One branch of a bank has 849 customers who have credit balances in a certain type of current account. The sizes of the balances in these accounts (to the nearest pound) have been arranged in the following grouped frequency distribution:

Size of balance (£)	Number of accounts
0–249	88
250–499	153
500–749	202
750–999	174
1000–1499	160
1500–1999	72

(a) Plot a histogram to represent this distribution.
(b) Find the cumulative relative frequency for each class.
(c) Plot a cumulative relative frequency distribution of the distribution.

2.12   The monthly membership fees (in pounds) for 22 health clubs are:

34   **43**   44   **22**   73   69   48   67   33   56   67
27   78   60   63   **32**   67   41   65   **48**   48   77

(a) Compile a stem and leaf display of these data.
(b) The clubs whose fees appear in bold do not have a swimming pool. Highlight them in your display.

2.13 The monthly membership fees (in pounds) for 17 fitness centres in local authority leisure centres are:

28   50   44   32   31   55   21   36   24
55   51   55   32   39   42   28   55

(a) Compile a stem and leaf display to show these figures and the set of data in the previous question. List the leaf digits for this distribution to the left of the stem digits and the leaf digits for the data in question 2.12 to the right.
(b) Compare the two distributions.

2.14 The hourly wages (in pounds) of 32 jobs advertised by a 'temp' agency are:

6.26   4.90   4.52   5.11   5.94   5.82   7.14   7.28   5.15
7.04   4.47   4.67   6.90   5.85   5.65   5.50   4.12   5.27
5.25   6.43   5.65   4.65   5.37   4.24   6.45   4.70   5.09
4.82   6.23   5.40   6.22   5.26

(a) Compile a stem and leaf display to present these figures using the figures in pounds (4, 5, 6, 7) as stem digits and a single line for each stem digit.
(b) Modify your stem and leaf display so that there are two stem lines for each stem digit.

2.15 The prices (in pounds) of 27 second-hand 'supermini' cars on sale at a garage are:

4960   1720   2350   2770   3340   4240   4850   4390
3870   2990   3740   2230   1690   2750   1590   4990
3660   1900   4250   4390   3690   1760   4800   1730
2040   4070   2670

(a) Compile a stem and leaf display for these figures using thousands as stem digits.
(b) Modify your display by using two stem lines for each stem digit.
(c) Construct a histogram using classes based on the stem lines used in (b).

2.16* The levels of expenditure on domestic fuel (in $000 millions) and the populations (in millions) of 9 countries are:

Expenditure (£000m)	5.2	4.1	1.9	1.4	27.2	0.5	11.1	10.2	20.4
Population (m)	10.6	5.4	10.3	4.2	55.9	0.4	15.3	40.1	56.3

(a) Plot a scatter diagram to portray these figures.
(b) Describe the relationship between the two variables.

2.17 A catalogue shop sells ten brands of television sets with 14-inch screens. The prices of these (to the nearest pound), and the number of each sold are:

Price (£)	75	80	85	100	100	120	140	200	220
Number sold	48	31	39	28	24	17	11	6	2

(a) Plot a scatter diagram to represent these sets of data.
(b) Is the relationship between the two variables direct or inverse?

2.18 The sales of organic vegetables (in £000) by a fruit and vegetable wholesaler over 10 years were:

Year	1992	1993	1994	1995	1996	1997	1998	1999	2000	2001
Sales	0.0	0.0	1.2	1.7	3.2	5.1	10.4	12.2	26.9	47.1

Construct a time series plot to present this set of data.

2.19 The quarterly sales (in £000) of greeting cards in a supermarket were:

Year	Quarter			
	1	2	3	4
1	12.0	14.8	9.6	19.2
2	13.1	16.3	9.2	20.8

Produce a time series plot to show these figures.

2.20 Select which of the statements listed below on the right-hand side describe the words listed on the left-hand side.

(a) histogram   (i) can only take a limited number of values

(b) time series   (ii) segments or slices represent categories

(c) pictograph   (iii) each plotted point represents a pair of values

(d) discrete data   (iv) separates parts of each observation

(e) stem and leaf display   (v) each block represents a class

(f) scatter diagram   (vi) data collected at regular intervals over time

(g) pie chart   (vii) comprises a set of small pictures

Summarizing univariate data

Chapter Objectives

This chapter will help you:

- To understand why summarizing data is important.
- To distinguish location and spread.
- To produce various methods of summarizing data.
- To interpret the different ways of summarizing data.
- To know when to use the different ways of summarizing data.
- To appreciate the role of summary techniques in monitoring quality.

In this chapter you will find:

- A discussion of the different approaches to summarizing data.
- Measures of location.
- Measures of spread.
- Diagrams to display order statistics and quality performance.
- Guidance on using computer software to produce summary measures.

This chapter is about using figures known as *summary measures* to represent or *summarize* quantitative data. Because they are used to describe sets of data they are also called *descriptive measures*. The summary measures that you will come across are very effective and widely used methods of communicating the essence or gist of a set of observations in just one or two figures, particularly when it is important to compare two or more distributions. Knowing how to interpret them and when to use them will help you become a much more effective communicator and user of statistical information.

There are two basic ways of summarizing a set of data. The first is to use a figure to give some idea of what the values within a set of data are like. This is the idea of an average, something you are probably familiar with; you may have achieved an average mark, you may be of average build etc.

The word average suggests a 'middle' or 'typical' level. An average is a representative figure that summarizes a whole set of numbers in a single figure. There are two other names for averages that you will meet. The first is the phrase *measures of location*, used because averages tell us where the data is positioned or *located* on the numerical scale, so they measure the location of the data. The second is the phrase *measures of central tendency*, used because averages provide us with some idea of the *centre* or middle of a set of data.

The second basic way of summarizing a set of data is to measure how widely the figures are spread out or dispersed. Summary measures that do this are therefore known as *measures of spread* or *measures of dispersion*. They are single figures that tell us how broadly a set of observations is scattered.

These two types of summary measures, measures of location and measures of spread, are not alternatives; they are complementary to each other. That is, we don't use either a measure of location or a measure of spread to summarize a set of data. More often than not we use both a measure of location and a measure of spread to convey an overall impression of a set of data, in the same way that suspects in US police series on television might be described by both their height and their weight.

3.1 Measures of location

There are various averages, or measures of location, that you can use to summarize or describe a set of data. The simplest both to apply and to interpret is the mode.

3.1.1 The mode

The *mode*, or *modal value*, is the most frequently occurring value in a set of observations. You can find the mode of a set of data by simply inspecting the observations.

Example 3.1

The ages of the 15 staff working at a fast food restaurant are:

17 18 21 18 16 19 17 28 16 20 18 17 17 19 17

What is the mode?

The value 17 occurs more often (5 times) than any other value, so 17 is the mode.

If you want an average to represent a set of data that consists of a fairly small number of discrete values in which one value is clearly the most frequent, then the mode is a perfectly good way of describing the data. Looking at the data in Example 3.1 you can see that using the mode, and describing these workers as having an average age of 17, would give a useful impression of the data.

The mode is much less suitable if the data we want to summarize consists of a larger number of different values, especially if there is more than one value that occurs the same number of times.

Example 3.2

The ages of the 18 checkout operators working in a supermarket are:

39 17 44 22 39 45 40 37 31
33 39 28 32 32 31 31 37 42

What is the mode?

The values 31 and 39 each occur three times.

The data in Example 3.2 is *bimodal*; that is, it has two modes. If another person aged 32 joined the workforce there would be three modes. The more modes there are, the less useful the mode is to use. Ideally we want a single figure as a measure of location to represent a set of data.

If you want to summarize a set of continuous data, using the mode is going to be even more inappropriate; usually continuous data consists of different values so every value would be a mode because it occurs as often as every other value. If two or more observations take exactly the same value it is something of a fluke.

3.1.2 The median

Whereas you can only use the mode for some types of data, the second type of average or measure of location, the *median*, can be used for any set of data.

The median is the middle observation in a set of data. We find the median by first arranging the data in order of magnitude, that is, listed in order from the lowest to the highest values. Such a list is called an *array*. Each observation in an array may be represented by the letter '*x*' and the position of the observation in the array is put in round brackets, for instance $x_{(3)}$ would be the third observation in the array and $x_{(n)}$ would be the last.

Example 3.3

Find the median of the data in Example 3.1.

Array   16   16   17   17   17   17   17   **18**   18   18   19   19   20   21   28

Since there are 15 observations, the middle one is the 8th, the first 18, which is shown in bold type. There are seven observations to the left of it in the array, and seven observations to the right of it.

You can find the exact position of the median in an array by taking the number of observations, represented by the letter *n*, adding one and then dividing by two.

Median position $= (n + 1)/2$

In Example 3.3 there are 15 observations, that is, $n = 15$, so:

Median position $= (15 + 1)/2 = 16/2 = 8$

The median is in the 8th position in the array, in other words the 8th highest value, 18. The median age of these workers is 18.

Example 3.4

Find the median of the data in Example 3.2.

Array   17 22 28 31 31 31 32 32 **33** **37** 37 39 39 39 40 42 44 45

In this case there are 18 observations, that is, $n = 18$, so:

Median position $= (18 + 1)/2 = 9.5$th

Although we can find a ninth observation and a tenth observation there is clearly no 9.5th observation. The median position of 9.5th means that the median lies half-way between the ninth and tenth observations, 33 and 37, which appear in bold type in the array. To find the half-way mark between these observations, add them together and divide by two.

Median $= (33 + 37)/2 = 35$

The median age of this group of workers is 35.

When we are dealing with an odd number of observations there will be a median, that is, a value in the middle. However, if there are an even number of observations in a set of data there will be no single middle value, we always have to split the difference between the middle pair of observations.

3.1.3 The arithmetic mean

Although you have probably come across averages before, and you may already be familiar with the mode and the median, neither of them are likely to be the first thing to come to mind if someone asked you how to find the average of a set of data. Faced with such a request you might well say something about adding the observations together and then dividing by the number of observations there are.

This is what many people think of as 'the average', although actually it is one of several averages. We have already dealt with two of them, the mode and the median. This third average, or measure of location, is called the *mean* or more specifically the *arithmetic* mean in order to distinguish it from other types of mean. Like the median, the arithmetic mean can be used with any set of quantitative data.

The procedure for finding the arithmetic mean involves calculation so you may find it more laborious than finding the mode, which only involves inspecting data, or finding the median, which only involves arranging data. You have to first get the sum of the observations and then divide by n, the number of observations in the set of data.

Arithmetic mean = $\Sigma x/n$

The symbol x is used here to represent an observed value of the variable X, so Σx represents the sum of the observed values of the variable X. The arithmetic mean of a sample is represented by the symbol $\bar{x}$, 'x-bar'. The arithmetic mean of a population is represented by the Greek letter μ, 'mu'.

The mean is one of several statistical measures you will meet which have two different symbols, one of which is Greek, to represent them. The Greek symbol is always used to denote the measure for the population. Rarely do we have the time and resources to calculate a measure for a whole population so almost invariably the ones we do calculate are for a sample.

Example 3.5

In one month the total costs (to the nearest pound) of the calls made by 23 male mobile phone owners were:

17 17 14 16 15 24 12 20 17 17 13 21
15 14 14 20 21   9 15 22 19 27 19

Find the mean monthly cost:

The sum of these costs: $\Sigma x = 21 + 19 + 22 + \ldots + 5 + 17 = 398$

The arithmetic mean: $\Sigma x/n = 398/23 = 17.304$ (to 3 decimal places)

You can use MINITAB to find a mean by choosing **Column Statistics** from the **Calc** menu. In the command window select **Mean** and specify the column location of your data in the box alongside **Input variable**. You can obtain the median and a variety of other measures using **Column Statistics**.

Alternatively, in EXCEL select **Data Analysis** from the **Tools** menu then choose **Descriptive Statistics** from the menu in the command window. Specify the cell locations of your data in the box alongside **Input Range** and tick **Summary statistics** which will give you a selection of representative figures including the mean, median and mode.

3.1.4 Choosing which measure of location to use

The whole point of using a measure of location is that it should convey an impression of a distribution in a single figure. If we need to communicate this to an audience it won't help if we quote the mode, median and mean and then invite our audience to please themselves which one to pick. It is important to use the right sort of average.

Picking which average to use might depend on a number of factors:

- The type of data we are dealing with
- Whether the average needs to be easy to find
- The shape of the distribution
- Whether the average will be the basis for further work on the data.

As far as the type of data is concerned, unless you are dealing with fairly simple discrete data the mode is redundant. If you do have such data to analyse the mode may be worth considering particularly if it is important that your measure of location is a feasible value for the variable to take.

Example 3.6

The numbers of days that 16 employees were absent through illness were:

1 1 6 0 2 1 1 4 0 2 4 1 4 3 2 1

Find the mode, median and mean for this set of data.

The modal value is 1, which occurs six times.

Array 0 0 1 1 1 1 1 1 2 2 2 3 4 4 4 6

The median position is: $(16 + 1)/2 = 8.5$th position,

The median is: (8th value + 9th value)/2 = $(1 + 2)/2 = 1.5$

The arithmetic mean = $(0 + 0 + 1 + 1 + . .. + 4 + 6)/16 = 33/16 = 2.0625$

In Example 3.6 it is only the mode that has a value that is both feasible and actually occurs, 1. Although the value of the median, 1.5, may be feasible if the employer recorded half-day absences, it is not one of the observed values. The value of the mean, 2.0625, is not feasible and therefore cannot be one of the observed values.

The only other reason you might prefer to use the mode rather than the other measures of location, assuming that you are dealing with discrete data made up of a relatively few different values, is that it is the easiest of the measures of location to find. All you need to do is to look at the data and count how many times the values occur. Often with the sort of simple data that the mode suits it is pretty obvious which value occurs most frequently and there is no need to count the frequency of each value.

There are more reasons for not using the mode than there are for using the mode. First, it is not appropriate for some types of data. Second, there is no guarantee that there is only one mode; there may be two or more in a single distribution. Third, only the observations that have the modal value 'count', the rest of the observations in the distribution are not taken into account at all. In contrast, when we calculate a mean we add all the values in the distribution together; none of them are excluded.

In many cases you will find that the choice of average boils down to either the median or the mean. The shape of the distribution is a factor that could well influence your choice. If you are dealing with a distribution that has a skewed rather than a symmetrical shape, the median is likely to be the more realistic and reliable measure of location to use.

Example 3.7

Produce a histogram to display the data from Example 3.6 and comment on the shape of the distribution.

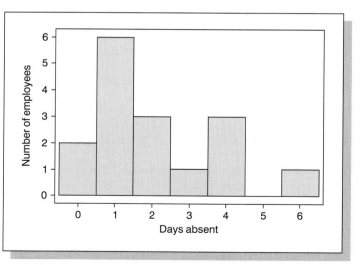

Figure 3.1
Histogram of the number of days absence through illness

The distribution of absences is positively skewed, with the majority of the observations occurring to the left of the distribution.

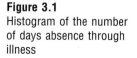

The median and mean for the data in Example 3.6 were 1.5 and 2.0625 respectively. There is quite a difference between them, especially when you consider that the difference between the lowest and highest values in the distribution is only 6. The difference between the median and the mean arises because the distribution is skewed.

When you find a median you concentrate on the middle of the distribution, you are not concerned with the observations to either side of the middle, so the pattern of the distribution at either end of the distribution does not have any effect on the median. In Example 3.6 it would not matter if the highest value in the distribution were 66 rather than 6, the median would still be 1.5. The value of the median is determined by how many observations lie to the left and right of it, not the values of those observations.

The mean, on the other hand, depends entirely on all the values in the distribution, from the lowest to the highest; they all have to be added together in order to calculate the mean. If the highest value in the distribution were 66 rather than 6 it would make a considerable difference to the value of the mean (in fact it would increase to 5.8125).

Because calculating the mean involves adding all the observations together the value of the mean is sensitive to unusual values or *outliers*. Every observation is equal in the sense that it contributes 1 to the value of n, the number of observations. However, if an observation is much lower than the rest, when it is added into the sum of the values it will contribute relatively little to the sum and make the value of the mean lower. If an observation is much higher than the rest, it will contribute disproportionately more to the sum and make the value of the mean higher.

Example 3.8

One of the observed values in the data in Example 3.6 has been recorded wrongly. The figure '6' should have been '2'. How does this affect the values of the mode, median and mean?

The mode is unaffected, the value '1' still occurs more frequently than the other values.

The median is unaffected because the 8th and 9th values will still be '1' and '2' respectively.

The mean will be affected because the sum of the observations will reduce by 4 to 29, so the mean is 29/16 = 1.8125.

In Example 3.8 only one value was changed yet the mean drops from 2.0625 to 1.8125.

In a skewed distribution there are unusual values so if you use a mean to represent a skewed distribution you should bear in mind that it will be disproportionately influenced or 'distorted' by the relatively extreme values or outliers in the distribution. This is why the median for the data in Example 3.6 was 1.5 and the mean was 2.0625. The higher values in the distribution, the '6' and the '4's, have in effect pulled the mean away from the median.

So, should you use the median or the mean to represent a skewed distribution? The answer is that the median is the more representative of the two. Look carefully at the values of the median and mean in relation to the figures in Example 3.6. The median, 1.5, is by definition in the middle of the distribution with eight observations below it and eight observations above it. In contrast the mean, 2.0625, has eleven observations below it and only five above it.

If you are dealing with a symmetrical distribution you will find that the mean is not susceptible to distortion because by definition there is roughly as much numerical 'ballast' to one side of the distribution as there is to the other. The mean and median of a symmetrical distribution will therefore be close together.

Example 3.9

Produce a histogram to portray the data in Example 3.5. Find the median and compare it to the mean.

See Figure 3.2.

There are 23 observations so the median is the (23 + 1)/2 = 12th observation.

Array   9   12   13   14   14   14   15   15   15   16   17   **17**   17   17   19
                19   20   20   21   21   22   24   27

The median is 17, which also happens to be the mode and is close to the mean, 17.304.

Figure 3.2 shows a much more symmetrical distribution than we saw in Figure 3.1. This symmetry has resulted in the mean and the median being close together.

There is one further factor to consider when you need to choose a measure of location, and that is whether you will be using the result as the basis for further statistical analysis. If this were the case you would be well advised to use the mean because it has a more extensive role within statistics as a representative measure than the median.

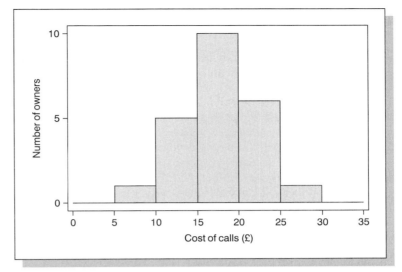

Figure 3.2
Histogram of the monthly costs
of calls

You will find that choosing the right measure of location is not always straightforward. The conclusions from the discussion in this section are:

- Use a mode if your data is discrete and has only one mode.

- It is better to use a median if your data is skewed.

- In other cases use a mean.

3.1.5 Finding measures of location from classified data

You may find yourself in a situation where you would like to use a measure of location to represent a distribution but you only have the data in some classified form, perhaps a frequency distribution or a diagram. Maybe the original data has been mislaid or discarded, or you want to develop work initiated by someone else and the original data is simply not available to you.

If the data is classified in the form of a stem and leaf display finding a measure of location from it is no problem since the display is also a list of the observed values in the distribution. Each observation is listed, but in a detached form so all you have to do is to put the stems and their leaves back together again to get the original data from which they were derived.

You can find the mode of a distribution from its stem and leaf display by looking for the most frequently occurring leaf digits grouped together on a stem line. Finding the median involves counting down (or up) to the middle value. To get the mean you would have to reassemble each observation in order to add them up.

Example 3.10

Construct a stem and leaf display to show the data in Example 3.5. Use the display to find the mode, median and mean of the distribution.

Stem-and-leaf of cost of calls $n = 23$

Leaf unit = 1.0

```
0    9
1    2 3 4 4 4
1    5 5 5 6 7 7 7 7 8 9 9
2    0 0 1 1 2 4
2    7
```

The modal value is 17, the leaf digit '7' appears four times on the lower of the two stem lines for the stem digit '1'.

We know from the calculation $(23 +1)/2 = 12$ that the median is the 12th observation, which is also 17. To find it we can count from the top. The leaf digit on the first stem line, which represents the observed value '9' is the 1st observed value in the distribution in order of magnitude. The five leaf digits on the next stem line, the first of the two stem lines for the stem digit '1', are the 2nd to the 6th observed values in order of magnitude. The first leaf digit on the third stem line, the second of the two for the stem digit '1', is the 7th observed value, so if we count a further five values along that stem line we come to the 12th observation, the median value. The leaf digit that represents the median value in the display is shown in bold type.

To get the mean we have to put the observed values back together again and add 9, 12, 13, 14, 14 etc. to get the sum of the values, 398, which when divided by 23, the number of values, is 17.304, the mean (to three decimal places).

In Example 3.10 you can see that we can get the same values for the mode, median and mean as we obtained from the original data because the stem and leaf display is constructed from the parts of the original data. Even if the stem and leaf display were made up of rounded versions of the original data we would get a very close approximation of the real values of the measures of location.

Finding these measures of location from a stem and leaf display is relatively straightforward. It is therefore a very useful way of deciding which measure is the most appropriate for a set of data.

But what if you didn't have a stem and leaf display to work with? If you had a frequency distribution that gave the frequency of every value in the distribution, or a bar chart that depicted the frequency distribution, you could still find the measures of location.

Example 3.11

Use Figure 3.1 to find the mode, median and mean of the distribution of days absence through illness.

Figure 3.1 shows the frequency with which each number of days absence occurs, in the form of a bar. By checking the height of the bar against the vertical axis we can tell exactly how many times that number of days absence has occurred. We can put that information in the form of a frequency distribution:

Number of days absent	Frequency
0	2
1	6
2	3
3	1
4	3
5	0
6	1

We can see that the value '1' has occurred six times, more than any other level of absence, so the mode is 1.

The median position is (16+1)/2 = 8.5th. To find the median we have to find the 8th and 9th values and split the difference. We can find these observations by counting down the observations in each category, in the same way as we can with a stem and leaf display. The first row in the table contains two '0's, the 1st and 2nd observations in the distribution in order of magnitude. The second row contains the 3rd to the 8th observations, so the 8th observation is a '1'. The third row contains the 9th to the 11th observations, so the 9th observation is a '2'. The median is therefore half-way between the 8th value, 1, and the 9th value, 2, which is 1.5.

To find the mean from the frequency distribution we could add each number of days absence into the sum the same number of times as its frequency. We add two '0's, six '1's and so on. There is a much more direct way of doing this involving multiplication, which is after all collective addition. We simply take each sales level and multiply it by its frequency, then add the products of this process together. If we use the letter 'x' to represent sales, and the letter 'f' to represent frequency we can describe this procedure as Σfx. Another way of representing n, the number of observations, is Σf, the sum of the frequencies, so the procedure for calculating the mean can be represented as $\Sigma fx / \Sigma f$.

Number of days absent (x)	Frequency (f)	fx
0	2	0
1	6	6
2	3	6
3	1	3
4	3	12
5	0	0
6	1	6
	$\Sigma f = 16$	$\Sigma fx = 33$

The mean $= \Sigma fx / \Sigma f = 33/16 = 2.0625$.

You can see that the results obtained in Example 3.11 are exactly the same as those found in Example 3.6 from the original data. This is possible because every value in the distribution is itself a category in the frequency distribution so we can tell exactly how many times it occurs.

But suppose you need to find measures of location for a distribution that is only available to you in the form of a grouped frequency distribution? The categories are not individual values but classes of values. We can't tell from it exactly how many times each value occurs, only the number of times each class of values occurs. From such limited information we can find measures of location but they will be approximations of the true values that we would get from the original data.

Because the data used to construct grouped frequency distributions usually includes many different values, hence the need to divide them into classes, finding an approximate value for the mode is a rather arbitrary exercise. It is almost always sufficient to identify the modal class, which is the class that contains most observations.

Example 3.12

Use Figure 3.2 to find the modal class, median and mean of the monthly costs of calls.

The grouped frequency distribution used to construct Figure 3.2 was:

Cost	Frequency
5 and under 10	1
10 and under 15	5
15 and under 20	10
20 and under 25	6
25 and under 30	1

The modal class is '15 and under 20' because it contains more values, ten, than any other class.

To find a value for the median we first need to locate the class that contains the median value. There are 23 observations in the distribution so the median is the $(23 + 1)/2 = 12$th value in order of magnitude. Clearly the median value does not belong to the first class, '5 and under 10', which contains only the 1st, the lowest observed value in the distribution. Neither does it belong to the second class, which contains the 2nd to the 6th values. The median is in the third class, which contains the 7th to the 16th values. But which one of the ten observations in the class is the median value? We know that the median will be the sixth observation in the median class but if we only have the grouped frequency we simply don't know what that observation is. All we know is that it is at least 15 because that is where the median class begins so all ten observations in it are no lower than 15.

We can approximate the median by assuming that all ten observations in the median class are distributed evenly through it. If that were the case the median would be 6/10ths the way along the median class. So to get an approximate value for the median:

Begin at the start of the median class 15
Add 6/10ths of the width of the median class   6/10 × 5 $\underline{3}$
18

This is quite close to the real value we obtained from the original data, 17.

To obtain an approximate value for the mean from the grouped frequency distribution we apply the same frequency-based approach as we used in Example 3.11, but once again we have to get around the problem of not knowing the exact values of the observations in a class.

In the absence of this knowledge we assume that all the observations in a class take, on average, the value in the middle of the class, known as the class midpoint. The set of class midpoints are then used as the values of the variables, x, that are contained in the distribution. So, for the purposes of calculating $\Sigma fx/\Sigma f$, the observation in the first class is assumed to have the value 7.5, that is the half-way mark or midpoint of the first class, '5 and under 10' and so on.

Cost of calls	Midpoint (x)	Frequency (f)	fx
5 and under 10	7.5	1	7.5
10 and under 15	12.5	5	62.5
15 and under 20	17.5	10	175.0
20 and under 25	22.5	6	135.0
25 and under 30	27.5	1	27.5
		$\Sigma f = 23$	$\Sigma fx = 407.5$

The approximate value of the mean = $\Sigma fx/\Sigma f$ = 407.5/23 = 17.717 (to three decimal places), which is close to the actual value, 17.304 (to three decimal places).

There is an alternative method that you can use to find the approximate value of the median from data presented in the form of a grouped frequency distribution. It is possible to estimate the value of the median from a cumulative frequency graph or a cumulative relative frequency graph of the distribution. These graphs are described in section 2.3.3 of Chapter 2.

To obtain a value for the median, plot the graph and find the point along the vertical axis that represents half the total frequency. Draw a horizontal line from that point to the line that represents the cumulative frequency and then draw a vertical line down from that point to the horizontal axis. The point at which your vertical line meets the horizontal axis is the approximate value of the median.

Example 3.13

Draw a cumulative relative frequency graph to represent the grouped frequency distribution in Example 3.12 and use it to find the approximate value of the median monthly cost of calls.

Cost	Frequency	Cumulative frequency	Cumulative relative frequency
5 and under 10	1	1	0.04
10 and under 15	5	6	0.26
15 and under 20	10	16	0.70
20 and under 25	6	22	0.96
25 and under 30	1	23	1.00

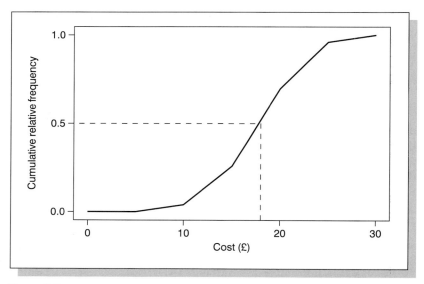

Figure 3.3
Monthly costs of calls made by male mobile phone owners

The starting point of the horizontal dotted line in the graph in Figure 3.3 is '0.5' on the vertical axis, midway on the cumulative relative frequency scale. At the point where the horizontal dotted line meets the cumulative relative frequency line, the vertical dotted line has been drawn down to the horizontal axis. The point where this vertical dotted line reaches the horizontal axis is about 17.5, which is the estimate of the median. The graph suggests that half of the values in the distribution are accumulated below 17.5 and half are accumulated above 17.5.

If you look back to Example 3.9 you will find that the actual median is 17.

3.2 Measures of spread

Just as there are several measures of location you can use to convey the central tendency of a distribution, there are several measures of spread you can use to convey the dispersion of a distribution. They are very often used alongside measures of location in order to give an overall impression of a distribution; where its middle is and how widely scattered the observations are around the middle. Indeed the two most important ones are closely linked to the median and the mean.

3.2.1 The range

The simplest measure of spread is the *range*. The range of a distribution is the difference between the lowest and the highest observations in the distribution, that is:

$$\text{Range} = \text{highest observed value} - \text{lowest observed value}$$

$$= x_{(n)} - x_{(1)}$$

The range is very easy to use and understand, and is often a perfectly adequate method of measuring dispersion. However, it is not a wholly reliable or thorough way of assessing spread because it is based on only two observations. If, for instance, you were asked to compare the spread in two different sets of data you may find that the ranges are very similar but the observations are spread out very differently.

Example 3.14

Two independent estate agencies each employ 9 people. The number of years' experience in the property sector that the employees of these companies have is

Agency A   0   4   4   5   7   8   10   11   15
Agency B   0   0   4   4   7   10   10   14   15

Find the range of each set of data and compare them. Plot histograms for each set of data.

Range (A) = 15 – 0
Range (B) = 15 – 0

The ranges are exactly the same, but this does not necessarily mean that the observations in the two distributions are spread out in exactly the same way.

If you compare Figure 3.4 and Figure 3.5 you can see that the distribution of experience of the staff at Agency A has a much more pronounced centre whereas the distribution of experience of staff at Agency B has much more pronounced ends.

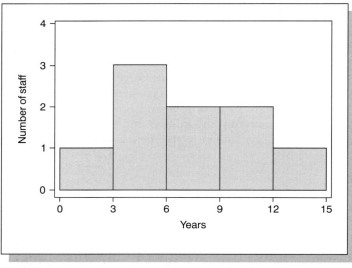

Figure 3.4
Experience (in years) of staff at Agency A

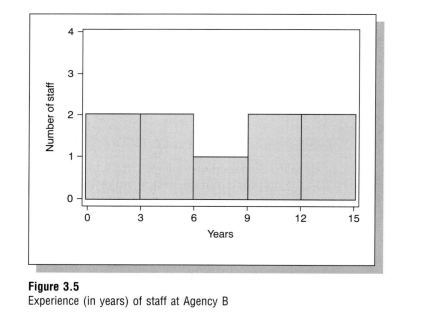

Figure 3.5
Experience (in years) of staff at Agency B

Although the ranges for the distributions in Example 3.14 are identical, the distributions show different levels of dispersion. The figures for Agency B are more widely spread or dispersed than the figures for Agency A.

3.2.2 Quartiles and the semi-interquartile range

The second measure of dispersion at our disposal is the *semi-interquartile range*, or SIQR for short. It is based on *quartiles*, which are a development from the idea of the median.

One way of looking at the median, or middle observation, of a distribution is to regard it as the point which separates the distribution into two equal halves, one consisting of the lower half of the observations and the other consisting of the upper half of the observations. The median, in effect, cuts the distribution in two.

If the median is a single cut that divides a distribution in two, the quartiles are a set of three separate points in a distribution that divide it into four equal quarters. The first, or lower quartile, known as Q1, is the point that separates the lowest quarter of the observations in a distribution from the rest. The second quartile is the median itself; it separates the lower two quarters (i.e. the lower half) of the observations in the distribution from the upper two quarters (i.e. the upper half). The third, or upper quartile, known as Q3, separates the highest quarter of observations in the distribution from the rest.

The median and the quartiles are known as *order statistics* because their values are determined by using the order or sequence of observations in a distribution. You may come across other order statistics such as *deciles*, which divide a distribution into tenths, and *percentiles*, which divide a distribution into hundredths.

You can find the quartiles of a distribution from an array or a stem and leaf display of the observations in the distribution. The quartile position is half-way between the end of the distribution and the median, so it is defined in relation to the median position, which is $(n + 1)/2$, where n is the number of observations. To find the approximate position of the quartiles take the median position, round it down to the nearest whole number if it is not already a whole number, add one and divide by two, that is:

Quartile position = (median position + 1)/2

Once you know the quartile position you can find the lower quartile by counting up to the quartile position from the lowest observation and the upper quartile by counting down to the quartile position from the highest observation.

Example 3.15

In one month the total costs (to the nearest pound) of the calls made by 23 female mobile phone owners were

14   5 15   6 17 10 22 10 12 17 13 29
7 27 33 16 30   9 15   7 33 28 21

Find the median and upper and lower quartiles for this distribution.

Array   5   6   7   7   9 10 10 12 13 14 15 15 16 17 17
21 22 27 28 29 30 33 33

The median position = (23 + 1)/2 = 12th position, so the median value is the value '15'. This suggests that the monthly cost of calls for half the female owners is below £15, and the monthly costs for the other half is above £15.

The quartile position = (12 +1)/2 = 6.5th position, that is midway between the 6th and 7th observations.

The lower quartile is half-way between the observations 6th and 7th from the lowest, which are both 10, so the lower quartile is 10. This suggests that the monthly cost of calls for 25 per cent of the female owners is below £10.

The upper quartile is half-way between the observations 6th and 7th from the highest, which are 27 and 22 respectively. The upper quartile is mid-way between these values, i.e. 24.5, so the monthly cost of calls for 25 per cent of the female owners is above £24.50.

If the upper quartile separates off the top quarter of the distribution and the lower quartile separates off the bottom quarter, the difference between the lower and upper quartiles is the range or span of the middle half of the observations in the distribution. This is called the *interquartile range*, which is the range between the quartiles. The semi-interquartile range (SIQR) is, as its name suggests, half the interquartile range, that is:

$$SIQR = (Q3 - Q1)/2$$

Example 3.16

Find the semi-interquartile range for the data in Example 3.15.

The lower quartile monthly cost of calls is £10 and the upper quartile monthly cost of calls is £24.5.

$$SIQR = (£24.5 - £10)/2 = £14.5/2 = £7.25$$

The semi-interquartile range is a measure of spread. The larger the value of the SIQR, the more dispersed the observations in the distribution are.

Example 3.17

Find the SIQR of the data in Example 3.5 and compare this to the SIQR of the data in Example 3.15.

Array   9 12 13 14 14 14 15 15 15 16 17 17 17 17 19
        19 20 20 21 21 22 24 27

There are 23 observations, so the median position is the $(23 + 1)/2 = 12$th position.

The quartile position is the $(12 + 1)/2 = 6.5$th position.

$Q1 = (£14 + £15)/2 = £14.5$ $Q3 = (£20 + £20)/2 = £20$
$SIQR = (£20 - £14.5)/2 = £2.75$

The SIQR for the data for the males (£2.75) is far lower than the SIQR for the data for the females (£7.25) indicating that there is more variation in the cost of calls for females.

There is a diagram called a *boxplot*, which you might find a very useful way of displaying order statistics. In a boxplot the middle half of the values in a distribution is represented by a box, which has the lower quartile at one end and the upper quartile at the other. A line inside the box represents the median. The top and bottom quarters are represented by straight lines called 'whiskers' protruding from each end of the box. A boxplot is a particularly useful way of comparing distributions.

Example 3.18

Produce boxplots for the monthly costs of calls for females and males.

Look carefully at the boxplot to the right in Figure 3.6, which represents the monthly costs of calls for males. The letter (a) indicates the position of the lowest observation, (b) indicates the position of the lower quartile, (c) is the median, (d) is the upper quartile, and (e) is the highest value.

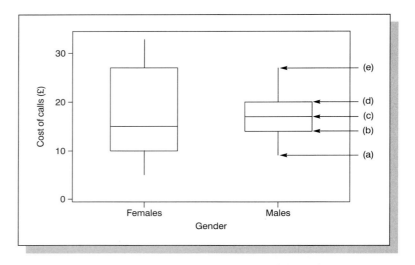

Figure 3.6
Monthly costs of calls for
female and male mobile phone
owners

In Figure 3.6 the diagram representing the costs of calls for females is larger than the diagram representing the costs of calls for males, emphasizing the greater variation in costs for females. The fact that the median line in the costs of calls for females box is positioned low down within the box suggests that the middle half of the distribution is skewed. The quarter of observations between the median and the upper quartile are more widely spread than the quarter of observations between the median and the lower quartile. In contrast, the median line in the box that represents the costs of calls for males is mid-way between the top and the bottom of the box indicates that the spread of values in the middle half of the costs for males is symmetrical.

A boxplot is a particularly useful for identifying outliers, observed values that seem detached from the rest of the distribution. If you have outliers in a distribution it is impor-tant to check first, that they have not been written down wrongly and second, assuming that they are accurately recor-ded, what reasons might explain such unusual observations.

Example 3.19

If lowest value in the set of monthly costs of calls for male owners was wrongly recorded as £9 but was actually £4, how does the boxplot change?

The lowest observation, 4, is now represented as an asterisk to emphasize its relative isolation from the rest of the observations.

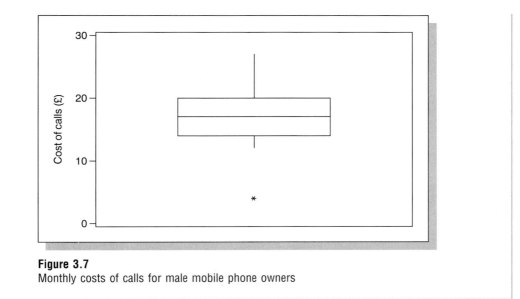

Figure 3.7
Monthly costs of calls for male mobile phone owners

You can produce a boxplot using MINITAB by selecting **Boxplot** from the **Graph** menu.

Quartiles and the SIQR are useful ways of measuring spread, and together with the median they are often the best way of summarizing skewed distributions. However, like the range, they focus on a very few observations in a distribution. So it is possible that the SIQR, like the range, cannot always detect differences in dispersion.

Example 3.20

Find the SIQR for each of the two sets of data in Example 3.14.

There are nine observations in each distribution, so the median position is $(9 + 1)/2 = 5$th in both cases. The quartile position is $(5 + 1)/2 = 3$rd position.

| Agency A | 0 | 4 | 4 | 5 | 7 | 8 | 10 | 11 | 15 |
| Agency B | 0 | 0 | 4 | 4 | 7 | 10 | 10 | 14 | 15 |

In both cases the lower quartile is 4 and the upper quartile is 10, giving an SIQR of 3 for each distribution. Despite the identical SIQR results, Figures 3.4 and 3.5 clearly show that these distributions are not spread out in the same way.

3.2.3 The standard deviation

In order to avoid the shortcomings of the range and the SIQR we have to turn to a measure of spread that is based on including every observation rather than selecting just a few. That measure, the most important measure of spread in Statistics, is known as the *standard deviation*.

As the name suggests, the standard deviation is based on the idea of measuring the typical, or standard, amount of deviation, or difference, in a set of observations. But deviation from what? In fact the deviation from the arithmetic mean.

We find the standard deviation by first calculating the mean and then finding how far each observation is from it.

Example 3.21

Six newsagents sell the following number of boxes of plain potato crisps in a particular week

2   5   6   4   3   4

The mean, $\bar{x} = 24/6 = 4$

Observation (x)	Mean ($\bar{x}$)	Deviation (x − $\bar{x}$)
2	4	−2
5	4	1
6	4	2
4	4	0
3	4	−1
4	4	0

To get a single measure of spread from deviation figures like those in Example 3.21 it would be very convenient to add up the deviations and divide the sum of the deviations by the number of them to get a sort of 'average' deviation. Unfortunately, as you will find out if you try it with the deviations in Example 3.21, it doesn't work because the deviations add up to zero.

This will always happen because the mean is, in effect, the centre of gravity of a distribution. In the same way that the centre of gravity of an object has as much weight to one side as it does to the other, the mean has as much numerical 'weight' below it as it has above it. The result is that the deviations between the mean and the observations that are lower than the mean, which are always negative, cancel out the deviations between the mean and the observations that are higher than the mean, which are always positive. You can see in Example 3.21 that the negative deviations (−1 and −2) would be cancelled out by the positive deviations (1 and 2) if we added all the deviations together.

To get round this problem we square the deviations before adding them up, since any number squared is positive. The sum of the squared deviations, $\Sigma(x - \bar{x})^2$, is the basis of the standard deviation.

Example 3.22

Find the sum of the squared deviations, $\Sigma(x - \bar{x})^2$, from the mean for the data in Example 3.21.

Observation (x)	Mean ($\bar{x}$)	Deviation ($x - \bar{x}$)	Squared deviation ($x - \bar{x})^2$
2	4	−2	4
5	4	1	1
6	4	2	4
4	4	0	0
3	4	−1	1
4	4	0	0

$\Sigma(x - \bar{x})^2 = 4 + 1 + 4 + 0 + 1 + 0 = 10$

Now we have a way of measuring total deviation it would be convenient to simply divide by the number of deviations that have been added together, which is the same as n, the number of observations. However, we actually divide the sum of the squared deviations by one less than n instead of n itself.

Any set of data starts off with the same number of *degrees of freedom* as it has observations, n. The implication is that if you wanted to specify all the figures in the set of data yourself you can do so freely. However, once you have found the mean you could only specify one less than the number of figures freely. The last one would have to be the only figure that combines with the ones you have specified to keep the mean the same, so you have 'lost' a degree of freedom. For instance, if we know that the mean of a set of three figures is 5, and we suggest that 2 and 7 are the first two figures in the set, the third value has to be 6 in order that the mean is still 5. Choose any other value for third figure and the mean will be different.

When we calculate a standard deviation we are using the mean, so we lose one degree of freedom. Therefore the procedure that we use to calculate the standard deviation, s, of a sample involves dividing the sum of squared deviations by $(n - 1)$. The only exception is the rare occasion when we need to calculate the population standard deviation, σ (the lower case of the Greek letter s), in which case the sum of squared deviations is divided by n.

In later work you will find that a sample standard deviation can be used as an estimate of a population standard deviation. This can save time and money, but it can only be done if the sample standard deviation is calculated properly.

The final part of the procedure you follow to obtain a sample standard deviation is to take the square root of the sum of squared deviations divided by $(n - 1)$. You have to do this to get a figure that is in the same units as your original data. For instance, the squared deviation figures in Example 3.22 are in 'boxes of crisps squared'. It is much more useful to have a figure measured in boxes of crisps.

We can sum up the procedure that is used to obtain a sample standard deviation in the following expression:

$$s = \sqrt{\frac{\Sigma(x - \bar{x})^2}{(n - 1)}}$$

Example 3.23

Calculate the standard deviation for the data in Example 3.21.

The sum of squared deviations is 10 and the number of observations is 6, so the standard deviation of this sample is:

$$s = \sqrt{10/5} = \sqrt{2} = 1.414 \text{ to three decimal places}$$

The expression for the population standard deviation is

$$\sigma = \sqrt{\Sigma(x - \mu)^2/n}$$

If you use either of these expressions to calculate the standard deviation of a set of data with many observations you will find the experience laborious. It really is a task that should be carried out with the aid of a calculator or computer software.

If you have a calculator with statistical functions look for a key with **s** or **x** σ_{n-1} or σ_{xn-1} on or alongside it. Alternatively you can use the **Descriptive Statistics** facility in the **Data Analysis** option from the **Tools** menu in EXCEL, or choose **Standard deviation** from the **Column Statistics** option on the **Calc** menu in MINITAB.

In later statistical work you may encounter something called a *variance*. The variance is the square of the standard deviation. The expression for the variance looks like the expression for the standard deviation and in fact the only difference is that finding the variance does not involve taking a square root.

The sample variance, $\qquad s^2 = \Sigma(x - \bar{x})^2/(n - 1).$

The population variance, $\qquad \sigma^2 = \Sigma(x - \mu)^2/n.$

The standard deviation is widely used with the mean to provide an overall summary or description of a distribution. Indeed for many distributions the mean and the standard deviation are the key defining characteristics or *parameters* of the distribution.

One of the reasons it has become such an important measure of spread is that it is a reliable way of detecting dispersion.

Example 3.24

Find the mean and the standard deviation of the data from Example 3.14 and compare the results for the two agencies.

Agency A $\qquad$ Mean $= (0 + 4 + 4 + 5 + 7 + 8 + 10 + 11 + 15)/9 = 7.11$

Experience (x)	Mean $(\bar{x})$	$(x - \bar{x})$	$(x - \bar{x})^2$
0	7.11	−7.11	50.55
4	7.11	−3.11	9.67
4	7.11	−3.11	9.67
5	7.11	−2.11	4.45
7	7.11	−0.11	0.01
8	7.11	0.89	0.79
10	7.11	2.89	8.35
11	7.11	3.89	15.13
15	7.11	7.89	62.25
		$\Sigma(x - \bar{x})^2 =$	160.87

$s = \sqrt{\Sigma(x - \bar{x})^2/(n - 1)} = \sqrt{160.87/(9 - 1)}$

$= \sqrt{160.87/8} = \sqrt{20.11} = 4.48$ to two decimal places

Agency B $\qquad$ Mean $= (0 + 0 + 4 + 4 + 7 + 10 + 10 + 14 + 15)/9 = 7.11$

Experience (x)	Mean $(\bar{x})$	$(x - \bar{x})$	$(x - \bar{x})^2$
0	7.11	−7.11	50.55
0	7.11	−7.11	50.55
4	7.11	−3.11	9.67
4	7.11	−3.11	9.67
7	7.11	−0.11	0.01
10	7.11	2.89	8.35
10	7.11	2.89	8.35
14	7.11	6.89	47.47
15	7.11	7.89	62.25
		$\Sigma(x - \bar{x})^2 =$	246.87

$$s = \sqrt{\Sigma(x - \bar{x})^2/(n - 1)} = \sqrt{246.87/(9 - 1)}$$
$$= \sqrt{246.87/8} = \sqrt{30.86} = 5.56 \text{ to two decimal places}$$

The means are the same, 7.11, but the standard deviation for Agency B is higher than the standard deviation for Agency A, 5.56 compared to 4.48. The difference between the standard deviations reflects the contrasting spread that we could see in Figures 3.4 and 3.5.

The mean and standard deviation can be used to approximate the overall spread of observations in a distribution. Typically nearly all the observations will lie between the point three standard deviations below the mean and the point three standard deviations above the mean. Another way of saying this is to say that almost the entire distribution is located within three standard deviations of the mean. Another rule of thumb is that 90 per cent or so of a distribution will be within two standard deviations of the mean.

In further work you will find that the mean and the standard deviation can be used to define the positions of values in a distribution. For instance, if we have a distribution that has a mean of 4 and a standard deviation of 2 we could describe the value '8' as being two standard deviations above the mean. The value '1' could be described as being one and a half standard deviations below the mean.

3.2.4 Finding measures of spread from classified data

You may need to determine measures of spread for data that is already classified. The ease of doing this and the accuracy of the results depend in part on the type of data and the form in which it is presented.

If you have a frequency distribution that shows the number of times each one of a small number of discrete values occurs then you will be able to identify all the values in the distribution and carry out the appropriate procedures and calculations on them. Similarly, if you have data in the form of a stem and leaf display you should be able to identify at least the approximate values of the data. In either case the results you obtain should be identical or at least very close to the real values.

If, however, the data you have is in the form of a grouped frequency distribution then it is possible to find measures of spread, but these will be approximations. Here we will consider how to find an approximate value of a standard deviation from a grouped frequency distribution and how to find approximate values for quartiles, and hence the semi-interquartile range, from a cumulative relative frequency graph.

A grouped frequency distribution shows how many observed values in the distribution fall into a series of classes. It does not show the actual values of the data. Since calculating a standard deviation does usually require the actual values we have to find some way of representing the actual values based on the classes to which they belong. In fact the midpoint of each class is used as the approximate value of every value in the class. This is the same approach as we used to find the mean from a grouped frequency distribution in section 3.1.5 of this chapter.

The approximate value of the standard deviation is:

$$s = \sqrt{\frac{1}{(\Sigma f) - 1}\left[\Sigma fx^2 - \frac{(\Sigma fx)^2}{\Sigma f}\right]}$$

where f represents the frequency of a class and x its midpoint.

Example 3.25

Find the approximate value of the standard deviation of the data represented in the grouped frequency distribution in Example 3.12.

Cost of calls	Midpoint (x)	Frequency (f)	fx	x^2	fx^2
5 and under 10	7.5	1	7.5	56.25	56.25
10 and under 15	12.5	5	62.5	156.25	781.25
15 and under 20	17.5	10	175.0	306.25	3062.50
20 and under 25	22.5	6	135.0	506.25	3037.50
25 and under 30	27.5	1	27.5	756.25	756.25
		$\Sigma f = 23$	$\Sigma fx = 407.5$		$\Sigma fx^2 = 7693.75$

$$s = \sqrt{\frac{1}{23 - 1}[7693.75 - \frac{(407.5)^2}{23}]}$$

$$= \sqrt{1/22\,[7693.75 - (166056.25/23)]}$$

$$= \sqrt{1/22\,[7693.75 - 7219.837]}$$

$$= \sqrt{21.5415}$$

$$= 4.641 \text{ to three decimal places}$$

You may like to work out the actual standard deviation using the original data, which appears in Example 3.5. You should find that it is 4.128, to three decimal places.

You can find the approximate values of the quartiles of a distribution from a cumulative frequency graph or a cumulative relative frequency graph by employing the same approach as we used to find the approximate value of the median in section 3.1.5 of this chapter. The difference is that to approximate the quartiles we start from points one-quarter and three-quarters the way up the vertical scale.

Example 3.26

Use the cumulative relative frequency graph shown in Example 3.13, Figure 3.3, to estimate the values of the lower and upper quartiles for the distribution and produce an approximate value of the semi-interquartile range.

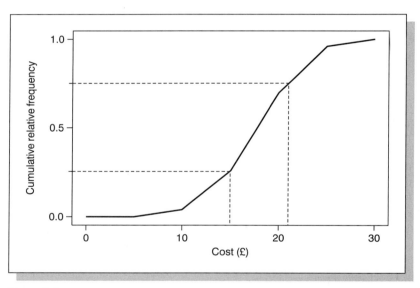

Figure 3.8
Monthly costs of calls made by male mobile phone owners

The approximate value of the lower quartile is the point where the vertical dotted line to the left meets the horizontal axis, at about £15. The approximate value of the upper quartile is the point where the vertical dotted line to the right meets the horizontal axis, at about £21. The semi-interquartile range is half the difference between these two, £3.0.

If you look back at Example 3.17 you will see that the true values of the lower and upper quartiles are £14.5 and £20 respectively, and that the semi-interquartile range is £2.75.

3.3 Measuring quality and consistency

In many fields of business, more and more attention is devoted to increasing the quality of the product. Improving quality is often interpreted to mean increasing the consistency of the product, or to put it another way, reducing the variation of the product. Measures of spread like the standard deviation and the variance can be important factors in product quality because they measure variation. Increasing consistency may mean implementing changes that reduce standard deviations or variances. Monitoring quality may involve comparing current performance with previous performance, which is described using a mean and standard deviation.

One well-established way of monitoring quality is the *control chart*, which is based on the distribution of the variable being measured to assess quality. Such a chart consists of a horizontal line representing the mean of the variable, which is the performance target, and lines three standard deviations above and below the mean, which are the control limits. As products are produced or services delivered they are measured and the observations plotted on the chart. If a plotted point lies beyond either of the control limits, the process is considered to be out of control and we need to take corrective action or shut it down.

Example 3.27

A 'while-you-wait' shoe repair service offers to replace certain types of heels on ladies' shoes in three minutes. Long experience has shown that the mean replacement time for

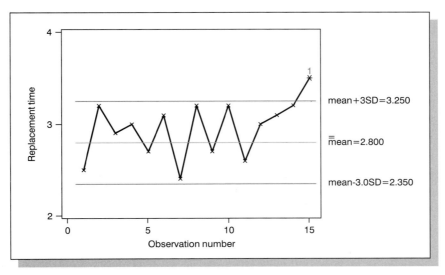

Figure 3.9
Control chart for heel replacement times

these heels is 2.8 minutes and the standard deviation is 0.15 minutes. Construct a control chart using these figures and use it to assess the following sequence of replacement times achieved by a trainee:

2.5 3.2 2.9 3.0 2.7 3.1 2.4 3.2 2.7 3.2 2.6 3.0 3.1 3.2 3.5

Figure 3.9 shows that the replacement times are erratic but within the control limits until the last observation, which suggests the process is going out of control, perhaps because the trainee is tiring.

In practice control charts are rather more complicated than in Example 3.27 because the monitoring process involves taking samples rather than individual values, but the role of the standard deviation is essentially the same. For a good introduction to statistical quality control, see Montgomery (2000).

Review questions

Answers to these questions, including fully worked solutions to those questions marked with an asterisk (*), are on pages 341–343.

3.1 The numbers of credit cards carried by 25 shoppers are

3 5 2 0 4 3 0 1 1 7 1 4 1
2 9 4 1 4 1 5 5 2 3 1 1

(a) Find the mode and median of this distribution.
(b) Calculate the mean of the distribution and compare it to the mode and median. What can you conclude about the shape of the distribution?
(c) Draw a bar chart to represent the distribution and confirm your conclusions in (b).

3.2 A supermarket sells kilogram bags of apples. The number of apples in 22 bags were

7   9 8 8 10 10 8 10 10 8 8
10 7 9 9   9   7 8   7   8 9 8

(a) Find the mode, median and mean for this set of data. Compare your results.
(b) Plot a simple bar chart to portray the data.

3.3 Twenty-six dental patients require the following numbers of fillings during their current course of treatment

2 3 2 2 3 1 2 2 1 3 2 2 2
2 4 3 2 2 2 2 2 1 1 0 1 1

(a) Identify the mode, find the median, and calculate the mean of these figures.
(b) Compile a bar chart to display the distribution.

3.4* A supermarket has one checkout for customers who wish to purchase 9 items or less. The number of items presented at this checkout by a sample of 19 customers were

5 8 7 7 6 6 10 8 9 9
9 6 5 9 8 9   5 5 6

(a) Find the median and quartiles for this set of data.
(b) Determine the semi-interquartile range.
(c) Calculate the mean and standard deviation for this set of data.

3.5 The crowd sizes for the 22 home league games played by Athletico Almaz were

1976 2162 1502 1782 1523 2033 1564 1320 1951
1714 1841 1648 1345 1837 1718 2047 1954 2000
1479 2571 1739 1781

The crowd sizes for the 22 home fixtures played by a rival club, Red Star Rubine, were

1508 2055 2085 2098 1745 1939 2116 1956 2075
1702 1995 2391 1964 1879 1813 2144 1958 2203
2149 2064 1777 1989

(a) Find the median, quartiles and semi-interquartile range for each team.
(b) Compare and contrast the two distributions using your results from (a).

3.6 Two neighbours work at the same place. One travels to work by bus, the other cycles to work. The times taken (in minutes) by each to get to work on a sample of 8 days were

| Bus passenger | 33 | 28 | 40 | 32 | 41 | 32 | 38 | 42 |
| Cyclist | 26 | 33 | 27 | 31 | 31 | 30 | 28 | 24 |

Calculate the mean and standard deviation for each set of times and use them to compare the travel times for the two commuters.

3.7 Three companies supply the domestic electricity supply market in a particular region; Iskra, Moogom, and Provod. Each company has produced an analysis of the distribution of the size of its customers' bills over the last financial year. The following results have been published:

Company	Mean bill size	Standard deviation of bill sizes
Iskra	£359	£72
Moogom	£412	£47
Provod	£307	£61

Are the following statements true or false?

(a) Provod bills are on average the smallest and vary more than those from the other companies.
(b) Moogom bills are on average the largest and vary more than those from the other companies.
(c) Iskra bills are on average larger than those from Provod and vary more than those from Moogom.
(d) Iskra bills are on average smaller than those from Moogom and vary less than those from Provod.
(e) Moogom bills are on average larger than those from Iskra and vary more than those from Provod.
(f) Provod bills vary less than those from Iskra and are on average smaller than those from Moogom.

3.8 Two friends want to take a summer holiday before going to college in the autumn. They are looking for somewhere with plenty of clubs where they can party all night. Unfortunately they have left it rather late to book and there are only two resorts, Medlena and Bistry, available within their budget. When they ask about the ages of the holiday-makers at these resorts their travel agent says the only thing he can tell them is that that the mean age of people going to Medlena is 19 whereas the mean age of visitors to Bistry is 22. Just as they are about to book holidays in Medlena because it seems to attract the sort of young crowd they want to be with the travel agent says. 'I've got some more figures, the standard deviation of the ages of visitors to Medlena is 8 and the standard deviation of the ages of visitors to Bistry is 2'.

Should they change their minds on the basis of this new information, and if so, why?

3.9* The kilocalories per portion in 32 different breakfast cereals were recorded and collated into the following grouped frequency distribution:

Kcal per portion	Frequency
80 and under 120	3
120 and under 160	11
160 and under 200	9
200 and under 240	7
240 and under 280	2

Determine approximate values for the mean and median of the distribution, and compare them.

3.10 The playing times of a sample of 57 contemporary pop albums and a sample of 48 reissued classic pop albums are summarized in the following grouped frequency distributions:

Playing time (minutes)	Frequency (contemporary)	Frequency (reissue)
30 and under 35	0	4
35 and under 40	7	9
40 and under 45	13	17
45 and under 50	22	15
50 and under 55	10	3
55 and under 60	4	0
60 and under 65	1	0

(a) Find approximate values of the median and mean for each distribution.

(b) Calculate approximate values for the standard deviations of each distribution.

(c) Compare the distributions using your results from (a) and (b).

3.11 The time in seconds that a sample of 79 callers trying to contact an insurance company had to wait was recorded. After introducing new procedures the waiting time for a sample of 61 callers was recorded. The results are presented in the following grouped frequency distribution:

Waiting time (seconds)	Frequency (before change)	Frequency (after change)
0 and under 10	2	7
10 and under 20	15	19
20 and under 30	23	31
30 and under 40	24	3
40 and under 50	11	1
50 and under 60	4	0

(a) Determine values for the mean and median of the distributions.

(b) Find an approximate value for the standard deviation of each distribution.

(c) Use the figures you obtain for (a) and (b) to compare the two distributions.

3.12 The total spend of a sample of 110 customers of the Peeshar supermarket and the total spend of a sample of 128 customers of the Peevar supermarket were analysed and the following grouped frequency distribution produced:

Total spend (£)	Frequency (Peeshar)	Frequency (Peevar)
0.00 to 19.99	13	35
20.00 to 39.99	27	61
40.00 to 59.99	41	17
60.00 to 79.99	17	14
80.00 to 99.99	10	1
100.00 to 119.99	2	0

(a) Find approximate values for the mean and standard deviation of each distribution and use them to compare the distributions.

(b) One of these supermarkets attracts customers doing their weekly shopping whereas the other attracts customers seeking occasional alcoholic beverage and luxury food purchases. From your answers to (a), which supermarket is which?

3.13 The stem and leaf display below shows the Friday night admission prices for 31 clubs.

Stem	Leaves
0	44
0	5555677789
1	000224444
1	5555588
2	002

Leaf unit = £1.0

Find the values of the median and semi-interquartile range.

3.14 The costs of work done at a garage on 33 vehicles to enable them to pass the MOT test of roadworthiness were

482 471 277 230 357 491 213 386 357 141 282
184 324 426 408 213 155 287 415 499 470 461
233 314 240 107 113 314 242 112 289 283 389

Identify the median and quartiles of this set of data and use them to compile a boxplot to represent the data.

3.15 The amounts (in pounds) spent in a month by 42 women on hair-care products were

13.23	11.19	14.49	6.51	10.07	18.91	13.14	15.90
16.11	12.89	9.12	12.27	8.16	10.84	9.33	10.36
15.02	8.45	12.92	6.79	13.02	6.85	13.76	8.92
11.40	10.88	8.99	9.46	8.67	8.52	11.17	5.79
9.17	9.16	5.24	7.11	7.37	10.60	13.21	10.61
4.65	8.94						

Construct a boxplot to represent this set of data.

3.16* The credit balances in the current accounts of customers of a bank are summarized in the following grouped relative frequency distribution:

Balance (£)	Relative frequency
0 and under 500	0.12
500 and under 1000	0.29
1000 and under 1500	0.26
1500 and under 2000	0.19
2000 and under 2500	0.09
2500 and under 3000	0.05

Plot a cumulative relative frequency graph to portray this distribution and use it to find approximate values of the median, quartiles and semi-interquartile range.

3.17 A report on usage of glass recycling bins contains the following grouped relative frequency distribution:

Weight of glass deposited per week (kg)	Proportion of bins
0 and under 400	0.23
400 and under 800	0.34
800 and under 1200	0.28
1200 and under 1600	0.11
1600 and under 2000	0.04

(a) Compile a cumulative relative frequency graph for this distribution.
(b) Determine approximate values of the median, quartile and semi-interquartile range using your graph.

3.18 The prices of a pint of ordinary bitter in each of 30 public houses in one city in the North of the UK and another city in the South of the UK were recorded and the following boxplot were produced to portray the two distributions.

Look carefully at the diagram and say whether each of the statements beneath it is true or false.

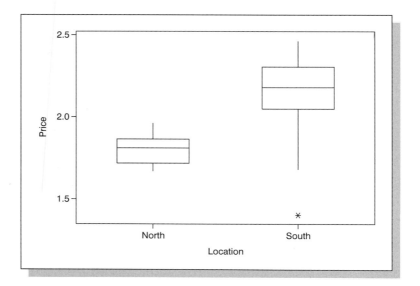

(a) The lowest price is to be found in the North.
(b) The SIQR for the figures from the South is larger.
(c) There is one outlier, the lowest price in the South.
(d) The middle half of the prices in the North is more symmetrically distributed.
(e) The highest price in the North is lower than the first quartile price in the South.
(f) The range of the prices in the South is smaller.
(g) The upper quartile of prices in the North is about £1.85.
(h) The median price in the South is about £2.40.

3.19 A film-processing shop promises to deliver photographs in half an hour. The mean and standard deviations of the processing times are 22 minutes and 3 minutes respectively. The layout of the machines in the shop has been altered. The processing times of the first ten films to be developed after the reorganization are

32.6   28.2   30.8   28.1   27.0   25.1   23.2   32.5   24.9   32.8

Plot a control chart and use it to ascertain whether the reorganization has affected the processing times.

3.20 Select which of the statements on the right-hand side best
define the words on the left-hand side.

(a) Median   (i)   the square of the standard deviation
(b) Range   (ii)   a diagram based on order statistics
(c) Variance   (iii)   the most frequently occurring value
(d) Boxplot   (iv)   the difference between the extreme observations
(e) SIQR   (v)   the middle value
(f) Mode   (vi)   half the difference between the quartiles

'An aircraft doesn't fly on one wing . . .'

Summarizing bivariate data

This chapter will help you:

- To understand why summarizing bivariate data is important.
- To investigate the connection between two variables.
- To measure changes over time.
- To adjust figures for the effects of inflation.
- To analyse time series.
- To predict future values of time series.

In this chapter you will find:

- Measures of correlation.
- Simple linear regression analysis.
- Price indices.
- Analysis of the components of time series.
- Guidance on using computer software.

This chapter is about techniques that you can use to study the relationship between two variables. The type of data that these techniques are intended to analyse is called *bivariate* data because they consist of observed values of two variables. The techniques themselves make up what is known as bivariate analysis.

Bivariate analysis is of great importance to business. The results of this sort of analysis have indeed affected many aspects of business considerably. The establishment of the relationship between smoking and health problems transformed the tobacco industry. The analysis of survival rates of micro-organisms and temperature is crucial to the setting of appropriate refrigeration levels by food retailers. Marketing strategies of many organizations are often based on the analysis of consumer expenditure in relation to age or income. Sometimes time itself is an important variable; for instance, the timing of advertising and promotional activities for patent medicines is based on the analysis of the incidence of illnesses such as colds over time.

The chapter will introduce you to some of the techniques that companies and other organisations use to summarize bivariate data. The first set of techniques you will meet, *correlation* and *regression*, are general techniques that can be used with any bivariate data. The second set of techniques, which consists of price indices and basic time series analysis, are designed to summarize sets of bivariate data in which one of the variables is time.

4.1 Correlation and regression

Suppose you have a set of bivariate data that consists of observations of one variable, X, and the associated observations of another variable, Y, and you want to see if X and Y are related. For instance, the Y variable could be sales of ice cream per day and the X variable the daily temperature, and you want to investigate the connection between temperature and ice cream sales. In such a case correlation analysis enables us to assess whether there is a connection between the two variables and, if so, how strong that connection is.

If correlation analysis tells us there is a connection we can use regression analysis to identify the exact form of the relationship. It is essential to know this if you want to use the relationship to make predictions, for instance if we want to predict the demand for ice cream when the daily temperature is at a particular level.

The assumption that underpins bivariate analysis is that one variable depends on the other. The letter Y is used to represent the *dependent* variable, the one whose values are believed to depend on the other variable. This other variable, represented by the letter X, is called the *independent* variable. The Y or dependent variable is sometimes known as the *response* because it is believed to *respond* to changes in the value of the X. The X or independent variable is also known as the *predictor* because it might help us to predict the values of Y.

4.1.1 Correlation analysis

Correlation analysis is a way of investigating whether two variables are correlated, or connected with each other. We can study this to some extent by using a scatter diagram to portray the data, but such a diagram can only give us a visual 'feel' for the association between two variables, it doesn't actually measure the strength of the connection. So, although a scatter diagram is the thing you should begin with to carry out bivariate analysis, you need to calculate a *correlation coefficient* if you want a precise way of assessing how closely the variables are related.

The correlation coefficient is similar to the standard deviation in that it is based on the idea of dispersion or spread. The comparison isn't complete because bivariate data is spread out in two dimensions; if you look at a scatter diagram you will see that the points representing the data are scattered both vertically and horizontally.

The letter r is used to represent the correlation coefficient of sample data. Its Greek counterpart, the letter ρ ('rho'), is used to represent the correlation coefficient of population data. As is the case with other summary measures it is exceedingly unlikely that you will ever have to find the value of a population correlation coefficient because of the cost and practical difficulty of studying entire populations.

The correlation coefficient is a ratio; it compares the co-ordinated scatter to the total scatter. The co-ordinated scatter is the extent to which the observed values of one variable, X, vary in co-ordination with the observed values of a second variable, Y. We use the *covariance* of the values of X and Y, Cov_{XY} to measure the degree of co-ordinated scatter.

To calculate the covariance you have to multiply the amount that each x deviates from the mean of the X values, $\bar{x}$, by the amount that its corresponding y deviates from the mean of the Y values, $\bar{y}$. That is, for every pair of x and y observations you calculate:

$$(x - \bar{x})(y - \bar{y})$$

The result will be positive whenever the x and y values are both bigger than their means, because we will be multiplying two positive deviations together. It will also be positive if both the x and y values are smaller than their means, because both deviations will be negative and the result of multiplying them together will be positive. The result will only be negative if one of the deviations is positive and the other negative.

The covariance is the total of the products from this process divided by n, the number of pairs of observations, minus one. We have to divide by $n - 1$ because the use of the means in arriving at the deviations results in the loss of a degree of freedom.

$$\text{Cov}_{XY} = \Sigma \, (x - \bar{x})(y - \bar{y})/(n - 1)$$

The covariance is positive if values of X below $\bar{x}$ tend to be associated with values of Y below $\bar{y}$, and values of X above $\bar{x}$ tend to be associated with values of Y above $\bar{y}$. In other words if high x values occur with high y values and low x values occur with low y values we will have a positive covariance. This suggests that there is a positive or *direct* relationship between X and Y, that is, if X goes up we would expect Y to go up as well, and vice versa. If you compared the income of a sample of consumers with their expenditure on clothing you would expect to find a positive relationship.

The covariance is negative if values of X below $\bar{x}$ are associated with values of Y above $\bar{y}$, and vice versa. The low values of X occur with the high values of Y, and the high values of X occur with the low values of Y. This is a negative or *inverse* relationship. If you compared the prices of articles of clothing with demand for them you might expect to find an inverse relationship.

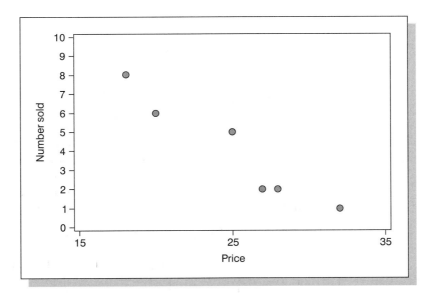

Figure 4.1
Prices of jackets and numbers sold

Example 4.1

A shop retails six brands of light shower-proof jacket. The prices in pounds and the numbers sold in a week are:

Price	18	20	25	27	28	32
Number sold	8	6	5	2	2	1

Plot a scatter diagram and calculate the covariance.

In Figure 4.1 Number sold has been plotted on the Y or vertical axis and Price has been plotted on the X or horizontal axis. We are assuming that Number sold depends on Price rather than the other way round.

To calculate the covariance we need to calculate deviations from the mean for every x and y value.

$$\bar{x} = (18+20+25+27+28+32)/6 = 150/5 = 25$$

$$\bar{y} = (8 +6+5+2+2+1+)/6 = 24/6 = 4$$

Price (x)	$\bar{x}$	$(x - \bar{x})$	Number sold (y)	$\bar{y}$	$(y - \bar{y})$	$(x - \bar{x})(y - \bar{y})$
18	25	−7	8	4	4	−28
20	25	−5	6	4	2	−10
25	25	0	5	4	1	0
27	25	2	2	4	−2	−4
28	25	3	2	4	−2	−6
32	25	7	1	4	−3	−21

$$\Sigma (x - \bar{x})(y - \bar{y}) = -69$$

Covariance $= \Sigma(x - \bar{x})(y - \bar{y})/(n - 1) = -69/5 = -13.8$

The other ingredient necessary to obtain a correlation coefficient is some measure of total scatter, some way of assessing the horizontal and vertical dispersion. We can do this by taking the standard deviation of the X values, which measures the horizontal spread, and multiplying by the standard deviation of the Y values, which measures the vertical spread.

The correlation coefficient, r, is the covariance of the X and Y values divided by the product of the two standard deviations.

$$r = Cov_{XY}/ (S_x \times S_y)$$

There are two things to note about r at this stage:

- It can be either positive or negative because the covariance can be negative or positive.

- It cannot be larger than 1 or –1 because the co-ordinated scatter, measured by the covariance, cannot be larger than the total scatter, measured by the product of the standard deviations.

Example 4.2

Calculate the correlation coefficient for the data in Example 4.1.

We need to calculate the sample standard deviations for X and Y.

Price (x)	$\bar{x}$	$(x - \bar{x})$	$(x - \bar{x})^2$	Number sold (y)	$\bar{y}$	$(y - \bar{y})$	$(y - \bar{y})^2$
18	25	–7	49	8	4	4	16
20	25	–5	25	6	4	2	4
25	25	0	0	5	4	1	1
27	25	2	4	2	4	–2	4
28	25	3	9	2	4	–2	4
32	25	7	49	1	4	–3	9
			136				38

From Example 4.1:   Covariance $= -13.8$

Sample standard deviation of X: $S_x = \sqrt{\Sigma(x - \bar{x})^2/(n - 1)} = \sqrt{136/5}$
$$= 5.22 \text{ to two decimal places}$$

Sample standard deviation of Y: $S_y = \sqrt{\Sigma(y - \bar{y})^2/(n - 1)} = \sqrt{38/5}$
$$= 2.76 \text{ to two decimal places}$$

Correlation coefficient: $r = (-13.8)/(5.22 \times 2.76) = -13.8/14.41$
$$= -0.96 \text{ to two decimal places}$$

As you can see, calculating a correlation coefficient, even for a fairly simple set of data is quite laborious. You can use MINITAB to produce a correlation coefficient by selecting **Basic Statistics** from the **Stat** menu. Choose **Correlation** from the sub-menu then give the column location of both sets of observations in the command window. In EXCEL you should select **Data Analysis** from the **Tools** menu, choose **Correlation** from the menu in the command window and specify the cell locations of your data.

What should we conclude from the analysis of the data in Example 4.1? The scatter diagram shows that the points representing the data almost lie along a straight line, in other words there is a pronounced linear pattern. The diagram also shows that this linear pattern goes from the top left of the diagram to the bottom right, suggesting that fewer of the more expensive garments are sold. This means there is an inverse relationship between the numbers sold and price.

What does the correlation coefficient in Example 4.2 tell us? The fact that it is negative, −0.96, confirms that the relationship between the numbers sold and price is indeed an inverse one. The fact that it is very close to the maximum possible negative value that a correlation coefficient can take, −1 indicates that there is a strong association between the variables.

The correlation coefficient measures linear correlation, that is, the extent to which there is a straight-line relationship between the variables. Every correlation coefficient will lie somewhere on the scale of possible values, that is, between −1 and +1 inclusive.

A correlation coefficient of +1 tells us that there is a perfect positive linear association between the variables. If we plotted a scatter diagram of data that has such a relationship we would expect to find all the points lying in the form of an upward-sloping straight line. You can see this sort of pattern in Figure 4.2. A correlation coefficient of −1 means we have perfect negative correlation, which is illustrated in Figure 4.3.

In practice you are unlikely to come across a correlation coefficient of +1 or −1, but you may well meet correlation coefficients that are positive and fairly close to +1 or negative and fairly close to −1. Such values reflect good positive and good negative correlation respectively. Figure 4.4 shows a set of data with a correlation coefficient of +0.9. You can see that although the points do not form a perfect straight line they form a pattern that is clearly linear and upward sloping.

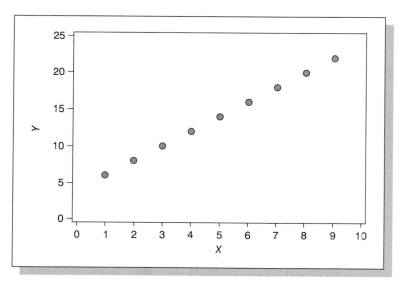

Figure 4.2
Perfect positive correlation

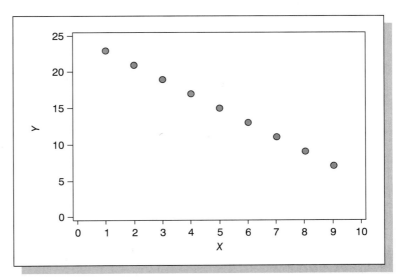

Figure 4.3
Perfect negative correlation

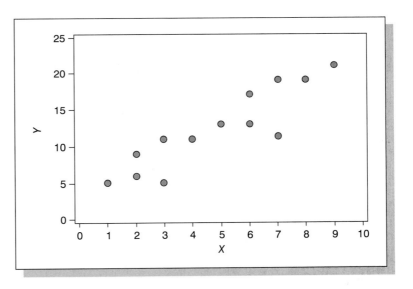

Figure 4.4
Good positive correlation

Figure 4.5 portrays bivariate data that has a correlation coefficient of −0.9. In this case you can see a clear downward linear pattern.

The closer your correlation coefficient is to +1 the better the positive correlation. The closer it is to −1, the better the negative correlation. It follows that the nearer a correlation coefficient is to zero, the weaker the connection between the two variables. Figure 4.6 shows a sample of observations of two variables with a correlation coefficient of −0.1, which provides little evidence for any correlation.

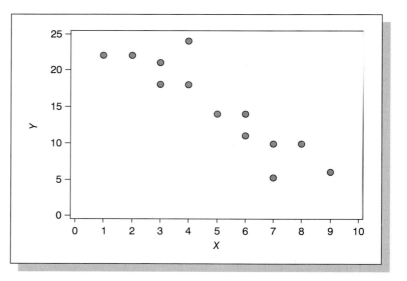

Figure 4.5
Good negative correlation

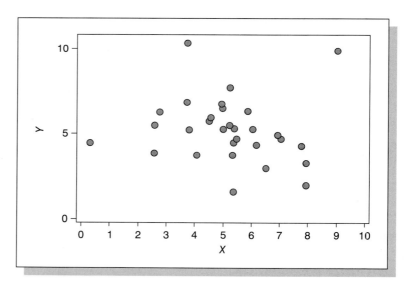

Figure 4.6
Negligible correlation

It is important to bear in mind that the correlation coefficient assesses the strength of linear relationships between two variables. It is quite possible to find a low or even zero correlation coefficient yet the scatter diagram shows a strong connection. This happens when the relationship between the two variables does not assume a linear form. Figure 4.7 shows that a clear non-linear relationship exists between the variables yet the correlation coefficient for the data it portrays is 0.

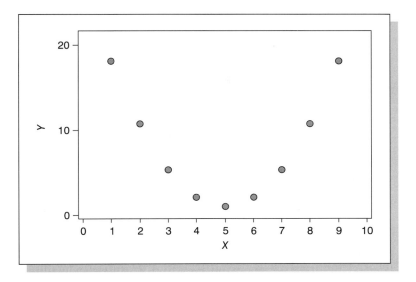

Figure 4.7
A non-linear relationship

The things to remember about the sample correlation coefficient, r, are that:

- It measures the strength of the connection or association between observed values of two variables.

- It can take any value from −1 to +1 inclusive.

- If it is positive it means there is a direct or upward-sloping relationship.

- If it is negative it means there is an inverse or downward-sloping relationship.

- The further it is from zero, the stronger the association.

- It only measures the strength of linear relationships.

4.1.2 The coefficient of determination

The square of the correlation coefficient is also used as a way of assessing the connection between variables. Although it is the square of r, the symbol used to represent it is R^2. It is called the *coefficient of determination* because it can help you to measure how much the values of one variable are decided or *determined* by the values of another.

As we saw, the correlation coefficient is based on the standard deviation. Similarly the square of the correlation coefficient is based on the square of the standard deviation, the variance.

Like the correlation coefficient, the coefficient of determination is a ratio, the ratio of the amount of the variance that can be explained by the relationship between the variables to the total variance in the data. Because it is a ratio it cannot exceed one and because it is a square it is always a positive value. For convenience it is often expressed as a percentage.

Example 4.3

Calculate the coefficient of determination, R^2, for the data in Example 4.1.

The correlation coefficient for the data was -0.96. The square of -0.96 is 0.92 (to two decimal places) or 92 per cent. This is the value of R^2. It means that 92 per cent of the variation in the numbers of jackets sold can be explained by the variation in the prices.

You may find R^2 an easier way to communicate the strength of the relationship between two variables. Its only disadvantage compared to the correlation coefficient is that the figure itself does not convey whether the association is positive or negative. However, there are other ways of showing this, including the scatter diagram.

4.1.3 Simple linear regression analysis

Measuring correlation tells you how strong the linear relationship between two variables might be but it doesn't tell us exactly what that relationship is. If we need to know about the way in which two variables are related we have to use the other part of basic bivariate analysis, *regression analysis*.

The simplest form of this technique, *simple linear regression* (which is often abbreviated to SLR), enables us to find the straight line most appropriate for representing the connection between two sets of observed values. Because the line that we 'fit' to our data can be used to represent the relationship it is rather like an average in two dimensions, it summarizes the link between the variables.

Simple linear regression is called *simple* because it analyses two variables, it is called *linear* because it is about finding a straight line, but why is it called *regression*, which actually means going backwards? The answer is that the technique was first developed by the genetics pioneer Francis Galton, who wanted a way of representing how the height of children was genetically restrained or 'regressed' by the height of their parents.

In later work you may encounter *multiple* regression, which is used to analyse relationships between more than two variables, and *non-linear* regression, which is used to analyse relationships that do not have a straight-line pattern.

You might ask why it is necessary to have a technique to fit a line to a set of data. It would be quite easy to look at a scatter diagram like Figure 4.1, lay a ruler close to the points and draw a line to represent the relationship between the variables. This is known as fitting a line 'by eye' and is a perfectly acceptable way of getting a quick approximation particularly in a case like Figure 4.1 where there are few points which form a clear linear pattern.

The trouble with fitting a line by eye is that it is inconsistent and unreliable. It is inconsistent because the position of the line depends on the judgement of the person drawing the line. Different people will produce different lines for the same data.

For any set of bivariate data there is one line that is the most appropriate, the so-called 'best-fit' line. There is no guarantee that fitting a line by eye will produce the best-fit line, so fitting a line by eye is unreliable.

We need a reliable, consistent way of finding the line which best fits a set of plotted points, which is what simple linear regression analysis is. It is a technique that finds the line of best-fit, the line that travels as closely as possible to the plotted points. It identifies the two defining characteristics of that line, its *intercept*, or starting point, and its *slope*, or rate of increase or decrease. These are illustrated in Figure 4.8.

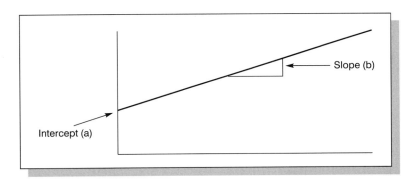

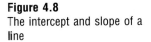

Figure 4.8
The intercept and slope of a line

We can use these defining characteristics to compose the equation of the line of best-fit, which represents the line using symbols. The equation enables us to plot the line itself.

Simple linear regression is based on the idea of minimizing the differences between a line and the points it is intended to represent. Since all the points matter, it is the sum of these differences that needs to be minimized. In other words the best-fit line is the line that results in a lower sum of differences than any other line would for that set of data.

The task for simple linear regression is a little more compli-cated because the difference between a point and the line is positive if the point is above the line, and negative if the point is below the line. If we were to add up these differences we would find that the negative and positive differences cancel each other out.

This means the sum of the differences is not a reliable way of judging how well a line fits a set of points. To get around this problem, simple linear regression is based on the squares of the differences because they will always be positive.

Example 4.4

The sales of ice-cream in an American-style ice-cream shop (in £000) and the midday temperatures (in degrees Celsius) for three days were:

Sales	(Y)	4	3	6
Temperature	(X)	15	20	25

Which of the two lines best fits the data, the one in Figure 4.9 or the one in Figure 4.10?

The deviations between the points and the line in Figure 4.9 are, from left to right, +1.5, −1.5 and 0. The total deviation is:

$$+1.5 + (-1.5) + 0 = 0$$

The deviations between the points and the line in Figure 4.10 are, from left to right, +1, −1 and +1. The total deviation is:

$$+1 + (-1) + 1 = 1$$

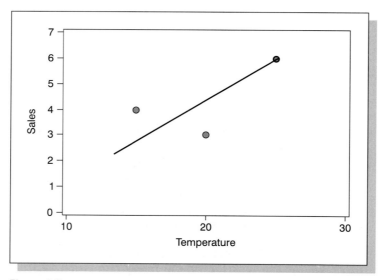

Figure 4.9
Sales and temperature

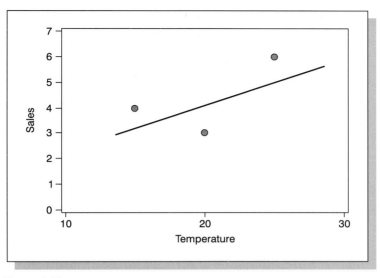

Figure 4.10
Sales and temperature

The fact that the total deviation is smaller for Figure 4.9 suggests that its line is the better fit. But if we take the sum of the squared deviations the conclusion is different.

Total squared deviation in Figure 4.9 $= 1.5^2 + (-1.5)^2 + 0^2 = 2.25 + 2.25 + 0 = 4.5$

Total squared deviation in Figure 4.10 $= 1^2 + (-1)^2 + 1^2 = 1 + 1 + 1 = 3$

This apparent contradiction has arisen because the large deviations in Figure 4.9 cancel each other out when we add them together.

The best-fit line that simple linear regression finds for us is the line which takes the path which results in there being the least possible sum of squared differences between the points and the line. For this reason the technique is sometimes referred to as *least squares regression*.

For any given set of data, as you can imagine, there are many lines from which the best-fit line could be chosen. To pick the right one we could plot each of them in turn and measure the differences using a ruler. Fortunately such a laborious procedure is not necessary. Simple linear regression uses calculus, the area of mathematics that is partly about finding minimum or maximum values, to find the intercept and slope of the line of best-fit directly from the data.

The procedure involves using two expressions to find first the slope and then the intercept. Since simple linear regression is almost always used to find the line of best-fit from a set of sample data the letters used to represent the intercept and the slope are a and b respectively. The equivalent Greek letters, α and β, are used to represent the intercept and slope of the population line of best-fit.

According to simple linear regression analysis the slope of the line of best fit:

$$b = \frac{\Sigma xy - (\Sigma x \times \Sigma y)/n}{\Sigma x^2 - (\Sigma x)^2/n}$$

and the intercept:

$$a = (\Sigma y - b\Sigma x)/n$$

These results can then be combined to give the equation of the line of best fit, which is known as the *regression equation*:

$$Y = a + bX$$

The expressions for getting the slope and intercept of the line of best fit look daunting, but this need not worry you. If you have to find a best fit line you can use a statistical or a spreadsheet package, or even a calculator with a good statistical facility to do the hard work for you. They are quoted here, and used in Example 4.5 below merely to show you how the procedure works.

Example 4.5

Find the equation of the line of best fit for the data in Example 4.1.

We need to find four summations; the sum of the x values, the sum of the y values, the sum of the x squared values and the sum of the products of each pair of x and y values multiplied together. We also need to know n, the number of pairs of observations.

Price (x)	x^2	Number sold (y)	xy
18	324	8	144
20	400	6	120
25	625	5	125
27	729	2	54
28	784	2	56
32	1024	1	32
$\Sigma x = 150$	$\Sigma x^2 = 3886$	$\Sigma y = 24$	$\Sigma xy = 531$ $n = 6$

$$b = \frac{\Sigma xy - (\Sigma x \times \Sigma y)/n}{\Sigma x^2 - (\Sigma x)^2/n} = \frac{531 - (150 \times 24)/6}{3886 - 150^2/6} = \frac{531 - 3600/6}{3886 - 22\,500/6}$$

$$= \frac{531 - 600}{3886 - 3750} = \frac{-69}{136} = -0.507 \text{ to three decimal places}$$

$$a = (\Sigma y - b\Sigma x)/n = (24 - (-0.507)150)/6 = (24 + 76.103)/6$$

$$= 100.103/6 = 16.684 \text{ to three decimal places}$$

The equation of the line of best fit is: $Y = 16.684 - 0.507X$

This is a laborious procedure, even with a relatively simple set of data. You can use MINITAB to perform this type of analysis by selecting **Regression** from the **Stat** menu. Choose **Regression** from the **Regression** sub-menu. Specify the column locations of the **Response,** i.e. the values of Y, and the **Predictor,** i.e. the values of X. Click **OK** and the output that appears has the regression equation, the equation of the line of best fit, at the top.

If you want a scatter diagram with the line of best-fit superimposed on the scatter, follow the **Stat – Regression** sequence in MINITAB and choose **Fitted Line Plot** from the **Regression** sub-menu. The diagram that appears includes the regression equation and the value of R^2 for the data.

To produce a regression equation in EXCEL choose **Data Analysis** from the **Tools** pull-down menu. Select **Regression** from the **Data Analysis** menu and specify the input ranges for the values of X and Y in the command window. The output that appears includes the intercept and slope of the line of best-fit in a column headed **Coefficient** towards the bottom. In this column you will see the intercept in the first row and the slope, labelled **X variable**, in the second row.

Example 4.6

Produce a fitted line plot for the data in Example 4.1.

You can see two insertions above the graph in Figure 4.11 The lower of the two is the value of the coefficient of determination, R^2, which is written R-Sq, 92.1 per cent. This is a slightly more precise version of the result we saw in Example 4.3. The other insertion is the regression equation:

Number sold $= 16.6838 - 0.507353$Price

This is the same equation as we obtained by calculation in Example 4.5, except that here the slope and the intercept are given more precisely.

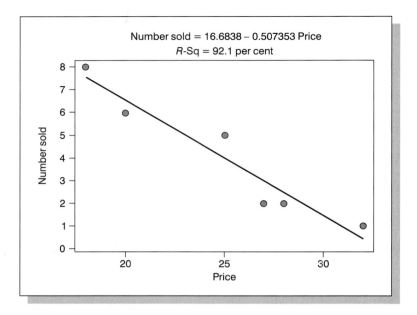

Number sold = 16.6838 – 0.507353 Price
R-Sq = 92.1 per cent

Figure 4.11
Fitted line plot of prices of
jackets and number sold

This is a regression 'model' that represents how the two variables are connected based on the sample evidence in Example 4.1. It is the best linear model that can be found for that set of data.

We can use the equation to predict values of Y that should occur with values of X. These are known as *expected* values of Y because they are what the line leads us to *expect* to be associated with the X values. The symbol $\hat{y}$, 'y-hat', is used to represent a value of Y that is predicted using the regression equation, so that we can distinguish it from an actual y value.

That is, the regression equation $Y = a + bX$ can be used to predict an individual y value that is expected to occur with an observed x value:

$$\hat{y} = a + bx$$

Example 4.7

Use the regression equation from Example 4.6 to find how many new jackets the shop can expect to sell if they are priced at £23.50.

The regression equation tells us that: Number sold = 16.6838 − 0.507353 Price

If we put the figure '23.5' in where the word 'Price' appears in the equation we can work out what, according to the equation, the number sold should be.

$$\text{Number sold (if price is 23.5)} = 16.6838 - 0.507353\,(23.5)$$

$$= 16.6838 - 11.9228 = 4.761 \text{ to three decimal places}$$

This suggests the number sold will be 5, as jackets sales are measured in whole numbers.

4.2 Summarizing data collected over time

Data collected over time, time series, is very important for the successful performance of organizations. For instance, such data can reveal trends in consumer expenditure and taste that companies need to follow.

Businesses use information based on data collected by other agencies over time to help them understand and evaluate the environment in which they operate. Perhaps the most important and widespread example of this is the use of *index numbers* to monitor general trends in prices and costs. For instance, the Retail Price Index is used as a benchmark figure in the context of wage bargaining, and Share Price Indices are reference points in financial decisions companies face.

Businesses also produce a variety of data that is collected over time in order to understand and communicate its progress. For instance, every company report contains charts and tables showing data that demonstrate its development over the period of a year: sales, profits, number of employees etc.

4.2.1 Index numbers

Most businesses attach a great deal of importance to changes in the costs of things they buy and the prices of things they sell. During periods of high inflation these changes are more dramatic, in periods of low inflation they are modest. Over recent decades, when the level of inflation has fluctuated so much, companies have got used to tracking general price and cost movements carefully. To help them do this they have turned to index numbers.

Index numbers can be used to represent movements of many things over time in a series of single figures. A simple index number is the value of something at one point in time, maybe the current value, in relation to its value at another point in time, the base-period, multiplied by 100 to give a percentage (although the per cent sign is not usually written alongside it).

$$\text{Simple price index} = \frac{\text{current price}}{\text{base period price}} \times 100 = \frac{p_c}{p_0} \times 100$$

where p_c represents the price in the current year and p_0 represents the price in the base year (i.e. period 0).

Example 4.8

Full exhaust systems cost a garage proprietor £156 each in 2000. They cost £125 in 1997. Calculate a simple price index to represent the change in price over the period.

$$\text{Simple price index} = \frac{\text{current price}}{\text{base period price}} \times 100 = \frac{p_c}{p_0} \times 100$$

$$= \frac{156}{125} \times 100 = 124.8$$

This tells us that the price of an exhaust system has increased by 24.8 per cent over this period.

However, businesses usually buy and sell more than a single item so this type of index number is of limited use. Of much greater importance are *aggregate* indices that summarize price movements of many items in a single figure.

We can calculate a simple aggregate price index for a combination of goods by taking the sum of the prices for the goods in the current period and dividing it by the sum of the prices of the same goods in the base period. That is:

$$\text{Simple aggregate price index} = \frac{\Sigma p_c}{\Sigma p_0} \times 100$$

Example 4.9

The garage proprietor in Example 4.8 regularly buys exhaust systems, car batteries, and tyres. The prices of these goods in 2000 and 1997 were:

	1997	2000
Exhaust system	£125	£156
Battery	£25	£35
Tyre	£28	£32

Calculate a simple aggregate price index to compare the prices in 2000 to the prices in 1997.

Simple aggregate price index:

$$\frac{\Sigma p_c}{\Sigma p_0} \times 100 = \frac{156 + 35 + 32}{125 + 25 + 28} \times 100 = \frac{223}{178} \times 100 = 125.3 \text{ to one decimal place}$$

This result indicates that prices paid by the garage proprietor increased by 25.3 per cent from 1997 to 2000.

The result we obtained in Example 4.9 may well be more useful because it is an overall figure that includes all the commodities. However, it does not differentiate between prices of items that may be purchased in greater quantity than other items, which implies that their prices are of much greater significance.

In a simple aggregate price index each price is given equal prominence, you can see in Example 4.9 that each price appears once in the expression. Its numerical 'clout' depends simply on whether it is a large or small price. In Example 4.9 the result, 125.3, is close to the value of the simple price index of the exhaust system calculated in Example 4.8, 124.8. This is because the exhaust system happens to have the largest price in the set.

In practice the importance of the price of an item is a reflection of the quantity that is bought as well as the price itself. To measure changes in movements of prices in a more realistic way we need to *weight* each price in proportion to the quantity purchased. We can then calculate a weighted aggregate price index.

There are two ways we can do this. The first is to use the quantity figure from the base period, represented by the symbol q_0, to weight the price of each item. This type of index is known as the Laspeyre price index. To calculate it we need to work out the total cost of the base period quantities at current prices, divide that by the total cost of the base period quantities at base period prices, and multiply the result by 100:

$$\text{Laspeyre price index} = \frac{\Sigma q_0 p_c}{\Sigma q_0 p_0} \times 100$$

Example 4.10

The garage records show that in 1997 50 exhaust systems, 400 batteries, and 1000 tyres were purchased. Use these figures and the price figures from Example 4.9 to produce a Laspeyre price index to compare the prices of 2000 to those of 1997.

$$\frac{\Sigma q_0 p_c}{\Sigma q_0 p_0} \times 100 = \frac{(50 \times 156) + (400 \times 35) + (32 \times 1000)}{(50 \times 125) + (400 \times 25) + (28 \times 1000)} \times 100$$

$$= \frac{53\,800}{44\,250} \times 100$$

$$= 121.6 \text{ to one decimal place}$$

This suggests that the prices have increased by 21.6 per cent between 1997 and 2000.

The result is lower than the figure obtained in Example 4.9, 125.3, because the exhaust system price has the lowest weighting and tyres, which have the lowest price change, have the highest weighting.

The Laspeyre technique uses quantities that are historical. The advantage of this is that such figures are usually readily available. The disadvantage is that they may not accurately reflect the quantities used in the current period.

The alternative approach, which is more useful when quantities used have changed considerably, is to use quantity figures from the current period, represented by the symbol q_c. This type of index is known as the Paasche price index. To calculate it you work out the total cost of the current period quantities at current prices, divide that by the total cost of the current period quantities at base period prices, and multiply the result by 100:

$$\text{Paasche price index} = \frac{\Sigma q_c p_c}{\Sigma q_c p_0} \times 100$$

Example 4.11

In 2000 the garage purchased 50 exhaust systems, 600 batteries, and 750 tyres. Use these figures and the price figures from Example 4.9 to produce a Paasche price index to compare the prices of 2000 to those of 1997.

$$\Sigma q_c p_c / \Sigma q_c p_0 \times 100 = \frac{(50 \times 156) + (600 \times 35) + (750 \times 32)}{(50 \times 125) + (600 \times 25) + (750 \times 28)} \times 100$$

$$= \frac{52\,800}{42\,250} \times 100 = 125.0 \text{ to one decimal place}$$

This result suggests that the prices have increased by 25.0 per cent between 1997 and 2000.

The figure is higher than the result in Example 4.10 because there is a greater weighting on the battery price, which has changed most, and a lower weighting on the tyre price, which has changed least.

The advantage of using a Paasche price index is that the quantity figures used are more up to date and therefore realistic. But it is not always possible to get current period quantity figures, particularly when there is a wide range of items and a large number of organizations or consumers that buy them.

The other disadvantage of using the Paasche price index is that new quantity figures must be available for each period we want to compare with the base period. If the garage proprietor wants a Paashce price index for prices in 2001 compared to 1997 you could not provide one until you know both the quantities and the prices used in 2001. In contrast, to calculate a Laspeyre price index for 2001 you only need to know the prices in 2001 because you would use quantities from 1997.

If you look carefully at Examples 4.10 and 4.11 you will see that whichever index is used the same quantity figures weight the prices from the different years. This is an important point, they are *price* indices, and they are used to compare prices across the time period, not quantities.

Organizations tend to use index numbers that have already been compiled rather than construct their own. Probably the most common use of index numbers that you will meet is in the adjustment of financial amounts to take into account changes in price levels.

A sum of money in one period is not necessarily the same as the same amount in another period because its purchasing power changes. This means that if we want to compare an amount from one period with an amount from another period we have to make some adjustment for price changes. The most common way of doing this is to use the Retail Price Index (RPI), an index the Office for National Statistics (ONS) calculates to monitor price changes, changes in the cost of living.

Example 4.12

The annual salary of the manager of a sports goods store has changed in the following way between 1997 and 2000. Use the RPI figures for those years to see whether the increases in her salary have kept up with the cost of living.

	1997	1998	1999	2000
Salary (£000)	24	26	27	28
RPI (1987 = 100)	157.5	162.9	165.4	170.3

(Source: 'Retail Price Index', ONS. Crown Copyright. Reproduced with the permission of HMSO and the Queen's Printer for Scotland)

We can 'deflate' the figures for 1998, 1999 and 2000 so that they are expressed in '1997 pounds' by multiplying each of them by the ratio between the RPI for 1997 and the RPI for the year concerned.

Adjusted 1998 salary $= 26 \times 157.5/162.9$

$= 25.138$ to three decimal places, i.e. £25,138

Adjusted 1999 salary $= 27 \times 157.5/165.4$

$= 25.710$ to three decimal places, i.e. £25,710

Adjusted 2000 salary $= 28 \times 157.5/170.3$

$= 25.895$ to three decimal places, i.e. £25.895

These results suggest that her salary has increased more than the cost of living throughout the period.

4.2.2 Basic time series analysis

Organizations collect time series data, which is data made up of observations taken at regular intervals, as a matter of course. Look at the operations of any organization and you will usually find figures such as daily receipts, weekly staff absences, and monthly payroll. If you look at the report it produces to present its performance you will find more time series data such as quarterly turnover and annual profit.

Sometimes each observed value of a time series is only looked at when it is collected. But often organizations need to look at the sequence that is unfolding as more observed values are collected. This can help them review their performance over the period covered by the time series and it can help them predict future values of the time series.

It is possible to do both of these things using a time series chart, a graph that shows the progression of observations in a time series. You can look for an overall movement, a *trend*, and recurrent fluctuations around the trend.

This is a good way to get a 'feel' for the way the time series is behaving, but to analyse a time series properly we need to use a more systematic approach. One way of doing this is called *decomposition*, which involves breaking down or *decomposing* the series into different parts. This approach is suitable for time series data that has a repeated pattern, which includes many time series that occur in business.

The decomposition approach assumes that a time series is made up, or composed, of three types of parts, or *components*. These are

- A trend, an underlying longer-term movement in the series.

- A recurrent component, which may be daily, weekly, monthly, seasonal or cyclical.

- An error, the amount that isn't part of either the trend or recurrent components.

The type of recurrent component we find in a time series depends on how regularly the data is collected. We would expect to find daily components in data collected each day, weekly components in data collected each week and so on. Seasonal components are usually a feature of data collected quarterly, whereas cyclical components, patterns that recur over many years, crop up in data collected annually.

It is possible that a time series includes more than one recurrent component, for instance weekly figures may exhibit a regular monthly fluctuation as well as a weekly one. However, usually the decomposition of a time series involves looking for the trend and just one recurrent component.

Example 4.13

The revenue (in pounds) from newspaper sales at a new service station for the morning, afternoon and evening periods of the first three days of operation are:

	Morning	Afternoon	Evening
Day 1	320	92	218
Day 2	341	101	224
Day 3	359	116	272

Construct a time series chart and examine it for evidence of a trend and a recurrent component for parts of the day.

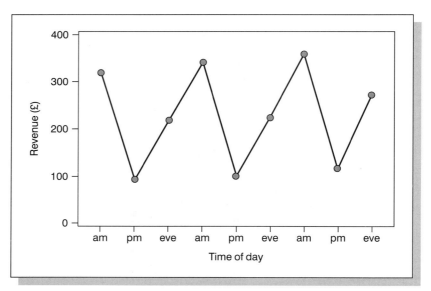

Figure 4.12
Newspaper sales revenue over three days

If you look carefully at Figure 4.12 you can see that there is a gradual upward drift in the points that represent the time series. This suggests the trend is that the revenue from newspaper sales is increasing.

You can also see that within the figures for each day there is considerable variation. The points for the mornings tend to peak whilst the figures for the afternoons tend to dip.

The first stage we take in decomposing a time series is to try to separate out the trend. We can do this by calculating a set of *moving averages* for the series. Moving averages are sequential, they are averages calculated from sequences of values in a time series.

A moving average (MA) is the mean of one of each time period in the time series. For the data in Example 4.13 each moving average will be the mean of one morning figure, one afternoon figure and one evening figure. Because in this case the moving average is calculated from three observations it is called a *three-point* moving average.

The first moving average in the set will be the mean of the figures for the first day. The second moving average is the mean of the figures from the afternoon and evening of the first day and the morning of the second day. The result will still be the mean of three figures, one from each part of the day. We continue doing this, dropping the first value of the sequence out and replacing it with a new figure until we reach the end of the series.

Example 4.14

Calculate moving averages for the data in Example 4.13.

The first MA $= (320 + 92 + 218)/3 = 630/3 = 210$

The second MA $= (92 + 218 + 341)/3 = 651/3 = 217$

The third MA $= (218 + 341 + 101)/3 = 660/3 = 220$

and so on.

The complete set of moving averages is:

210   217   220   222   228   233   249

If you count the number of moving averages in Example 4.14 you will find there are only seven, two fewer than the number of observations in the time series. This is because each moving average summarizes three observations that come from different points in time.

Like any other average, we can think of a moving average as being in the middle of the set of data from which it has been derived. In the case of moving averages we can think of them as belonging to the middle of the period covered by the observations that we used to calculate it. The first moving average therefore belongs to the afternoon of the first day because that is the middle of the three parts of the day, the parts of the day whose observed values were used to calculate it.

If the first moving average belongs to the first afternoon, we don't have a moving average that belongs to the first morning. Similarly, the last moving average belongs to the last afternoon and we have no moving average for the last evening.

The process of positioning the moving averages in line with the middle of the observations they summarize is called *centring*.

Example 4.15

Centre the moving averages in Example 4.14.

Day	Time	Revenue	Moving average
1	am	320	
1	pm	92	210
1	eve	218	217
2	am	341	220
2	pm	101	222
2	eve	224	228
3	am	359	233
3	pm	116	249
3	eve	272	

The process of centring is a little more complicated if you have a time series with a *periodicity* of four, that is, where each larger time period is split into four periods as in quarterly data. To centre the moving averages for quarterly data you have to split the difference between two moving averages because the moving averages you calculate are 'out of phase' with the time series observations.

Example 4.16

Calculate and centre the moving averages for the data below. They are the sales of beachwear (in £000) in a department store over two years.

	Winter	Spring	Summer	Autumn
Year 1	14.2	31.8	33.0	6.9
Year 2	15.3	34.7	36.2	7.3

Moving averages for these figures will be four-point moving averages.

First MA $= (14.2 + 31.8 + 33.0 + 6.9)/4 = 85.9/4 = 21.475$

Second MA $= (31.8 + 33.0 + 6.9 + 15.3)/4 = 87.0/4 = 21.75$

and so on.

Year	Quarter	Sales	Moving average
1	Winter	14.2	
1	Spring	31.8	
			21.475
1	Summer	33.0	
			21.750
1	Autumn	6.9	
			22.475
2	Winter	15.3	
			23.275
2	Spring	34.7	
			23.375
2	Summer	36.2	
2	Autumn	7.3	

The moving averages straddle two quarters because the middle of four periods is between two of them. To centre them, that is, to bring them in line with the series itself, we have to split the difference between pairs of them.

The centred four-point MA for the Summer of Year 1 = (21.475 + 21.750)/2

= 21.6125

The centred four-point MA for the Autumn of Year 1 = (21.750 + 22.475)/2

= 22.1125

and so on.

Year	Quarter	Sales	Moving average	Centred moving average
1	Winter	14.2		
1	Spring	31.8		
			21.475	
1	Summer	33.0		21.6125
			21.750	
1	Autumn	6.9		22.1125
			22.475	
2	Winter	15.3		22.8750
			23.275	
2	Spring	34.7		23.3250
			23.375	
2	Summer	36.2		
2	Autumn	7.3		

Centring moving averages is important because the moving averages are the figures that we need to use as estimates of the trend at particular points in time. We want to be able to compare them directly with observations in order to separate out other components of the time series.

The procedure we adopt to separate the components of a time series depends on how we assume they are combined in the observations. The simplest case is to assume that the components are added together, that is, each observation, y, is the sum of a set of components:

$$y = \text{Trend component } (T) + \text{Recurrent component } (R)$$
$$+ \text{ Error component } (E)$$

This is called the *additive* model of a time series. You may also come across the *multiplicative* model. If you want to analyse a time series which you assume is additive, you have to subtract the components from each other to decompose the time series. If you assume it is multiplicative, you have to divide to decompose it.

We begin the process of decomposing a time series assumed to be additive by subtracting the centred moving averages, the estimated trend values, from the observations they sit alongside. What we are left with are deviations from the trend, a set of figures that contain only the recurrent and error components, that is,

$$y - T = R + E$$

Example 4.17

Subtract the centred moving averages in Example 4.14 from the observations in Example 4.13.

Day	Time	Revenue (y)	Moving average (T)	y – T
1	am	320		
1	pm	92	210	–118
1	eve	218	217	1
2	am	341	220	121
2	pm	101	222	–121
2	eve	224	228	–4
3	am	359	233	126
3	pm	116	249	–133
3	eve	272		

The next stage is to arrange these $y - T$ results by the parts of the day and calculate the mean of the deviations from the trend for each part of the day. These will be our estimates for the recurrent component for each part of the day, the differences we expect between the trend and the observed value in each part of the day.

Example 4.18

Find the estimates for the recurrent daily components from the figures in Example 4.17. What do they tell us about the pattern of newspaper sales?

		Morning	Afternoon	Evening
Day 1	$y - T$		−118	1
Day 2	$y - T$	121	−121	−4
Day 3	$y - T$	126	−133	

The estimated components for the parts of the day are:

In mornings $(121 + 126)/2$ $= 123.5$

In afternoons $((-118) + (-121) + (-133))/3 = -124.0$

In evenings $(1 + (-4))/2$ $= -1.5$

These three figures (123.5, −124.0, and −1.5) add up to −2. Because they are variations around the trend they really should add up to 0, otherwise when they are used together they suggest a deviation from the trend. To overcome this problem, we simply divide the total by 3, as there are three recurrent components, and add this amount to each component. After this modification the components should add up to zero:

Adjusted morning component $= 123.5 + 0.667 = 124.167$

Adjusted afternoon component $= -124.0 + 0.667 = -123.333$

Adjusted evening component $= -1.5 + 0.667 = \underline{-0.833}$

                                                        0.001

The adjusted components do not add up to precisely zero because two adjusted components have been rounded down and one rounded up. Nevertheless the results sum to very nearly zero.

These components suggest that newspaper sales are regularly higher in mornings, lower in the afternoons and almost the same as the trend in the evenings.

We can take the analysis a stage further by subtracting the recurrent components, R, from the $y - T$ figures to isolate the error components, E. That is:

$$E = y - T - R$$

Example 4.19

Find the error components for the data in Example 4.13 using the table produced in Example 4.17 and the recurrent components from Example 4.18.

Day	Time	Revenue (y)	Moving average (T)	y − T	R	E = (y − T) − R
1	am	320				
1	pm	92	210	−118	−123.333	5.333
1	eve	218	217	1	−0.833	1.833
2	am	341	220	121	124.167	−3.167
2	pm	101	222	−121	−123.333	2.333
2	eve	224	228	−4	−0.833	−3.167
3	am	359	233	126	124.167	1.833
3	pm	116	249	−133	−123.333	−9.667
3	eve	272				

The error terms enable us to review the performance over the period. A large negative error component suggests we have under-performed in that period and might lead us to investigate reasons that may explain why. A large positive error component suggests we have performed better than expected and we would look for reasons to explain the success. This type of evaluation should enable us to improve the performance because we can tackle the factors that lead us to under-perform and build on the factors that lead us to perform well.

Occasionally the analysis of a time series results in a very large error component that reflects the influence of some unusual and unexpected external influence such as a fuel shortage or a sudden rise in exchange rates. You can usually spot the impact of such factors by looking for prominent peaks or troughs, sometimes called spikes when the series is plotted.

The error components in Example 4.19 suggest newspaper sales in the morning of the second day were disappointing compared to the morning sales on the third day. Perhaps copies of a particular paper did not arrive on the second day. The evening sales on the second day were disappointing compared to the evening sales on the first day. The afternoon sales were good on the first day, reasonable on the second but poor on the third.

As well as using the results of decomposition to review performance we can use them to construct forecasts for future periods. There are two stages in doing this. The first is to project the trend into the periods we want to predict, and the second is to add the appropriate recurrent components to the trend projections. We can represent the process as:

$$\hat{y} = T + R$$

where $\hat{y}$ is the estimated future value, T and R are the trend and recurrent components respectively. You can see there is no error component. The error components are, by definition, unpredictable.

You could produce trend projections by plotting the centred moving averages and fitting a line to them by eye, then simply continuing the line into the future periods you want to predict. However, a much better way is to use regression analysis to get the equation of the line that best fits the moving averages and using the equation to project the trend. The regression equation in this context is called the *trend line equation*.

Example 4.20

Find a trend line equation for the moving averages in Example 4.15 and use the equation to predict the trend values on day 4 and construct forecasts for day 4 by adding the recurrent components from Example 4.18.

We have to use numbers for the regression analysis so we cannot use the names of the parts of the day. Instead we number the periods, starting with period 1 for the morning of day 1, period 2 for the afternoon of day 1, and so on.

MA	210	217	220	222	228	233	249
Period	2	3	4	5	6	7	8

Using regression analysis the trend line equation is:

Trend = 197.54 + 5.61 Period

Day 4 will consist of periods 10 to 12.

Forecast trend at period 10 (am day 4) = 197.54 + 5.61 (10) = 253.64

Forecast trend at period 11 (pm day 4) = 197.54 + 5.61 (11) = 259.25

Forecast trend at period 12 (eve day 4) = 197.54 + 5.61 (12) = 264.86

Adding the appropriate recurrent components gives the forecast values for day 4:

Forecast for period 10 (am day 4) = 253.64 + 124.167   = 377.807   round to £377.81

Forecast for period 11 (pm day 4) = 259.25 + (−123.333) = 135.917   round to £135.92

Forecast for period 12 (eve day 4) = 264.86 + (−0.833)   = 264.027   round to £264.03

Forecasts like the ones we have obtained in Example 4.20 can be used as the basis for setting budgets, for assessing future order levels and so forth. In practice computer software would be used to derive them.

In MINITAB there is a **Decomposition** facility that you can enter via the **Time Series** option in the **Stat** menu. It can produce graphics like Figure 4.13 to portray the process.

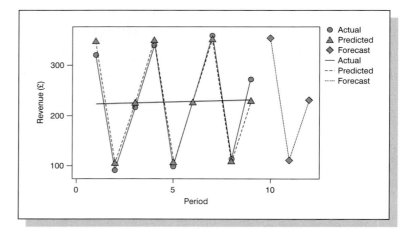

Figure 4.13
Newspaper sales revenue

In Figure 4.13 the solid line that zigzags depicts the original series, the smooth line running upwards through it is the trend line, and the broken line that follows the original series closely is a plot of the trend plus the components for the parts of the day. The differences between the latter line and the line representing the original values are the error components. The dotted line on the right-hand side is a plot of the predictions the package has made for the periods of day 4.

Note that the **Decomposition** function in MINITAB finds the trend line for time series data by applying regression analysis to the series values themselves. This means that the resulting trend line will differ somewhat from the trend line you would obtain by using regression analysis on moving averages calculated from the series, as in Example 4.20, or by fitting a line to such moving averages by eye.

In EXCEL the **Moving average** facility in the **Data Analysis** option from the **Tools** menu can provide you with moving averages for a time series. If you tick the **Chart output** box in the **Moving average** command window you can get a plot of the time series alongside its moving averages.

In this section we have concentrated on using one technique, known as decomposition to analyse time series data. The field of time series analysis is substantial and contains a variety of techniques. If you would like to read more about it, Chatfield (1996) and Cryer (1986) are useful introductory texts.

Review questions

Answers to these questions, including fully worked solutions to those questions marked with an asterisk (*), are on pages 344–347.

4.1   Consider which of the relationships below are likely to have a positive and which are likely to have a negative correlation coefficient.

(a) The distance a vehicle travels and the fuel consumed
(b) The demand for laptop computers and their price
(c) The average temperature of countries and the sales of warm clothing
(d) The amount consumers spend on motor insurance and their age
(e) The population of countries and the amount of waste they generate
(f) The income of people and the amount of income tax they pay.

4.2*   The cost of placing a full-page colour advertisement (in £000) and the circulation figures (in £000) of nine magazines are:

Cost:	9	43	16	17	19	13	20	44	35
Circulation:	135	2100	680	470	450	105	275	2250	695

(a) Which of these variables should be the dependent variable, and why?
(b) Plot a scatter diagram to portray the data.
(c) Determine the correlation coefficient and assess its value.

4.3   The outstanding balances on the monthly bills of 12 credit card accounts (in £) and the household income of the account holders (in £000) are:

Balance:	250	1630	970	2190	410	830	0	550	0	682	0	0
Income:	15	23	26	28	31	35	37	38	42	42	45	46

Portray these figures on a scatter diagram taking the outstanding balance as the dependent variable and then calculate the correlation coefficient and comment on its value.

4.4 Car parking spaces in a city centre are in short supply. The cost of parking a car for a whole day in ten public car parks within the city (in £) and the distances between the car parks and the monument that is always considered the centre of the city (in km) are:

Cost	5	5	7	8	10	12	15	15	18	20
Distance	1.5	1.2	1.0	1.1	0.8	0.5	0.4	0.2	0.1	0.1

Assuming that the cost of parking is dependent on the distance the car park is from the city centre, plot the data on a scatter diagram. Find the value of the correlation coefficient and indicate what conclusions should be drawn from it.

4.5 The weekly turnover and the total display area, in square metres, of eight 'late night' grocery shops are:

Turnover (£000)	23	37	33	41	47	86	72	95
Display area (m²)	15	21	30	45	61	77	79	92

(a) Identify which variable is the dependent variable.
(b) Plot a scatter diagram to portray these figures.
(c) Calculate the correlation coefficient and discuss its value.

4.6 A consumer group has tested ten makes of personal stereo. The prices and the score (out of 100) awarded to them by a panel of experts the group commissioned to test them, are:

Price (£)	95	69	18	32	27	70	49	35	50	29
Score	74	63	28	33	37	58	38	43	50	31

(a) Plot a scatter diagram to portray the data taking score as the dependent variable.
(b) Find the equation of the line of best fit using simple linear regression.
(c) Plot the line of best fit on the scatter diagram produced for (a).
(d) Use the regression equation from (c) to predict the score that the panel of experts would award to a personal stereo priced £40.

4.7 Eight prominent football teams play in the same division. The total number of goals scored by each team last season and the league position each was in at the end of the season are:

Goals scored   75   60   56   44   43   40   37   52

League position   2   5   9   10   14   16   17   22

(a) Produce a scatter diagram to display the data taking league position as the dependent variable.
(b) Using simple linear regression, determine the line of best fit and plot it on your scatter diagram.
(c) Predict the final position of a team that scored 50 goals using your regression equation.

4.8   In a survey of commuting patterns ten respondents say that they cycle to work. The distances they travel (in miles) and the mean journey times (in minutes) they report are:

Distance   2   2   3   4   5   6   7   8   8   10

Mean journey time   10 15 15 20 25 25 30 40 45 50

(a) Portray the data on a scatter diagram.
(b) Calculate the slope and intercept of the line of best fit using simple linear regression analysis.
(c) Plot the line of best fit and use it to estimate the time that a journey of 9 miles would take.

4.9   The classified advertisement columns of a local paper contain details of twelve used cars of a particular make and model. The prices of these cars (in £000) and the numbers of miles they have travelled (in 000) are:

Price   6.8 6.2 5.7 4.7 6.0 5.9 7.0 4.5 5.0 3.0 3.8 3.5

Mileage 9   13   11   33   14   11   3   19   22   35   40   44

(a) Present these figures in the form of a scatter diagram.
(b) Find the least squares line of best fit and plot it on your scatter diagram.
(c) Predict the price of a car of this type that has travelled 25 000 miles.

4.10 A pizza manufacturer purchases cheese, pepperoni, and tomato paste. The prices of these ingredients in 1997, 1999, and 2001 were:

	Year		
Ingredient	1997	1999	2001
Cheese (per kg)	£1.75	£2.65	£3.10
Pepperoni (per kg)	£2.25	£2.87	£3.55
Tomato paste (per litre)	£0.60	£1.10	£1.35

(a) Calculate a simple aggregate price index for the prices in 1999 and 2001 using 1997 as the base period.

(b) What additional information would you need in order to calculate a weighted aggregate price index to measure these price changes?

4.11* A cab driver pays for fuel, vehicle servicing and maintenance every 3 months, and an annual operating licence. The prices of these in 2000 and in 1996, together with the quantity of each that was purchased during 1996 are:

Item	Price in 2000 (£)	Price in 1996 (£)	Quantity bought in 1996
Fuel (litre)	0.76	0.48	4100
Servicing	115.00	83.00	4
Licence	750.00	500.00	1

(a) Calculate the weighted aggregate price index for the prices in 2000 based on the prices in 1996 using the Laspeyre method.

(b) In 2000 the driver purchased 4000 litres of fuel, had the vehicle serviced four times and bought the annual licence. Use these figures to calculate the weighted aggregate price index for 2000 with 1996 as the base year using the Paasche method.

(c) Compare the results to (a) and (b) and advise the driver, who is not good at keeping records, which method of assessing overall changes in costs would be more suitable.

4.12 A textile manufacturer makes casual jackets. The company buys lining fabric, interfacing fabric and outer fabric. These fabrics are cut and machined to make the garments. The prices per metre of these materials in 1998, 1999 and 2000 were:

	Year		
Fabric	1998	1999	2000
Lining	£2.20	£2.30	£2.35
Interfacing	£0.92	£0.95	£1.00
Outer	£6.50	£7.25	£7.95

In 1998 the company purchased 2500 metres of lining fabric, 400 metres of interfacing fabric, and 2750 metres of outer fabric. In 1999 these quantities were 2800, 500, and 3200 respectively. In 2000 they were 3000, 500, and 5000 respectively.

(a) Calculate Laspeyre price indices for 1999 and 2000 using 1998 as the base period.
(b) Calculate Paasche price indices for 1999 and 2000 using 1998 as the base period.
(c) Compare your answers to (a) and (b) and account for any differences between the values of the price indices.

4.13   A confectioner buys cocoa, cocoa butter, sugar, and milk solids. The prices per kilogram of these ingredients in 1994, 1997, and 2000 were:

	Year		
Ingredient	1994	1997	2000
Cocoa	£1.50	£1.45	£1.70
Cocoa butter	£1.30	£1.95	£2.05
Sugar	£0.45	£0.50	£0.55
Milk solids	£0.35	£0.62	£0.68

The quantities that were purchased in 1994 were 7500 kg of cocoa, 4200 kg, of cocoa butter, 12 000 kg of sugar, and 5700 kg of milk solids. The purchased amounts of these items in 1997 were 8000 kg, 4000 kg, 13 000 kg, and 6000 kg respectively. In 2000 they were 8800 kg, 3100 kg, 15 000 kg, and 4500 kg respectively.

(a) Compile Laspeyre price indices for 1997 and 2000 using 1994 as the base year.
(b) Compile Paasche price indices for 1997 and 2000 using 1994 as the base year.
(c) Compare your results for (a) and (b) suggesting reasons for any differences between them.

4.14   The turnover figures provided in the annual accounts of a large retail grocer over the six years from 1995 to 2000 were:

Year	1995	1996	1997	1998	1999	2000
Turnover (£m)	7022	7101	7350	7844	8249	8598

The values of the Retail Price Index (RPI) for this period were:

Year	1995	1996	1997	1998	1999	2000
RPI	149.1	152.7	157.5	162.9	165.4	170.3

Use the RPI values to deflate the turnover figures so that they are all expressed in 1995 pounds.

4.15 An enthusiast paid £5000 for a classic car in 1990. Since that time the car has been kept carefully and been valued every two years. The valuations were:

Year	1992	1994	1996	1998	2000
Valuation (£)	5800	5200	5500	6200	6000

The values of the Retail Price Index (RPI) for these years were:

Year	1992	1994	1996	1998	2000
RPI	138.5	144.1	152.7	162.9	170.3

Use the values of the RPI to adjust the valuations of the car so that they are all expressed in 1990 pounds. The value of the RPI in 1990 was 126.1.

4.16 Sales of alcoholic beverages at an off-licence during the course of three days were:

Day	Morning	Afternoon	Evening
1	204	450	939
2	261	459	1056
3	315	522	1113

(a) Plot a graph to display the time series.
(b) Calculate three-point moving averages for the series.
(c) Determine the recurrent components for each part of the day.
(d) Find estimates for the values of the trend in day 4 using regression analysis.
(e) Compile forecasts for the sales that can be expected on each part of day 4.

4.17 A body-piercing and tattoo studio is open each day of the week except Sundays and Mondays. The number of customers visiting the studio per day over a period of three weeks is:

Week	Tuesday	Wednesday	Thursday	Friday	Saturday
1	5	8	9	18	34
2	4	8	11	22	39
3	7	9	14	21	42

(a) Plot the time series.
(b) Calculate five-point moving averages for the series.
(c) Estimate daily components for the series.
(d) Produce estimates for the values of the trend in week 4 using regression analysis.
(e) Compile forecasts for the number of visitors the studio should expect on each day in week 4.

4.18* The amounts of gas (in thousands of gigawatt hours) sold to domestic consumers by a regional energy company over three years were:

	Quarter			
Year	Winter	Spring	Summer	Autumn
1	28	12	7	23
2	27	14	7	24
3	28	13	6	24

(a) Produce a graph to represent the figures.
(b) Determine centred four-point moving averages for the time series.
(c) Find the seasonal component for each quarter.
(d) Compile forecasts for the four quarters of year 4.

4.19 A High Street chemist sells travel first aid packs. The numbers of these sold over three years were:

	Quarter			
Year	Winter	Spring	Summer	Autumn
1	11	37	61	18
2	13	49	58	16
3	16	53	66	18

(a) Plot a graph to portray the data.
(b) Calculate centred four-point moving averages for the time series.
(c) Determine the seasonal component for each quarter.
(d) Compile forecasts for the four quarters of the fourth year.

4.20 Select the appropriate definition for each term on the left-hand side from the list on the right hand side.

(a) A regression equation

(b) A correlation coefficient

(c) A moving average

(d) An inverse relationship

(e) A predictor

(f) A response

(g) A trend

(h) A weighted price index

(i) is another name for the dependent variable, Y

(ii) is an underlying movement in a time series

(iii) measures price changes over time

(iv) is another name for the independent variable, X

(v) is a mean of a sequence of time series values

(vi) measures association between two variables

(vii) is when Y goes down as X goes up

(viii) represents the line of best fit

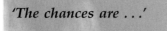

C H A P T E R   5

Assessing risk

This chapter will help you:

- To understand why probability is important.
- To appreciate how chance and risk can be measured.
- To identify different types of probability.
- To analyse the chances of sequences and combinations.

In this chapter you will find:

- The scale of probability.
- Different approaches to assessing probabilities.
- Analysis of simple and compound probabilities.
- The addition rule of probability.
- The multiplication rule of probability and dependency.
- Bayes' rule.
- Probability trees and Venn diagrams.

This chapter is intended to introduce you to the subject of probability, the branch of mathematics that is about finding out how likely real events or theoretical results are to happen. The subject originated in gambling, in particular the efforts of two seventeenth-century French mathematical pioneers, Fermat and Pascal, to calculate the odds of certain results in dice games.

The science of probability may well have remained a historical curiosity within the field of mathematics that was little known outside casinos and race-tracks if it were not for the fact that probability has proved to be invaluable in fields as varied as psychology, economics, physical science, market research and medicine. In these and other fields, probability offers us a way of analysing chance and allowing for risk so that it can be taken into account whether we are investigating a problem or trying to make a decision.

Probability makes the difference between facing *uncertainty* and coping with *risk*. Uncertainty is a situation where we know that it is possible that things could turn out in different ways but we simply don't know how probable each result is. Risk, on the other hand, is when we know there are different outcomes but we also have some idea of how likely each one is to occur.

Business organizations operate in conditions that are far from certain. Economic circumstances change, customer bases shift, employees move to other jobs. New product development and investment ventures are typically something of a gamble.

As well as these examples of what we might call normal commercial risk, there is the added peril of unforeseen risk. A developing market may be torn apart by war, demand for certain food products may be undermined by contamination, there may be an accident that disrupts transport etc.

The topics that you will meet in this chapter will help you to understand how organizations can measure and assess the risks they have to deal with. But there is a second reason why probability is a very important part of your studies; because of the role it plays in future statistical work.

Almost all the statistical research that you are likely to come across at college and in your future career, whether it is intended to investigate consumer behaviour, employee attitudes, product quality, or whatever, will have one important thing in common; it will involve the collection and analysis of a sample.

In almost every case both the people who commission the research and those who carry it out want to know about an entire population. They may want to know the opinions of all customers, the attitudes of all employees, the characteristics of all products, but it would be far too expensive or time-consuming or simply impractical to study every item in a population. The only alternative is to study a sample and use the results to gain some insight into the population.

This can work very well, but only if we have a sample that is random and we take account of the risks associated with sampling.

A sample is called a random sample if every item in the population has the same chance of being included in the sample as every other item in the population. If a sample is not random it is of very little use in helping us to understand a population.

Taking samples involves risk because we can take different random samples from a single population. These samples will be composed of different items from the population and produce different results. Some samples will produce results very similar to those that we would get from the population itself if we had the opportunity to do so. Other samples will produce results that are not typical of the population as a whole.

To use sample results effectively we need to know how likely they are to be close to the population results even though we don't actually know what the population results are. Assessing this involves the use of probability.

5.1 Measuring probability

A *probability*, usually represented by a capital *P*, is a measure of the likelihood of a particular result or outcome. It is a number on a scale that runs from zero to one inclusive, although it can be expressed as a percentage.

If there is a probability of zero that an outcome will occur it means there is literally no chance that it will happen. At the other end of the scale, if there is a probability of one that something will happen, it means that it is absolutely certain to occur. Half-way between these extremes, a probability of one half means that a result is equally likely to occur as not to occur. Sometimes such a probability is described as a fifty–fifty chance.

So how do we decide what the probability of something happening is? The answer is that there are three distinct approaches that can be used to attach a probability to a particular outcome. We can describe these as the *judgemental*, *experimental*, and *theoretical* approaches to identifying probabilities.

The judgemental approach means evaluating the chance of something happening on the basis of opinion alone. Usually the something is relatively uncommon, which rules out the use of the experimental approach, and doesn't occur within a context of definable possibilities, which rules out the use of the theoretical approach. The opinion on which the probability is based is usually someone with relevant expertise.

You will often find judgemental probabilities in assessments of political stability and economic conditions, perhaps concerning investment prospects or currency fluctuations. You could, of course, use a judgemental approach to assessing the probability of any outcome even when there are more sophisticated means available. For instance, some people assess the chance that a horse wins a race solely on their opinion of the name of the horse when they could investigate the horse's record.

If you did investigate the horse's record you would be using an experimental approach, looking into the results of the previous occasions when the 'experiment', in this case the horse entering a race, was conducted. You could work out the number of times the horse has won a race as a proportion of the total number of races it has entered. This is the *relative frequency* of wins and this can be used to estimate the probability that the horse wins its next race.

A relative frequency based on a limited number of experiments is only an estimate of the probability because it approximates the 'true' probability, which is the relative frequency based on an infinite number of experiments.

Example 5.1

The horse 'Starikon' has entered sixteen races and won five of them. What is the probability that it will win its next race?

The relative frequency of wins is the number of wins, five, divided by the total number of races, sixteen:

Relative frequency = 5/16 = 0.3125 or 31.25 per cent

We can conclude therefore that on the basis of its record, the probability that the horse wins its next race:

P (Starikon wins its next race) = 0.3125

In other words a little less than a one-third or a one in three chance.

Of course, Example 5.1 is a simplified version of what horse racing analysts actually do. They would probably consider ground conditions, other horses in the race and so on, but essentially they base their assessment of a horse's chances on the experimental approach to setting probabilities.

There are other situations when we want to establish the probability of a certain result of some process and we could use the experimental approach. Perhaps we could consult the results of previous 'experiments', or conduct some ourselves.

The results we found would provide a suitable relative frequency figure for us to use as the probability, but we need not go to the trouble of using the experimental approach if we can deduce the probability using the theoretical approach. You can deduce the probability of a particular outcome if the process that produces it has a constant, limited and identifiable number of possible outcomes, one of which must occur whenever the process takes place.

There are many examples of this sort of process in gambling, including those where the number of possible outcomes is very large indeed such as bingo and lotteries. However, even then the number of outcomes is finite, the possible outcomes remain the same whenever the process takes place, and they could all be identified if we had the time and patience to do it.

Probabilities of specific results in bingo and lotteries can be deduced because the same number of balls and type of machine are used each time. In contrast, probabilities of horses winning races can't be deduced because different horses enter each race, the lengths of races vary and so on.

Example 5.2

A 'Wheel of Fortune' machine in an amusement arcade has thirty-six segments. Ten of the segments would give the player a cash prize. What is the probability that you win a cash prize if you play the game?

To answer this we could build a wheel of the same type, spin it thousands of times and work out what proportion of the results would have given us a cash prize. Alternatively we could question people who have played the game previously and find out what proportion of them won a cash prize. These are two ways of finding the probability experimentally.

It is far simpler to deduce the probability. Ten outcomes out of a possible thirty-six would give us a cash prize so:

P (cash prize) $= 10/36 = 0.2778$ or 27.78 per cent

This assumes that the wheel is fair, in other words that each outcome is as likely to occur as any other outcome.

Gambling is a rich source of illustrations of the use of probabilities because it is about games of chance. However, it is by no means the only field where you will find probabilities. Whenever you buy insurance you are buying a product whose price has been decided on the basis of the rigorous and extensive use of the experimental approach to find probabilities.

5.2 Different types of probabilities

So far the probabilities that you have met in this chapter have been what are known as *simple* probabilities. Simple probabilities are probabilities of single outcomes. In Example 5.1 we wanted to know the chance of the horse winning its next race. The probability that the horse wins its next two races is a *compound* probability.

A compound probability is the probability of a compound or combined outcome. In Example 5.2 winning a cash prize is a simple outcome, but winning a cash or a non-cash prize, like a cuddly toy, is a compound outcome.

To illustrate the different types of compound probability we can apply the experimental approach to bivariate data. That is, we can estimate compound probabilities by finding appropriate relative frequencies from data that has been tabulated by categories of attributes, or classes of values of variables.

Example 5.3

A survey of the type of goods purchased and methods of payment of 500 customers at a service station produced the following results.

Payment	Sandwiches	Magazines	Fuel	Total
Cash	87	189	15	291
Debit card	11	5	62	78
Credit card	4	12	115	131
Total	102	206	192	500

What is the probability that a customer will pay by credit card?

What is the probability that a customer will purchase fuel?

These are both simple probabilities because they each relate to only one variable, method of payment in the first case, type of goods purchased in the second.

The totals column on the right of the table tells us that in all 131 of the 500 customers paid by credit card.

P (Payment by credit card) $= 131/500 = 0.262$, or 26.2 per cent, which is the relative frequency of credit card payment.

Similarly, by using the totals row along the bottom of the table,

P (Customer purchases fuel) $= 192/500 = 0.384$, or 38.4 per cent, which is the relative frequency of fuel purchases.

If we want to use a table such as in Example 5.3 to find compound probabilities we must use figures from the cells within the table, rather than the column and row totals, to produce relative frequencies.

Example 5.4

What is the probability that a customer in the service station in Example 5.3 purchases sandwiches and pays by cash?

The number of customers in the survey who purchased sandwiches with cash was 87 so:

P (Customer purchases sandwiches and pays cash) $= 87/500$

$$= 0.174 \quad \text{or 17.4 per cent}$$

It is rather laborious to write descriptions of the outcomes in full so they are normally abbreviated; we could use 'S' to represent the purchase of sandwiches, 'M' for the purchase of magazines and 'F' for the purchase of fuel. Likewise we could use 'Ca' for cash payment, 'Cr' for credit card payment and 'D' for debit card payment. So we can express the probability in Example 5.4 in a more convenient way.

P (Customer purchases sandwiches and pays with cash) $= P$ (S and Ca) $= 0.174$

The type of compound probability in Example 5.4, which includes the word 'and', measures the chance of the *intersection* of two outcomes. The relative frequency we have used as the probability is based on the number of people who are in two specific categories of the 'type of goods purchased' and 'method of payment' characteristics. It is the number of people who are at the 'crossroads' or intersection between the 'purchases sandwiches' and the 'cash' categories.

Finding the probability of an intersection of two outcomes is quite straightforward if we are assessing it by applying the experimental approach to bivariate data. In other situations, for instance where we only have simple probabilities to go on, we need to use the *multiplication rule* of probability, which we will discuss later in the chapter.

There is a second type of compound probability, which measures the probability that one out of two or more alternative outcomes occurs. This type of compound probability includes the word 'or' in the description of the outcomes involved.

Example 5.5

Use the data in Example 5.3 to find the probability that a customer purchases fuel or pays by debit card.

The probability that one (and by implication, both) of these outcomes occurs is based on the relative frequency of all the people who are in one or other category. This implies that we should add the number of customers who purchased fuel to the number of customers who paid by debit card, and divide the result by the total number of customers in the survey.

Number of customers who purchased fuel $= 15 + 62 + 115 = 192$

Number of customers who paid by debit card $= 11 + 5 + 62 = 78$

If you look carefully you will see that the number 62 appears in both of these expressions. This means that if we use the sum of the number of customers who purchased fuel and the number of customers who paid by debit card to get our relative frequency figure we will double count the 62 customers who purchased fuel and paid by debit card. This means the probability we get will be too big.

The problem arises because we have added the 62 customers who purchased fuel and paid by debit card in twice so to correct this we have to subtract the same number once.

$$P \text{ (F or D)} = \frac{(15 + 62 + 115) + (11 + 5 + 62) - 62}{500} = \frac{192 + 78 - 62}{500}$$

$$= 208 = 0.416 = 208/500 = 0.416 \quad \text{or } 41.6 \text{ per cent}$$

The type of compound probability in Example 5.5 measures the chance of a *union* of two outcomes. The relative frequency we have used as the probability is based on the combined number of people who are in two specific categories of the 'type of goods purchased' and 'method of payment' characteristics. It is the number of customers who are in the union or 'merger' between the 'purchases fuel' and the 'debit card' categories. To get a probability of a union of outcomes from other probabilities, rather than by applying the experimental approach to bivariate data, we use the *addition rule* of probability. You will find this discussed later in the chapter.

The third type of compound probability is the *conditional* probability. Such a probability measures the chance that one outcome occurs given that, or on *condition* that, another outcome has already occurred.

Example 5.6

Use the data in Example 5.3 to find the probability that a customer who has purchased magazines pays by cash.

Another way of describing this is as the probability that a customer pays by cash given that he or she has purchased magazines. It is represented as:

P (Ca|M)

where the '|' symbol is shorthand for 'given that'.

We find this probability by taking the number of people who paid cash and purchased magazines as a proportion of the total number of people who purchased magazines.

P (Ca|M) $= 189/206 = 0.9175$ or 91.75 per cent

This is a proportion of a subset of the 500 customers in the sample. The majority of them, the 294 people who did not purchase magazines, are excluded because they didn't meet the condition on which the probability is based, i.e. purchasing magazines.

It is always possible to identify compound probabilities directly from the sort of bivariate data in Example 5.3 by the experimental approach. But what if we don't have this sort of data? Perhaps we have some probabilities that have been obtained judgementally or theoretically and we want to use them to find compound probabilities. Perhaps there are some probabilities that have been obtained experimentally but the data is not at our disposal.

5.3 The rules of probability

In situations where we do not have recourse to appropriate experimental data we need to have some method of finding compound probabilities. These are the two rules of probability: the addition rule and the multiplication rule.

5.3.1 The addition rule

The addition rule of probability specifies the procedure for finding the probability of a union of outcomes, that is, a compound probability defined using the word 'or'.

According to the addition rule the compound probability of one or both of two outcomes, which we will call A and B for convenience, is the simple probability that A occurs added to the simple probability that B occurs. From this total we subtract the compound probability of the intersection of A and B, the probability that both A and B occur. That is:

$$P \text{ (A or B)} = P \text{ (A)} + P \text{ (B)} - P \text{ (A and B)}$$

Example 5.7

Use the addition rule to calculate the probability that a customer coming into the service station in Example 5.3 purchases fuel or pays by debit card.

Applying the addition rule:

$$P \text{ (F or D)} = P \text{ (F)} + P(D) - P \text{ (F and D)}$$

The simple probability that a customer purchases fuel: $P \text{ (F)} = 192/500$

The simple probability that a customer pays by debit card: $P \text{ (D)} = 78/500$

The probability that a customer purchases fuel and pays by debit card:

$$P \text{ (F and D)} = 62/500$$

So: $P \text{ (F or D)} = 192/500 + 78/500 - 62/500$

$$= \frac{192 + 78 - 62}{500} = 208/500 = 0.416 \quad \text{or } 41.6 \text{ per cent}$$

If you compare this answer to the answer we obtained in Example 5.5 you will see they are exactly the same. In this case the addition rule is an alternative means of getting to the same result. In some ways it is more convenient because it is based more on row and column totals of the table in Example 5.3 rather than numbers from different cells within the table.

The addition rule can look more complicated than it actually is because it is called the addition rule yet it includes a subtraction. It may help to represent the situation in the form of a *Venn* diagram; the sort of diagram used in part of mathematics called *set theory*.

In a Venn diagram the complete set of outcomes that could occur, known as the *sample space*, is represented by a rectangle. Within the rectangle circles are used to represent sets of outcomes.

In Figure 5.1 the circle on the left represents the purchasing fuel outcome, and the circle on the right represents the payment by debit card outcome. The combined area of both circles represents the probability that a customer purchases fuel or pays by debit card. The area of overlap represents the probability that a customer purchases fuel and pays by debit card.

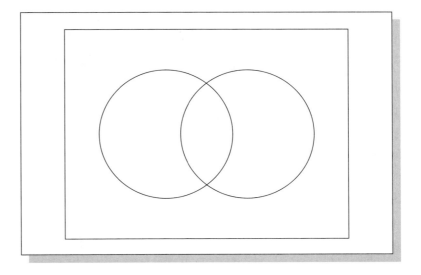

Figure 5.1
A Venn diagram to illustrate
Example 5.7

By definition the area of overlap is part of both circles. If you simply add the areas of the two circles together to try to get the combined area of both circles, you will include the area of overlap twice. If you subtract it once from the sum of the areas of the two circles you will only have counted it once.

The addition rule would be simpler if there were no overlap; in other words there is no chance that the two outcomes can occur together. This is when we are dealing with outcomes that are known as *mutually exclusive*. The probability that two mutually exclusive outcomes both occur is zero.

In this case we can alter the addition rule:

$$P(A \text{ or } B) = P(A) + P(B) - P(A \text{ and } B)$$

to $\qquad P(A \text{ or } B) = P(A) + P(B)$

because $\quad P(A \text{ and } B) = 0$

Example 5.8

One weekend a total of 178 prospective homebuyers visit a new housing development. They are offered a choice of three different types of house: the 2-bedroom 'Ambience', the 3-bedroom 'Bermuda', or the 4-bedroom 'Casa'. When invited to select the type of house they would most like, 43 chose the 'Ambience', 61 the 'Bermuda', and 29 the 'Casa'.

What is the probability that a prospective homebuyer from this group has chosen the 'Bermuda' or the 'Casa'?

We can assume that the choices are mutually exclusive because each prospective homebuyer was asked to choose only one type of house. We can therefore use the simpler form of the addition rule.

For convenience we can use the letter A for 'Ambience', B for 'Bermuda' and C for 'Casa'.

$$P \text{ (B or C)} = P \text{ (B)} + P \text{ (C)} = 61/178 + 29/178 = 90/178$$

$$= 0.5056 \quad \text{or } 50.56 \text{ per cent}$$

If you read Example 5.8 carefully you can see that although the three choices of types of house are mutually exclusive, they do not constitute all the alternative outcomes. That is, they are not *collectively exhaustive*. As well as choosing one of the three types of house each prospective homebuyer has a fourth choice, to decline to express a preference. If you subtract the number of prospective homebuyers expressing a preference from the total number of prospective homebuyers you will find that 45 of the prospective homebuyers have not chosen one of the types of house.

A footnote to the addition rule is that if we have a set of mutually exclusive and collectively exhaustive outcomes their probabilities must add up to one. A probability of one means certainty, which reflects the fact that in a situation where there are a set of mutually exclusive and collectively exhaustive outcomes, one and only one of them is certain to occur.

Example 5.9

What is the probability that one of the prospective homebuyers in Example 5.8 chooses the 'Ambience' or the 'Bermuda' or the 'Casa' or expresses no preference? For convenience we will use the letter N to denote the latter.

The simple probability that a prospective homebuyer picks 'Ambience' $= P(A)$
$= 43/178$

The simple probability that a prospective homebuyer picks 'Bermuda' $= P(B)$
$= 61/178$

The simple probability that a prospective homebuyer picks 'Casa' $= P(C)$
$= 29/178$

The simple probability that a prospective homebuyer makes no choice $= P(N)$
$= 45/178$

$$P(A \text{ or } B \text{ or } C \text{ or } N) = \frac{43 + 61 + 29 + 45}{178} = 178/178 = 1$$

This footnote to the addition rule can be used to derive probabilities of one of a set of mutually exclusive and collectively exhaustive outcomes if we know the probabilities of the other outcomes.

Example 5.10

Deduce the probability that a prospective homebuyer in Example 5.8 expresses no preference using the simple probabilities of the other outcomes.

$$P(\text{Prospective homebuyer makes no choice}) = 1 - P(A) - P(B) - P(C)$$
$$= 1 - 43/178 - 61/178 - 29/178$$
$$= 1 - 0.2416 - 0.3427 - 0.1629$$
$$= 1 - 0.7472 = 0.2528 \quad \text{or 25.28 per cent}$$

The result we obtained in Example 5.10, 0.2528, is the decimal equivalent of the figure of 45/178 that we used for $P(N)$ in Example 5.9.

5.3.2 The multiplication rule

The multiplication rule of probability specifies the procedure for finding the probability of an intersection of outcomes, that is, a compound probability defined using the word 'and'.

According to the multiplication rule the compound probability that two outcomes both occur is the simple probability that the first one occurs multiplied by the *conditional* probability that the second outcome occurs, given that the first outcome has already happened. That is:

$$P \text{ (A and B)} = P \text{ (A)} \times P \text{ (B} \mid \text{A)}$$

The multiplication rule is what bookmakers use to work out odds for 'accumulator' bets, that is, bets that a sequence of outcomes, like several specific horses winning races, occurs. To win the bet the first horse must win the first race; the second horse must win the second race and so on. The odds of this sort of thing happening are often something like five hundred to one. The numbers, like five hundred, are large because they are obtained by multiplication.

Example 5.11

Use the multiplication rule to calculate the probability that a customer at the service station in Example 5.3 purchases sandwiches and pays by cash.

We will use the abbreviations S for the purchase of sandwiches and Ca for payment by cash.

$$P \text{ (S and Ca)} = P \text{ (S)} \times P \text{ (Ca} \mid \text{S)}$$

From the table in Example 5.3:

$$P \text{ (S)} = 102/500$$

the relative frequency of customers purchasing sandwiches and

$$P \text{ (Ca} \mid \text{S)} = 87/102$$

the relative frequency of customers purchasing sandwiches who pay by cash.

So

$$P \text{ (S and Ca)} = 102/500 \times 87/102 = 0.204 \times 0.853 = 0.174 \text{ or } 17.4 \text{ per cent}$$

If you compare this answer to the answer we obtained in Example 5.4 you will see that they are exactly the same.

The multiplication rule can look more complex than it actually is because it includes a conditional probability. We use a conditional probability for the second outcome because the chances of it occurring could be influenced by the first outcome. This is called *dependency*; in other words one outcome is dependent on the other.

A useful way of telling whether two outcomes are dependent is to compare the conditional probability of one outcome given that the other has happened, with the simple probability that it happens. If the two figures are different the outcomes are dependent.

Example 5.12

A promotional stall in a shopping centre offers passers-by the opportunity to taste bison meat. A total of 200 people try the product and 122 of them stated that they liked it. Of these, 45 said they would buy the product. Overall 59 of the 200 passers-by said they would buy the product.

Are liking the product and expressing the intention to buy it dependent?

The simple probability that a passer-by expresses an intention to buy is 59/200 or 29.5 per cent.

The conditional probability that a passer-by expresses an intention to buy given that he or she liked the product is 45/122 or 36.9 per cent.

You can see that there is a difference between these two figures, which suggests that the expression of an intention to buy is dependent on liking the product.

The multiplication rule can be rearranged to provide us with a way of finding a conditional probability. That is:

$$\text{if} \quad P (A \text{ and } B) = P (A) \times P (B|A)$$

then if we divide both sides by $P (A)$ we get

$$P (A \text{ and } B)/P (A) = P (B|A)$$

that is:

$$P (B|A) = P (A \text{ and } B)/P (A)$$

Example 5.13

What is the probability that a customer at the service station in Example 5.3 pays by cash given that he or she has purchased magazines?

We will use the abbreviations M for the purchase of magazines and Ca for cash.

$$P(Ca \mid M) = P(Ca \text{ and } M) / P(M)$$

From the table in Example 5.3

$$P(Ca \text{ and } M) = 189/500 = 0.378$$

and $P(M) = 206/500 = 0.412$

so $P(Ca \mid M) = 0.378/0.412 = 0.9175$ or 91.75 per cent

You might like to compare this to the answer we obtained in Example 5.6.

If there had been no difference between the two probabilities in Example 5.12 there would be no dependency; that is, the outcomes would be *independent*.

In situations where outcomes are *independent*, the conditional probabilities of the outcomes are the same as their simple probabilities. This means we can simplify the multiplication rule when we are dealing with independent outcomes. We can replace the conditional probability of the second outcome given that the first outcome has occurred with the simple probability that the second outcome occurs. That is, instead of

$$P(A \text{ and } B) = P(A) \times P(B \mid A)$$

we can use $P(A \text{ and } B) = P(A) \times P(B)$

because $P(B) = P(B \mid A)$.

Example 5.14

What is the probability that a player who plays the Wheel of Fortune in Example 5.2 twice wins cash prizes both times?

Ten of the thirty-six segments give a cash prize, so the probability of a cash prize in any one game is 10/36.

The probability that a player gets a cash prize in their second game given that they have won a cash prize in their first game is also 10/36. The outcomes are independent; in other words the result of the second game is not influenced by the result of the first. (If this is not clear because you feel there is a connection, you might ask yourself how the Wheel of Fortune remembers what it did the first time!)

We will use the letter C to represent a cash prize. The first cash prize the player wins can then be represented as C_1, and the second as C_2.

$$P \ (C_1 \text{ and } C_2) \ = \ P \ (C) \times P \ (C) \ = \ 10/36 \times 10/36 \ = \ 0.077 \text{ or } 7.7 \text{ per cent}$$

5.3.3 Bayes' rule

In the previous section we looked at how the multiplication rule, which enables us to find the compound probability that both of two outcomes occur, could be rearranged to provide a definition of the conditional probability that the second outcome occurs given that the first outcome had already occurred. That is:

$$\text{if} \quad P \ (A \text{ and } B) \ = \ P \ (A) \times P \ (B \,|\, A)$$

$$\text{then} \quad P \ (B \,|\, A) \ = \ P \ (A \text{ and } B)/P \ (A)$$

In this context we normally assume that outcome A occurs before outcome B, for instance the probability that a person succumbs to a lung disease given that they have smoked tobacco.

Thanks to the work of the eighteenth-century clergyman and mathematician Thomas Bayes we can develop this further to say that:

$$P \ (B \text{ and } A) \ = \ P \ (B) \times P \ (A \,|\, B)$$

$$\text{so} \quad P \ (A \,|\, B) \ = \ P \ (B \text{ and } A)/ \ P \ (B)$$

This means that we can find the probability that outcome A happened given that we know outcome B has subsequently happened. This is known as a *posterior* or 'after-the-event' probability. In contrast, the simple probability that outcome A happens is a *prior*, or 'before-the-event' probability.

The compound probability that both A and B occur is the same whether it is described as the probability of A and B or the probability of B and A. That is:

$$P \text{ (A and B)} = P \text{ (B and A)}$$

The multiplication rule tells us that:

$$P \text{ (A and B)} = P \text{ (A)} \times P \text{ (B} | \text{A)}$$

We can therefore express the conditional probability that A has occurred given that we know B has subsequently occurred as:

$$P \text{ (A} | \text{B)} = \frac{P \text{ (A)} \times P \text{ (B} | \text{A)}}{P \text{ (B)}}$$

This definition of the posterior probability of an outcome is known as Bayes' rule or Bayes' theorem.

Example 5.15

A financial services ombudsman is investigating the mis-selling of pension schemes some years previously. Some buyers of these pension schemes were sold the schemes on the basis of misleading information, and would have been better off had they made alternative arrangements.

The pension schemes being investigated were provided by one company but actually sold by two brokers, Copilka, who sold 80 per cent of the schemes, and Denarius who sold 20 per cent of the schemes. Some of the pension schemes sold by these brokers were appropriate for the customers who bought them, but the ombudsman has established that 30 per cent of the schemes sold by Copilka and 40 per cent of the schemes sold by Denarius have turned out to be inappropriate for the customers who bought them.

The ombudsman wishes to apportion liability for compensation for mis-sold pension scheme between the two brokers and wants to do so on the basis of the following:

(a) If a pension scheme was mis-sold what was the probability that it was sold by Copilka?

(b) If a pension scheme was mis-sold what was the probability that it was sold by Denarius?

We will use M to represent a pension scheme that was mis-sold, C to denote that a pension scheme was sold by Copilka, and D to denote that a pension scheme was sold by Denarius.

The first probability that the ombudsman needs to know is $P \text{ (C} | \text{M)}$.

Using Bayes' rule:

$$P(C|M) = \frac{P(C) \times P(M|C)}{P(M)}$$

We know that the probability that a pension scheme was sold by Copilka, $P(C)$, is 0.8. We also know that the probability that a pension scheme was mis-sold given that it was sold by Copilka, $P(M|C)$ is 0.3. The only other probability that we need in order to apply Bayes' rule in this case is $P(M)$, the probability that a pension scheme was mis-sold.

A pension scheme that was mis-sold must have been sold by either Copilka or Denarius. The probability that a pension scheme was mis-sold must therefore be the sum of the probability that a pension scheme was mis-sold and it was sold by Copilka and the probability that a pension scheme was mis-sold and it was sold by Denarius. That is:

$$P(M) = P(C \text{ and } M) + P(D \text{ and } M)$$

Although we do not know these compound probabilities we can derive them by applying the multiplication rule:

$$P(C \text{ and } M) = P(C) \times P(M|C) = 0.8 \times 0.3 = 0.24$$

The probability that a pension scheme was sold by Denarius, $P(D)$, is 0.2, and the probability that a pension scheme was mis-sold given that it was sold by Denarius, $P(M|D)$, is 0.4, so:

$$P(D \text{ and } M) = P(D) \times P(M|D) = 0.2 \times 0.4 = 0.08$$

so $P(M) = 0.24 + 0.08 = 0.32$

We can now work out the first of the two probabilities that the ombudsman needs, the probability that if a pension scheme was mis-sold it was sold by Copilka, $P(C|M)$:

$$P(C|M) = \frac{P(C) \times P(M|C)}{P(M)} = \frac{0.8 \times 0.3}{0.32} = \frac{0.24}{0.32} = 0.75$$

A mis-sold pension scheme must have been sold by Denarius if it was not sold by Copilka, they are mutually exclusive and collectively exhaustive outcomes. This means that we can deduce that the probability that if a pension scheme was mis-sold it was sold by Denarius, $P(D|M)$ is one less $P(C|M)$. That is:

$$P(D|M) = 1 - 0.75 = 0.25$$

On the basis of these results the ombudsman should apportion 75 per cent of the liability for compensation to Copilka and 25 per cent of the liability for compensation to Denarius.

5.3.4 Applying the rules of probability

Although we have dealt separately with different types of probability, rules of probability and so on, when it comes to applying them to solve problems involving sequences of outcomes you may well have to use them together. You may like to look at Example 5.16, which brings together many of the topics that you have met in this chapter to solve an apparently straightforward problem.

Example 5.16

Twenty-five graduates join a company at the same time. During their induction and training programme friendships are established and they decide that when one of them has a birthday they will all dine at a restaurant chosen by the person whose birthday is being celebrated. One of the graduates asks what will happen if two or more of them share a birthday. In response another graduate says that it won't happen because there are only 25 of them and 365 days in the year.

What is the probability that there will be at least one clash of birthdays in a year?

This is quite a complex question because of the sheer variety of ways in which there could conceivably be a clash of birthdays. We could have a clash on 1 January, 2 January and so on. Maybe three graduates could share the same birthday? It would be extremely difficult and tedious to work out all these probabilities separately.

In fact we don't need to. One of the phrases you met during the discussion of the addition rule was 'mutually exclusive and collectively exhaustive'. Such outcomes rule each other out and have probabilities that add up to one. We can make use of this here.

We have two outcomes: either some birthdays clash or none do. They are mutually exclusive because it is impossible to have both clashes and no clashes. They are collectively exhaustive because we must have either one or more clashes or no clashes.

This makes things easier. We want the probability of clashes, but to get that we would have to analyse many different combinations of outcomes and put their probabilities together. Instead we can work out the probability than there are no clashes and take it away from one. This is easier because there is only one probability to work out.

What is the probability that there are no clashes?

Imagine if there was just one graduate and we introduced the others one at a time. This one graduate can have a birthday on any day because at this stage there are no other graduates whose birthdays could clash with theirs.

The probability that the second graduate has a birthday on another day is 364/365 because one day is already 'occupied' by the birthday of the first graduate, leaving 364 'free' days.

The probability that the third graduate has a birthday on a different day to the other two graduates assuming that the first two graduates' birthdays don't clash is 363/365. This is the conditional probability that the third graduate's birthday misses those of the first and second graduates, given that the birthdays of the first and second graduates don't clash. The number 363 appears because that is the number of 'free' days that remain if the birthdays of the first two graduates don't clash.

Continuing the process, the probability that the fourth graduate's birthday doesn't clash with those of the first three, assuming they are on different days, is 362/365. The probability that the fifth graduate's birthday doesn't clash with those of the first four is 361/365, and so on.

Eventually we reach the probability that the twenty-fifth graduate's birthday doesn't clash with those of the other twenty-four, which is 341/365.

The probabilities that we now have are probabilities that the birthdays of specific graduates don't clash with those of other specific graduates. What we want is the probability that there are no clashes at all. To get this we have to put these probabilities together. But how? Should we multiply or add?

The answer is that we multiply them together. We want the probability that the second graduate's birthday misses that of the first graduate **and** the third graduate's birthday misses those of the first two and so on.

So $\quad P$ (no clashes) $= 364/365 \times 363/365 \times 362/365 \times \ldots \times 342/365 \times 341/365$

$$= 0.4252 \quad \text{or } 42.52 \text{ per cent}$$

This is the probability that there are no clashes, but we wanted to find the probability that there is at least one clash. For this we use the addition rule. It is certain that there is either at least one clash **or** no clash. That is:

$\quad P$ (at least one clash) $+ P$ (no clash) $= 1$

So $\quad P$ (at least one clash) $= 1 - P$ (no clash)

$$= 1 - 0.4252 = 0.5748 \quad \text{or } 57.48 \text{ per cent}$$

5.4 Tree diagrams

If you have to investigate the probabilities of sequences of several outcomes it can be difficult to work out the different combinations of outcomes in your head. It helps if you write down all the different variations, and you may find a Venn diagram a useful way of arranging them in order to work out probabilities of certain types of combinations. But perhaps the best way of sorting out this kind of problem is to use a *tree diagram*.

A tree diagram, which is sometimes called a *probability tree*, represents the different sequences of outcomes in the style of a tree that 'grows' from left to right. Each branch of the tree leads to a particular outcome.

On the right-hand side of the diagram, at the end of each branch, we can insert the combination of outcomes that the sequence of branches represents and, using the multiplication rule, the probability that the sequence of outcomes happens.

Example 5.17

Three friends start Higher Education courses at the same time in the same institution. Angela is studying Accounting, Bashir is studying Business and Charlie is studying Computing. Seventy per cent of students who begin the Accounting course complete it successfully, 80 per cent of students who begin the Business course complete it successfully, and 60 per cent of students who begin the Computing course complete it successfully. Construct a tree diagram and use it to work out:

- The probability that all three friends successfully complete their courses.

- The probability that two of the friends successfully complete their courses.

- The probability that only one of the friends successfully completes their course.

We will use A to represent Angela, B for Bashir and C for Charlie. To indicate someone failing their course we will use the appropriate letter followed by a 'mark, so A' represents the outcome that Angela fails her course, whereas A alone represents the outcome that Angela completes her course successfully.

The completion rate suggests the probability that Angela passes the Accounting course is 0.7, and given that the 'pass' and 'fail' outcomes are mutually exclusive and collectively exhaustive, the probability she fails is 0.3. The probability that Bashir passes the Business course is 0.8, and the probability that he fails is 0.2. The probability that Charlie passes the Computing course is 0.6 and the probability that he fails is 0.4.

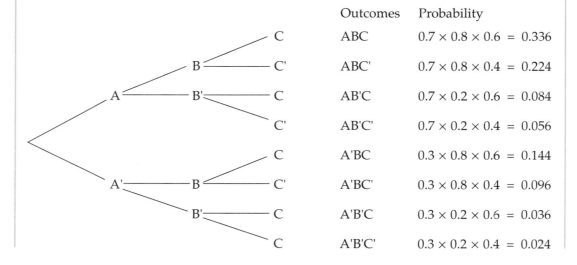

	Outcomes	Probability
C	ABC	$0.7 \times 0.8 \times 0.6 = 0.336$
C'	ABC'	$0.7 \times 0.8 \times 0.4 = 0.224$
C	AB'C	$0.7 \times 0.2 \times 0.6 = 0.084$
C'	AB'C'	$0.7 \times 0.2 \times 0.4 = 0.056$
C	A'BC	$0.3 \times 0.8 \times 0.6 = 0.144$
C'	A'BC'	$0.3 \times 0.8 \times 0.4 = 0.096$
C	A'B'C	$0.3 \times 0.2 \times 0.6 = 0.036$
C	A'B'C'	$0.3 \times 0.2 \times 0.4 = 0.024$

The probability that all three pass, that is P (ABC), is the probability at the top on the right-hand side, 0.336 or 33.6 per cent.

The probability that two of the friends pass is the probability that one of three sequences, either ABC′ or AB′ C or A′BC occurs. Since these combinations are mutually exclusive we can apply the simpler form of the addition rule:

P (ABC′ or AB′C or A′BC) $= 0.224 + 0.084 + 0.144 = 0.452$ or 45.2 per cent

The probability that only one of the friends passes is the probability that either AB′C′ or A′BC′ or A′B′C occurs. These combinations are also mutually exclusive so again we can apply the simpler form of the addition rule:

P (AB′C′ or A′BC′ or A′B′C) $= 0.056 + 0.096 + 0.036 = 0.188$ or 18.8 per cent

A tree diagram should include all possible sequences. One way you can check that it does is to add up the probabilities on the right-hand side. Because these outcomes are mutually exclusive and collectively exhaustive their probabilities should add up to one. We can check that this is the case in Example 5.16.

$$0.336 + 0.224 + 0.084 + 0.056 + 0.144 + 0.096 + 0.036 + 0.024 = 1$$

Review questions

Answers to these questions, including fully worked solutions to those questions marked with an asterisk (*), are on pages 347–349.

5.1 An electrical goods retailer sold video recorders to 8200 customers last year and extended warranties to 3500 of these customers. When the retailer sells a video recorder, what is the probability that:

(a) The customer will buy an extended warranty?
(b) The customer will not buy an extended warranty?

5.2 Since it was set up 73 825 people have visited the website of a fashion designer and 6301 of them purchased goods on-line. When someone visits the site what is the probability that:

(a) they do not purchase goods on-line?
(b) they do purchase goods on-line?

5.3 A direct marketing company produces leaflets offering membership of a book club. These leaflets are then inserted into the magazine sections of two Sunday newspapers, the

Citizen and the *Despatch*. 360 000 leaflets are put in copies of the *Citizen* and 2 130 000 are put in copies of the *Despatch*. The company receives 19 447 completed leaflets from *Citizen* readers and 58 193 completed leaflets from *Despatch* readers. What is the probability that:

(a) A *Citizen* reader returns a leaflet?
(b) A *Despatch* reader returns a leaflet?

5.4* A garage offers a breakdown recovery service for motorists that is available every day of the year. According to their records the number of call-outs they received per day last year were:

Number of call-outs	0	1	2	3	4
Number of days	68	103	145	37	12

What is the probability that:

(a) They receive two call-outs in a day?
(b) They receive two or fewer call-outs in a day?
(c) They receive one or more call-outs in a day?
(d) They receive less than four call-outs in a day?
(e) They receive more than two call-outs in a day?

5.5 Last year 12 966 people opened new accounts at a building society. Of these 5314 were branch-based accounts, 4056 were postal accounts, and 3596 were e-accounts. What is the probability that when a customer opens a new account:

(a) It is a postal account?
(b) It is an e-account?
(c) It is either branch-based or postal?

5.6* The 120 employees at a factory were asked which would best improve their working life: better promotion prospects, higher pay or more respect from other staff. The results are tabulated below.

	Job type:		
Response	Manual	Clerical	Managerial
Better promotion prospects	12	12	3
Higher pay	53	19	2
More respect	7	6	6

(a) What is the probability that an employee selected more respect?

(b) What is the probability that an employee is a clerical worker or selected better promotion prospects?

(c) What is the probability that a manual employee selected higher pay?

(d) What is the probability that an employee selected more respect and is a manager?

(e) What is the probability that a managerial employee selected higher pay?

5.7 A safety agency analysed road traffic accidents involving injury to pedestrians by private cars and produced the following table:

	Type of car:		
Degree of injury	4×4	Sports	Other
Fatal	8	5	14
Serious	21	9	38
Non-serious	13	7	95

What is the probability that:

(a) An injury to a pedestrian proves fatal?

(b) An accident involved a sports car?

(c) An accident involved a 4×4 car or resulted in a non-serious injury?

(d) An accident resulted in serious injury and involved an 'other' type of car?

(e) An accident that involved a 4×4 car resulted in a fatal injury? Compare this figure and your answer to (a), and comment on whether the type of car and degree of injury are independent.

5.8 The following survey results show the social class and type of main holiday destination of 250 adult holidaymakers.

	Social class:		
Destination	AB	C1C2	DE
UK	13	25	26
The rest of Europe	29	60	23
Other	55	14	5

Use these figures to estimate

(a) The probability that a holidaymaker belongs to social class DE.

(b) The probability that a holidaymaker takes a main holiday in the UK.

(c) The probability that a holidaymaker is in social class AB or takes a main holiday outside Europe.

(d) The probability that a holidaymaker takes a main holiday in the rest of Europe or is in social class DE.

(e) The probability that a holidaymaker is in social class C1C2 and takes a main holiday in the UK.

(f) The probability that a holidaymaker takes a main holiday in the rest of Europe and is in social class AB.

(g) The probability that a holidaymaker in social class DE takes a main holiday outside Europe.

(h) The probability that a holidaymaker in social class DE takes a main holiday in the UK.

(i) Compare your answers to (b) and (h). Are social class and main holiday destination independent?

5.9 A final-year undergraduate applies for a well-paid job with a large and reputable organization in a highly desirable location. Competition for the job is expected to be fierce. The probability that a candidate is selected for first interview is 0.10. The probability that a candidate is then selected for second interview is 0.4. The probability that a candidate then passes the psychometric test is 0.8. The probability that a candidate then passes the selection procedure at the assessment centre and is offered the job is 0.25. What is the probability that the undergraduate will get the job?

5.10 A commuter's journey to work consists of driving her car to her local train station, taking a train to the city, and catching a bus to her place of work. If her car trip is delayed she misses the train and is late for work. If the train is delayed, she misses the bus and is late for work. If the bus is delayed she is late for work. The probability that her car journey is delayed is 0.05, the probability that the train is delayed is 0.1, and the probability that the bus is delayed is 0.07.

(a) What is the probability that she arrives at work on time?

(b) What is the probability that she is late for work?

(c) What is the probability that she is late for work because the bus is delayed?

5.11* Declan, Emily and Farid each intend to start their own business after leaving college. Declan wants to start a computer software company, Emily intends to open a recruitment agency, and Farid would like to launch a graphic design business. According to available evidence 60 per cent of computer software companies, 75 per cent of recruitment agencies, and 80 per cent of graphic design businesses fail within their first trading year. What is the probability that:

(a) The businesses that Declan, Emily and Farid start all stay in operation for at least a year?
(b) The businesses that two of them start are still trading after a year?
(c) All three businesses fail within a year?

5.12 Bella is taking her friend out for the evening but has forgotten to take some cash out of her bank account. She reaches the cash machine, but can't remember the exact sequence of her PIN number. She knows that the digits in her PIN number are 2, 7, 8, and 9.

(a) What is the probability that Bella enters the correct PIN number?
(b) Bella's friend Mel offers to draw some cash out of her account instead. She also cannot remember her PIN number but recalls that there are two fours and two sixes in it. What is the probability that Mel enters the correct PIN number?

5.13 Two friends have a favourite compilation CD that contains some of their all-time favourite tracks. There are 20 tracks on the album. Sam likes five tracks and Chris likes six other tracks. If they program their CD player to play three tracks selected at random from the album, and assuming that the CD player can only select a track once, what is:

(a) The probability that none of their favourites is selected?
(b) The probability that at least one of Sam's favourites is selected?
(c) The probability that at least one of Chris's favourites is selected?

5.14 Every morning Jack makes tea for the other four people in his section. Two of them take sugar. Jack always forgets which teas he has sugared. One of the two senior members of the section, Alicia, takes sugar in her tea; the other, Ben, does not. If Jack takes tea first to Alicia and then to Ben, what is the probability that:

(a) He gives them both the right tea?
(b) He gets one wrong?
(c) He gets both wrong?

5.15 As a result of flood damage a supermarket has a very large stock of tins without labels. Forty per cent of the tins contain soup, 30 per cent contain carrots, 25 per cent contain raspberries, and 5 per cent contain asparagus. The tins are to be offered for sale at three for 50 pence. When a customer buys three tins what is the probability that:

(a) None of the tins contain asparagus?
(b) All three tins contain soup?
(c) One tin contains raspberries?
(d) Two tins contain carrots?
(e) The contents of the three tins are different?

5.16 Thursday, Friday and Saturday are the busiest nights at the Jopper pub. Police records show that on 12 of the last 50 Thursdays, 15 of the last 50 Fridays, and 16 of the last 50 Saturdays they were summoned to deal with a disturbance at the pub. Construct a tree diagram and use it to find the probability that over the next Thursday, Friday and Saturday nights there will be:

(a) No trouble
(b) Trouble on Thursday only
(c) Trouble on one night only
(d) Trouble on Friday and Saturday only
(e) Trouble on two nights only

Assume that events on any one night are independent of events on any other night.

5.17 You win a prize in a charity raffle. The prize, donated by a small hotel chain, is a voucher entitling you to a free double room for a weekend at each of the three hotels in the chain, the Xerxes, the York and the Zetland. The room you stay in at each hotel will be picked at random by the hotel manager. The Xerxes has 12 double rooms, 7 of which are en suite. The York has 28 double rooms, 16 of which are en suite. The Zetland has 18 double rooms, of which 13 are en suite.

(a) What is the probability that none of the rooms you get is en suite?
(b) What is the probability that one of the rooms you get is en suite?
(c) What is the probability that two or more of the rooms you get are en suite?

5.18 Heidi's High Couture shop and Maggie's market stall both sell a particular style of sweatshirt. They are the only outlets for the garment in the area, with Heidi's accounting for 70 per cent of the total number sold and Maggie's accounting for the remainder. Unfortunately colour dye that faded prematurely was used to manufacture the first batches of the product. The supplier estimates that 15 per cent of the stock supplied to Heidi and 25 per cent of the stock supplied to Maggie have this problem. Use Bayes' rule to find the probability that if a sweatshirt is defective it was sold by Maggie.

5.19 An insurance company offers quotations for motor insurance by telephone. The company employs permanent staff to do this work but as a result of a dramatic rise in the number of telephone inquiries 35 per cent of quotations are provided by temporary staff. Unfortunately 22 per cent of the quotations provided by temporary staff prove to be wrong, compared to the 8 per cent of the quotations provided by full-time staff that turn out to be wrong. Under the contract with the agency supplying the temporary staff, the agency will pay a proportion of total costs arising from the mistakes based on the proportion of mistakes that are made by the temporary staff. Use Bayes' rule to determine the probability that if a mistake has been it has been made by one of the temporary staff and use it to suggest what proportion of the total costs of mistakes the agency should pay.

5.20 Select the appropriate definition for each term on the left-hand side from the list on the right-hand side.

(a)	compound probability	(i)	basing a probability on opinion
(b)	multiplication rule	(ii)	outcomes that cannot occur together
(c)	collectively exhaustive	(iii)	$P \text{ (A and B)} = P \text{ (A)} \times P \text{ (B\|A)}$
(d)	dependency	(iv)	a probability of a single outcome
(e)	judgmental	(v)	basing a probability on deduction
(f)	simple probability	(vi)	all possible outcomes
(g)	mutually exclusive	(vii)	$P \text{ (A or B)} = P \text{ (A)} + P \text{ (B)} - P \text{ (A and B)}$
(h)	experimental	(viii)	when $P \text{ (B\|A)}$ is not equal to $P \text{ (B)}$
(i)	addition rule	(ix)	a probability of more than one outcome
(j)	theoretical	(x)	basing a probability on evidence

CHAPTER

6

Putting
probability
to work

This chapter will help you:

- To understand and use probability distributions.
- To analyse discrete random variables.
- To find and interpret summary measures of probability distributions.
- To apply probability in the analysis of business decisions.

In this chapter you will find:

- Simple discrete probability distributions.
- The binomial distribution.
- The Poisson distribution.
- Mean and standard deviation of probability distributions.
- Expectation.
- Decision trees.
- Guidance on using computer software to access probability distributions.

The early parts of this chapter are intended to show you how we can *model* or represent the chances of different combinations of outcomes using the same sort of approach as we use to arrange data into frequency distributions. The later sections are designed to illustrate how probability can be used in making decisions, especially when there are several stages in the decision process, such as investment in new capacity.

6.1 Simple probability distributions

In Chapter 2 we looked at how we could present data in the form of a frequency distribution. This involved listing categories of values that occurred in the set of data and finding out how many observed values fell into each category, in other words the frequency of each category of values in the set of data. The results of this process enabled us to see how the observations were distributed over the range of the data, hence the term frequency distribution.

A *probability distribution* is very similar to a frequency distribution. Like a frequency distribution, a probability distribution has a series of categories, but instead of categories of values it has categories of types of outcomes. The other difference is that each category has a probability instead of a frequency.

In the same way as a frequency distribution distribution tells us how frequently each type of value occurs, a probability distribution tells us how probable each type of outcome is.

In Chapter 2 we saw how a histogram could be used to portray a frequency distribution. We can use a similar type of diagram to portray a probability distribution.

In Chapter 3 we used summary measures including the mean and standard deviation to summarize distributions of data. We can use the mean and standard deviation to summarize distributions of probabilities.

Just as we need the set of data to construct a frequency distribution, we need to identify the set of compound outcomes in order to create a probability distribution. We also need the probabilities of the simple outcomes that make up the combinations of outcomes.

Example 6.1

The Sales Director of a large organization requires all members of sales staff to attend a team-building event at an outward-bound centre. Teams of three staff will be selected by drawing names out of a hat. If there are equal numbers of females and males employed in the sales force, what are the chances that a team of three includes zero, one, two and three females?

Because there are equal numbers of females and males the probability that a female is selected is 0.5 and the probability that a male is selected is also 0.5.

The probability that a team includes no females is the probability that a sequence of three males is selected.

$$P \text{ (MMM)} = 0.5 \times 0.5 \times 0.5 = 0.125$$

The probability that one female is selected in a team of three is a little more complicated because we have to take into account the fact that the female could be the first or the second or the third person to be selected.

So: P (1 Female) = P (FMM or MFM or MMF)

Because these three sequences are mutually exclusive, according to the addition rule:

$$P \text{ (1 Female)} = P \text{ (FMM)} + P \text{ (MFM)} + P \text{ (MMF)}$$

Since the probability that a female is selected is the same as the probability that a male is selected each of these three ways of getting one female will have the same probability. That is:

$$P \text{ (FMM)} = P \text{ (MFM)} = P \text{ (MMF)} = 0.5 \times 0.5 \times 0.5 = 0.125$$

So: P (1 Female) = 0.125 + 0.125 + 0.125 = 0.375

We get the same answer for the probability that two females are selected.

$$P \text{ (2 Females)} = P \text{ (FFM or FMF or MFF)}$$
$$= P \text{ (FFM)} + P \text{ (FMF)} + P \text{ (MFF)}$$
$$= 0.125 + 0.125 + 0.125 = 0.375$$

Finally P (3 Females) = $0.5 \times 0.5 \times 0.5 = 0.125$

We can bring these results together and present them in the form of a probability distribution.

Number of females (x)	P (x)
0	0.125
1	0.375
2	0.375
3	0.125

In Example 6.1 the probability distribution presents the number of females as a variable, X, whose values are represented as x. The variable X is a *discrete random variable*. It is discrete because it can only take a limited set of values. It is random because the values occur as the result of a random process.

The symbol '$P(x)$' represents the probability that the variable X takes a particular value, x. For instance, we can represent the probability that the number of females is one, as

$$P(X = 1) = 0.375$$

Figure 6.1 shows the probability distribution we compiled in Example 6.1 in graphical form.

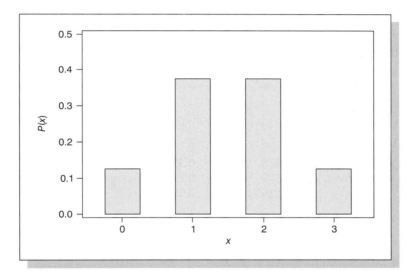

Figure 6.1
The probability distribution of
X, the number of females

We can find summary measures to represent this distribution, in the same way as we could use summary measures to represent distributions of data. However, we don't have a set of data to use to get our summary measures. Instead we have to use the probabilities to 'weight' the values of X, just as we would use frequencies to obtain the mean from a frequency distribution.

You can get the mean of a probability distribution by multiplying each x value by its probability and then adding up the results:

$$\mu = \Sigma x\, P(x)$$

Notice that we use the Greek symbol μ here to represent the mean of the distribution. The mean of a probability distribution is a population mean because we are dealing with a distribution that represents the probabilities of all possible values of the variable.

Once we have found the mean we can proceed to find the variance and standard deviation. We can obtain the variance, σ^2, by squaring each x value, multiplying the square of it by its probability and adding the results. From this sum we subtract the square of the mean:

$$\sigma^2 = \Sigma x^2 \, P\,(x) - \mu^2$$

You can get the standard deviation, σ by taking the square root of the variance.

Again you can see that we are using a Greek letter to represent the variance and the standard deviation because they are population measures.

Example 6.2

Calculate the mean and the standard deviation for the probability distribution in Example 6.1.

x	$P\,(x)$	$x\,P\,(x)$	x^2	$x^2\,P\,(x)$
0	0.125	0	0	0
1	0.375	0.375	1	0.375
2	0.375	0.750	4	1.500
3	0.125	0.375	9	1.125
		1.500		3.000

The mean, μ, is 1.5, the total of the $x\,P(x)$ column.

The variance, σ^2, is 3, the total of the $x^2\,P(x)$ column minus the square of the mean:

$$\sigma^2 = 3 - 1.5^2 = 3 - 2.25 = 0.75$$

The standard deviation: $\sigma = \sqrt{\sigma^2} = \sqrt{0.75} = 0.866$ to three decimal places

The mean of a probability distribution is sometimes referred to as the *expected value* of the distribution. Unlike the mean of a set of data, which is based on what the observed values of a variable actually were, the mean of a probability distribution tells us what the values of the variable are likely, or *expected* to be.

We may need to know the probability that a discrete random variable takes a particular value or a lower value. This is known as a *cumulative* probability because in order to get it we have to add up or *accumulate* other probabilities. You can calculate cumulative probabilities directly from a probability distribution.

Example 6.3

Calculate a set of cumulative probabilities from the probability distribution in Example 6.1.

Suppose we want the probability that X, the number of females, is two or less than two. Another way of saying this is the probability that X is less than or equal to two. We can use the symbol '$\leq$' to represent 'less than or equal to', so we are looking for $P(X \leq 2)$. (It may help you to recognize this symbol if you remember that the small end of the '$<$' part is pointing at the X and the large end at the 2, implying that X is smaller than 2.)

We can find the cumulative probabilities for each value of X by taking the probability that X takes that value and adding the probability that X takes a lesser value. You can see these cumulative probabilities in the right-hand side column of the following table.

Number of females (x)	P (xv	P (X $\leq$ x)
0	0.125	0.125
1	0.375	0.500
2	0.375	0.875
3	0.125	1.000

The cumulative probability that X is zero or less, $P(X \leq 0)$ is the probability that X is zero, 0.125, plus the probability that X is less than zero. Since it is impossible for X to be less than zero we do not have to add anything to 0.125.

The second cumulative probability, the probability that X is one or less, $P(X \leq 1)$, is the probability that X is one, 0.375, plus the probability that X is less than one, in other words that it is zero, 0.125. Adding these two probabilities together gives us 0.5.

The third cumulative probability is the probability that X is two or less, $P(X \leq 2)$. We obtain this by adding the probability that X is 2, 0.375, to the probability that X is less than 2, in other words that it is one or less. This is the previous cumulative probability, 0.5. If we add this to the 0.375 we get 0.875.

The fourth and final cumulative probability is the probability that X is three or less. Since we know that X can't be more than three (there are only three members in a team), it is certain to be three or less, so the cumulative probability is 1. We would get the same result arithmetically if we add the probability that X is three, 0.125, to the cumulative probability that X is less than 3, in other words that it is 2 or less, 0.875.

The cumulative probabilities like those we worked out in Example 6.3 are perfectly adequate if we want the probability that a variable takes a particular value or a lower one, but what if we need to know the probability that a variable is higher than a particular value?

We can use the same cumulative probabilities if we manipulate them using our knowledge of the addition rule of probability. If, for instance, we want to know the probability that a variable is more than two, we can find it by taking the probability that it is two or less away from 1.

$$P\,(X > 2) \,=\, 1 - P\,(X \leq 2)$$

We can do this because the two outcomes (X being greater than two and X being less than or equal to two) are mutually exclusive and collectively exhaustive. One and only one of them must occur. There are no other possibilities so it is certain that one of them happens.

In the expression $P\,(X > 2)$, which represents the probability that X is greater than two, we use the symbol '>' to represent 'greater than'. It may help you to recognize this symbol if you remember that the larger end of it is pointing to the X and the smaller end is pointing to the 2, implying than X is bigger than 2.

Although the situation described in Example 6.1, picking teams of just three people, was quite simple, the approach we used to obtain the probability distribution was rather laborious. Imagine that you had to use the same approach to produce a probability distribution if there were five or six members of a team instead of just three. We had to be careful enough in identifying the three different ways of selecting two females in a team of three. Listing the different ways two females could be selected in a team of five is far more tedious.

Fortunately there are methods of analysing such situations that do not involve strenuous mental gymnastics. These involve using a type of probability distribution known as the *binomial* distribution.

6.2 The binomial distribution

The binomial distribution is the first of a series of 'model' statistical distributions that you will meet in this chapter and the two that follow it. The distribution was first derived theoretically but is widely used in dealing with practical situations. It is particularly useful because it enables you not only to answer a specific question but also to explore the consequences of altering the situation without actually doing it.

You can use the binomial distribution to solve problems that have what is called a *binomial structure*. These types of problems arise in situations where a series of finite, or limited number of 'experiments', or 'trials' take place repeatedly. Each trial has the same two mutually exclusive and collectively exhaustive outcomes, as the *bi* in the word binomial might suggest. These two outcomes are generally referred to as 'success' and 'failure'.

To analyse a problem using the binomial distribution you have to know the probability of each outcome and it must be the same for every trial. In other words the results of the trials must be independent of each other.

Words like 'experiment' and 'trial' are used to describe binomial situations because of the origins and widespread use of the binomial distribution in science. Although the distribution has become widely used in many other fields, these scientific terms have stuck.

The situation in Example 6.1 has a binomial structure. Selecting a team of three is in effect conducting a series of three trials. In each trial, that is, each time a name is selected from the hat, there can be only one of two outcomes, either a female or a male is picked.

In practice we would use computer software or printed tables such as those in Table 1 in Appendix 1 (page 332) to apply the binomial distribution. These have been produced using an equation, called the binomial equation, which you will see below. You won't need to remember it, and you shouldn't need to use it. We will look at it here purely to show that it works.

We will use the symbol X to represent the number of 'successes' in a certain number of trials, n. X can be described as a binomial random variable. The probability of success in any one trial is represented by the letter p.

The probability that there are x successes in n trials is:

$$P\,(X\,=\,x)\,=\,\frac{n!}{x!\,(n\,-\,x)!}\times p^x(1\,-\,p)^{n-x}$$

You will see that an exclamation mark is used several times in the equation. It represents a *factorial*, that is, a number multiplied by one less than itself then multiplied by two less itself and so on until we get to one. For instance, four factorial, 4!, is four times three times two times one, $4 \times 3 \times 2 \times 1$, which comes to 24.

Example 6.4

Use the binomial equation to find the first two probabilities in the probability distribution for Example 6.1.

We will begin by identifying the number of trials to insert in the binomial equation.

Selecting a team of three involves conducting three 'trials', so $n = 3$.

The variable X is the number of females selected in a team of three. We need to find the probabilities that X is 0, 1, 2, and 3, so these will be the x values.

If we define 'success' as selecting a female, p, the probability of success in any one trial, is 0.5.

We can now put these numbers into the equation. We will start by working out the probability that no females are selected in a team of three, that is, $X = 0$.

$$P(X = 0) = \frac{3!}{0!(3-0)!} \times 0.5^0 (1-0.5)^{3-0}$$

This expression can be simplified considerably. Any number raised to the power zero is one, so $0.5^0 = 1$. Conveniently zero factorial, $0!$, is also one. We can also clear up some of the subtractions.

$$P(X = 0) = \frac{3!}{1(3)!} \times 1 (0.5)^3$$

$$= \frac{3 \times 2 \times 1}{3 \times 2 \times 1} \times (0.5 \times 0.5 \times 0.5) = 1 \times 0.125 = 0.125$$

If you look back at Example 6.1 you will find that this is the same as the first figure in the probability distribution. The figure below it, 0.375, is the probability that one female is selected in a team of three, that is, $X = 1$. Using the binomial equation:

$$P(X = 1) = \frac{3!}{1!(3-1)!} \times 0.5^1 (1-0.5)^{3-1}$$

$$= \frac{3 \times 2 \times 1}{1(2!)} \times 0.5 (0.5)^2$$

$$= \frac{6}{1(2 \times 1)} \times 0.5 (0.25) = 3 \times 0.125 = 0.375$$

You may like to try using this approach for $P(X = 2)$ and $P(X = 3)$ as well.

You will find it much easier to use computer software to get these figures. You can do it in MINITAB by selecting the **Probability Distributions** option from the **Calc** menu. Pick the **Binomial** option from the sub-menu. You can choose to obtain probabilities or cumulative probabilities. You will need to specify the **Number of trials** and the **Probability of success**, as well as the column location of the x values.

Alternatively you can obtain the probabilities one at a time in EXCEL. Move the cursor to an empty cell then type **=BINOM-DIST(x,n,p,FALSE)** in the Formula Bar. The numbers you put in for x, n and p depend on the problem. **FALSE** denotes that we don't want a cumulative probability, **TRUE** denotes that we do.

To get the probability that one female is selected in a team of three we would type **=BINOMDIST(1,3,0.5,FALSE)**

Finding binomial probabilities using software or using printed tables means we don't have to undertake laborious calculations to obtain the figures we are looking for. We can use software or printed tables to help us analyse far more complex problems than Example 6.1. We will use tables to analyse the problem in Example 6.5, but it is well worth learning how to produce tables using software because limitations of space means that printed tables only contain a limited number of binomial distributions.

Example 6.5

Malenky Aviation operates commuter flights using aircraft that can take ten passengers. During each flight passengers are given a hot drink and a 'Snack Pack' that contains a ham sandwich and a cake. The company is aware that some of their passengers may be vegetarians and therefore every flight is stocked with one vegetarian Snack Pack that contains a cheese sandwich in addition to ten that contain ham.

If 10 per cent of the population are vegetarians, what is the probability that on a fully booked flight there will be at least one vegetarian passenger who will be dissatisfied with their Snack Pack?

This problem has a binomial structure. We will define the variable X as the number of vegetarians on a fully booked flight. Each passenger is a 'trial' that can be a 'success', a vegetarian, or a 'failure', a non-vegetarian. The probability of 'success', in this case the probability that a passenger is a vegetarian, is 0.1. There are ten passengers on a fully booked flight, so the number of trials, n is 10.

The appropriate probability distribution for this problem is the binomial distribution with $n = 10$ and $p = 0.1$. Table 1 on page 332 contains the following information about the distribution:

FOR 10 TRIALS ($n = 10$)

		$p = 0.1$	
		$P(x)$	$P(X \leq x)$
$x =$	0	0.349	0.349
$x =$	1	0.387	0.736
$x =$	2	0.194	0.930
$x =$	3	0.057	0.987
$x =$	4	0.011	0.998
$x =$	5	0.001	1.000
$x =$	6	0.000	1.000
$x =$	7	0.000	1.000
$x =$	8	0.000	1.000
$x =$	9	0.000	1.000
$x =$	10	0.000	1.000

The column headed $P(x)$ provides the probabilities that a specific number of 'successes', x occurs, e.g. the probability of three 'successes' in ten trials, $P(3)$, is 0.057. The column headed $P(X \leq x)$ provides the probability that x or fewer 'successes' occur, e.g. the probability that there are three or fewer 'successes', $P(X \leq 3)$, is 0.987.

If there is only one vegetarian passenger they can be given the single vegetarian Snack Pack available on the plane. It is only when there is more than one vegetarian passenger that at least one of them will be dissatisfied with their Snack Pack. So we need the probability that there is more than one vegetarian passenger, that is the probability that X is greater than one, $P(X > 1)$. We could get it by adding up all the probabilities in the $P(x)$ column except the first and second ones, the probability that X is zero, $P(0)$ and the probability that X is one, $P(1)$. However, it is easier to take the probability of one or fewer, $P(X \leq 1)$, away from one. That is:

$$P(X > 1) = 1 - P(X \leq 1) = 1 - 0.736 = 0.254 \quad \text{or 25.4 per cent}$$

We can show the binomial distribution we used in Example 6.5 in graphical form.

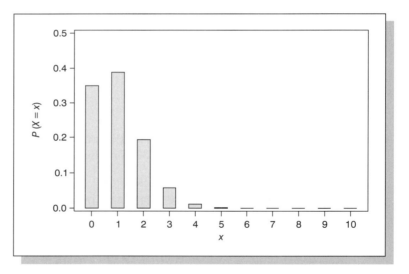

Figure 6.2
The binomial distribution for n = 10 and $p = 0.1$

In Figure 6.2 the block above 0 represents the probability that $X = 0$, $P(0)$, 0.349. The other blocks combined represent the probability that X is larger than 0, $P(X > 0)$, 0.651.

It is quite easy to find the mean and variance of a binomial distribution. The mean, μ, is simply the number of trials multiplied by the probability of success, that is, $\mu = np$. The variance is the number of trials multiplied by the probability of success times one minus the probability of success, $\sigma^2 = np(1-p)$.

Example 6.6

Calculate the mean, variance and standard deviation of the binomial distribution in Example 6.5.

In Example 6.5 the number of trials, n, was 10, and the probability of success, p, was 0.1.

The mean: $\mu = np = 10 \times 0.1 = 1.0$

The variance: $\sigma^2 = np\,(1 - p) = 10 \times 0.1\,(1 - 0.1) = 1.0 \times 0.9 = 0.9$

The standard deviation: $\sigma = \sqrt{\sigma^2} = \sqrt{0.9} = 0.949$ to three decimal places

The binomial distribution is called a *discrete probability distribution* because it describes the behaviour of some discrete random variables, binomial variables. These variables concern the number of times things happen in the course of a finite number of trials.

But what if we need to analyse how many things happen over a period of time? For this sort of situation we use another type of discrete probability distribution known as the *Poisson* distribution.

6.3 The Poisson distribution

Some types of business problem involve the analysis of incidents that are unpredictable. Usually they are things that can happen over a period of time such as the number of telephone calls coming through to an office. However, it could be a number of things over an area such as the number of stains in a carpet.

The Poisson distribution describes the behaviour of variables like the number of calls per hour or the number of stains per square metre. It enables us to find the probability that a specific number of incidents happen over a particular period.

Using the Poisson distribution is quite straightforward. In fact you may find it easier than using the binomial distribution because we need to know fewer things about the situation. To identify which binomial distribution to use we had to specify the number of trials and the probability of success, these were the two defining characteristics, or *parameters* of the binomial distribution. In contrast, the Poisson distribution is a single parameter distribution, the one parameter being the mean.

If we have the mean of the variable we are investigating we can obtain the probabilities of the Poisson distribution using computer software or printed tables such as those in Table 2 on page 333.

In MINITAB select **Probability Distributions** from the **Calc** menu, and then pick **Poisson** from the sub-menu. In the command window you can choose to obtain probabilities or cumulative probabilities. You will need to provide the **Mean** as well as the column location of your x values.

You can also obtain the Poisson distribution probabilities in EXCEL. Move the cursor to an empty cell then type **=POISSON(x, Mean,FALSE)** in the Formula Bar. The numbers you put in for x and the mean depend on the problem. **FALSE** denotes that we don't want a cumulative probability, **TRUE** denotes that we do.

Example 6.7

The first aid tent at a music festival has the capacity to deal with up to three people requiring treatment in any one hour. The mean number of people requiring treatment is two per hour. What is the probability that they will not be able to deal with all the people requiring treatment in an hour?

The variable X in this case is the number of people per hour that require treatment. We can use the Poisson distribution to investigate the problem because it involves a discrete number of occurrences, or incidents over a period of time. The mean of X is 2.

The first aid facility can deal with three people an hour, so the probability that there are more people requiring treatment than they can handle is the probability that X is more than 3, $P\,(X > 3)$.

The appropriate distribution is the Poisson distribution with a mean of 2. Table 2 on page 333 contains the following information about the distribution:

$$\mu = 2.0$$

	$P\,(x)$	$P\,(X \le x)$
$x = 0$	0.135	0.135
$x = 1$	0.271	0.406
$x = 2$	0.271	0.677
$x = 3$	0.180	0.857
$x = 4$	0.090	0.947
$x = 5$	0.036	0.983
$x = 6$	0.012	0.995
$x = 7$	0.003	0.999
$x = 8$	0.001	1.000

The column headed $P\,(x)$ provides the probabilities that a specific number of incidents, x, occurs, e.g. the probability of four incidents, $P\,(4)$, is 0.090. The column headed $P\,(X \le x)$ provides the probability that x or fewer incidents occur, e.g. the probability that there are four or fewer incidents, $P\,(X \le 4)$, is 0.947.

To obtain the probability that more than three people require treatment at the first aid tent, $P(X > 3)$, we can subtract the probabilities that X is 3 or fewer, $P(X \leq 3)$, that is, the probability that the number of people requiring treatment in an hour can be dealt with, from one.

$$P(X > 3) = 1 - P(X \leq 3) = 1 - 0.857 = 0.143 \quad \text{or } 14.3 \text{ per cent}$$

If we had to produce the Poisson probabilities in Example 6.7 without the aid of computer software or printed tables we could calculate them using the formula for the distribution. You won't have to remember it, and probably won't need to use it, but it may help your understanding if you know where the figures come from.

The probability that the number of incidents, X, takes a particular value, x, is:

$$P(X = x) = \frac{e^{-\mu}\,\mu^x}{x!}$$

You can see the letter e, which represents a mathematical constant known as Euler's number. The value of this, to four places of decimals, is 2.7183, so we can put this in the formula.

$$P(X = x) = \frac{2.7183^{-\mu}\,\mu^x}{x!}$$

The symbol μ represents the mean of the distribution and x is the value of X whose probability we want to know. In Example 6.7 the mean is 2, so the probability that there are no people requiring treatment, in other words the probability that X is zero, is:

$$P(X = 0) = \frac{2.7183^{-\mu}\,\mu^0}{0!} = \frac{2.7183^{-2} \times 2^0}{1}$$

To work this out you need to know that if you raise any number (in this case μ) to the power zero the answer is one. So:

$$P(X = 0) = \frac{2.7183^{-2} \times 2^0}{1} = \frac{2.7183^{-2} \times 1}{1}$$

The first part of the expression, 2.7183^{-2}, becomes $1/2.7183^2$. Any number raised to a negative power is a reciprocal, which is one divided by the number, for instance 2^{-2} is $1/2^2$, in other words $1/4$. So:

$$P(X = 0) = 1/2.7183^2 = 0.135 \text{ to three decimal places}$$

If you look back to the extract from Table 2 in Example 6.7 you can check that this is the correct figure. The figure below $P(0)$, 0.135, in the extract from Table 2 is $P(1)$, 0.271, which can be calculated as follows:

$$P(X = 1) = \frac{2.7183^{-\mu} \mu^1}{1!} = \frac{2.7183^{-2} \times 2}{1} = 2/2.7183^2 = 0.271$$

We can portray the Poisson distribution used in Example 6.7 in graphical form.

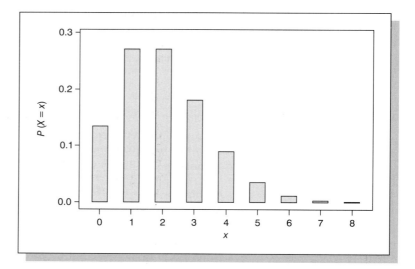

Figure 6.3
The Poisson distribution for μ = 2.0

6.4 Expectation

Earlier in the chapter we referred to the mean of a probability distribution as the expected value of the distribution because it can be used as a guide to what we could expect or predict that the values will be like. In fact one of the most important uses of probabilities is to make predictions. The production of predicted, or expected, values is called *expectation*.

A probability assesses the chance of a certain outcome in general. To use it to make predictions we have to apply it to something specific. If the probability refers to a process that is repeated, we can predict how many times the outcome will occur if the process happens a specific number of times by multiplying the probability by the number of times the process happens.

Example 6.8

In Example 6.1 the probability that a team of three members of the sales force chosen at random contained one female was 0.375. If there are enough sales staff for 200 teams, how many teams will contain exactly one female?

Selecting these teams is a process that is to be repeated 200 times so we can work out how many teams include one female by multiplying the probability that a team contains one female, 0.375, by the number of times the process is repeated, 200.

Expected number of teams with one female $= 0.375 \times 200 = 75$

So we would expect 75 of the teams to contain one female.

The result we obtained in Example 6.8 is a prediction, and like any prediction it won't always be true. We shouldn't therefore interpret the result as meaning that every time 200 teams are selected at random there will be exactly 75 teams that contain one female.

What the result in Example 6.8 does mean is that if 200 teams were to be selected at random many times over, in the long run we would expect that the average number of teams that contain one female will be 75.

Expectation also allows us to predict incidences over time. To do this you multiply the probability that a certain number of incidences occur over a period of time by the time you want your prediction to cover.

Example 6.9

In Example 6.7 we found the probability that the number of people requiring treatment at the first aid tent was more than three in any hour was 0.143. If the music festival lasts 10 hours, in how many hours will there be more than three people seeking treatment?

We can obtain the answer by multiplying the probability of more than three people requiring treatment in an hour by the number of hours the music festival lasts.

Expected hours with more than three people requiring treatment $= 0.143 \times 10 = 1.43$

Since the first aid tent can only treat three people an hour, we would expect them to have to summon help during 1 or 2 hours of the music festival.

In some situations the outcomes are associated with specific financial results. In these cases the probabilities can be applied to the monetary consequences of the outcomes to produce a prediction of the amount of money that the process will generate. These types of prediction are often called *expected monetary values* (*EMVs*).

Example 6.10

A rail operating company incurs extra costs if its long-distance trains are late. Passengers are given a voucher to put towards the cost of a future journey if the delay is between thirty minutes and two hours. If the train is more than two hours late the company refunds the cost of the ticket for every passenger. The cost of issuing vouchers costs the company £500. The cost of refunding all the fares costs the company £6000.

The probability that a train is between thirty minutes and two hours late is 10 per cent and the probability a train is more than two hours late is 2 per cent. What is the expected monetary value of the operating company's extra costs?

To answer this we need to take the probability of each of the three possible outcomes (less than thirty minutes late, thirty minutes to two hours late, more than two hours late) and multiply them by their respective costs (£0, £500, and £6000). The expected monetary value is the sum of these results.

$$EMV = (0.88 \times 0) + (0.1 \times 500) + (0.02 \times 6000) = 0 + 50 + 120 = 170$$

The company can therefore expect that extra costs will amount to £170 per journey.

6.5 Decision trees

Expected monetary values play an important part in models that can be used to analyse business situations that involve a number of stages of outcomes and decisions. These models are called *decision trees*.

As their name might suggest, decision trees depict the different sequences of outcomes and decisions in the style of a tree spreading from left to right. Each branch of the tree represents an outcome or a decision. The junctions, or points at which branches separate, are called *nodes*. If the branches that stem from a node represent outcomes, the node is called a *chance node* and depicted using a small circle. If the branches represent different decisions that could be made at that point, the node is a *decision node* and depicted using a small square.

All the paths in a decision tree should lead to a specific monetary result that may be positive (an income or a profit) or negative (a cost or a loss). The probability that each outcome occurs is written at the end of the branch that represents the outcome. We use the probabilities and the monetary results to work out the expected monetary value (EMV) of each possible decision. We write the EMV of a decision alongside the branch that represents it. The final task is to select the decision, or series of decisions if there is more than one stage of decision-making, that yields the highest EMV.

Example 6.11

A retail grocery company is interested in opening a new supermarket in a disused cinema on the outskirts of a major town. Because of local opposition to the proposal there is only a 65 per cent chance that planning permission will be granted. If planning permission is obtained there is an 80 per cent chance that a major competitor will build a rival establishment close enough to seriously affect the prospects of the supermarket.

Financial planners at the company say that the venture would make a profit of £20 m in its first five years of operation if the rival establishment is not built, and a loss of £4 m over the five years if the rival establishment is built.

Assuming that the company takes all investment decisions on the basis of financial prospects over the first five years of any venture, should they proceed with their plan?

We can begin by distinguishing between the decisions the company can take and the outcomes they could face. The decisions are to open the supermarket or not to open the supermarket. The outcomes are whether they get planning permission or not, and whether the rival establishment is built or not.

Although granting planning permission and building the rival establishment are decisions, they are decisions taken by people outside the company. As far as the company is concerned they are outcomes and they do not have direct control over them.

In the diagram we will use the abbreviations:

- 'O' for opening the supermarket and 'No O' for not opening it
- 'PP' for planning permission and 'No PP' for no planning permission
- 'RE' for a rival establishment and 'No RE' for no rival establishment

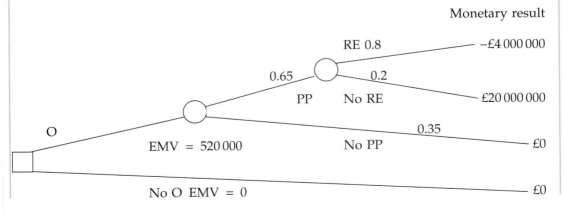

We can start with the EMV of the 'No open' decision. If they decide not to open the supermarket the monetary result is certain to be zero.

If they decide to open the supermarket there is a probability of 0.35 that they fail to get planning permission and hence obtain a monetary result of zero. The probability that they make a loss of £4 000 000 is the probability that they get planning permission and that the rival establishment is built. The probability that they make a profit of £20 000 000 is the probability that they get planning permission and that the rival establishment is not built.

The EMV of opening the supermarket is the sum of these probabilities multiplied by their respective monetary results.

$$\text{EMV (Open)} = (0.35 \times 0) + (0.65 \times 0.8 \times (-4\,000\,000)) + (0.65 \times 0.2 \times 20\,000\,000)$$

$$= 0 + (-2\,080\,000) + 2\,600\,000 = 520\,000$$

Since the expected monetary value of opening the supermarket, £520 000, is greater than the expected monetary value of not opening it, £0, they should open the supermarket.

Although decision trees can be useful approaches to weighing up decisions, they do have some shortcomings as techniques for taking decisions.

Their first weakness is that they are only as good as the information that you put into them. If the probabilities and monetary figures are not reliable then the conclusion is also unreliable. This is an important issue when, as in Example 6.11, the figures are speculative assessments of future events over a considerable period of time.

The second shortcoming is that they take no account of the attitude that the people making the decision have towards risk. For instance, if the retail grocery company in Example 6.11 has high profits and is cash-rich it might be prepared to accept the risk of a loss more readily than if it has low profits and a liquidity problem.

The third drawback is that it is difficult to introduce factors that are non-quantifiable or difficult to quantify into the process. For instance, the location where the company in Example 6.11 wants to open the supermarket may be in an area where recruiting part-time staff for peak periods is easier than in a city-centre location.

Despite these weaknesses decision trees can help to investigate decisions and their consequences, especially when we are interested in the effects of altering some of the figures to see whether the conclusion changes.

Example 6.12

The rival company in Example 6.11 publishes financial results that show an improvement in profits. As a result the retail grocery company that wants to open the supermarket now puts the probability that a rival establishment will be built at 0.9. Should the company change its mind about opening the supermarket?

We need to put the new probability that there is no rival establishment, 0.1, into the expression for the expected monetary value of the decision to open the supermarket.

$$\text{EMV (Open)} = (0.35 \times 0) + (0.65 \times 0.9 \times (-4{,}000{,}000)) + (0.65 \times 0.1 \times 20{,}000{,}000)$$

$$= 0 + (-2\,340\,000) + 1\,300\,000 = -1\,040\,000$$

The expected monetary value of opening the supermarket is now negative, −£1 040 000, which means it is lower than the expected monetary value of not opening the supermarket, £0. In this case they should not open the supermarket

Review questions

Answers to these questions, including fully worked solutions to those questions marked with an asterisk (*), are on pages 349–351.

6.1*   The employees of the Brecht Bank decide to put on a five-a-side football tournament to raise money for charity. If the teams are chosen at random and four tenths of the employees are women, what is the probability that:

(a) A team consists entirely of males?
(b) There are three females in a team?
(c) There are three or fewer females in a team?
(d) The majority of a team are female?

6.2   'Fast' Gary and Mickey 'the Mule' import alcoholic beverages from France into the UK. They are offered a consignment of packs of bottled beers. Each pack contains ten bottles. The price for the consignment is low because due to problems at the bottling plant 20 per cent of the bottles have no labels. What is the probability that in a pack from this consignment:

(a) No bottles are without labels?
(b) Three or fewer bottles are without labels?
(c) More than one bottle is without a label?
(d) Less than five bottles are without labels?
(e) The majority of bottles are without labels?

6.3 A lingerie manufacturer produces ladies' knickers in packs of five pairs. Quality control has been erratic and they estimate that one in every ten pairs of knickers leaves the factory without the trim sewn on. What is the probability that in a pack of five pairs of knickers:

(a) There are no pairs without the trim?
(b) There are two or fewer pairs without the trim?
(c) There is more than one pair without the trim?
(d) The majority of pairs are without the trim?

6.4 The producers of a TV survival programme advertise for potential participants and then select random samples of ten people to appear in the programme. If 30 per cent of the people who apply to take part in the programme are smokers, what is the probability that:

(a) A team consists entirely of non-smokers?
(b) A team includes only one smoker?
(c) A team includes no more than three smokers?
(d) A team includes more than four smokers?
(e) The majority of a team are non-smokers?

6.5 An egg-packing company thinks that a tenth of all the eggs they buy from farms are contaminated with harmful bacteria that could result in food poisoning. What is the probability that in a pack of ten eggs:

(a) None of the eggs contain harmful bacteria?
(b) More than two eggs contain harmful bacteria?
(c) Half the eggs contain harmful bacteria?
(d) Less than two eggs contain harmful bacteria?

6.6 A large party of Russian managers is to visit a car plant in the UK. They will be shown round the plant in small groups of five. Twenty per cent of the managers speak English. If the groups are selected at random, what is the probability that:

(a) There is no English speaker in a group?
(b) There is at least one English speaker in a group?
(c) All but one of the group speaks English?

6.7 The mean number of accidents per day at a large building site is 1.0. What is the probability that a day passes when there are:

(a) No accidents?
(b) Two accidents?
(c) Four or fewer accidents?
(d) More than three accidents?

6.8 An office worker receives an average of 22.5 e-mail messages per day. If his working day lasts seven and a half hours, what is the probability that:

(a) He receives no e-mails in an hour?
(b) He receives one e-mail in an hour?
(c) He receives two or fewer e-mails in an hour?
(d) He receives more than four e-mails in an hour?

6.9 The mean number of violent incidents at the Koshmar pub is 14 per week. As a result of being injured at work the pub bouncer will be off for a day.

(a) What is the probability that the day passes without any violent incidents?
(b) What is the probability that the day passes with no more than one violent incident?
(c) If his doctor says the bouncer needs two days off work, what is the probability that these two days pass without any violent incidents?
(d) What is the probability that these two days pass with more than one violent incident?

6.10 Everyone working in a large open-plan office takes cups of tea or coffee back to their desk to drink. The mean number of spilled cups of hot drinks in an eight-hour working day is 24. What is the probability that an hour passes in which:

(a) There are no spillages?
(b) There are two spillages?
(c) There are less than four spillages?
(d) There is at least one spillage?

6.11 A company produces mouse mats that are 20 cm long and 20 cm wide. These mats are cut from sheets of material that are one metre long and one metre wide. Precise machine setting means that 25 mouse mats can be cut from each sheet of material. Problems that have arisen in the laminating process mean that the sheets of material contain small holes. The mean number of holes per sheet is 25. What is the probability that:

(a) A mouse mat has no holes?
(b) A mouse mat has two or fewer holes?
(c) A mouse mat has more than one hole?

6.12* A pharmaceuticals company marketed a drug that proved to be an effective treatment but unfortunately resulted in side effects for some patients. On the basis of initial clinical research the probability that a patient who is treated with the drug suffers no side effect is 0.85, the probability of a minor side effect is 0.11, and the probability of a major side effect is 0.04. Under an agreement with the appropriate authorities the company has agreed to pay £2500 in compensation to patients who suffer a minor side effect and £20 000 in compensation to patients who suffer a major side effect. What is the expected value of the compensation per patient?

6.13 A graduate wants to pursue a career in a profession. She will need to gain membership of the professional institute by passing three stages of examinations. If she becomes a full member of the institute she anticipates that she will be able to earn £50 000 per year. If she fails the final stage of the examinations, but passes the first two stages she can become an associate member of the institute. An associate member earns about £32 000 per year. If she fails at the second stage but passes the initial stage she can obtain a certificate of competence from the institute and probably earn £24 000. If she fails the initial stage of the examinations she will have to consider other employment and anticipates that she would be able to earn £18 000. The pass rates for the initial, second and final stages of the institute's examinations are 70 per cent, 55 per cent, and 80 per cent. What is the expected value of her annual earnings?

6.14 An insurance company calculates that the probability that in a year a motor insurance policyholder makes a claim arising from a major accident is 0.03, the probability that he or she makes a claim as a result of a minor accident is 0.1, and the probability that he or she makes a claim as a result of vehicle theft is 0.05. The typical payment for a major accident claim is £4500, for a minor accident claim is £800, and for theft £4000. The probability that a policyholder makes more than one claim in a year is zero. What is the expected value of claims per policy?

6.15 A film production company is about to release a new movie. They estimate that there is 5 per cent chance that the film will make a profit of $14 m, a 30 per cent chance that it will make a $1 m profit, a 25 per cent chance that it will break even, and a 40 per cent chance that it will make a loss of $2 m. What is the expected return from the film?

6.16* A sportswear company markets a premium brand of trainers. At present the revenue from sales of these trainers is £17 m a year. They have been negotiating with representatives of a top US sports star in order to obtain his endorsement of the product. The cost to the company of the endorsement would be £3 m a year, a cost that would be met from the sales revenue from the trainers. If the star endorses the trainers the company expects that the sales revenue will rise to £30 m a year. However, just as the deal is about to be signed a regional US news agency runs a story alleging that the star has taken bribes. The sportswear company understand from their US representatives that there is a 60 per cent chance that the star will be able to refute the allegation, in which case sales of the trainers will still be £30 m. If the star is unable to refute the allegation the negative publicity is likely to reduce sales revenue from the trainers to £10 m a year.

(a) Should the company cancel or complete the endorsement deal?
(b) What should the company do if the chance of the star refuting the allegation is 40 per cent?

6.17 A member of a successful girl band is considering leaving the band to pursue a solo career. If she stays with the band she estimates that there is a 60 per cent chance that the band will continue to be successful and she would earn £1.7 m over the next three years. If the band's success does not continue she would still earn £0.6 m over the next three years under her existing contract. If she embarks on a solo career she estimates that the chance of success is 20 per cent. A successful solo career would bring her £4 m in the next three years. If her solo career is not successful she can expect to earn only £0.25 m in the next three years. What should she do?

6.18 An arable farmer is thinking of sowing scientifically modified crops next year. She believes that if she did so her profits would be £75 000, compared to £50 000 if she sowed unmodified crops. A neighbouring farmer has made it clear that if his crops are contaminated he will demand compensation. The arable farmer guesses that the probability of contamination to be 40 per cent. In the event that the neighbouring farmer claims compensation there is a 30 per cent chance that the arable farmer would have to pay £25 000 in compensation and a 70 per cent chance she would have to pay £50 000 in compensation.

(a) Construct a decision tree and use it to advise the arable farmer.
(b) An expert puts the probability that there will be contamination of the crops of the neighbouring farmer at 60 per cent. Should the arable farmer change her strategy in the light of this information?

6.19 Eagraville United are the last lower-division football club in the quarter-finals of a major cup competition. The other teams are all prominent clubs with large numbers of supporters. The commercial manager at Eagraville has to place the order for programmes to sell at the game before the draw for the next stage of the competition takes place. She can place a small or a large order. If she places a large order and the game is played at Eagraville she anticipates a profit of £10 000. If she places a small order and the game is played at Eagraville she anticipates a profit of £3000. If a large order is placed and the game is played elsewhere she estimates a loss of £2500. If a small order is placed and the game is played elsewhere she estimates a loss of £1000. There is a 50 per cent chance that Eagraville will get a home game in the draw, but if they do they expect that the larger club will apply for the fixture to be relocated because of the modest size of the Eagraville ground. The probability that such an application will succeed is 0.4. Use a decision tree to represent the situation and use it to recommend whether the commercial manager should place a large or a small order.

6.20 Select the appropriate description for each term on the left-hand side from the list on the right-hand side.

(a) cumulative probability
(b) expected value
(c) binomial distribution
(d) Poisson distribution
(e) EMV
(f) decision trees

(i) consists of probabilities of incidents over time
(ii) the expected monetary value of a decision
(iii) the probability of one value or a lower one
(iv) consists of probabilities of successes in trials
(v) represent decisions and outcomes
(vi) a name for a probability distribution mean

CHAPTER 7

Modelling populations

In the last chapter we looked at how two different types of theoretical probability distributions, the binomial and Poisson distributions, can be used to model or simulate the behaviour of discrete random variables. These types of variable can only have a limited or finite number of values, typically only whole numbers like the number of defective products in a pack or the number of telephone calls received over a period of time.

Discrete random variables are not the only type of random variable. You will also come across continuous random variables, variables whose possible values are not confined to a limited range. In the same way as we used discrete probability distributions to help us investigate the behaviour of discrete random variables we use continuous probability distributions to help us investigate the behaviour of continuous random variables. Continuous probability distributions can also be used to investigate the behaviour of discrete variables that can have many different values.

The most important continuous probability distribution in Statistics is the Normal distribution. As the name, which is written with a capital N, suggests, this distribution represents the pattern of many 'typical' or 'normal' variables.

However, the Normal distribution has a very special place in Statistics because as well as helping us to investigate variables that behave in the way that the Normal distribution portrays, it is used to model the way in which results from random samples vary. This is of great importance when we want to use sample results to make predictions about entire populations.

7.1 The Normal distribution

Just as we saw that there are different binomial distributions that describe the patterns of values of binomial variables, and different Poisson distributions that describe the behaviour of Poisson variables, there are many different Normal distributions that display the patterns of values of Normal variables.

Each binomial distribution is defined by n, the number of trials and p, the probability of success in any one trial. Each Poisson distribution is defined by its mean. In the same way, each Normal distribution is identified by two defining characteristics or parameters: its mean and standard deviation.

The Normal distribution has three distinguishing features:

- It is unimodal, in other words there is a single peak.

- It is symmetrical, one side is the mirror image of the other.

- It is asymptotic, that is, it tails off very gradually on each side but the line representing the distribution never quite meets the horizontal axis.

Because the Normal distribution is a symmetrical distribution with a single peak, the mean, median and mode all coincide at the middle of the distribution. For this reason we only need to use the mean as a measure of location for the Normal distribution. Since the average we use is the mean, the measure of spread that we use for the Normal distribution is the standard deviation.

The Normal distribution is sometimes described as bell-shaped. Figure 7.1 illustrates the shape of the Normal distribution. It takes the form of a smooth curve. This is because it represents the probabilities that a continuous variable takes values right across the range of the distribution.

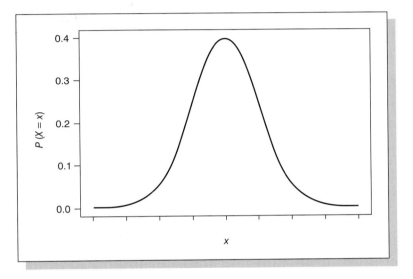

Figure 7.1
The Normal distribution

If you look back at the diagrams we used to represent discrete probability distributions in Figures 6.1 and 6.2 in Chapter 6 you will see that they are bar charts that consist of separate blocks. Each distinct block represents the probability that the discrete random variable in question takes one of its distinct values. Because the variable can only take discrete, or distinct, values we can represent its behaviour with a diagram consisting of discrete, or distinct, sections.

If we want to use a diagram like Figures 6.1 or 6.2 to find the probability that the discrete variable it describes takes a specific value, we could measure the height of the block against the vertical axis. In contrast, using the smooth or continuous curve in Figure 7.1 to find the probability that the continuous variable it describes takes a particular value is not so easy.

To start with, we need to specify a range rather than a single value. For instance, we would have to say what is the probability that the variable X is between 3.500 and 4.499 rather that the probability that X is 4. This probability would be represented in a diagram by that part of the area below the curve that lies between the points 3.500 and 4.499 on the horizontal axis, as a proportion of the total area below the curve. Because this sort of thing is very difficult to measure even approximately on a graph, using the Normal distribution inevitably involves software or printed tables of probabilities.

In Chapter 6 we saw how we could produce tables of binomial or Poisson probabilities using software as long as we could specify the necessary parameters. We could use the software to produce probabilities for any binomial or Poisson distribution. We can also use the software to produce probabilities for any Normal distribution.

You can do this in MINITAB by selecting the **Probability Distributions** option from the **Calc** menu. Pick the **Normal** option from the sub-menu. In the command window that appears you can choose to obtain probabilities or cumulative probabilities. Because of the nature of continuous variables you will nearly always need cumulative probabilities. You will need to specify the **Mean** and the **Standard deviation** of the Normal distribution you want, as well as the column location of the x values whose probabilities you want to know.

Alternatively you can obtain the probabilities one at a time in EXCEL. Move the cursor to an empty cell then type **=NORMDIST (x,mean,standard deviation,TRUE)** in the Formula Bar. The number x is the value whose probability you want to find. The mean and the standard deviation are the parameters of the Normal distribution to which x belongs. **TRUE** denotes that we want a cumulative probability, putting **FALSE** denotes that we don't.

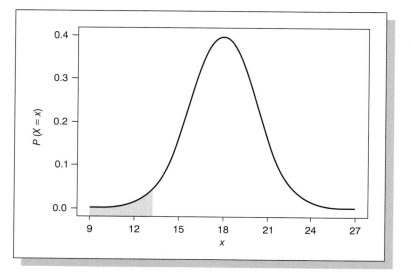

Figure 7.2
The distribution of times taken to use cash dispensers in Example 7.1

Example 7.1

According to a bank, the time taken by its customers to use cash dispensing machines is Normally distributed with a mean of 18 seconds and a standard deviation of 3 seconds. What is the probability that a customer selected at random takes less than 13 seconds?

The shaded area in Figure 7.2 represents the cumulative probability that the time that customers take to use cash dispensing machines is less than 13 seconds.

We can find it by typing =NORMDIST(13,18,3,TRUE)in the EXCEL Formula Bar. The result is 0.0478 or 4.78%.

The result in Example 7.1 can be interpreted to mean that 4.78 per cent of customers take less than 13 seconds. If we wanted to a more extensive profile of the probabilities of different amounts of time that customers take we could use MINITAB to obtain more details of the distribution.

Example 7.2

Find the probabilities that customers of the bank in Example 7.1 take:

(a) Less than 12 seconds

(b) Less than 15 seconds

(c) Less than 18 seconds

(d) Less than 21 seconds

(e) Less than 24 seconds

to use the cash dispensing machines.

You can do this by listing these values in a column in the MINITAB worksheet and specifying the mean, 18, the standard deviation, 3, and the column location of the values, in the command window of the **Normal** option from the **Probability Distributions** sub-menu of the **Calc** menu. You should get the following results.

Normal with mean = 18.0 and standard deviation = 3.0

x	$P(X < x)$
12.0	0.0228
15.0	0.1587
18.0	0.5000
21.0	0.8413
24.0	0.9772

In this output X represents the variable 'time taken by customers', and x represents a specific period of time taken by customers.

You can see from the table in Example 7.2 that the probability that a customer takes less than the mean, 18 seconds, is 0.5, or 50 per cent. This is not too surprising because the mean of the Normal distribution is the figure right in the middle of a symmetrical distribution. We would expect 50 per cent of the values in the distribution to be below it and the other half above it. The probability that any one value is below the mean is therefore exactly the same as the probability that that it is above the mean, 0.5.

If the probability that a customer takes less than 18 seconds is 0.5 and the probability that a customer takes more than 18 seconds is 0.5, what is the probability that a customer takes exactly 18 seconds? In theory the probability that a continuous variable has a precise value is infinitely small. The probability that X, the time that customers take, is precisely 18, that is, 18.000000 . . . is, for all practical purposes, zero. If we are more specific about what we mean by '18 seconds', which is probably '18 seconds to the nearest second', it is clear that we don't mean the probability that X is exactly 18, we mean the probability that X is more than 17.5 and less than 18.5.

An implication of the last point is that there is no tangible difference between the probability that X is less than an amount, and the probability that X is less than or equal to that amount.

The other values in Example 7.2 have been chosen because they are one or two standard deviations away from the mean. As a rule of thumb roughly two-thirds of the Normal distribution is between one standard deviation below the mean and one standard deviation above the mean and about 95 per cent of the distribution is within two standard deviations of the mean. Over 99 per cent of the distribution is within three standard deviations of the mean.

Example 7.3

Use the list of probabilities in Example 7.2 to find the proportion of customers that take:

(a) Between 15 and 21 seconds

(b) Between 12 and 24 seconds

to use the cash dispensers.

According to the table the probability that X, the time taken by customers, is below 21 seconds is 0.8413, or 84.13 per cent. The probability that X is below 15 seconds is 0.1587, or 15.87 per cent. To find the probability that X is less than 21 seconds and more than 15 seconds we have to subtract the probability that it is less than 15 seconds from the probability that it is less than 21 seconds.

$$P (21 > X > 15) = P (X < 21) - P (X < 15)$$

$$= 0.8413 - 0.1587 = 0.6826, \text{ or } 68.26 \text{ per cent}$$

This is illustrated in Figure 7.3.

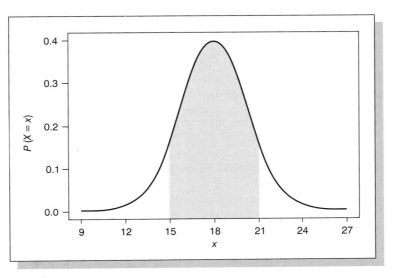

Figure 7.3
Example 7.3: $P (21 > X > 15)$

Similarly we can get the probability that X is less than 24 seconds and more than 12 seconds by subtracting the probability that X is less than 12 seconds from the probability that it is less than 24 seconds.

$$P (24 > X > 12) = P (X < 24) - P (X < 12)$$

$$= 0.9772 - 0.0228 = 0.9544, \text{ or } 95.44 \text{ per cent}$$

This is illustrated in Figure 7.4.

When we looked at the binomial and Poisson distributions in Chapter 6 we saw how it was possible to calculate probabilities in these distributions using the appropriate formulae. In fact in the days before the sort of software we now have became available, if you needed to use a binomial or a Poisson distribution you had to start by consulting published tables. However, because of the sheer number of distributions, the one that you wanted may not have appeared in the tables. In such a situation you often had to calculate the probabilities yourself.

Calculating the probabilities that make up discrete distributions is tedious but not impossible, especially if the number of

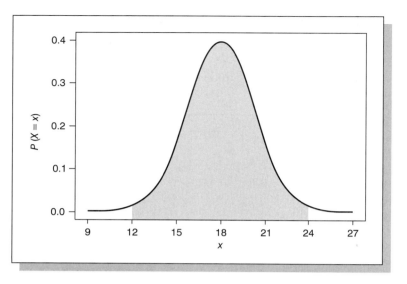

Figure 7.4
Example 7.3: $P (24 > X > 12)$

outcomes involved is quite small. The nature of the variables concerned, the fact that they can only take a limited number of values restricts the number of calculations involved.

In contrast, calculating the probabilities in continuous distributions can be daunting. The variables, being continuous, can have an infinite number of different values and the distribution consists of a smooth curve rather than a collection of detached blocks. This makes the mathematics involved very much more difficult and puts the task beyond the capabilities of many people.

Because it was so difficult to calculate Normal distribution probabilities, published tables were the only viable means of using the Normal distribution before computers were available to do the work. However, the number of different Normal distributions is literally infinite, so it was impossible to publish tables for all Normal distributions.

The solution to this problem was the production of tables describing a benchmark Normal distribution known as the *Standard Normal Distribution*. The advantage of this was that you could analyse any Normal distribution by comparing points in it with equivalent points in the Standard Normal Distribution. Once you had these equivalent points you could use published Standard Normal Distribution tables to assist you with your analysis.

Although modern software means that the Standard Normal Distribution is not quite as indispensable as it once was, it is important that you know something about it. Not only is it useful in case you do not have access to appropriate software, but more importantly, there are many aspects of further statistical work you will meet that are easier to understand if you are aware of the Standard Normal Distribution.

7.2 The Standard Normal Distribution

The Standard Normal Distribution describes the behaviour of the variable Z, which is Normally distributed with a mean of zero and a standard deviation of one. Z is sometimes known as the *Standard Normal Variable* and the Standard Normal Distribution is known as the *Z Distribution*. The distribution is shown in Figure 7.5.

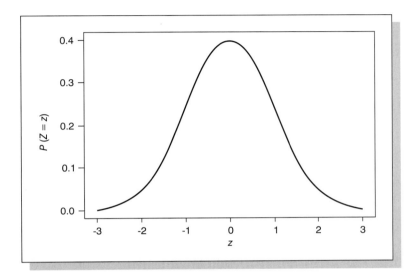

Figure 7.5
The Standard Normal Distribution

If you look carefully at Figure 7.5 you will see that the bulk of the distribution is quite close to the mean, 0. The tails on either side get closer to the horizontal axis as we get further away from the mean, but they never meet the horizontal axis. They are what are called asymptotic.

As you can see from Figure 7.5 half of the Standard Normal Distribution is to the left of zero, and half to the right. This means that half of the z values that make up the distribution are negative and half are positive.

Table 3 on pages 334–335 provides a detailed breakdown of the Standard Normal Distribution. You can use it to find the probability that Z, the Standard Normal Variable, is more than a certain value, z, or less than z. In order to show you how this can be done, a section of Table 3 is printed below:

z	0.00	0.01	0.02	0.03	0.04	0.05	0.06	0.07	0.08	0.09
0.0	0.5000	0.4960	0.4920	0.4880	0.4840	0.4801	0.4761	0.4721	0.4681	0.4641
0.1	0.4602	0.4562	0.4522	0.4483	0.4443	0.4404	0.4364	0.4325	0.4286	0.4247
0.2	0.4207	0.4168	0.4129	0.4090	0.4052	0.4013	0.3974	0.3936	0.3897	0.3859
0.3	0.3821	0.3783	0.3745	0.3707	0.3669	0.3632	0.3594	0.3557	0.3520	0.3483
0.4	0.3446	0.3409	0.3372	0.3336	0.3300	0.3264	0.3228	0.3192	0.3156	0.3121
0.5	0.3085	0.3050	0.3015	0.2981	0.2946	0.2912	0.2877	0.2843	0.2810	0.2776
0.6	0.2743	0.2709	0.2676	0.2643	0.2611	0.2578	0.2546	0.2514	0.2483	0.2451
0.7	0.2420	0.2389	0.2358	0.2327	0.2297	0.2266	0.2236	0.2206	0.2177	0.2148
0.8	0.2119	0.2090	0.2061	0.2033	0.2005	0.1977	0.1949	0.1922	0.1894	0.1867
0.9	0.1841	0.1814	0.1788	0.1762	0.1736	0.1711	0.1685	0.1660	0.1635	0.1611
1.0	0.1587	0.1562	0.1539	0.1515	0.1492	0.1469	0.1446	0.1423	0.1401	0.1379

Suppose you need to find the probability that the Standard Normal Variable, Z, is greater than 0.72, $P (Z > 0.72)$. Begin by looking for the value of z, 0.72, to just one decimal place, i.e. 0.7, among the values listed in the column headed z on the left-hand side. Once you have found 0.7 under z, look along the row to the right until you reach the figure in the column headed 0.02. The figure in the 0.7 row and the 0.02 column is the proportion of the distribution that lies to the right of 0.72, 0.2358. This area represents the probability that Z is greater than 0.72, so $P (Z > 0.72)$ is 0.2358 or 23.58 per cent.

If you require the probability that Z is less than 1.08, $P (Z < 1.08)$, look first for 1.0 in the z column and then proceed to the right until the figure in the column headed 0.08, 0.1401. This is the area to the right of 1.08 and represents the probability that Z is more than 1.08. To get the probability that Z is less than 1.08, subtract 0.1401 from 1, that is:

$$P (Z < 1.08) = 1 - P (Z > 1.08) = 1 - 0.1401$$

$$= 0.8599 \quad \text{or } 85.99 \text{ per cent}$$

In Example 7.4 you will find a further demonstration of the use of Table 3.

Example 7.4

Use Table 3 on pages 334–335 to find the following:

(a) The probability that Z is greater than 0.7, $P (Z > 0.7)$.

(b) The probability that Z is less than 0.7, $P (Z < 0.7)$.

(c) The probability that Z is greater than 2.27, $P (Z > 2.27)$.

(d) The probability that Z is greater than –1.35, $P (Z > -1.35)$.

(e) The probability that Z is less than –1.35, $P (Z < -1.35)$.

(f) The probability that Z is greater than 0.41 and less than 2.74, P (0.41 < Z < 2.74).

(g) The probability that Z is less than −0.82 and more than −1.98, P (−1.98 < Z < −0.82).

(h) The probability that Z is less than 1.53 and more than −0.69, P (−0.69 < Z < 1.53).

Until you are used to dealing with the Standard Normal Distribution you may find it helpful to make a small sketch of the distribution and identify on the sketch the z value(s) of interest and the area that represents the probability you want.

(a) The probability that Z is greater than 0.7, P (Z > 0.7).

The value of Z in this case is not specified to two places of decimals, so we take the figure to the immediate right of 0.7 in Table 3, in the column headed 0.00, which is 0.2420. This is the probability that Z is greater than 0.7. We could also say that 24.20 per cent of z values are greater than 0.7.

This is represented by the area shown in Figure 7.6.

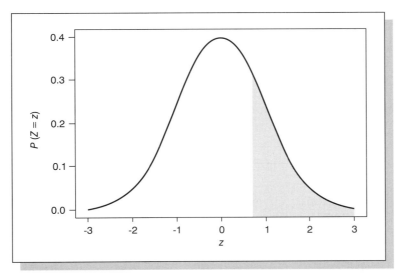

Figure 7.6
Example 7.4 (a): P (Z > 0.7)

(b) The probability that Z is less than 0.7, P (Z < 0.7).

From (a) we know that 24.20 per cent of z values are bigger than 0.7. This implies that 75.80 per cent of z values are less than 0.7, so the answer is 1 − 0.2420 which is 0.7580.

This is represented by the area shown in Figure 7.7.

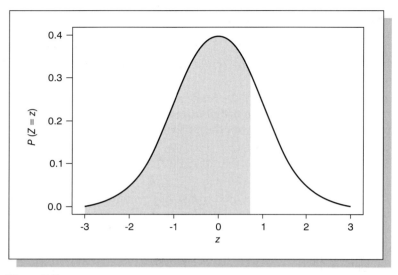

Figure 7.7
Example 7.4 (b): $P(Z < 0.7)$

(c) The probability that Z is greater than 2.27, $P(Z > 2.27)$.

The figure in the row to the right of 2.2 and in the column headed 0.07 in Table 3 is 0.0116. This means that 1.16 per cent of z values are bigger than 2.27. The probability that Z is bigger than 2.27 is therefore 0.0116.

This is represented by the area shown in Figure 7.8.

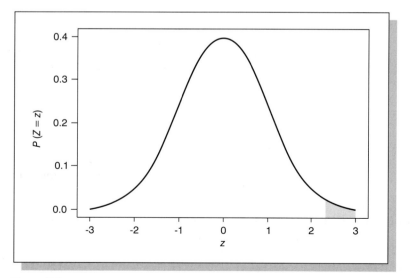

Figure 7.8
Example 7.4 (c): $P(Z > 2.27)$

(d) The probability that Z is greater than -1.35, $P\ (Z > -1.35)$.

The figure in the row to the right of -1.3 and the column headed 0.05 in Table 3 is 0.9115. This is the area of the distribution to the right of -1.35 and represents the probability that z is greater than -1.35.

Figure 7.9 depicts this area.

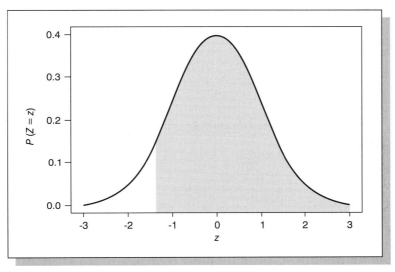

Figure 7.9
Example 7.4 (d): $P\ (Z > -1.35)$.

(e) The probability that Z is less than -1.35, $P\ (Z < -1.35)$.

From (d) we know that the probability that Z is greater than -1.35 is 0.9115, so the probability that Z is less than -1.35 (by which we mean -1.4, -1.5 and so on) is $1 - 0.9115$, which is 0.0885.

This is shown in Figure 7.10.

(f) The probability that Z is greater than 0.41 and less than 2.74, $P\ (0.41 < Z < 2.74)$.

The probability that Z is greater than 0.41, $P\ (Z > 0.41)$, is shown in Table 3 in the row for 0.4 and the column headed 0.01, 0.3409. You will find the probability that Z is greater than 2.74 in the row for 2.7 and the column headed 0.04, 0.0031. We can obtain the probability that Z is more than 0.41 and less than 2.74 by taking the probability that Z is more than 2.74 away from the probability that Z is more than 0.41, that is:

$$P\ (0.41 < Z < 2.74) = P\ (Z > 0.41) - P\ (Z > 2.74) = 0.3409 - 0.0031 = 0.3378$$

This probability is shown in Figure 7.11.

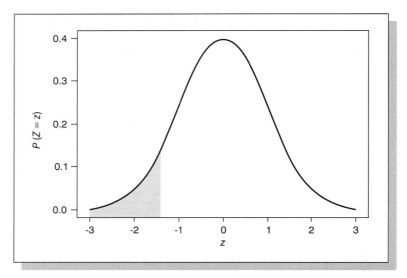

Figure 7.10
Example 7.4 (e): $P\ (Z < -1.35)$

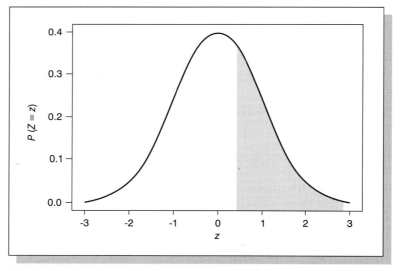

Figure 7.11
Example 7.4 (f): $P\ (0.41 < Z < 2.74)$

Another way of approaching this is to say that if 34.09 per cent of the area is to the right of 0.41 and 0.31 per cent of the area is to the right of 2.74, then the difference between these two percentages, 33.78 per cent is the area between 0.41 and 2.74.

(g) The probability that Z is greater than -1.98 and less than -0.82, $P\ (-1.98 < Z < -0.82)$.

From Table 3 we can establish by looking for figure in the -1.9 row and the 0.08 column that the probability that Z is more than -1.98, $P\ (Z > -1.98)$, is 0.9761. The probability that

Z is more than –0.82, P (Z > –0.82) is the figure in the –0.8 row and the 0.02 column, 0.7939. The probability that Z is between –1.98 and –0.82 is the probability that Z is more than –1.98 minus the probability that Z is more than 0.82. That is:

$$P(-1.98 < Z < -0.82) = P(Z > -1.98) - P(Z > -0.82) = 0.9761 - 0.7939 = 0.1822$$

This is illustrated in Figure 7.12.

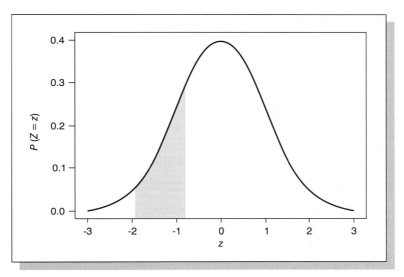

Figure 7.12
Example 7.4 (g): $P(-1.98 < Z < -0.82)$

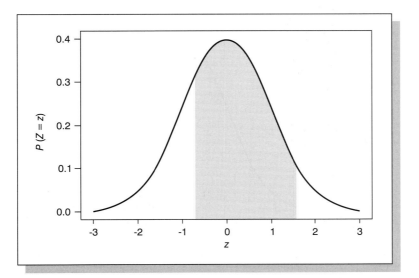

Figure 7.13
Example 7.4 (h): $P(-0.69 < Z < 1.53)$

(h) The probability that Z is greater than -0.69 and less than 1.53, $P(-0.69 < Z < 1.53)$.

The probability that Z is greater than -0.69, $P(Z > -0.69)$, is in the -0.6 row and the 0.09 column of Table 3, 0.7549. $P(Z > 1.53)$ is in the row for 1.5 and the column headed 0.03, 0.0630. The probability that Z is between -0.69 and 1.53 is the probability that Z is greater than -0.69 minus the probability that Z is greater than 1.53:

$$P(-0.69 < Z < 1.53) = P(Z > -0.69) - P(Z > 1.53) = 0.7549 - 0.0630 = 0.6919$$

This is depicted in Figure 7.13.

Sometimes we need to use the Standard Normal Distribution in a rather different way. Instead of starting with a value of Z and finding a probability, we may have a probability and need to know the value of Z associated with it.

Example 7.5

Use Table 3 on pages 334–335 to find the specific value of Z, which we will call z_α, so that the area to the right of z_α, the probability that Z is greater than z_α, $P(Z > z_\alpha)$, is:

(a) 0.4207

(b) 0.0505

(c) 0.0250

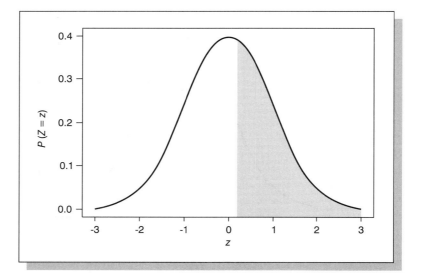

Figure 7.14
Example 7.5 (a): $0.4207 = P(Z > 0.2)$

(a) If you look carefully down the list of probabilities in Table 3, you will see that 0.4207 appears to the right of the z value 0.2, so in this case the value of z_α is 0.2. The probability that Z is greater than 0.2, $P\,(Z > 0.2)$, is 0.4207.

This is shown in Figure 7.14.

(b) To find the value of Z that has an area of 0.0505 to the right of it you will have to look further down Table 3. The figure 0.0505 appears in the row for 1.6 and the column headed 0.04, 0.0505 is the probability that Z is more than 1.64, $P\,(Z > 1.64)$.

This is shown in Figure 7.15.

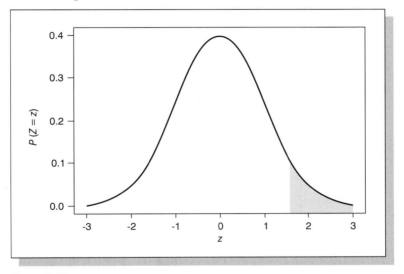

Figure 7.15
Example 7.5 (b): $0.0505 = P\,(Z > 1.64)$

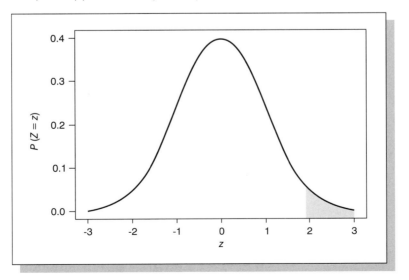

Figure 7.16
Example 7.5 (c): $0.0250 = P\,(Z > 1.96)$

(c) The value of Z that has an area of 0.0250, or 2.5 per cent of the distribution, to the right of it is 1.96 because the figure 0.0250 is in the row for 1.9 and the column headed 0.06 in Table 3. So 0.0250 is the probability that Z is more than 1.96, $P (Z > 1.96)$.

This is illustrated in Figure 7.16.

The symbol we used in Example 7.5 to represent the value of Z we wanted to find, z_α, is a symbol that you will come across in later work. The α in this symbol represents the area of the distribution beyond z_α, in other words the probability that z is beyond z_α.

$$P (Z > z_\alpha) = \alpha$$

In Example 7.5 (c), α is 0.0250 and z_α is 1.96, that is $P (Z > 1.96)$ = 0.0250. 1.96 is the value of Z and 0.0250 or 2.5 per cent is the area of the distribution beyond 1.96. As you can see from Figure 7.16 this is a small area in the right-hand tail of the distribution, so we sometimes refer to such an area as a *tail area*.

Sometimes it is convenient to represent a particular value of Z by the letter z followed by the tail area beyond it in the distribution in the form of a suffix. For instance, the z value 1.96 could be written as $z_{0.0250}$ because there is a tail of 0.0250 of the distribution beyond 1.96. We might say that the z value 1.96 'cuts off' a tail area of 0.0250 from the rest of the distribution.

In later work you will find that particular z values are often referred to in this style because it is the area of the tail that leads us to use a particular z value and we may want to emphasize the fact. Values of Z that cut off tails of 5 per cent, 2.5 per cent, 1 per cent and $\frac{1}{2}$ per cent crop up in the topics we will look at in the next chapter. The z values that cut off these tail areas, 1.64, 1.96, 2.33 and 2.58 are frequently referred to as $z_{0.05}$, $z_{0.025}$, $z_{0.01}$ and $z_{0.005}$ respectively.

7.2.1 Using the Standard Normal Distribution

To use the Standard Normal Distribution to analyse other Normal distributions we need to be able to express any value of a Normal distribution that we want to investigate as a value of Z, which is known as finding its *Z-equivalent* or *Z score*.

The Z-equivalent of a particular value, x, of a Normal variable, X, is the difference between x and the mean of X, μ, divided by the standard deviation of X, σ.

$$Z = \frac{x - \mu}{\sigma}$$

Because we are dividing the difference between the value, x, and the mean of the distribution it belongs to, μ, by the standard deviation of the distribution, σ, to get it, the Z-equivalent of a value is really just the number of standard deviations the value is away from the mean.

Once we have found the Z-equivalent of a value in another Normal distribution we can refer to the Standard Normal Distribution table, Table 3 on pages 334–335, to assess probabilities associated with it.

Example 7.6

A pub offers a '10 oz Steak Special'. If the steaks they use for these meals have uncooked weights that are Normally distributed with a mean of 9.8 ounces and a standard deviation of 0.5 ounces, what is the probability that a customer will get:

(a) A steak that has an uncooked weight of more than 10 ounces?

(b) A steak that has an uncooked weight of more than 9.5 ounces?

(c) A steak that has an uncooked weight of less than 10.5 ounces?

(a) If X represents the uncooked weights of the steaks, we want to find $P(X > 10)$. This is shown in Figure 7.17.

The Z-equivalent of $x = 10$ is

$$z = \frac{10 - 9.8}{0.5} = 0.4$$

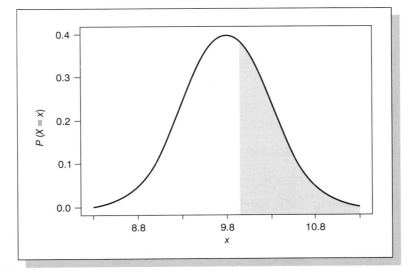

Figure 7.17
Example 7.6 (a): $P(X > 10)$

So the probability that X is more than 10 is equivalent to the probability that Z is more than 0.4. From Table 3 on pages 334–335:

$$P(Z > 0.4) = 0.3446 \quad \text{or } 34.46 \text{ per cent}$$

(b) The Z-equivalent of 9.5 is

$$z = \frac{9.5 - 9.8}{0.5} = -0.6$$

So the probability that X is more than 9.5 is equivalent to the probability that Z is more than −0.6. From Table 3:

$$P(Z > -0.6) = 0.7257 \quad \text{or } 72.57 \text{ per cent}$$

(c) The Z-equivalent of 10.5 is

$$z = \frac{10.5 - 9.8}{0.5} = 1.4$$

The probability that X is less than 10.5 is the same as the probability that Z is less than 1.4. According to Table 3 the probability that Z is more than 1.4 is 0.0808, so the probability that Z is less than 1.4 is $1 - 0.0808$ which is 0.9192, or 91.92 per cent.

In some situations you may need to find a specific point in the Normal distribution that cuts off a particular tail area. To do this, you first have to select the value of Z that cuts off the same area in the Standard Normal Distribution. Once you have established this z value, find the point that number of standard deviations away from the mean. If the z value is positive, add that number of standard deviations to the mean, if it is negative, take them away.

Example 7.7

In the population of uncooked steaks in Example 7.6, what is:

(a) The minimum weight of the heaviest 20 per cent of steaks?

(b) The maximum weight of the lightest 10 per cent of steaks?

To answer (a), begin by looking at the cumulative probabilities in Table 3. Look down the table until you come to the figure closest to 0.2, 0.2005. This figure is in the row for 0.8 and the column headed 0.04, which means that the value of Z that cuts off a 20 per cent tail on the right-hand side of the distribution is 0.84. In other words $P(Z > 0.84)$ is 0.2005. If 20 per cent of the Standard Normal Distribution lies to the right of 0.84,

20 per cent of any Normal distribution, including the one representing the distribution of uncooked weights of steaks in Example 7.6, lies to the right of a point 0.84 standard deviations above the mean. The mean of the distribution of uncooked weights of steaks is 9.8 ounces and the standard deviation is 0.5 ounces, so 20 per cent of uncooked steaks weigh more than:

$$9.8 + (0.84 \times 0.05) = 10.22 \text{ ounces}$$

We can conclude that the heaviest 20 per cent of the steaks weigh more than 10.22 ounces.

The figure for (b), the maximum weight of the lightest 10 per cent of steaks, is also the minimum weight of the heaviest 90 per cent of steaks. From Table 3 the value of Z that cuts off 90 per cent of the area to the right of it is −1.28. If 90 per cent of the Standard Normal Distribution is above −1.28 then 10 per cent is below it. This means that the lowest 10 per cent of any Normal distribution is 1.28 standard deviations below the mean, so the lightest 10 per cent of steaks will weigh less than:

$$9.8 - (1.28 \times 0.5) = 9.16 \text{ ounces}$$

Normal distributions are important statistical distributions because they enable us to investigate the very many continuous variables that occur in business and many other fields, whose values are distributed in a Normal pattern. What makes Normal distributions very important, perhaps even the most important distributions in Statistics, is that they enable us to understand how samples results vary. This is because many *sampling distributions* have a Normal pattern.

7.3 Sampling distributions

Sampling distributions are distributions that show how sample results vary, they portray the 'populations' of sample results. Such distributions play a crucial role in statistical work because they enable us to use data from a random sample to make predictions or judgements about a population. There are considerable advantages in doing this especially when the population is too large to be accessible, or if investigating the population is too expensive or time-consuming.

A sample is a subset of a population, that is, it consists of some observations taken from the population. A random sample is a sample that consists of values taken at random from the population.

You can take many different random samples from the same population, even samples that consist of the same number of observations. Unless the population is very small the number of samples that you could take from it is infinitesimal. A 'parent' population can produce an infinite number of 'offspring' samples.

These samples will have different means, standard deviations and so on. So if we want to use say a sample mean to predict the value of the population mean we will be using something that varies, the sample mean, to predict something that is fixed, the population mean.

To do this effectively we have to know how the sample means vary from one sample to another. We have to regard sample means as observations, $\bar{x}$, of a variable, $\bar{X}$, and consider how they are distributed. What is more we need to relate the distribution of sample means to the parameters of the population the samples come from so that we can use sample statistics to predict population measures. The distribution of sample means is a sampling distribution.

We will start looking at this by taking the simplest case, in which we assume that the parent population is Normally distributed. If this is the case, what will the sampling distributions of means of samples taken from the population be like?

If you took all possible random samples consisting of n observations from a population that is Normal, with a mean μ and a standard deviation σ, and analysed them you would find that the means of all these samples will themselves be Normally distributed.

You would also find that the mean of the distribution of all these different sample means is exactly the same as the population mean, μ, and that the standard deviation of all these sample means is the population standard deviation divided by the square root of the size of the samples, $\sigma/\sqrt{n}$.

So the sample means of all the samples size n that can be taken from a Normal population with a mean μ and a standard deviation σ are distributed Normally with a mean of μ and a standard deviation of $\sigma/\sqrt{n}$. In other words the sample means are distributed around the same mean as the population itself but with a smaller spread.

We know that the sample means will be less spread out than the population because n will be more than one, so $\sigma/\sqrt{n}$ will be less than σ. For instance, if there are four observations in each sample, $\sigma/\sqrt{n}$ will be $\sigma/2$, that is, the sampling distribution of means of samples which have four observations in them will have half the spread of the population distribution.

The larger the size of the samples, the less the spread in the values of their means, for instance if the samples each consist of 100 observations the standard deviation of the sampling distribution will be $\sigma/10$, a tenth of the population distribution.

This is an important logical point. In taking samples we are 'averaging out' the differences between the values in the population. The larger the samples, the more this happens. For this reason it is better to use larger samples to make predictions about a population.

Next time you see an opinion poll look for the number of people that the pollsters have canvassed. It will probably be at least one thousand. The results of an opinion poll are a product that the polling organization wants to sell to media companies. In order to do this they have to persuade them that their poll results are likely to be reliable. They won't be able to do this if they only ask a very few people for their opinions!

The standard deviation of a sampling distribution, $\sigma/\sqrt{n}$, is also known as the *standard error* of the sampling distribution because it helps us anticipate the error we will have to deal with if we use a sample mean to predict the value of the population mean.

If we know the mean and standard deviation of the parent population distribution we can find the probabilities of different sample means by using software or the Standard Normal Distribution.

Example 7.8

A group of four friends visit the pub in Example 7.6 and each of them orders a Steak Special. What is the probability that the mean uncooked weight of the steaks they order is more than 10 ounces?

The uncooked weights of the steaks in the pub in Example 7.6 are Normally distributed with a mean of 9.8 ounces and a standard deviation of 0.5 ounces.

Imagine we took every possible sample of four steaks from the population of steaks at the disposal of the pub (which we will assume is infinite) and calculated the mean weight of each sample. We would find that the sampling distribution of all these means has a mean of 9.8 and a standard error of $0.5/\sqrt{4}$, which is 0.25.

The probability that one sample of four steaks has a mean of more than 10 is the probability that a Normal variable with a mean of 9.8 and a standard deviation of 0.25 is greater than 10.

The Z-equivalent of the value 10 in the sampling distribution is:

$$Z = \frac{\bar{x} - \mu}{\sigma/\sqrt{n}} = \frac{10 - 9.8}{0.5/\sqrt{4}} = \frac{0.2}{0.25} = 0.8$$

From Table 3 on pages 334–335 we find that the probability that Z is more than 0.8 is 0.2119 or 21.19%.

We can conclude that there is a little more than a one in five chance that four steaks chosen at random have a mean uncooked weight of more than 10 ounces. You might like to compare this with the result in Example 7.6 (a), which suggests than the chance that a single steak has an uncooked weight of more than 10 ounces is 34.46 per cent.

The procedure we used in Example 7.8 can be applied whether we are dealing with small samples or with very much larger samples. As long as the population the samples come from is Normal we can be sure that the sampling distribution will be distributed Normally with a mean of μ and a standard deviation of $\sigma/\sqrt{n}$.

But what if the population is not Normal? There are many distributions that are not Normal, such as distributions of wealth of individuals or distributions of waiting times.

Fortunately, according to a mathematical finding known as the Central Limit Theorem, as long as n is large (which is usually interpreted to mean more than 30) the sampling distribution of sample means will be Normal in shape and have a mean of μ and a standard deviation of $\sigma/\sqrt{n}$. This is true whatever the shape of the population distribution.

Example 7.9

The times that passengers at a busy railway station have to wait to buy tickets during the rush hour follow a skewed distribution with a mean of 2 minutes 46 seconds and a standard deviation of 1 minute 20 seconds. What is the probability that a random sample of 100 passengers will, on average have to wait more than 3 minutes?

The sample size, 100, is larger than 30 so the sampling distribution of the sample means will have a Normal shape. It will have a mean of 2 minutes 46 seconds, or 166 seconds, and a standard error of $80/\sqrt{100}$.

$$P\ (\bar{X} > 180 \text{ seconds}) = P(Z > \frac{180 - 166)}{80/\sqrt{100}}$$

$$= P(Z > 14/8) = P(Z > 1.75)$$

From Table 3 the probability that Z is more than 1.75 is 0.0401. So the probability that a random sample of 100 passengers will have to wait on average more than 3 minutes is 4.01 per cent, or a little more that a one in twenty-five chance.

If the samples taken from a population that is not Normal consist of fewer than 30 observations then the Central Limit Theorem does not apply. The sampling distributions of means of small samples taken from such populations don't have a Normal pattern.

7.3.1 Estimating the standard error

The main reason for being interested in sampling distributions is to help us use samples to assess populations because studying the whole population is not possible or practicable. Typically we will be using a sample, which we do know about, to investigate a population, which we don't know about. We will have a sample mean and we will want to use it to assess the likely value of the population mean.

So far we have measured sampling distributions using the mean and the standard deviation of the population, μ and σ. But if we need to find out about the population using a sample, how can we possibly know the values of μ and σ?

The answer is that in practice we don't. In the case of the population mean, μ, this doesn't matter because usually it is the thing we are trying to assess. But without the population standard deviation, σ, we do need an alternative approach to measuring the spread of a sampling distribution.

Because we will have a sample, the obvious answer is to use the sample standard deviation, s, in place of the population standard deviation, σ. So the standard error of the sampling distribution becomes $s/\sqrt{n}$ instead of $\sigma/\sqrt{n}$.

This is fine as long as the sample concerned is large, in practice that n, the sample size, is at least 30. If we are dealing with a large sample we can use $s/\sqrt{n}$ as an approximation of $\sigma/\sqrt{n}$. The means of samples consisting of n observations will be Normally distributed with a mean of μ and an approximate standard error of $s/\sqrt{n}$. The Central Limit Theorem allows us to do this even if the population the sample comes from is not itself Normal in shape.

Example 7.10

The mean volume of draught beer served in pint glasses in a particular pub is known to be 0.564 litres. A consumer organization takes a random sample of 64 pints of draught beer and finds that the standard deviation of this sample is 0.025 litre. What is the probability that the mean volume of the sample will be more than a pint (0.568 litre)?

The population mean, μ, in this case is 0.564 and the sample standard deviation, s, is 0.025. We want the probability that $\bar{X}$ is more than 0.568, $P(\bar{X} > 0.568)$. The z-equivalent of 0.568 is:

$$z = \frac{\bar{x} - \mu}{s/\sqrt{n}} = \frac{0.568 - 0.564}{0.025/\sqrt{64}} = \frac{0.004}{0.003125} = 1.28$$

So $P(\bar{X} > 0.568) = P(Z > 1.28)$

If you look at Table 3 you will find that the probability that Z is greater than 1.28 is 0.1003, so the probability that the sample mean is more than a pint is 0.1003 or 10.03 per cent.

As $s/\sqrt{n}$ is not the real standard error it is referred to as the *estimated standard error*, but because the standard deviation of a large sample will be reasonably close to the population standard deviation the estimated standard error will be close to the actual standard error.

7.4 The *t* distribution

In section 7.3.1 we looked at how you can analyse sampling distributions using the sample standard deviation, s, in the likely event that you do not know the population standard deviation, σ. As long as the sample size, n, is 30 or more the estimated standard error will be a sufficiently consistent measure of the spread of the sampling distribution, whatever the shape of the parent population.

If, however, the sample size, n, is less than 30 the estimated standard error is not so close to the actual standard error, and the smaller the sample size, the greater will be the difference between the two. In this situation it is possible to model, or simulate, the sampling distribution using the estimated standard error, as long as the population the sample comes from is Normal, but we have to use a modified Normal distribution in order to do it.

This modified Normal distributions is known as the *t distribution*. The development of the distribution in the early twentieth century by an executive of the Guinness Brewery, William S. Gosset was a real breakthrough in Statistics because it made it possible to investigate populations using small sample results. Small samples are generally much cheaper and quicker to gather than large sample so *t* distributions transformed the way in which people used Statistics.

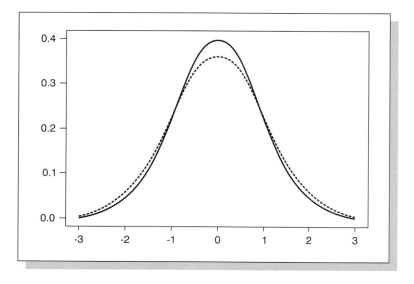

Figure 7.18
The Standard Normal
Distribution (solid line) and the
t distribution (dotted line)

A *t* distribution is a Normal distribution that is more spread out. The difference between the two is illustrated in Figure 7.18.

The greater spread is to compensate for the greater variation in sample standard deviations between small samples than between large samples.

The smaller the sample size, the more compensation is needed, so there are a group of 'standard' *t* distributions. The one that should be used in a particular context depends on the number of degrees of freedom, represented by the symbol v (nu, the Greek letter n), which is the sample size minus one, $n - 1$.

To work out the probability that the mean of a small sample taken from a Normal population is more, or less than a certain amount we first need to find its *t*-equivalent, or *t* value. The procedure is very similar to the way we work out a *z*-equivalent:

$$t = \frac{\bar{x} - \mu}{s/\sqrt{n}}$$

Once we have the *t* value equivalent to the sample mean we can use computer software to find the probability associated with it. In MINITAB choose **Probability Distributions** from the **Calc** menu, then **t** from the **Probability Distributions** sub-menu. In the command window you will have to select the **Cumulative probability** options and provide the number of **Degrees of freedom** (the sample size minus one) and the **Input column**, that is, the column location of your *t* value(s). The result that you see in the Session window will be the probability that *t* is less than the value(s) in the **Input column**.

You can also find probabilities of *t* distributions using EXCEL. The command that you need to type in the Formula Bar is **=TDIST(x,degrees of freedom,tails)**, where *x* is the *t* value you are interested in and 'tails' can be either one or two. If you simply want the probability that *t* is bigger than a certain value, specify just one tail. In some circumstances it is useful to know the probability that *t* is more than a certain value or less than its negative equivalent in which case we would specify two tails.

Example 7.11

A customer visiting the pub in Example 7.10 purchases nine pints of real ale. The volumes of the pints served are known to be Normally distributed with a mean of 0.564 litres and the standard deviation of the volumes of the nine pints bought by the customer is 0.048 litre. What is the probability that the mean volume of the nine pints is more than a pint (0.568 litre)?

The population mean, μ, is 0.564 and the sample standard deviation, s, is 0.048. We want the probability that $\bar{X}$ is more than 0.568, $P(\bar{X} > 0.568)$. The *t* value equivalent to 0.568 is:

$$t = \frac{\bar{x} - \mu}{s/\sqrt{n}} = \frac{0.568 - 0.564}{0.048/\sqrt{9}} = \frac{0.004}{0.016} = 0.25$$

So $P(\bar{X} > 0.568) = P(t > 0.25)$

We can find the probability that t is more than 0.25 by putting **=TDIST(0.25,8,1)** in the EXCEL Formula Bar. The figure 8 is the number of degrees of freedom, which is one less than the sample size, 9. The result is 0.4044, so the probability that the mean volume of nine 'pints' is more than a pint is 40.44 per cent.

The t value that led to the result we obtained in Example 7.11 could be written as $t_{0.4044,8}$ because it is the value of t that cuts off a tail area of 40.44 per cent in the t distribution that has 8 degrees of freedom. In the same way, $t_{0.05,15}$ represent the t value that cuts off a tail area of 5 per cent in the t distribution that has 15 degrees of freedom.

You will find that the way t distributions are used in further work depends on tail areas. For this reason, and also because there are 'standard' t distributions for the different degrees of freedom, printed tables do not provide full details of t distributions in the same way that Standard Normal Distribution tables give full details of the Standard Normal Distribution. Table 4 on page 336 gives selected values of t from t distributions with different degrees of freedom for the most commonly used tail areas.

Example 7.12

Use Table 4 to find:

(a) t with four degrees of freedom that cuts off a tail area of 0.10, $t_{0.10,4}$

(b) t with ten degrees of freedom that cuts off a tail area of 0.01, $t_{0.01,10}$

(c) t with seventeen degrees of freedom that cuts off a tail area of 0.025, $t_{0.025,17}$

(d) t with one hundred degrees of freedom that cuts off a tail area of 0.005, $t_{0.005,100}$.

From Table 4:

(a) You will find $t_{0.10,4}$ in the row for 4 degrees of freedom and the column headed 0.10, 1.533. This means that the probability that t, with 4 degrees of freedom, is greater than 1.533 is 0.10 or 10 per cent.

(b) $t_{0.01,10}$ is the figure in the row for 10 degrees of freedom and the column headed 0.01, 2.764.

(c) $t_{0.025,17}$ is in the row for 17 degrees of freedom and the 0.025 column, 2.110.

(d) $t_{0.005,100}$ is in the row for 100 degrees of freedom and the 0.005 column, 2.626.

7.5 Choosing the correct model for a sampling distribution

The Normal distribution and the t distribution are both models that you can use to model sampling distributions, but how can you be sure that you use the right one? This section is intended to provide a brief guide to making the choice.

The first question to ask is; are the samples whose results make up the sampling distribution drawn from a population that is distributed Normally? In other words, is the parent population Normal? If the answer is yes then it is always possible to model the sampling distribution. If the answer is no then it is only possible to model the sampling distribution if the sample size, n, is 30 or more.

The second question is whether the population standard deviation, σ, is known. If the answer to this is yes then as long as the parent population is Normal the sampling distribution can be modelled whatever the sample size. If the answer is no the sampling distribution can be modelled using the Normal distribution only if the sample size is 30 or more. In the absence of the population standard deviation, you have to use the sample standard deviation to approximate the standard error.

Finally, what if the parent population is Normal, the population standard deviation is not known, and the sample size is less than 30? In these circumstances you should use the t distribution and approximate the standard error using the sample standard deviation. Note that if the parent population is not Normal and the sample size is less than 30 neither the Normal distribution nor the t distribution can be used to model the sampling distribution, and this is true whether or not the population standard deviation is known.

Review questions

Answers to these questions, including fully worked solution to those questions marked with an asterisk (*), are on pages 351–354.

7.1 Find the areas of the Standard Normal Distribution that represent the following probabilities:

(a) $P(Z > 1.44)$
(b) $P(Z > -0.29)$
(c) $P(Z < 2.06)$
(d) $P(Z < -1.73)$
(e) $P(0.52 < Z < 1.99)$
(f) $P(-2.31 < Z < -1.08)$
(g) $P(-0.97 < Z < 0.65)$

7.2* A confectionery company produces 100-gram 'Real Chocolate' bars that have a mean chocolate content of 70 grams with a standard deviation of 0.8 gram. The variation in chocolate content follows a Normal distribution. What is the probability that a chocolate bar chosen at random contains:

(a) More than 71 grams?
(b) More than 68 grams?
(c) Less than 70 grams?
(d) Between 69 and 72 grams?

7.3 The colour dye used in the manufacture of certain garments fades after a mean of 96 machine washes, with a standard deviation of 7 washes. If the number of washes before fading follows a Normal distribution, what proportion of the garments will first fade:

(a) After 100 washes?
(b) Before 90 washes?
(c) Between 95 and 105 washes?

7.4 An automobile manufacturer produces a certain model of car. The fuel economy figures of these cars are Normally distributed with a mean mileage per gallon (mpg) of 36.8 and a standard deviation of 1.3.

(a) What is the probability that one of these cars will have an mpg of more than 37.5?
(b) What is the probability that one of these cars will have an mpg of less than 35?
(c) What is the probability that one of these cars will have an mpg of less than 40?
(d) What is the probability that one of these cars will have an mpg of between 34 and 38 mpg?
(e) What is the minimum mpg of the 15 per cent most fuel efficient cars?
(f) What is the maximum mpg of the 40 per cent least fuel efficient cars?

7.5 A large company insists that all job applicants who are invited for interview take a psychometric test. The results of these tests follow a Normal distribution with a mean of 61 per cent and the standard deviation of 7.2 per cent.

(a) What proportion of applications would be expected to score over 70 per cent?
(b) What proportion of applications would be expected to score under 40 per cent?
(c) What proportion of applications would be expected to score between 50 per cent and 65 per cent?

(d) What score is exceeded by 20 per cent of applicants?

(e) What is the highest score achieved by the 5 per cent of applicants who do least well in the test?

7.6   A bed linen company manufactures duvets that have a mean TOG rating (a measure of thermal effectiveness) of 11.5 with a standard deviation of 0.18. If the TOG ratings are Normally distributed, what is the probability that a duvet selected at random has a TOG rating:

(a) Above 12?

(b) Above 11.3?

(c) Below 11.6?

(d) Below 11.1?

(e) Between 11.2 and 11.4?

(f) Between 11.5 and 11.9?

7.7   The weight losses that members of a slimming club can expect to achieve follow a Normal distribution with a mean of 24.7 lb and a standard deviation of 5.2 lb.

(a) What proportion of members can expect to lose more than 25 lb?

(b) What proportion of members can expect to lose more than 20 lb?

(c) What proportion of members can expect to lose less than 35 lb?

(d) What proportion of members can expect to lose less than 15 lb?

(e) What proportion of members can expect to lose between 12 lb and 30 lb?

(f) What is the most weight that the least successful 40 per cent of slimmers can expect to lose?

(g) What is the least weight that the most successful 30 per cent of slimmers can expect to lose?

7.8   The times taken by a traditional barber to cut hair are Normally distributed with a mean of 15.6 minutes and a standard deviation of 3.4 minutes. What is the probability that he can cut a customer's hair in:

(a) Less than 20 minutes?

(b) Less than 10 minutes?

(c) Between 8 and 14 minutes?

(d) Between 17 and 22 minutes?

(e) Between 12 and 18 minutes?

7.9   A drinks vending machine dispenses a variety of hot and cold beverages. The volumes of the drinks dispensed follow a Normal pattern with a mean of 149.7 ml and a standard deviation of 1.2 ml.

(a) What proportion of drinks will be over 150 ml?
(b) What proportion of drinks will be over 147.5 ml?
(c) What proportion of drinks will be under 148 ml?
(d) What proportion of drinks will be under 152 ml?
(e) What proportion of drinks will be between 149 ml and 152.5 ml?
(f) What is the most that can be expected in the smallest 5 per cent of drinks?
(g) What is the least that can be expected in the largest 25 per cent of drinks?

7.10 The amount of time that visitors to a web site browse the site is assumed to be Normally distributed with a mean of 8.75 minutes and a standard deviation of 3.1 minutes. What is the probability that a randomly selected visitor browses the site for:

(a) Less than 5 minutes?
(b) More than 10 minutes?
(c) Less than 15 minutes?
(d) Between 3 and 7 minutes?
(e) Between 10 and 14 minutes?
(f) Between 8 and 12 minutes?

7.11* The mean legal lifetime (the number of miles travelled before the tyre is worn down to the legal limit) of car tyres of a certain brand is 23 450 miles. The standard deviation is 1260 miles. If the lifetimes of the tyres are Normally distributed, what is the probability that a random sample of four tyres fitted to a vehicle will have a mean legal lifetime of:

(a) More than 25 000 miles?
(b) More than 22 000 miles?
(c) Less than 24 000 miles ?
(d) Less than 23 000 miles?
(e) Between 22 500 and 24 500 miles?
(f) Between 23 400 and 24 200 miles?

7.12 The playing time of C180 videocassettes produced by one manufacturer varies Normally with a mean of 182.4 minutes and a standard deviation of 1.3 minutes. What proportion of packs of five of these videocassettes will have a mean playing time of:

(a) Longer than 183 minutes?
(b) Longer than 182 minutes?

(c) Shorter than 184 minutes?

(d) Shorter than 181 minutes?

(e) Between 181.5 and 182.5 minutes?

(f) Between 181.3 and 182.3 minutes?

7.13 As part of a charity event a radio DJ plans to broadcast a selection of 12 tracks chosen at random from the very large stock of music CDs stored at the radio station. The lengths of the tracks on these CDs are Normally distributed with a mean of 3 minutes 9 seconds and a standard deviation of 43 seconds.

(a) What is the probability that the mean track length of the selected sample is longer than 3 minutes?

(b) What is the probability that the mean track length of the sample of tracks selected is shorter than 2 minutes 50 seconds?

(c) What is the probability that the mean track length of the sample of tracks selected is longer than 3 minutes 30 seconds?

(d) What is the probability that the mean track length of the sample of tracks selected is between 2 minutes 45 seconds and 3 minutes 15 seconds?

(e) If the DJ has a hour for the show and 20 minutes are required for advertising slots and messages, what is the probability that the show will run over time?

7.14 A large administrative centre is replacing its IT facilities. As part of this operation all standard client files are to be stored temporarily on floppy disks as a precaution. The disk spaces that these files require are Normally distributed with a mean of 0.20 mb and a standard deviation of 0.085 mb. The capacity of the floppy disks that are to be used is 1.44 mb. Staff are instructed to save six files on to each disk. Assuming that the selection of files can be assumed to be random:

(a) Work out the maximum mean disk space per file that is available and find the probability that there is insufficient disk space on a disk for six files.

(b) What is the probability that a there is insufficient disk space if only five files are stored per disk?

7.15 Multi-Purpose Vehicles (MPVs) produced by a manufacturer can accommodate seven adults. The load capacity of the passenger compartment is 1240 lb. If the weights of adults are distributed Normally with a mean of 170 lb and a standard deviation of 18 lb, what is the probability that the mean weight of a sample of seven adults will exceed the maximum average weight that the load capacity permits?

7.16 The delays to scheduled airline departures at an international airport are known to follow a skewed distribution with a mean of 11 minutes and a standard deviation of 7 minutes. What is the probability that the mean delay of a random sample of 40 flights is:

(a) More than 12 minutes?
(b) More than 10 minutes?
(c) Less than 8 minutes?
(d) Less than 11 minutes?
(e) Between 9 minutes and 10.5 minutes?
(f) Between 11.5 and 12.5 minutes?
(g) Between 9.5 and 14 minutes?

7.17 The amount of analgesic per pill in a proprietary brand of painkiller follows a Normal pattern with a mean of 7.5 mg. The pills are sold in bottles of 50. If the standard deviation of the analgesic content of the 50 pills in one bottle is 0.4 mg, what is the probability that the mean analgesic content of 50 pills is:

(a) Above 7.35 mg?
(b) Above 7.6 mg?
(c) Below 7.55 mg?
(d) Below 7.45 mg?
(e) Between 7.4 and 7.65 mg?

7.18* The contents of pots of a certain brand of yoghurt are Normally distributed with a mean of 101.4 grams. The yoghurts are sold in packs of four. The contents of each pot in one pack of four were measured and the standard deviation was found to be 3.1 grams.

(a) What mean amount of content will be exceeded by 10 per cent of packs?
(b) What mean amount of content will be exceeded by 5 per cent of packs?
(c) What mean amount of content will be exceeded by 1 per cent of packs?

7.19 The times taken by buses to travel between two stops on a route follow a Normal pattern of variation with a mean of 13.9 minutes. A commuter makes this journey ten times each week. One week she times the ten journeys and works out that the standard deviation of them is 1.7 minutes. Treating the ten journeys in a week as a random sample:

(a) What mean journey time will be exceeded one week in twenty?
(b) What mean journey time will be exceeded one week in forty?
(c) What mean journey time will not be exceeded 90 per cent of the time?

7.20 Select the appropriate description for each term on the left-hand side from the list on the right-hand side.

(a) the Normal distribution

(b) the Z distribution

(c) z_α

(d) $z_{0.05}$

(e) a sampling distribution

(f) $\sigma/\sqrt{n}$

(g) $s/\sqrt{n}$

(h) a t distribution

(i) the z value for which $P(Z > z) = 0.05$

(ii) the estimated standard error

(iii) a distribution used for small samples

(iv) a symmetrical continuous distribution

(v) the standard error

(vi) the z value for which $P(Z > z) = \alpha$

(vii) the Standard Normal Distribution

(viii) shows how sample results vary

'How to understand mountains by studying molehills . . .'

Statistical decision making

This chapter will help you:

- To use sample results to make predictions about populations.
- To test hypotheses about populations.
- To decide how large a sample needs to be.

In this chapter you will find:

- Interval estimates of population means.
- Interval estimates of population proportions.
- Methods of setting the minimum sample size.
- Tests of hypotheses about the population mean.
- Tests of hypotheses about the difference between two population means.
- Tests of hypotheses about the population proportion.
- Non-parametric testing of hypotheses about the population median.
- Guidance on using computer software for statistical inference.

Businesses often use statistical analysis in order to help them study and solve problems. In almost every case the data they use in this analysis will be sample data. Usually it is too expensive, or too time-consuming or simply impossible to obtain population data.

So if there is a problem of customer dissatisfaction they will study data from a sample of customers, not all customers. If there is a problem with product quality they will study a sample of the products, not all of them. If a large organization has a problem with staff training they will study the experiences of a sample of their staff rather than all their staff.

Of course, they will analyse the sample data in order to draw general conclusions about the population from their analysis. As long as the samples they use are random samples, in other words they consist of observed values chosen at random from the population, it is quite possible to do this.

The use of sample data in drawing conclusions, or making deductions, about populations is known as *statistical inference* from the word *infer* which means to deduce or conclude. It is also referred to as *statistical decision making*, which reflects the fact that this sort of analysis helps organizations and individuals take decisions.

In the last chapter we looked at sampling distributions. These distributions are the theoretical foundations on which statistical inference is built because they connect the behaviour of sample results to the distribution of the population the samples came from. Now we will consider the procedures involved in statistical inference.

There are two types of statistical inference technique that you will encounter in this chapter. The first is *estimation*; the use of sample data to predict population measures like means and proportions. The second is *hypothesis testing*; the use of sample data to verify or refute claims made about population measures.

Collecting sample data can be time-consuming and expensive so in practice organizations don't like to gather more data than they need, but, on the other hand, they don't want to end up with too little in case they haven't enough for the sort of conclusive results they want. You will find a discussion of this aspect of planning statistical research in this chapter.

8.1 Estimation

Statistical estimation is the use of sample measures such as means or proportions to predict the values of their population counterparts. The easiest way of doing this is to simply take the sample measure and use it as it stands as a prediction of the population equivalent. So we could take the mean of a sample and use it as our estimate of the population mean. This type of prediction is called *point estimation*. It is widely used to get a 'feel' for the population value and it is a perfectly valid use of the sample result.

The main shortcoming of point estimation is given away by its name; it is a single point, a single shot at estimating one number using another. It is a crude way of estimating a population measure because not only is it uncertain whether it will be a good estimate, in other words close to the measure we want it to estimate, but we have no idea of the chance that it is a good estimate.

The best way of using sample information to predict population measures is to use what is known as *interval estimation*, which is the preparation of a range or *interval* as the estimate. The aim is to be able to say how likely it is that the interval we construct is accurate, in other words how *confident* we are that the interval does include within it the population measure. Because the probability that the interval includes the population measure, or the confidence we should have in the interval estimate, is an important issue, interval estimates are often called *confidence intervals*.

Before we look at how interval estimates are constructed and why they work, it will be helpful if we reiterate some key points about sampling distributions. For convenience we will concentrate on sample means for the time being.

- A sampling distribution of sample means shows how all the means of the different samples of a particular size, n, are distributed.

- Sampling distributions that describe the behaviour of means of samples bigger than 30 are always approximately Normal.

- The mean of a sampling distribution is the population mean, μ.

- The standard deviation of a sampling distribution, called the standard error, is the population standard deviation divided by the square root of the sample size, $\sigma/\sqrt{n}$.

The sampling distributions that are Normal in shape have the same features as other Normal distributions. One of these features is that if we take one point two standard deviations to the left of the mean and another point two standard deviations to the right of the mean, the area between the two points is roughly 95 per cent of the distribution.

To be more precise, if these points were 1.96 standard deviations below and above the mean the area would be exactly 95 per cent of the distribution. In other words 95 per cent of the observations in the distribution are within 1.96 standard deviations from the mean.

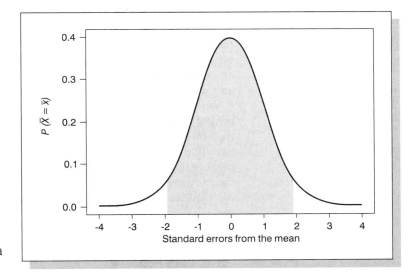

Figure 8.1
Ninety-five per cent of the area
of a sampling distribution

This is also true for Normal sampling distributions. Ninety-five per cent of the sample means in a sampling distribution that is Normal will be between 1.96 standard errors below and 1.96 standard errors above the mean. You can see this illustrated in Figure 8.1.

The limits of this range, or interval are:

$$\mu - 1.96 \; \sigma/\sqrt{n} \text{ on the left-hand side}$$

and

$$\mu + 1.96 \; \sigma/\sqrt{n} \text{ on the right-hand side.}$$

The largest possible distance between any of the middle 95 per cent of sample means and the population mean, μ, is 1.96 standard errors, 1.96 $\sigma\sqrt{n}$. The probability that any one sample mean is within 1.96 standard errors of the mean is:

$$P \; (\mu - 1.96 \; \sigma/\sqrt{n} < \overline{X} < \mu + 1.96 \; \sigma/\sqrt{n}) \; = \; 0.95$$

The sampling distribution allows us to predict values of sample means like this, using the population mean. But in practice we wouldn't be interested in doing this because we wouldn't know the value of the population mean. Indeed typically the population mean is the thing we want to find out about using a sample mean rather than the other way round.

The thing that makes sampling distributions so useful is that we can use them to predict population measures using sample results.

As we have seen, adding and subtracting 1.96 standard errors to and from the population mean creates a range that encompasses 95 per cent of the sample means in the distribution. But what would happen if, instead of adding and subtracting this amount to the population mean, we add and subtract this amount to and from every sample mean in the distribution?

We would create a range around every sample mean. In 95 per cent of cases, the ranges based on the 95 per cent of sample means that are closest to the population mean (those nearest the middle of the distribution), the range would encompass the population mean itself. In the other 5 per cent of cases, those means furthest away from the population mean and far from the centre of the distribution, the range would not encompass the population mean.

So, suppose we take the mean of a large sample and create a range around it by adding 1.96 standard errors to get an upper figure, and subtracting 1.96 standard errors to get a lower figure. There is a 95 per cent chance that the range between the upper and lower figures will encompass the mean of the population. Such a range is called a *95 per cent confidence interval* or a *95 per cent interval estimate* because it is an interval, or range, that we are 95 per cent confident, or certain, includes the population mean.

Example 8.1

The total bill sizes of shoppers at a supermarket have a mean of £50 and a standard deviation of £12.75. A group of researchers, who do not know that the population mean bill size is £50, finds the total bill sizes of a random sample of 100 shoppers.

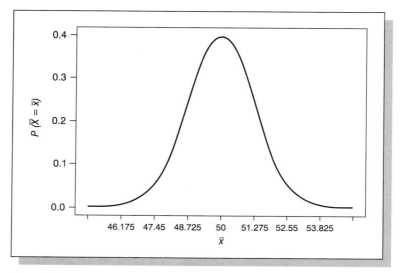

Figure 8.2
The sampling distribution in Example 8.1

The sampling distribution that the mean of their sample belongs to is shown in Figure 8.2. The standard error of this distribution is $12.75/\sqrt{100} = 1.275$.

Ninety-five per cent of the sample means in this distribution will be between 1.96 standard errors below the mean, which is:

$$50 - (1.96 \times 1.275) = 47.50 \text{ to two decimal places}$$

and 1.96 standard errors above the mean, which is:

$$50 + (1.96 \times 1.275) = 52.50 \text{ to two decimal places.}$$

This is shown in Figure 8.3.

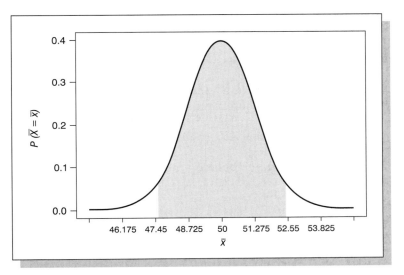

Figure 8.3
The middle 95 per cent of the sampling distribution in Example 8.1

Suppose the researchers calculate the mean of their sample and it is £49.25, a figure inside the range 47.50 to 52.50 that encompasses the 95 per cent of sample means that are within 1.96 standard errors of the population mean. If they add and subtract the same number of standard errors to and from their sample mean:

$$49.25 \pm (1.96 \times 1.275) = 49.25 \pm 2.50 = £46.75 \text{ to } £51.75 \text{ to two decimal places}$$

The interval they create does include the population mean, £50.

Notice the symbol '±' in the expression we have just used. It means we have to carry out two operations: we have to both add *and* subtract the amount that follows it. The addition produces the higher figure, in this case 51.75, and the subtraction produces the lower figure, 46.75.

Imagine they take another random sample of 100 shoppers and find that the mean expenditure of this second sample is a little higher, but still within the central 95 per cent of the sampling distribution, say £51.87. If they add and subtract 1.96 standard errors to and from this second mean:

$$51.87 \pm (1.96 \times 1.275) = 51.87 \pm 2.50 = £49.37 \text{ to } £54.37 \quad \text{to two decimal places}$$

This interval also includes the population mean.

If the researchers in Example 8.1 took many samples and created an interval based on each one by adding and subtracting 1.96 standard errors they would find that only occasionally would the interval not include the population mean.

Example 8.2

The researchers in Example 8.1 take a random sample that yields a mean of £47.13. Calculate a 95 per cent confidence interval using this sample mean.

$$47.13 \pm (1.96 \times 1.275) = 47.13 \pm 2.50 = £44.63 \text{ to } £49.63 \quad \text{to two decimal places}$$

This interval does not include the population mean of £50.

How often will the researchers in Example 8.1 produce an interval that does not include the population mean? The answer is every time they have a sample mean that is among the lowest $2\frac{1}{2}$ per cent or the highest $2\frac{1}{2}$ per cent of sample means. If their sample mean is among the lowest $2\frac{1}{2}$ per cent the interval they produce will be too low, as in Example 8.2. If the sample mean is amongst the highest $2\frac{1}{2}$ per cent the interval will be too high.

As long as the sample mean is among the 95 per cent of the distribution between the lowest $2\frac{1}{2}$ per cent and the highest $2\frac{1}{2}$ per cent, the interval they produce will include the population mean, in other words it will be an accurate estimate of the population mean.

Of course, usually when we carry out this sort of research we don't know what the population mean is, so we don't know which sample means are among the 95 per cent that will give us accurate estimates and which are amongst the 5 per cent that will give us inaccurate estimates. The important point is that if we have a sample mean and we create an interval in this way there is a 95 per cent chance that the interval will be accurate. To put it another way, on average 19 out of every 20 samples will produce an accurate estimate, and 1 out of 20 will not. That is why the interval is called a 95 per cent interval estimate or a 95 per cent confidence interval.

We can express the procedure for finding an interval estimate for a population measure as taking a sample result and adding and subtracting an *error*. This error reflects the uncertainties involved in using sample information to predict population measures.

$$\text{Population measure estimate} = \text{sample result} \pm \text{error}$$

The error is made up of two parts, the standard error and the number of standard errors. The number of standard errors depends on how confident we want to be in our estimation.

Suppose you want to estimate the mean of a Normal population. If you know the population standard deviation, σ, and you want to be $(100 - \alpha)$ per cent confident that your interval is accurate, then:

$$\text{Estimate of } \mu = \bar{x} \pm (z_{\alpha/2} \times \sigma/\sqrt{n})$$

The letter 'z' appears because we are dealing with sampling distributions that are Normal, so we can use the Standard Normal Distribution, the Z distribution, to model them. You have to choose which z value to use on the basis of how sure you want or need to be that your estimate is accurate.

If you want to be 95 per cent confident in your estimate, that is $(100 - \alpha)$ per cent = 95 per cent, then α is 5 per cent and $\alpha/2$ is $2\frac{1}{2}$ per cent or 0.025. To produce your estimate you would use $z_{0.025}$, 1.96, the z value that cuts off a $2\frac{1}{2}$ per cent tail in the Standard Normal Distribution. This means that a point 1.96 standard deviations (or standard errors in the case of sampling distributions) away from the mean of any Normal distribution will cut off a tail area of $2\frac{1}{2}$ per cent of the distribution. So:

$$95 \text{ per cent interval estimate of } \mu = \bar{x} \pm (1.96 \times \sigma/\sqrt{n})$$

This is the procedure we used in Example 8.1.

The most commonly used level of confidence in interval is probably 95 per cent, but what if you wanted to construct an interval based on a higher level of confidence, say 99 per cent? A 99 per cent level of confidence means we want 99 per cent of the sample means in the sampling distribution to provide accurate estimates.

To obtain a 99 per cent confidence interval the only adjustment we make is the z value that we use. If $(100 - \alpha)$ per cent = 99 per cent, then α is 1 per cent and $\alpha/2$ is $\frac{1}{2}$ per cent or 0.005. To produce your estimate you would use $z_{0.005}$, 2.576, the z value that cuts off a $\frac{1}{2}$ per cent tail in the Standard Normal Distribution.

$$99 \text{ per cent interval estimate of } \mu = \bar{x} \pm (2.576 \times \sigma/\sqrt{n})$$

Table 8.1
Selected levels of confidence
and associated z values

Level of confidence $(100 - \alpha)$ per cent	$\alpha/2$	$z \alpha/2$
90 per cent	0.05	1.645
95 per cent	0.025	1.960
99 per cent	0.005	2.576

The most commonly used confidence levels and the z values you need to construct them are given in Table 8.1.

Example 8.3

Use the sample result in Example 8.2, £47.13, to produce a 99 per cent confidence interval for the population mean.

From Table 8.1 the z value that cuts off a 0.005 tail area is 2.576, so the 99 per cent confidence interval is:

$$47.13 \pm (2.576 \times 1.275) = 47.13 \pm 3.28 = £43.85 \text{ to } £50.41 \quad \text{to two decimal places}$$

Notice that the confidence interval in Example 8.3 includes the population mean, £50, unlike the 95 per cent interval estimate produced in Example 8.2 using the same sample mean, £47.13. This is because this sample mean, £47.13, is not among the 95 per cent closest to the population mean, but it is among the 99 per cent closest to the population mean.

Changing the level of confidence to 99 per cent has meant the interval is accurate, but it is also wider. The 95 per cent interval estimate was £44.63 to £49.63, a width of £5.00. The 99 per cent interval estimate is £43.85 to £50.41, a width of £6.56.

You can obtain the z values necessary for other levels of confidence by looking for the appropriate values of $\alpha/2$ in the body of Table 3 on page 335 and finding the z values associated with them.

Example 8.4

Use the sample result in Example 8.2, £47.13, to produce a 98 per cent confidence interval for the population mean.

From Table 3 the z value that cuts off a tail area of 0.01 is 2.33, so the 98 per cent confidence interval is:

$$47.13 \pm (2.33 \times 1.275) = 47.13 \pm 2.97 = £44.16 \text{ to } £50.10 \quad \text{to two decimal places}$$

8.1.1 Determining sample size

All other things being equal, if we want to be more confident that our interval is accurate we have to accept that the interval will be wider, in other words less precise. If we want to be more confident and retain the same degree of precision, the only thing we can do is to take a larger sample.

In the examples we have looked at so far the size of the sample was already decided. But what if, before starting a sample investigation, you wanted to ensure that you had a big enough sample to enable you to produce a precise enough estimate with a certain level of confidence? To see how to do this, we need to start with the expression we have used for the error of a confidence interval:

$$\text{Error} = z_{\alpha/2} \times \sigma / \sqrt{n}$$

Until now we have assumed that we know the three elements to the right of the equals sign and so we can work out the error. But what if we wanted to set the error and find the necessary sample size, n? We can change the expression for the error around so that it provides a definition of the sample size:

$$\text{Error} = z_{\alpha/2} \times \sigma / \sqrt{n}$$

Exchange error and $\sqrt{n}$: $\sqrt{n} = z_{\alpha/2} \times \sigma / \text{error}$

So $n = (z_{\alpha/2} \times \sigma / \text{error})^2$

This means that as long as you know the degree of precision you need (the error), the level of confidence (to find $z_{\alpha/2}$), and the population standard deviation (σ), you can find out what sample size you need to use.

Example 8.5

If the researchers in Example 8.1 want to construct 99 per cent confidence intervals that are £5 wide, what sample size should they use?

If the estimates are to be £5 wide that means they will have to be produced by adding and subtracting £2.50 to and from the sample mean. In other words the error will be 2.5. If the level of confidence is to be 99 per cent then the error will be 2.576 standard errors.

If $(100 - \alpha)$ per cent = 99 per cent, $z_{\alpha/2} = 2.576$. We know $\sigma = 12.75$, so:

$n = (2.576 \times 12.75 / 2.50)^2$

$n = (13.1376)^2 = 172.6$ to one decimal place.

Round this up to 173. When deciding sample size it is always better to play safe and round the calculated sample size up to the next whole number.

We can conclude that if the researchers want 99 per cent interval estimates that are £5 wide they would have to take a sample of 173 bills.

8.1.2 Estimating without σ

Example 8.1 is artificial because we assumed that we knew the population mean, μ. This helped to explain how and why interval estimation works. In practice we wouldn't know the population mean, and neither would we know the population standard deviation, σ.

Practical interval estimation is based on sample results alone, but it is very similar to the procedure we explored in Example 8.1. The main difference is that we have to use a sample standard deviation, s, to produce an estimate for the standard error of the sampling distribution the sample belongs to. Otherwise, as long as the sample concerned is quite large, which we can define as containing 30 or more observations, we can follow exactly the same procedure as before.

That is, instead of: estimate of $\mu = \bar{x} \pm (z_{\alpha/2} \times \sigma/\sqrt{n})$

we use: estimate of: $\mu = \bar{x} \pm (z_{\alpha/2} \times s/\sqrt{n})$.

Example 8.6

The mean weight of the cabin baggage checked in by a random sample of 40 passengers at an international airport departure terminal was 3.47 kilograms. The sample standard deviation was 0.82 kilogram. Construct a 90 per cent confidence interval for the mean weight of cabin baggage checked in by passengers at the terminal.

In this case α is 10 per cent, so $\alpha/2$ is 5 per cent or 0.05 and according to Table 8.1 $z_{0.05}$ is 1.645.

$$90 \text{ per cent interval estimate of } \mu = \bar{x} \pm (1.645 \times s/\sqrt{n})$$
$$= 3.47 \pm (1.645 \times 0.82/\sqrt{40})$$
$$= 3.47 \pm (1.645 \times 0.82/6.32)$$
$$= 3.47 \pm 0.213$$
$$= 3.257 \text{ to } 3.683 \text{ kg} \quad \text{to three decimal places}$$

In Example 8.6 we are not told whether the population that the sample comes from is Normal or not. This doesn't matter because the sample size is over 30. In fact given that airlines tend to restrict cabin baggage to 5 kg per passenger the distribution in this case would probably be skewed.

8.1.3 Estimating with small samples

If we want to produce an interval estimate based on a smaller sample, one with less than 30 observations in it, we have to be much more careful. First, for the procedures we will consider in this section to be valid, the population that the sample comes from must be Normal. Second, because the sample standard deviation of a small sample is not a reliable enough estimate of the population standard deviation to enable us to use the Z distribution, we must use the appropriate t distribution to find how many standard errors are to be added and subtracted.

Instead of: estimate of $\mu = \bar{x} \pm (z_{\alpha/2} \times \sigma/\sqrt{n})$

we use: estimate of $\mu = \bar{x} \pm (t_{\alpha/2,v} \times s/\sqrt{n})$

The number of degrees of freedom, v, which is the sample size less one ($n-1$), determines the t distribution you use. You will be able to find the values you need to produce confidence intervals in Table 4 on page 336.

You may recall from Chapter 7 that t distributions are modifications of the Z distribution. If you compare the figures in the bottom row of the 0.05, 0.025, and 0.005 columns of Table 4 with the z values in Table 8.1, that is, 1.645, 1.960 and 2.576, you can see that they are the same. If, however, you compare these z values with the equivalent t values in the top row of Table 4, the ones from the t distribution with just one degree of freedom, which we would have to use for samples of only 2, you can see that the differences are substantial.

Example 8.7

A random sample of 15 employees of a call centre was taken and each employee took a competency test. The mean of the scores achieved by these employees was 56.3 per cent with a standard deviation of 7.1 per cent. Results of this test have been found to be Normally distributed in the past. Construct a 95 per cent confidence interval for the mean test score of all the employees of the call centre.

Here α is 5 per cent so $\alpha/2$ is 2.5 per cent or 0.025 and the number of degrees of freedom, v, is $n-1$, 14.

$$\text{Estimate of } \mu = \bar{x} \pm (t_{\alpha/2,v} \times s/\sqrt{n}).$$
$$95 \text{ per cent estimate of } \mu = \bar{x} \pm (t_{0.025,14} \times s/\sqrt{n})$$

From Table 4, $t_{0.025,14}$ is 2.145, so:

$$95 \text{ per cent estimate of } \mu = 56.3 \pm (2.145 \times 7.1/\sqrt{15})$$
$$= 56.3 \pm 3.93$$
$$= 52.37 \text{ per cent to } 60.23 \text{ per cent} \quad \text{to two decimal places}$$

8.1.4 Estimating using computer software

You can produce confidence intervals using EXCEL or MINI-TAB. In EXCEL you can find the error, that is the amount that needs to be added and subtracted to create the interval around the sample measure, by typing **=CONFIDENCE(alpha, standard deviation,size)** in the Formula Bar. Alpha is 100 per cent minus the level of confidence expressed as a proportion, standard deviation is the population standard deviation, and size is the sample size. As long as your sample size is at least 30, you can type this in as the population standard deviation. To produce the error for Example 8.6 we would have to type **=CONFIDENCE(0.10,0.82,40)**. This will produce the error to six places of decimals, in this case 0.213261. We would then apply this error to the sample mean as a separate numerical operation.

The **CONFIDENCE** command in EXCEL should only be used if you have a large sample. If you have a small sample you can't use it unless you know the population standard deviation, which is unlikely. However, you could obtain the appropriate t value and sample measures using the other statistical tools available in the package, then assemble the interval yourself.

To construct interval estimates using MINITAB you need to have the sample data. Put these into a worksheet column then select **Basic Statistics** from the **Stat** menu. Choose **1-Sample Z** from the **Basic Statistics** sub-menu. In the command window that appears specify the column location of the sample data and provide **Sigma**, the population standard deviation. If your sample consists of at least 30 observations you can type in the sample standard deviation instead. To change the confidence level from the default level, 95%, click the **Options** button in the command window and type in the level you require.

If you have a small sample follow the same procedure but choose **1-Sample t** from the **Basic Statistics** sub-menu. The command window is almost identical to the one for **1-Sample Z**, except that you do not have to specify **Sigma**, instead the package will calculate the sample standard deviation in the course of providing your interval estimate. Because you do not need to specify a standard deviation you may find **1-Sample t** easier whatever the size of your sample, indeed strictly speaking it is technically more correct to use a t distribution unless your sample consists of an infinite number of observations.

If you have access to both EXCEL and MINITAB you may find it convenient to use EXCEL when you want to produce an interval using results from a large sample, rather than the sample data and MINITAB when you want to produce an interval using small-sample data.

8.2 Estimating population proportions

Although so far we have concentrated on how to estimate population means, these are not the only population measures that can be estimated. You will probably also come across estimates of population proportions, indeed almost certainly you already have done.

If you have ever seen an opinion poll, perhaps about voting intentions or a specific issue, you will have seen an estimate of a population proportion. To produce the opinion poll result that you read in a newspaper or see on TV some organization has interviewed a sample of people and used the sample results to predict the voting intentions of the entire population.

In many ways estimating a population proportion is very similar to the estimation we have already considered. To start with, you need a sample; you calculate a sample result around which your estimate will be constructed; you add and subtract an error based on the standard error of the relevant sampling distribution, and how confident you want to be that your estimate is accurate.

We have to adjust our approach because of the different nature of the data. When we estimate proportions we are usually dealing with qualitative variables. The values of these variables are characteristics, for instance people voting for party A or party B. If there are only two possible characteristics, or we decide to use only two categories in our analysis, the variable will have a binomial distribution.

As you will see, this is convenient as it means we only have to deal with one sample result, the sample proportion, but it also means that we cannot produce reliable estimates from small samples, those consisting of less than 30 observations. This is because the distribution of the population that the sample comes from must be Normal if we are to use the *t* distribution, the device we have previously used to overcome the extra uncertainty involved in small-sample estimation.

The sampling distribution of sample proportions is approximately Normal in shape if the samples involved are large, that is, more than 30, as long as the sample proportion is not too small or too large. In practice because we do not know the sample proportion before taking the sample, it is best to use a sample size of over 100. If the samples are small, the sampling distribution of sample proportions is not Normal.

Provided that you have a large sample, you can construct an interval estimate for the population proportion, π (pi, the Greek letter p), by taking the sample proportion, p, and adding and subtracting an error. The sample proportion is the number of items in the sample that possess the characteristic of interest, x, divided by the total number of items in the sample, n.

$$\text{Sample proportion} \quad p = x/n$$

The error that you add to and subtract from the sample proportion is the z value appropriate for the level of confidence you want to use multiplied by the estimate standard error of the sampling distribution of sample proportions. The estimated standard error is based on the sample proportion.

$$\text{Estimated standard error} = \sqrt{\frac{p\,(1-p)}{n}}$$

$$\text{So the interval estimate of } \pi = p \pm z_{\alpha/2} \times \sqrt{\frac{p\,(1-p)}{n}}$$

Example 8.8

A study of a sample of 110 supermarkets reveals that 31 offer trolleys suitable for shoppers with limited mobility. Construct a 95 per cent interval estimate of the proportion of all supermarkets that have these trolleys.

$$p = 31/110 = 0.28 \text{ to two decimal places}$$

$$(100 - \alpha) \text{ per cent} = 95 \text{ per cent, so } z_{\alpha/2} = 1.96$$

interval estimate of π

$$= 0.28 \pm 1.96 \times \sqrt{\frac{0.28\,(1 - 0.28)}{110}}$$

$$= 0.28 \pm 1.96 \times \sqrt{\frac{0.28 \times 0.72}{110}}$$

$$= 0.28 \pm 1.96 \times 0.043 = 0.28 \pm 0.084$$

$$= 0.196 \text{ to } 0.364 \text{ to three decimal places}$$

These results suggest that we can be 95 per cent confident that the proportion of supermarkets with suitable trolleys for shoppers with limited mobility will be between 19.6 per cent and 36.4 per cent.

You can produce estimates of population proportions using MINITAB by selecting **Basic Statistics** from the **Stat** menu. Pick the **1 Proportion** option from the **Basic Statistics** sub-menu. In the command window you can choose to submit **Summarised data**. If you do this you will need to provide the **Number of trials** and the **Number of successes**. In Example 8.8 these numbers were 110 and 31 respectively.

8.2.1 Determining sample size

If you know how confident you want to be that your interval estimate is accurate and you need your estimate to have a certain precision, in other words the error has to be a particular amount, you can work out the sample size you will need to use.

The precision of the test depends on the estimated standard error of the sample proportions, $\sqrt{p(1-p)/n}$. The value of this depends on the value of p, the sample proportion. Clearly you cannot know this until the sample data has been collected yet you cannot collect the sample data until you have decided what sample size to use. It is therefore necessary to make a prior assumption about the value of the sample proportion.

To be on the safe side we will assume the worst-case scenario, which is that the value of p will be the one that produces the highest value of $p(1-p)$. The higher the value of $p(1-p)$, the wider the interval will be, for a given sample size. We need to avoid the situation where $p(1-p)$ turns out to be larger than we have assumed it is.

What is the largest value of $p(1-p)$? If you work out $p(1-p)$ when p is 0.1, you will find it is 0.09. If p is 0.2 $p(1-p)$ rises to 0.16. As you increase the value of p you will find that it keeps going up until p is 0.5, when $p(1-p)$ is 0.25, then it goes down again. So $p = 0.5$ is the worst-case scenario.

The error in an interval estimate of a population proportion is:

$$\text{Error} = z_{\alpha/2} \times \sqrt{\frac{p(1-p)}{n}}$$

If p is 0.5, in other words we assume the largest possible value of $p(1-p)$:

$$\text{Error} = z_{\alpha/2} \times \sqrt{\frac{0.5(1-0.5)}{n}} = z_{\alpha/2} \times \sqrt{\frac{0.5 \times 0.5}{n}}$$

$$= z_{\alpha/2} \times \frac{0.5}{\sqrt{n}}$$

This last expression can be rearranged:

If

$$\text{error} = z_{\alpha/2} \times \frac{0.5}{\sqrt{n}}$$

then

$$\sqrt{n} = \frac{z_{\alpha/2} \times 0.5}{\text{error}}$$

and

$$n = \left(\frac{z_{\alpha/2}}{2 \times \text{error}}\right)^2$$

Example 8.9

How many supermarkets would have to be included in the sample in Example 8.8 if the confidence interval of the proportion of establishments with trolleys suitable for shoppers with limited mobility has to be within 5 per cent of the actual population proportion with a 95 per cent degree of confidence?

For the error to be 5 per cent:

$$n = \left(\frac{1.96}{2 \times 0.05}\right)^2 = 19.6^2 = 384.16$$

This has to be rounded up to 385 to be on the safe side so a random sample of 385 supermarkets would have to be used.

8.3 Hypothesis testing

Usually when we make predictions or estimates about population measures we have no idea of the actual value of the measure we are trying to estimate. Indeed the purpose of estimation using sample results is to tell us what the actual value is likely to be.

Sometimes we use sample results to deal with a different situation. This is where the population measure is claimed to be a particular value and we want to see whether the claim is correct. Such a claim is known as a *hypothesis*, and the use of sample results to investigate whether it is true is called *hypothesis testing*. To begin with, we will concentrate on testing hypotheses about population means using a single sample. Later in this chapter you will find hypothesis tests for comparing the means of two samples, hypothesis testing of population proportions, and a way of testing hypotheses about population medians.

The procedure used in hypothesis testing begins with a formal statement of the claim being made for the population measure. This is known as the *null hypothesis* because it is the starting point in the investigation, and is represented by the symbol H_0, 'aitch-nought'.

We could find that a null hypothesis turns out to be wrong, in which case we should reject it in favour of an *alternative hypothesis*, represented by the symbol H_1, 'aitch-one'. The alternative hypothesis is the collection of explanations that contradict the claim made in the null hypothesis.

A null hypothesis may specify a single value for the population measure, in which case we would expect the alternative hypothesis to consist of other values both below and above it. Because of this 'dual' nature of the alternative hypothesis, the procedure to investigate such a null hypothesis is known as a *two-sided test*.

Table 8.2
Types of hypotheses

Null hypothesis	Alternative hypothesis	Type of test
$H_0: \mu = \mu_0$	$H_1: \mu \neq \mu_0$ (not equal)	Two-sided
$H_0: \mu \leq \mu_0$	$H_1: \mu > \mu_0$ (greater than)	One-sided
$H_0: \mu \geq \mu_0$	$H_1: \mu < \mu_0$ (less than)	One-sided

In this table μ_0 is used to represent the value of the population mean, μ, that is to be tested.

In other cases the null hypothesis might specify a minimum or a maximum value, in which case the alternative hypothesis consists of values below, or values above respectively. The procedure we use in these cases is called a *one-sided test*. Table 8.2 lists the three combinations of hypotheses.

The type of null hypothesis that should be used depends on the context of the investigation and the perspective of the investigator.

Example 8.10

A bus company promotes a 'one-hour' tour of a city. Suggest suitable null and alternative hypotheses for an investigation by:

(a) A passenger who wants to know how long the journey will take.

(b) A journalist from a consumer magazine who wants to see whether passengers are being cheated.

In the first case we might assume that the passenger is as concerned about the tour taking too much time as too little time. So appropriate hypotheses would be that the population mean of the times of the tours is either equal to one hour or not.

(a) H_0: $\mu = 60$ minutes H_1: $\mu \neq 60$ minutes

In the second case we can assume that the investigation is more focused. The journalist is more concerned that the trips might not take the full hour rather than taking longer than an hour, so appropriate hypotheses would be that the population mean tour time is either one hour or more, or it is less than an hour.

(b) H_0: $\mu \geq 60$ minutes H_1: $\mu < 60$ minutes

Once we have established the form of the hypotheses we can test them using the sample evidence at our disposal. We have to decide whether the sample evidence is compatible with the null hypothesis, in which case we cannot reject it. If the sample evidence contradicts the null hypothesis we reject it in favour of the alternative hypothesis.

To guide us in making this decision we need a *decision rule* that we can apply to our sample evidence. The decision rule is based on the assumption that the null hypothesis is true.

If the population mean really does take the value that the null hypothesis specifies, then as long as we know the value of the population standard deviation, σ, and the size of our sample, n, we can identify the sampling distribution that our sample belongs to.

Example 8.11

The standard deviation of the bus tours in Example 8.10 is known to be 6 minutes. If the duration of a random sample of 50 tours is to be recorded in order to investigate the operation, what can we deduce about the sampling distribution the mean of the sample belongs to?

The null hypotheses in both sections of Example 8.10 specified a population mean, μ, of 60 minutes. If this is true the mean of the sampling distribution, the distribution of means of samples consisting of 50 observations, is 60. The population standard deviation, σ, is 6 so the standard error of the sampling distribution, $\sigma/\sqrt{n}$, is $6/\sqrt{50}$, 0.85 minutes to two decimal places.

We can conclude that the sample mean of our sample will belong to a sampling distribution with a mean of 60 and a standard error of 0.85, if H_0 is true.

The next stage is to compare our sample mean to the sampling distribution it is supposed to come from if H_0 is true. If it seems to belong to the sampling distribution, in other words it is not too far away from the centre of the distribution, then we can regard the null hypothesis as plausible. If, on the other hand, the sample mean is located on one of the extremes of the sampling distribution we might regard the null hypothesis as suspect.

We can make this comparison by working out the z-equivalent of the sample mean and using it to find out the probability that a sample mean like the one we have comes from the sampling distribution that is based on the null hypothesis being true. Because we are using a z-equivalent, this type of hypothesis test is sometimes called a *z test*.

Example 8.12

The mean of the random sample in Example 8.11 is 61.87 minutes. What is the z-equivalent of this sample mean, assuming it belongs to a sampling distribution with a mean of 60 and a standard error of 0.85? Use the z-equivalent to find the probability that a sample mean of this magnitude comes from such a sampling distribution.

$$z = \frac{(\bar{x} - \mu)}{\sigma/\sqrt{n}} = \frac{61.87 - 60}{0.85} = 2.20$$

Using Table 3:

$$P\,(Z > 2.20) = 0.0139$$

This means $P\,(\bar{X} > 61.87) = 0.0139$ or 1.39 per cent

This is shown in Figure 8.4.

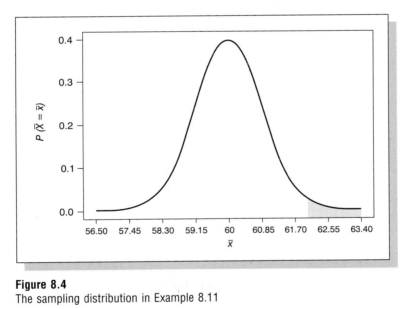

Figure 8.4
The sampling distribution in Example 8.11

Once we know how likely it is that our sample mean belongs to the sampling distribution implied by the null hypothesis, we can make a judgement about the null hypothesis. We have to distinguish between 'acceptable' sample results, those that are compatible with the null hypothesis, and 'unacceptable' sample results, those that conflict with the null hypothesis.

If the probability that a sample mean comes from the sampling distribution that H_0 implies is quite high then it would be 'acceptable'. If it were quite low it would be 'unacceptable'. In

Example 8.11 the probability that the sample mean comes from the sampling distributions that H_0 suggests is only 1.39 per cent, a low figure, so we may consider it to be 'unacceptable'.

But what exactly are 'quite high' and 'quite low' probabilities? When you get used to hypothesis testing you may well develop an intuitive 'feel' for what the appropriate dividing line is in a given situation, but until then you will need to apply a decision rule.

In many practical applications this type of testing is a way of establishing that goods and services meet standards agreed between a supplier and a customer, or between a head office and local management. In these circumstances it is important that a decision rule that defines acceptable sample test results is agreed between the parties involved.

A decision rule should define how low the likelihood of a sample mean has to be before we consider it 'unacceptable'. 'Unacceptable' sample results are often described as *significant*, in the sense that they are significantly different to what the null hypothesis says they should be like. The decision rule specifies what is called the *level of significance*, α.

If we say that we will use a 5 per cent level of significance in our testing we are saying that if there is less than a 5 per cent chance that a sample mean belongs to the sampling distribution based on H_0 then we will consider it 'unacceptable'. This is a little misleading because it is really the null hypothesis that we would have found to be unacceptable in the light of the sample evidence. So if our sample result is 'unacceptable' we should reject the null hypothesis.

A 5 per cent level of significance means that if the chance that the sort of sample mean our investigation produces does come from the sampling distribution H_0 implies is less than one in twenty, then it is such an unlikely result we believe that the sample evidence disproves the null hypothesis. Another way of putting it is to say that if our sample mean is among the 5 per cent least likely to come from the sampling distribution that it should belong to if H_0 were true then we will reject H_0.

The implication of rejecting H_0 is that the sample mean we have actually belongs to a different sampling distribution, because it is very unlikely to belong to the one that H_0 implies. It is very unlikely, but not impossible. The sort of sample mean that our decision rule says is significant, or 'unacceptable', could, just possibly, belong to the sampling distribution H_0 implies. In that case the decision to reject H_0 would be wrong. The level of significance that we specify in a decision rule is also therefore the risk we are prepared to take that we wrongly reject H_0.

When we apply our decision rule we need to take into account the type of null hypothesis we are dealing with. If it suggests that the population mean equals a particular figure we should conduct a two-sided test in order to assess it. That is, if the sample mean we produce is *either* too high *or* too low, then we should reject H_0.

In two-sided tests there are two types of 'unacceptable', or significant sample result. Because of this if we use a 5 per cent level of significance, the 5 per cent least likely sample means that would lead us to reject the null hypothesis will consist of the lowest $2\frac{1}{2}$ per cent of sample means and the highest $2\frac{1}{2}$ per cent of sample means. If therefore the probability that the sample mean we have belongs to the sampling distribution were less than $2\frac{1}{2}$ per cent, or 0.025, we would reject H_0. But because the test is two-sided we would say that we reject it *at the 5 per cent level*.

These lowest and highest extremes of the sampling distribution are called the *rejection regions*, since we reject the null hypothesis if our sample mean is located in one of those parts of the distribution. Another way of applying the decision rule is to use the *z* values that cut off the tails on the Standard Normal Distribution equivalent to the rejection regions as benchmarks that we compare to the *z*-equivalent of the sample mean. In this context the *z*-equivalent of the sample mean is sometimes called the *test statistic* and the *z* values that mark off the limits of the rejection regions are called the *critical values* of Z.

In a two-sided, or *two-tail*, test using a 5 per cent level of significance the rejection regions of the furthest $2\frac{1}{2}$ per cent on the left and right sides of the sampling distribution are the same as the areas of the Standard Normal Distribution beyond the critical *z* values, −1.96 and +1.96 respectively. If the *z*-equivalent of our sample mean, the test statistic, is either less than −1.96 or greater than +1.96, we should reject H_0. This is illustrated in Figure 8.5.

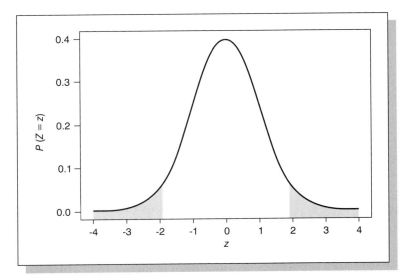

Figure 8.5
Rejection regions for a two-tail test at the 5 per cent level of significance

Example 8.13

Test the hypothesis that the population mean duration of the bus tours in Example 8.10 is 60 minutes, H_0: μ = 60. Use the sample mean given in Example 8.12 and apply a 5 per cent level of significance.

H_0: μ = 60 minutes H_1: $\mu \neq$ 60 minutes

The level of significance, α = 0.05

From Example 8.12 we know that the probability that the sample mean, 61.87, belongs to a sampling distribution with a mean of 60 and a standard error of 0.85 is 0.0139 or 1.39 per cent. Since this is less than $2\frac{1}{2}$ per cent we can reject the null hypothesis at the 5 per cent level.

Alternatively we can compare the test statistic, the z-equivalent of the sample mean, 2.20, to the critical values of Z that cut off $2\frac{1}{2}$ per cent tails of the Standard Normal Distribution, −1.96 and +1.96. Because it is larger than +1.96, we reject the null hypothesis; our sample evidence suggests that on average the tours take longer than 60 minutes.

If the null hypothesis suggests that the population mean is less than or equal to a particular figure we conduct a one-sided, or *one-tail*, test. If we do this using a 5 per cent level of significance we reject the null hypothesis if our sample mean is among the highest 5 per cent of samples in the sampling distribution that H_0 implies.

Since the null hypothesis includes the possibility that the population mean is lower than a particular value, a very low sample mean is compatible with the null hypothesis. It is only if the sample mean is very high that we would reject H_0.

The decision rule in this case means that if the probability that the sample mean comes from the sampling distribution implied by H_0 is less than 5 per cent or 0.05 and the sample mean is higher than the population mean specified in H_0, then we reject H_0. Alternatively we could say that if the test statistic, the z-equivalent of our sample mean, is higher than 1.645, the z value that cuts off a tail of 5 per cent on the right-hand side of the Standard Normal Distribution, we will reject H_0. This is illustrated in Figure 8.6.

If the null hypothesis states that the population mean is greater than or equal to a particular value, we would also conduct a one-tail test. But this time we would reject the null hypothesis if our sample mean were among the lowest 5 per cent of samples in the sampling distribution that H_0 implies.

If the null hypothesis includes the possibility that the population mean is higher than a particular value, a very high sample

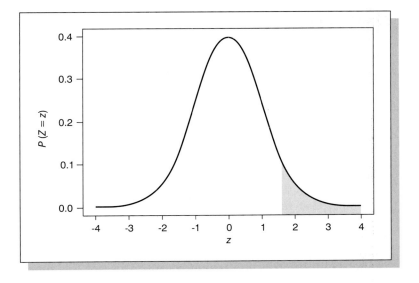

Figure 8.6
Rejection region for a one-tail
test of a 'less than or equal'
null hypothesis at the 5 per
cent level of significance

mean is compatible with the null hypothesis. It is only if the
sample mean is very low that we would reject H_0.

The decision rule is that if the probability that the sample mean
comes from the sampling distribution implied by H_0 is less than
5 per cent or 0.05 and the sample mean is lower than the
population mean specified in H_0, then we reject H_0. Alternatively
we could say that if the test statistic were less than -1.645, the z
value that cuts off a tail of 5 per cent on the left-hand side of the
Standard Normal Distribution, we would reject H_0. This is
illustrated in Figure 8.7.

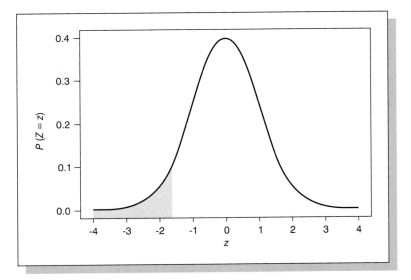

Figure 8.7
Rejection region for a one-tail
test of a 'greater than or equal'
null hypothesis at the 5 per
cent level of significance

Example 8.14

Use the sample mean in Example 8.12 to test the hypothesis that the tours in Example 8.10 take at least 60 minutes, H_0: $\mu \geq 60$, at the 5 per cent level of significance.

H_0: $\mu \geq 60$ minutes H_1: $\mu < 60$ minutes

The level of significance, $\alpha = 0.05$

The sample mean is 61.87 and in Example 8.12 we found that the probability that it comes from a sampling distribution with a mean of 60 and a standard error of 0.85 was 0.0139 or 1.39 per cent. However, because the null hypothesis includes the possibility that the population mean is larger than 60 we cannot reject it.

If we compare the test statistic, 2.20, with the z value that cuts off the 5 per cent tail on the left-hand side of the Standard Normal Distribution, −1.645 we can see that 2.20 cannot be in the rejection region because it is not less than −1.645.

In the same way that you can use different levels of confidence in estimation, you can use different levels of significance in hypothesis testing. The most commonly used levels of significance are 10 per cent, 5 per cent, 1 per cent, and 0.1 per cent. The lower the level of significance, the more rigorous the test. In circumstances where it is important that the result of a hypothesis test is robust, such as testing pharmaceutical products, it would be appropriate to use the 0.1 per cent level of significance.

The level of significance you use determines the size of the rejection region and the critical value of Z. Once you have decided which level of significance to use you can obtain the critical value by looking for the appropriate values of α (for a one-tail test) or $\alpha/2$ (for a two-tail test) in the body of Table 3 on page 335 and finding the z values associated with them. Alternatively you can find the probability that the sample result occurs if the null hypothesis is true by working out its z-equivalent and then referring to Table 3 to find the critical value.

Example 8.15

According to the label on packets of mixed nuts there should be 25 grams of cashew nuts in every packet. The standard deviation of the weight of cashew nuts per packet is known to be 2.2 grams and the weights are Normally distributed.

The mean weight of cashew nuts in a random sample of 15 packets is 23.5. Test the hypothesis that the information on the label is valid using a 1 per cent level of confidence.

$$H_0: \mu = 25 \text{ grams} \qquad H_1: \mu \neq 25 \text{ grams}$$

Level of significance, $\alpha = 0.01$

$$z = \frac{(\bar{x} - \mu)}{\sigma/\sqrt{n}} = \frac{23.5 - 25}{2.2/\sqrt{15}} = \frac{-1.5}{0.5658} = -2.64 \text{ to two decimal places}$$

According to Table 3 the value of Z that cuts off a tail area of 0.005, $z_{0.005}$, is between 2.57 and 2.58, so we will use −2.575 and +2.575 as the critical values for this test. The test statistic, −2.64, is beyond −2.575 on the left-hand side of the distribution and so falls in the rejection region. We should reject H_0 at the 1 per cent level of significance.

Alternatively we can use Table 3 to find that $P(Z < -2.64) = 1 - 0.9959 = 0.0041$. This means that the probability a sample mean is less than 23.5, $P(\bar{X} < 23.5)$, is 0.0041. Because this is less than 0.005 (half of α; this is a two-tail test), reject H_0 at the 1 per cent level of significance.

Note that in Example 8.15 the sample size, 15, is quite small. We do not need to alter the procedure used because the population the sample comes from is Normal, which means that the sampling distribution for means of sample size 15 will also be Normal, and the population standard deviation is known.

Any sample result that leads to the rejection of a null hypothesis is referred to as significant. If the sample result allows us to reject a null hypothesis at an exacting level of significance like 1 per cent such as in Example 8.15 we refer to the sample result as highly significant.

You may find that at first the most difficult thing about hypothesis testing is the decision rule, and in particular making sure you use the appropriate critical value. It may help if you remember the connection between the type of null hypothesis and the critical value.

- If you are testing $H_0: \mu = \mu_0$, reject it if the test statistic is below $-z_{\alpha/2}$ or above $z_{\alpha/2}$.

- If you are testing $H_0: \mu \leq \mu_0$, reject it if the test statistic is above z_{α}.

- If you are testing $H_0: \mu \geq \mu_0$, reject it if the test statistic is below $-z_{\alpha}$.

8.3.1 Hypothesis testing without σ

In the hypothesis testing we have looked at so far we have assumed that we know the population standard deviation, σ. This could be the case, particularly if you are trying to find out whether a change had an effect by comparing sample data collected after the change with a previous situation was well established and known. Perhaps a brewery wants to know if the refurbishment of a pub has a significant effect on trade. In such a case the brewery records are likely to be comprehensive and they could be used to calculate the population standard deviation of the turnover per week. You could then use this figure to calculate the standard error of the sampling distribution that would provide the context for the test.

However, in the majority of cases we are unlikely to know the population standard deviation. In these situations the sample size is the first key factor. If our sample evidence comes from a sample that consists of 30 or more observations the sample standard deviation will be sufficiently close to the population standard deviation to allow us to use a z test; that is, to base our decision rule on the Standard Normal Distribution. We simply use the sample standard deviation in place of the population distribution and calculate the estimated standard error, that is instead of $\sigma/\sqrt{n}$ we would use $s/\sqrt{n}$.

Example 8.16

A hair products company claims that a hair colouring treatment it produces lasts for an average of 45 days before fading. The company wants to check that its claim is valid. The hair of a random sample of 40 customers who had applied the treatment was monitored and the time that elapsed until the colouring faded was recorded. The mean time it took for the hair colouring to fade on these customers was 46.1 days with a standard deviation of 2.9 days. Do these results support the claim that the mean time the colouring lasts is 45 days? Use a 10 per cent level of significance.

We can assume that the company wants to ensure that the colouring lasts neither too short nor too long a period, so we will use a two-tail test.

$$H_0: \quad \mu = 45 \qquad H_1: \mu \neq 45$$

Level of significance, $\alpha = 0.1$

If $\mu = 45$, the means of samples size 40 will form a sampling distribution that has a mean of 45 and an estimated standard error of $2.9/\sqrt{40}$. The test statistic is:

$$z = \frac{46.1 - 45}{2.9/\sqrt{40}} = \frac{1.1}{0.459} = 2.40 \qquad \text{to two decimal places}$$

According to Table 3 the probability that Z is more than 2.40 is 0.0082, or 0.82 per cent.

If we apply a 10 per cent level of significance, this probability must be less than 0.05, or 5 per cent in order to reject H_0. In this case we can reject H_0.

The z values that cut off tails of 5 per cent are −1.645 and +1.645. H_0 should be rejected because the test statistic is outside these values.

8.3.2 Hypothesis testing with small samples

Suppose we want to test a hypothesis using the mean of a sample that consists of less than 30 observations and we don't know the population standard deviation. We can do this but we have to be reasonably sure that the population that the sample comes from is Normal.

The sample standard deviation from a small sample will not be close enough to the population standard deviation to allow us to simply substitute s for σ as we could do with larger samples. This means we have to use t distributions for benchmarks in comparing sample results to sampling distributions that null hypotheses imply. Because a t distribution is used you will find that hypothesis tests based on small samples are called t tests.

Example 8.17

On average 74.9 units of a brand alco-pop drink are sold at a city-centre pub each week. Sales are Normally distributed. The manager puts on a special promotion to boost sales of the product. During the five weeks following the promotion the mean sales were 82.4 units per week with a standard deviation of 7.3 units. Test the hypothesis that the promotion has improved sales using a 5 per cent level of significance.

We are only interested in proving that sales have improved, so we need to conduct a one-tail test. The null hypothesis assumes that the sales have not improved; the alternative hypothesis assumes that they have.

$$H_0: \ \mu \leq 74.9 \qquad H_1: \mu > 74.9$$

Level of significance, $\alpha = 0.05$

The test statistic is $t = \dfrac{(\bar{x} - \mu)}{s/\sqrt{n}} = \dfrac{82.4 - 74.9}{7.3/\sqrt{5}} = \dfrac{7.5}{3.26} = 2.30$ to two decimal places

According to Table 4 on page 336, $t_{0.05,4}$ is 2.132, which means that the top 5 per cent of values in a t distribution with 4 degrees of freedom will be greater than 2.132. Our test statistic is larger so we can conclude that there has been a significant increase in sales and H_0 should be rejected in favour of H_1.

8.3.3 Hypothesis testing using computer software

If you want to use MINITAB to test hypotheses about a population mean you need to use the same commands as you use to produce estimates, either **1-Sample Z** or **1-Sample t** from the **Basic Statistics** sub-menu in **Stat**. Both of these commands assume that you have stored your sample data in a column in the worksheet.

In the command window for **1-Sample Z** you should specify the column location of your data, then type into the box next to **Test mean** the value of the population mean you want to test, i.e. the population mean featured in the null hypothesis. Click **Options** and you will see **Alternative**, which invites you to select the type of alternative hypothesis you want to use. The default is **not equal** but if you click the pull-down menu you could select **less than** or **greater than** instead. You will have to type the value of the population standard deviation in the command window next to **Sigma**. If you click the **Graphs** button the package will offer you a selection of diagrams that will portray your data and superimpose on the diagram the population mean being tested. The output that you will see in the session window includes the test statistic, **Z**, and the probability that the test statistic occurs if the null hypothesis is true, **P**.

The command window for **1-Sample t** is very similar to the **1-Sample Z**; the main difference is that you don't have to specify the population standard deviation.

You can test a hypothesis in EXCEL by typing **=ZTEST(array,x,sigma)** in the Formula Bar. The **array** is the sample data, which must be bracketed, **x** is the population mean that you want to test, and **sigma** is the population standard deviation. The result you get, a **P-value**, is the probability that the sample mean belongs to the sampling distribution based on the population mean you are testing. *P*-value is an abbreviation of 'population value'.

If you do not provide the population standard deviation the package will use the sample standard deviation instead. This is sound enough if the sample size is at least 30, but the results you get with smaller samples should be treated as rough approximations. There is a separate **TTEST** facility within EXCEL but it performs more complex tests, such as comparisons between sample means, than the relatively straightforward t tests we have considered.

8.4 Testing hypotheses about two population means

In the previous section we looked at tests of the population mean based on a single sample mean. In this section we will consider tests designed to assess the difference between two population means. In businesses these tests are used to investigate whether, for instance, the introduction a new logo improves sales.

To use these tests you need to have a sample from each of the two populations. For the tests to be valid the samples must be random, but they can be *independent* or *dependent*.

Independent samples are selected from each population separately. If we selected a random sample of customers of one domestic gas supplier and a random sample of customers from a rival gas supplier the samples would be independent.

Dependent samples consist of matched or paired values. If we selected a sample of athletes and compared their pulse rates before and after an exercise routine the samples would be paired or dependent.

The choice of independent or dependent samples depends on the context of the test. Unless there is a good reason for using paired data, such as in the case of the athletes where using the same athletes before and after the exercise makes sense, use independent samples. We will begin by looking at tests for use with independent samples and deal with paired samples later in the section.

As with single sample tests the size of the samples is important because it determines the nature of the sampling distribution. In this section we will assume that the population standard deviations are not known.

8.4.1 Large independent samples

The null hypothesis you have to use in comparing population means is based on the difference between the means of the two populations, $\mu_1 - \mu_2$. The possible combinations of null and alternative hypotheses are shown in Table 8.3.

Table 8.3
Types of hypotheses for comparing population means

Null hypothesis	Alternative hypothesis	Type of test
H_0: $\mu_1 - \mu_2 = 0$	H_1: $\mu_1 - \mu_2 \neq 0$	Two-sided
H_0: $\mu_1 - \mu_2 \leq 0$	H_1: $\mu_1 - \mu_2 > 0$	One-sided
H_0: $\mu_1 - \mu_2 \geq 0$	H_1: $\mu_1 - \mu_2 < 0$	One-sided

The hypotheses listed in Table 8.3 all assume that the focus of the test is that there is no difference between the population means. This is very common but the same formats can be used to test whether the difference between two population means is a non-zero constant, e.g. H_0: $\mu_1 - \mu_2 = 6$.

If both samples contain 30 or more items the difference between their means, $\bar{x}_1 - \bar{x}_2$, belongs to the sampling distribution of $\overline{X}_1 - \overline{X}_2$. This sampling distribution is Normally distributed with a mean of $\mu_1 - \mu_2$, and a standard error of:

$$\sqrt{\frac{\sigma_1^2}{n_1} + \frac{\sigma_2^2}{n_2}}$$

where σ_1 and σ_2 are the standard deviations of the first and second populations, and n_1 and n_2 are the sizes of the samples from the first and second populations.

We are assuming that the population standard deviations are not known, in which case the estimated standard error of the sampling distribution is:

$$\sqrt{\frac{s_1^2}{n_1} + \frac{s_2^2}{n_2}}$$

The test statistic is:

$$z = \frac{(\bar{x}_1 - \bar{x}_2) - (\mu_1 - \mu_2)}{\sqrt{\frac{s_1^2}{n_1} + \frac{s_2^2}{n_2}}}$$

If the null hypothesis suggests that the difference between the population means is zero, we can simplify this to:

$$z = \frac{\bar{x}_1 - \bar{x}_2}{\sqrt{\frac{s_1^2}{n_1} + \frac{s_2^2}{n_2}}}$$

Once we have calculated the test statistic we need to compare it to the appropriate critical value from the Standard Normal Distribution.

Example 8.18

The mean and standard deviation of the times that it took for the 'Action' breakdown recovery service to assist a random sample of 47 motorists were 51 minutes and 7 minutes. The mean and standard deviations of the response times recorded by the rival 'Bistry' service in assisting a random sample of 39 motorists were 49 minutes and 5 minutes. Test the hypothesis that there is no difference between the mean response times of the two breakdown services. Use a 5 per cent level of significance.

$$H_0: \mu_1 - \mu_2 = 0 \quad H_1: \mu_1 - \mu_2 \neq 0$$

$$\text{Test statistic,} \quad z = \frac{51 - 49}{\sqrt{\dfrac{7^2}{47} + \dfrac{5^2}{39}}} = \frac{2}{\sqrt{\dfrac{49}{47} + \dfrac{25}{39}}}$$

$$= 2/1.298 = 1.54 \quad \text{to two decimal places}$$

This is a two-tail test using a 5 per cent level of confidence so the critical values are $\pm z_{0.025}$. Unless the test statistic is below -1.96 or above ± 1.96 the null hypothesis cannot be rejected. The test statistic, 1.54, is within ± 1.96 so we cannot reject H_0, the population mean response times of the two breakdown services could be equal.

Notice that in Example 8.17 we have not said anything about the distributions of response times. The Central Limit Theorem allows us to use the same two-sample z test whatever the shape of the populations from which the samples were drawn as long as the size of both samples is 30 or more.

8.4.2 Small independent samples

If the size of the samples you want to use to compare population means is small, less than 30, you can only follow the procedure outlined in the previous section if both populations are Normal and both population standard deviations known. In the absence of the latter it is possible to test the difference between two population means using small independent samples but only under certain circumstances.

If both populations are Normal and their standard deviations can be assumed to be the same, that is $\sigma_1 = \sigma_2$, we can conduct a two-sample t test. We use the sample standard deviations to produce a pooled estimate of the standard error of the sampling distribution of $\overline{X}_1 - \overline{X}_2$, s_p.

$$s_p = \sqrt{\frac{(n_1 - 1) s_1^2 + (n_2 - 1) s_2^2}{n_1 + n_2 - 2}}$$

The test statistic is $t = \dfrac{\bar{x}_1 - \bar{x}_2}{s_p \times \sqrt{\dfrac{1}{n_1} + \dfrac{1}{n_2}}}$

We then compare the test statistic to the appropriate critical value from the t distribution. The number of degrees of freedom for this test is $n_1 + n_2 - 2$, one degree of freedom is lost for each of the sample means.

Example 8.19

A cereal manufacturer produces packets of 'own-brand' muesli for a supermarket chain using the same production line as they use for their own premium brand. The mean and standard deviation of the oat content by weight of a random sample of 14 'own-brand' packets are 34.9 per cent and 1.4 per cent. The mean and standard deviation of the oat content of a random sample of 17 premium brand packets are 33.4 per cent and 1.1 per cent. Test the hypothesis that the mean oat content of the premium brand is no greater than the mean oat content of the 'own-brand' muesli using a 1 per cent level of significance. Oat content is Normally distributed in both brands.

We will define μ_1 as the population mean of the 'own-brand' and μ_2 as the population mean of the premium product.

$$H_0: \mu_1 - \mu_2 \leq 0 \qquad H_1: \mu_1 - \mu_2 > 0$$

First we need the pooled estimate of the standard error:

$$s_p = \sqrt{\frac{(14-1)\ 1.4^2 + (17-1)\ 1.1^2}{14 + 17 - 2}}$$

$$= \sqrt{\frac{(13 \times 1.96) + (16 \times 1.21)}{29}}$$

$$= \sqrt{(25.48 + 19.36)/29} = 1.243 \quad \text{to three decimal places}$$

Now we can calculate the test statistic:

$$t = \frac{34.9 - 33.4}{1.243 \times \sqrt{\dfrac{1}{14} + \dfrac{1}{17}}}$$

$$= \frac{1.5}{1.243 \times 0.361} = 3.344 \quad \text{to three decimal places}$$

This is a one-tail test so the null hypothesis will only be rejected if the test statistic exceeds the critical value. From Table 4 on page 336, $t_{0.01,29}$ is 2.462. Since the test statistic is greater than the critical value we can reject the null hypothesis at the 1 per cent level. The difference between the sample means is very significant.

You can test differences between population means in MINITAB. Pick **Basic Statistics** from the **Stat** menu then **2-Sample t** from the sub-menu. Click next to **Samples in different columns** and give the column locations of your first and second samples. If you want to use a pooled estimate of the standard error click next to **Assume equal variances**. Click **Options** and specify the null hypothesis value of the mean of the differences beside **Test mean** and the form of the alternative hypothesis beside **Alternative**. The output that you will see in the session window includes the test statistic, **T-value** and the probability that the test statistic occurs if the null hypothesis is true, **P-value**.

In the command **2-Sample t**, MINITAB uses the t distribution to conduct the test whatever the sample size. It is important to note that unless you propose to use a pooled estimate of the standard error the distribution of differences between small-sample means only follows the t distribution approximately and so the test is not entirely robust.

8.4.3 Paired samples

If you want to test the difference between population means using dependent or paired samples the nature of the data enables you to test the mean of the differences between all the paired values in the population, μ_d. This approach contrasts with the methods described in the earlier parts of this section where we have tested the difference between population means, $\mu_1 - \mu_2$.

The procedure involved in testing hypotheses using paired samples is very similar to the one-sample hypothesis testing we discussed in section 8.3. We have to assume that the differences between the paired values are Normally distributed with a mean of μ_d, and a standard deviation of σ_d. The sampling distribution of sample mean differences will consequently be Normally distributed with a mean of μ_d and a standard error of $\sigma_d/\sqrt{n}$, where n is the number of differences in the sample. Since we assume that σ_d is unknown we have to use the estimated standard error $s_d/\sqrt{n}$, where s_d is the standard deviation of the sample differences.

Table 8.4
Types of hypotheses for the mean of the population of differences

Null hypothesis	Alternative hypothesis	Type of test
$H_0: \mu_d = \mu_{d0}$	$H_1: \mu_d \neq \mu_{d0}$ (not equal)	Two-sided
$H_0: \mu_d \leq \mu_{d0}$	$H_1: \mu_d > \mu_{d0}$ (greater than)	One-sided
$H_0: \mu_d \geq \mu_{d0}$	$H_1: \mu_d < \mu_{d0}$ (less than)	One-sided

In this table μ_{d0} represents the value of the population mean that is to be tested.

Typically samples of paired data tend to be small so the benchmark distribution for the test is the t distribution. The test is therefore called *the paired t test*. Table 8.4 lists the three possible combinations of hypotheses.

The test statistic is:

$$t = \frac{\bar{x}_d - \mu_{d\,0}}{s_d/\sqrt{n}}$$

where $\bar{x}_d$ is the mean of the sample differences.

We then compare the test statistic to the appropriate critical value from the t distribution with $n-1$ degrees of freedom.

Example 8.20

A Business School claims that on average people who take their MBA programme will enhance their annual salary by at least £8000. A random sample of 12 graduates of the programme were asked for their annual salary prior to beginning the programme and their current annual salary. Use the sample data to test whether the mean difference in annual earnings is £8000 or more using a 10 per cent level of significance.

$$H_0: \mu_d \geq 8.00 \qquad H_1: \mu_d < 8.00 \text{ (£000)}$$

To conduct the test we first need to find the mean and standard deviation of the salary differences in the sample.

Graduate	1	2	3	4	5	6	7	8	9	10	11	12
Prior salary (£000)	22	29	29	23	33	20	26	21	25	27	27	29
Current salary (£000)	31	38	40	29	41	25	29	26	31	37	41	36
Salary difference (£000)	9	9	11	6	8	5	3	5	6	10	14	7

The mean and standard deviation of the sample differences are 7.75 and 3.05, to two decimal places. The test statistic is:

$$t = \frac{7.75 - 8.00}{3.05/\sqrt{12}} = \frac{-0.25}{0.88} = -0.28 \qquad \text{to two decimal places}$$

From Table 4 on page 336, $t_{0.10,11}$ is 1.363. The alternative hypothesis is that the population mean salary difference is less than £8000 so the critical value is −1.363. A sample mean that produces a test statistic less than this would lead us to reject the null hypothesis. In this case, although the sample mean is less than £8000, the test statistic, −0.28, is not less than the critical value and the null hypothesis cannot be rejected. The population mean of the salary differences could well be £8000.

You can use MINITAB to conduct a paired t test. Pick **Basic Statistics** from the **Stat** menu then **Paired t** from the sub-menu. Give the column locations of the first and second samples then click **Options** and specify the null hypothesis value of the mean of the differences beside **Test mean** and the form of the alternative hypothesis beside **Alternative**. The output that you will see in the session window includes the test statistic, **T-value** and the probability that the test statistic occurs if the null hypothesis is true, **P-value**.

8.5 Testing hypotheses about population proportions

In many respects the procedure we use to test hypotheses about population proportions is similar to the way we test other types of hypothesis. We begin with a null hypothesis that specifies a population proportion to be tested, which we represent by the symbol π_0 (the Greek letter pi, π, is the symbol for the population proportion). If the null hypothesis is one of the 'equal to' type we conduct a two-tail test. If it is 'less than' or 'greater than', we conduct a one-tail test. The three possible combinations of hypotheses are listed in Table 8.5.

Table 8.5
Types of hypotheses for the population proportion

Null hypothesis	Alternative hypothesis	Type of test
$H_0: \pi = \pi_0$	$H_1: \pi \neq \pi_0$ ('not equal')	Two-sided
$H_0: \pi \leq \pi_0$	$H_1: \pi > \pi_0$ ('greater than')	One-sided
$H_0: \pi \geq \pi_0$	$H_1: \pi < \pi_0$ ('less than')	One-sided

In this table π_0 represents the value of the population proportion that is to be tested.

We calculate the test statistic from the sample proportion, represented by the symbol p, which comes from the sample data that we want to use to test the hypothesis. We assume that the sample proportion belongs to a sampling distribution that has a mean of π_0 and a standard error of:

$$\sqrt{\frac{\pi_0 (1 - \pi_0)}{n}}$$

Notice that we use the proportion from the null hypothesis to calculate the standard error, not the sample proportion.

The test statistic is:

$$z = \frac{p - \pi_0}{\sqrt{\pi_0 (1 - \pi_0)/n}}$$

Sample proportions are distributed Normally if they come from large samples. As long as the sample size is large, preferably over 100, we can use the Standard Normal Distribution as the benchmark for the test; in other words it will be a z test.

As we have done before we use a decision rule that specifies a level of significance in order to assess the validity of the null hypothesis.

Example 8.21

In her annual report the general manager of a car rental business observes that commercial bookings constituted 32 per cent of the bookings received over the previous year. Out of a random sample of 146 bookings received for the current year, 40 are commercial bookings. Test the hypothesis that the proportion of commercial bookings in the current year is at least as high as the proportion received last year using a 5 per cent level of significance.

We are interested in proving that the proportion is no lower than it was, so we will use a one-tail test. The hypotheses are:

$$H_0: \pi_0 \geq 0.32 \qquad H_1: \pi_0 < 0.32$$

Level of significance, $\alpha = 0.05$

The sample proportion, $p = 40/146 = 0.274$

The test statistic, $z = \dfrac{p - \pi_0}{\sqrt{\pi_0 (1 - \pi_0)/n}} = \dfrac{0.274 - 0.32}{\sqrt{0.32 (1 - 0.32)/146}}$

$$= -0.046/0.039 = -1.19$$

From Table 3 on page 335, the probability that Z is -1.19 or less is 0.117, or 11.7 per cent. Since this is more than 5 per cent we cannot reject the null hypothesis.

Another way of assessing the test statistic is to compare it to the z value that cuts off a tail of 5 per cent on the left-hand side of the distribution, -1.645. Because the test statistic is not less than this, the sample result is not significant. We can conclude that, although the sample proportion is lower than the proportion last year, it is not significantly lower.

You can test a hypothesis about a population proportion in MINITAB if you select **1 Proportion** from the **Basic Statistics** selection in the **Stat** menu. You will have to specify whether you have **Sample data in columns** or **Summarised data**. You will also have to click the **Options** button and specify in the **Options** window, the **Test proportion** featured in the null hypothesis, and the style of the **Alternative** hypothesis. By default MINITAB tests proportions using the appropriate binomial distribution, so to use the Standard Normal Distribution you have to tick the box next to **Use test and interval based on normal approximation**.

8.6 A hypothesis test for the population median

For most of this chapter we have concentrated on testing population means. When sample sizes are large this is a generally applicable way of assessing the central tendency of populations. But as we have seen, it is not so straightforward when using small samples, samples that contain less than 30 items.

If you want to test a hypothesis about a mean using a small sample you have to be able to assume that the population that the sample comes from is Normal. In many situations this is not a reasonable assumption; patterns of wealth and income, for instance, form a skewed distribution.

When a distribution is skewed the sampling distributions for small samples based on it will also be skewed. You may recall that in the course of the discussion about averages in Chapter 3 we concluded that the median was a more effective measure of location to use with skewed distributions. In this section we will look at a test for the population median known as the *sign* test, which can be used with small samples drawn from non-Normal populations.

The idea at the heart of the sign test is quite a simple one. The definition of the median is that it is the midway point in the population. Exactly one half of the values in the population are above the median and the other half are below it. This means that the probability a randomly selected value is less than the median is $\frac{1}{2}$ and the probability it is more than the median is $\frac{1}{2}$. If we have a random sample the values in it will be either above or below the median. The total number of values in the sample that are above and below the median can therefore be modelled using the binomial distribution, with say 'success' being defined as a value above the median, and p, the probability of success, being 0.5.

You start with null and alternative hypotheses much the same as those we have already looked at, except that they involve the population median. As before, the null hypothesis must identify the specific value of the population median to be tested. You then have to allocate a plus to each value in the sample that is above the median and a minus to each value that is below the median. In the unlikely event that your sample contains a value exactly the same as the null hypothesis population median, you can allocate a sign on the basis of the toss of a coin.

Once every value has been assigned a plus or minus, you then count up the number of plus signs and the number of minus signs. Finally use the appropriate binomial distribution to define the rejection region in keeping with the desired level of significance.

Example 8.22

The times taken to serve customers in an off-licence follow a skewed distribution. The service times, in minutes, for a random sample of 10 customers were:

    2 6 1 4 2 5 1 1 3 2

Test the hypothesis that the population median service time is 2.5 minutes using a 5 per cent level of significance.

H_0: median $= 2.5$ H_1: median $\neq 2.5$

First we allocate signs to each value, minus for a value below 2.5 and plus for a value above 2.5.

    2 6 1 4 2 5 1 1 3 2
    − + − + − + − − + −

We have four plus signs and six minus signs. Table 1 on page 332 contains the probabilities for the binomial distribution for $n = 10$ and $p = 0.5$.

This is a two-tail test using a 5 per cent level of significance so there are two parts of the rejection region, each with a tail area of 0.025. We will reject the null hypothesis if there are too many pluses (too many values above the suggested population median) or too few. But what are too many or too few?

We are dealing with discrete distributions so the tail areas will be approximate. From Table 1 we can see that the probability of 0 or 1 successes (in this context values above the median, pluses) is 0.011, and we can work out that the probability of 9 or 10 successes is also 0.011. This means that if the population median really were 2.5, the probability of getting 0, 1, 9 or 10 pluses is 0.022 or 2.2 per cent. These numbers of pluses constitute the rejection region. As long as there are between 2 and 8 pluses inclusive, we cannot reject the null hypothesis.

In this case there are four pluses so we cannot reject H_0, the median could be 2.5.

Note that in effect we have used a 2.2 per cent level of significance in this test. It is as near as we can get to 5 per cent without exceeding it. If we were to include 2 and 8 in our rejection region the effective level of significance would be 11 per cent (Table 1 gives the probability of 0, 1 or 2 successes as 0.055).

You can use MINITAB to conduct a sign test. Pick **Non-parametrics** from the **Stat** menu then **1-Sample sign** from the sub-menu. Enter the column location of your data in the window below **Variables.** Click on the button beside **Test median** and enter the null hypothesis value of the median. Specify the form of the alternative hypothesis beside **Alternative**. The output that you will see in the session window includes counts of the numbers of values below, equal to and above the null hypothesis value of the population median, and the probability that the test statistic occurs if the null hypothesis is true, **P**.

The sign test is one of a wide range of tests that can be applied in a broader range of contexts than the more traditional or classical methods we looked at earlier in the chapter. These tests are known as *non-parametric* tests because they are not generally based on the parameters used in the classical methods, the mean and the standard deviation. They are also referred to as *distribution-free* methods because they do not depend on assumptions about the population distribution.

Non-parametric methods are simpler to use and more widely applicable than classical methods, but they are not as efficient. Typically a non-parametric test requires more data than a classical test for the same degree of rigour. We have only considered one of the many non-parametric tests that are available. You can find out more about them in Sprent (1989).

Review questions

Answers to these questions, including fully worked solutions to those questions marked with an asterisk (*), are on pages 354–356.

8.1*   The standard deviation of the fat content of a brand of flapjack is known to be 0.8 gram per 100-gram bar. The mean fat content of a random sample of 33 bars is 24.7 grams.

    (a) Construct a 95 per cent confidence interval for the population mean fat content of the bars of flapjack.
    (b) Construct a 99 per cent confidence interval for the population mean fat content of the bars of flapjack.

8.2   The burning times of aromatherapy candles are known to be Normally distributed with a standard deviation of 6 minutes. The mean burning time of a random sample of 18 candles was 3 hours 51 minutes. Set up:

    (a) A 90 per cent confidence interval for the mean burning time of the candles.
    (b) A 99 per cent confidence interval for the mean burning time of the candles.

8.3   To help shape her promotional strategy the General Manager of a regional airport wants to know how far passengers travel to use the airport. The mean and standard deviation of the distances travelled by a random sample of 61 passengers were 24.1 miles and 5.8 miles respectively.

(a) Find a 95 per cent confidence interval for the mean distance travelled by passengers.
(b) If the population standard deviation were later found to be 6.3 miles, what size sample would be needed in order to estimate the mean distance travelled by passengers for the error to be one mile with a 95 per cent level of confidence?

8.4 The distribution of rents of two-bedroom flats in the central district of a city is known to follow a skewed distribution with most flats being relatively cheap to rent but some, in prestige blocks, very expensive. The mean rent of a sample of 48 flats was £403 per month with a standard deviation of £65.

(a) Construct a 90 per cent interval estimate of the mean rent of two-bedroom flats in the area.
(b) The population standard deviation turns out to be £59. In the light of this new information, determine the size of sample necessary to enable the mean rent to be estimated to within £10, in other words for the error to be £10, with a 90 per cent level of confidence.

8.5 The weights of bags of pears sold to customers asking for one pound of pears at a market stall is known to be Normally distributed. The weights of bags served to a random sample of 15 customers were measured. The sample mean weight was 1.06 lb with a standard deviation of 0.11 lb.

(a) Produce a 95 per cent confidence interval for the weight of 'one pound' bags of pears.
(b) Produce a 99 per cent confidence interval for the weight of 'one pound' bags of pears.

8.6 A waste management consultant is investigating the waste generated by households. She is certain that the distribution of weights of household waste are distributed Normally. She selects a random sample of 12 households and measures the weight of the waste they put in their 'wheelie bin' one week. The results (to the nearest kilogram) are as follows:

28 41 36 50 17 39 21 64 26 30 42 12

(a) Use these figures to construct a 99 per cent confidence interval for the mean weight of waste in 'wheelie bins'.

(b) Does the interval suggest that the mean weight of the contents of all 'wheelie bins' can be assumed to be less than 40 kilograms?

8.7* In a UK survey of a random sample of 281 working women who had children, 175 reported that they felt that having children had held back their career prospects. In a similar study of 138 women in Denmark, 65 reported that having children had held back their career.

(a) Produce a 95 per cent confidence interval for the proportion of women in the UK who consider that having children held back their career prospects.

(b) Produce a 95 per cent confidence interval for the proportion of women in Denmark who consider that having children held back their career prospects.

(c) How do the two confidence intervals compare?

8.8 As part of a survey of a random sample of students, respondents were asked whether they were satisfied with the Students' Union Entertainments programme. Of the 109 respondents from the Arts Faculty 83 reported that they were satisfied with the Entertainments programme. Of the 116 respondents from the Business Faculty 97 reported that they were satisfied with the Entertainments programme.

(a) Construct a 90 per cent confidence interval for the proportion of students in the Arts Faculty who are satisfied with the Entertainments programme.

(b) Construct a 90 per cent confidence interval for the proportion of students in the Business Faculty who are satisfied with the Entertainments programme.

(c) Contrast the two confidence intervals.

8.9 A television audience research company intends to install monitoring devices in a random sample of households in order to produce 95 per cent interval estimates of the proportion of households watching specific programmes. If the company wants to estimate to within 2 per cent of the real figure, in other words so that the error is 2 per cent, in how many households will it have to install monitoring devices?

8.10*   The standard deviation of the recovery time of young adults who contract a strain of influenza is known to be 1.3 days. The sample mean recovery time of a random sample of 40 young adults is 12.9 days. Use this result to test the hypothesis that the mean duration of the illness is 12 days with a 5 per cent level of significance.

8.11   The alcohol content of bottles of an imported brand of flavoured vodka is presumed to follow a Normal distribution with a standard deviation of 0.83 per cent. The mean alcohol content of a random sample of 12 bottles is 64.6 per cent. Test the validity of the claim made by the importer that the average alcohol content is at least 65 per cent. Use a 5 per cent level of significance.

8.12   Office workers at a large organization are told that they should not work for more than one and a half hours at their PCs before taking a break. A survey of a random sample of 37 employees found that the mean time that they worked at their PCs before taking a break one morning was one hour 43 minutes with a standard deviation of 18 minutes. Test the hypothesis that on average the employees of this organization are working for no more than one and a half hours before taking a break using a 1 per cent level of significance.

8.13   In an advertisement it is claimed that a brand of domestic air freshener will last on average at least 70 days. The mean and standard deviation of the lifetimes of a sample of 19 air fresheners were 69.3 days and 2.9 days respectively.

(a) Test the claim made for the product using a 5 per cent level of significance.
(b) What assumption must be made for the test to be valid?

8.14   An IT Manager considers that the average number of hits per week on the company intranet pages should be 75. The mean number of hits per week on a random sample of 38 pages is 71.4 with a standard deviation of 31.9.

(a) Test a suitable hypothesis at the 10 per cent level of significance to assess the plausibility of the IT Manager's assertion.

(b) It later emerges that 13 of these pages are often visited by non-company users, and should therefore not be included in the sample. The mean and standard deviation of the remaining 25 pages are 65.8 and 28.3 respectively. Test the same hypothesis again at the 10 per cent level. What assumption must you make for the test to be valid?

8.15   A bus company claims that the mean journey time for the service from Paglashonny to Gorley is 53 minutes. A random sample of 35 journeys was chosen and each journey timed. The mean journey time of these journeys was 57 minutes with a standard deviation of 4.6 minutes.

(a) Test the bus company's claim at the 5 per cent level of significance and comment on the result.
(b) It appears that for nine of these journeys the regular driver was absent from work through illness and relief drivers, who were unfamiliar with the route, had to be used. The mean journey time for the remaining journeys was 55 minutes with a standard deviation of 3.1 minutes. Test the bus company's claim again at the 5 per cent level of significance using these figures and comment on the result.
(c) What do you need to assume about the population of journey times for the results from the second test to be valid?

8.16   A Trade Union official wants to find out if the wages in the Deshovy region of the country are lower than the wages in the Bugatty region. The mean and standard deviation of the basic weekly wages of a random sample of 58 workers in the Deshovy region were £315 and £47. The mean and standard deviation of the basic weekly wages of a random sample of 39 Bugatty workers were £361 and £53. Test the hypothesis that on average workers in Deshovy are paid no less than workers in Bugatty. Use a 1 per cent level of significance.

8.17   The speeds of a random sample of 28 cars travelling through a residential area were recorded. The mean speed of these cars was 31.7 mph with a standard deviation of 4.1 mph. After a major poster campaign urging motorists to reduce speed when driving through the area the speeds travelled by a random sample of 24 cars was recorded. The mean speed of this second sample was 29.5 mph with a standard deviation of 3.2. Test the hypothesis that the poster campaign has resulted in no reduction of speed in the area using a 5 per cent level of significance and a pooled estimate of the standard error.

8.18 A garage offers a 'clean and green engine makeover', which it promises will reduce the amount of CO_2 emissions from cars. A random sample of ten cars was tested for CO_2 emissions before and after the service. The emission figures (in grams of CO_2 per kilometre travelled) were:

Car	1	2	3	4	5	6	7	8	9	10
Before	174	160	196	214	219	149	292	158	186	200
After	169	158	183	210	204	148	285	155	179	183

Test the hypothesis that after the service emission levels are at least as high as before against the alternative that emission levels are lower. Use a 1 per cent level of significance.

8.19 Last year 61 per cent of total job applications received by a national recruitment agency were from female applicants. Out of a random sample of 192 application received this year, 105 were from females. Test the hypothesis that the proportion of applications from females has not changed using a 10 per cent level of significance.

8.20 A cinema manager claims that at least 25 per cent of customers buy popcorn during their visit to the cinema. If 38 out of a random sample of 176 customers buy popcorn, is the manager right? Use a 5 per cent level of significance.

8.21 The number of pairs of shoes owned by adult women is assumed to follow a skewed distribution. A random sample of 10 women was taken and each woman was asked how many pairs of shoes she owned. Their responses were:

7   24   15   7   18   15   9   13   8   10

Using this data test the hypothesis that the median number of pairs of shoes owned by adult women is 12. Apply the sign test with a 5 per cent level of significance.

8.22 Select the appropriate definition from the list on the right-hand side for the terms listed on the left-hand side.

(a) point estimate   (i) the likelihood that an estimate is accurate

(b) z interval   (ii) a result that refutes a null hypothesis

(c) error   (iii) another name for an interval estimate

(d) confidence   (iv) an interval estimate based on a small sample

(e) t interval   (v) a single figure estimate

(f) confidence interval   (vi) an interval estimate based on a large sample

(g) null hypothesis   (vii) what to add and subtract to create an interval estimate

(h) significant   (viii) a claim, to be tested, about a population measure.

'*Making the right connections . . .*'

Statistical decision making using bivariate data

Chapter Objectives

This chapter will help you:

- To analyse the connection between variables.
- To test bivariate models.
- To use bivariate models to make sophisticated predictions.

In this chapter you will find:

- Contingency tests for qualitative data.
- Tests of the correlation coefficient.
- Tests of components of bivariate models.
- Predictions with confidence intervals.
- Guidance on using computer software for statistical inference using bivariate data.

The purpose of this chapter is to introduce you to methods of statistical inference, or statistical decision making that enable us to draw conclusions about connections between variables in populations based on sample data. The sample data we will be using is described as *bivariate* data because it consists of observed values of two variables. This sort of data is usually collected in order to establish whether there is a connection between the two variables, and if so, what sort of connection it is.

Many organizations use this type of analysis to study consumer behaviour, patterns of costs and revenues, and other aspects of their operations. Sometimes the results of such analysis have far-reaching consequences. For example, if you look at a tobacco product you will see a health warning prominently displayed. It is there because some years ago researchers used these types of statistical methods to establish that there was a connection between tobacco consumption and certain medical conditions.

We shall consider two types of statistical decision-making techniques. The first, tests of association or *contingency*, are designed to investigate connections between qualitative variables, or characteristics. The second are tests that enable us to investigate connections between quantitative variables. The latter usually take the form of bivariate models, and we shall also be looking at how we can use such models to produce confidence intervals for predictions.

9.1 Contingency tests

These tests are used primarily with qualitative data, which is data that consists of different categories of attributes or characteristics. They can help us determine whether one characteristic is associated with, or *contingent* upon another characteristic. They are also suitable for use with quantitative data as long as it is discrete data which can take only a very few values, or the data is sorted into relatively few categories.

If you conduct a questionnaire survey, or have to analyse the results of questionnaire research, you may well want to find out from the data how different characteristics are related to each other. For instance, you may want to look into the possible connection between the socio-economic class of respondents and the newspapers they buy. You would need to conduct a contingency test in order to ascertain whether a connection you might find in your sample results is strong enough to enable you to conclude that there is a connection in the population at large, in other words to see if the sample results are *significant*.

Contingency tests are conducted in the same way as the hypothesis tests we looked at in the last chapter. We begin with a null hypothesis, H_0, which in contingency analysis says that there is no association between the characteristics, whereas the alternative hypothesis, H_1, says that there is an association between them.

The next stage is to analyse the sample results that we want to use to decide which hypothesis is the more plausible. We can start by putting the data into a *contingency table*.

Example 9.1

In a survey about television, a random sample of 100 respondents were asked if they thought there was too much or not enough sport on television. Of the 40 men in the sample, 15 said too much. Of the 60 women in the sample, 35 said too much. Is there a significant connection between gender and attitude to the amount of sport on television?

The first stage is to specify suitable hypotheses.

H_0: There is no association. H_1: There is association.

We begin the analysis of the sample results by arranging them in a contingency table.

	Men	Women	Total
Too much sport	15	35	50
Not enough sport	25	25	50
Total	40	60	100

To test the hypotheses the sample results must be combined to produce a measure of contingency, a *test statistic* that we can compare to a benchmark distribution. The test statistic that we use is known as *chi-square* after the Greek letter chi, χ^2.

The value of chi-square is calculated by comparing the sample results, which are referred to as the *Observed* frequencies and are represented by the letter O, to the results that we would expect if the null hypothesis were true. These values, which we have to work out, are known as the *Expected* frequencies and are represented by the letter E.

Example 9.2

Find the results that we would expect to see in the contingency table in Example 9.1 if there is no association between gender and attitude to the amount of sport on television.

We can deduce the figures we would expect to see. We know from the totals that the respondents are split equally between the 50 who think there is too much sport and the 50 who think there is not enough. If there is no association between the attitudes that people have towards the amount of sport on television and gender we would anticipate that both men and women would be evenly split on the issue. In other words if gender makes no difference to whether people think there is too much sport on television we would expect the same proportion of men as women to say so, and the same proportion of men as women to say there is not enough.

The contingency table would look like this:

	Men	Women	Total
Too much sport	20	30	50
Not enough sport	20	30	50
Total	40	60	100

If you look at the table you will see that each group, men and women, has been divided equally between the opposing viewpoints. These figures are the Expected figures we need to use in calculating the test statistic. Notice that, although the figures within the table are different, the row and column totals are unchanged.

If you would prefer a rather more formal way of finding expected frequencies you can multiply the row total by the column total and divide the product by the overall total. So to find how many men in Example 9.2 we would expect to say there is too much sport on television, assuming there is no association, we would multiply the total number saying there is too much sport on television by the total number of men and divide the result by 100, the total number of respondents in the sample. That is:

$$\text{Expected frequency} = \frac{\text{Row total} \times \text{column total}}{\text{Overall total}}$$

$$= \frac{50 \times 40}{100} = 20$$

Once we have the expected frequencies we can compare them to the observed frequencies, the actual sample results, by putting them together in a single table.

Example 9.3

Produce a contingency table that shows the observed frequencies from Example 9.1 alongside the expected frequencies from Example 9.2. Compare the two sets of frequencies.

In the table below the expected frequencies are shown in parentheses.

	Men	Women	Total
Too much sport	15 (20)	35 (30)	50
Not enough sport	25 (20)	25 (30)	50
Total	40	60	100

Fewer men than we would expect if there were no association say there is too much sport and more women than we would expect if there were no association say there is too much.

The conclusions from Example 9.3 suggest that there is some association in the sample results but is the association strong enough to be significant, in other words does the evidence point to association in the entire population? To find out we need to calculate the test statistic, χ^2.

To do this we subtract each expected frequency from its corresponding observed frequency and then square the result. We will be adding these differences between observed and expected frequencies, so we have to square them otherwise the positive and negative differences will cancel each other out and the test statistic will be of no use. We then divide each squared difference by its expected frequency. This is to the *standardize* the test statistic, in other words to enable us to compare it to a standard χ^2 distribution. Finally we add together the standardized squared differences, one for each section or cell of the contingency table. The total we get is the value of the test statistic, χ^2, for the sample results.

The procedure can be represented using the following formula:

$$\chi^2 = \Sigma \, (O - E)^2 / E$$

Example 9.4

Find the value of χ^2 for the sample data in Example 9.1.

We can work from the contingency table produced in Example 9.3.

	Men	*Women*
Too much sport	15 (20)	35 (30)
Not enough sport	25 (20)	25 (30)

We will start with men who say there is too much sport on television. The observed frequency, O, is 15 and the expected frequency, E, is 20, so:

$$(O - E)^2/E = (15 - 20)^2/20 = 25/20 = 1.25$$

Next we will consider the women who say there is too much sport on television.

$$(O - E)^2/E = (35 - 30)^2/30 = 25/30 = 0.833 \quad \text{to three decimal places}$$

Next the men who say there is not enough sport on television.

$$(O - E)^2/E = (25 - 20)^2/20 = 1.25$$

Last the women who say there is not enough sport on television.

$$(O - E)^2/E = (25 - 30)^2/30 = 0.833 \quad \text{to three decimal places}$$

The test statistic, χ^2, is the sum of these four results, that is:

$$\chi^2 = 1.25 + 0.833 + 1.25 + 0.833 = 4.167 \quad \text{to three decimal places}$$

Does the test statistic in Example 9.4 suggest that there is association between gender and attitude to the amount of sport on television among the whole population? We can only establish this by comparing the test statistic to a suitable benchmark distribution.

The type of distribution we will use to assess the test statistic is the *chi-square* distribution, and the procedure is often referred to as a chi-square test. This distribution describes the behaviour of the measure of contingency that we have used, whereas the Standard Normal and t distributions do not. The shape of the chi-square distribution is shown in Figure 9.1.

There are in fact many different chi-square distributions. The one we use depends on the number degrees of freedom we have in our sample results. We can work this out by taking the number of rows in the contingency table, subtracting one, and then

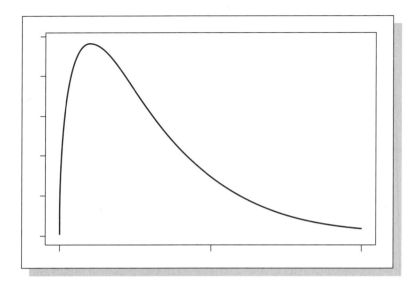

Figure 9.1
The chi-square distribution

multiplying by the number of columns in our contingency table minus one. If we use r to represent the number of rows and c to represent the number of columns:

$$\text{Degrees of freedom} = (r - 1) \times (c - 1)$$

The contingency table in Example 9.4 has two rows and two columns, so the benchmark chi-square distribution is the one that has one degree of freedom. This describes the pattern of chi-square values we would get if we took all the samples we possibly could from a population that had no association between two characteristics, each of which had only two categories, and calculated a chi-square value from each set of sample results.

We need to use the appropriate chi-square distribution to find how likely the test statistic is to arise if there is no association between the characteristics in the population. Using a decision rule that specifies a level of significance we will then be able to arrive at our conclusion.

Table 5 on page 337 provides information about chi-square distributions, with up to 10 degrees of freedom. In Table 5 the figure in the first row, the row for 1 degree of freedom, and the column headed 0.10 is 2.706. This means that 10 per cent of the distribution is to the right of 2.706. If we wanted to test the null hypothesis of no association at a 10 per cent level of significance, then the test statistic from our sample results would need to be larger than 2.706 in order to reject the null hypothesis.

Table 5 also shows that 5 per cent of the distribution is to the right of 3.841. If the test statistic is more than this we can reject the null hypothesis at the 5 per cent level of significance. In order to reject the null hypothesis at the 1 per cent level the test statistic would have to be larger than 6.635.

Notice that the larger our test statistic is, the stronger the evidence of association will be. Rejecting the null hypothesis at 1 per cent is far more conclusive than rejecting it at 10 per cent. This is not surprising because the test statistic, χ^2, is based on differences between the actual, or observed frequencies and those we would expect if there were no association. If there were association then we would anticipate large differences between observed and expected frequencies. If there were no association we would expect small differences.

The test statistic in Example 9.4 was 4.167, which is large enough (larger than 3.841) to enable us to reject the null hypothesis at the 5 per cent level of significance. The sample results suggest that there is association between gender and their attitude to the amount of sport on television.

An alternative approach is to use computer software to find exactly how likely it is that a χ^2 value of the size of the test statistic or larger occurs, if there is no association in the population. You can do this in MINITAB by selecting **Probability Distributions** from the **Calc** menu and picking the **Chi-Square** option from the sub-menu. In the command window you will need to select **Cumulative probability**, specify the **Degrees of freedom** and specify the test statistic as the **Input constant**. If you try this using the test statistic from Example 9.4, 4.16, you will find that the probability that χ^2 is below 4.16 is 0.9586, so the probability that it is more than 4.16 is 0.414 or 4.14 per cent. Since this is less than 5 per cent we can reject the null hypothesis at the 5 per cent level of significance and rule out the possibility of no association.

To produce the same figure using EXCEL, position the cursor in an empty cell and type **=CHIDIST(4.16,1)** in the Formula Bar. The result appears in the cell when you press the **Enter** key.

If you have raw data and you want to use MINITAB to produce a contingency table and test for association, select the **Tables** option from the **Stat** menu, then pick the **Cross Tabulation** option from the sub-menu. You will have to specify the column locations of your data in the command window and click the box to the left of **Chi-Square analysis** to obtain the test results. You should also click the button to the left of **Above and expected count** if you want the expected frequencies included in your output. Click **OK** and you should see the contingency table in the session window. Beneath it you should see values for Chi-Square (the test statistic), DF (the number of degrees of freedom), and P-Value (the chance of the test statistic occurring if there is no association).

If your data is already tabulated you can use MINITAB to test it for association by storing the table in the worksheet and picking the **Chi-Square Test** option from the **Tables** sub-menu. Specify the column locations of the tabulated data and click **OK**. The output will include the test statistic (Chi-Sq), the degrees of freedom (DF), and the probability of getting the test statistic if there were no association (P-Value).

You can produce a similar analysis in EXCEL by storing the observed frequencies, the 'actual range', in one set of spreadsheet cells, and the expected frequencies, the 'expected range' in another. Type **=CHITEST(actual range,expected range)** in the Formula bar, and by using the cursor or typing, give the cell locations of the **actual range** and the **expected range.**

The set of data we have used to illustrate chi-square tests for association is quite a simple one. In practice we are likely to have more rows and/or columns. Even in the example, we might have had another category of response, perhaps the view that the amount of sport on television is just right, to cope with. Although the table is more elaborate the procedure you have to follow is essentially the same. However, there are some important points to remember.

The first is that more rows and columns mean more degrees of freedom, so you must use the correct χ^2 distribution. The second concerns the amount of data. Like other types of statistical testing, all other things being equal, the more data we have, the firmer our conclusions will be. We should have enough data to ensure that none of the expected frequencies is less than 5; otherwise our results may not be dependable. If any expected frequencies are less than 1, the results of the test will be useless.

If one or more expected frequencies are too low there are two possible solutions. The first is to obtain more data. The second is to merge categories so that there are fewer rows and columns. If you are managing the project yourself you can avoid the problem by planning the research carefully, an issue we will consider in the next chapter.

Example 9.5

In a survey a random sample of 135 motorists were each asked about themselves and the cars they drove. Some of the results are summarized in the contingency table below.

Car type:	Performance	Sports	Supermini	Family car	Total
Drivers 40 or over	4	26	12	28	70
Drivers under 40	3	24	18	20	65
Total	7	50	30	48	135

Use these sample results to test for association between age category and type of car using a 5 per cent level of significance.

H_0: There is no association. H_1: There is association.

To test the null hypothesis we need to find the expected frequencies for each cell, but when we calculate the expected frequencies for the number of drivers who drive a performance car we find that for both categories of staff these figures are less than 5.

Expected number of drivers 40 or over in performance cars

$$= (70 \times 7)/135$$

$$= 3.63 \text{ to two decimal places}$$

Expected number of drivers under 40 in performance cars

$$= (65 \times 7)/135$$

$$= 3.37 \text{ to two decimal places}$$

These low expected frequencies would weaken the test. We can overcome this by merging the performance and sports categories.

	Performance/Sports	Supermini	Family car	Total
Drivers 40 or over	30	12	28	70
Drivers under 40	27	18	20	65
Total	57	30	48	135

The expected values are now (to two decimal places):

Expected number of drivers 40 or over in Performance/Sports cars $= (70 \times 57)/135$
$= 29.56$

Expected number of drivers under 40 in Performance/Sports cars $= (65 \times 57)/135$
$= 27.44$

Expected number of drivers 40 or over in superminis $= (70 \times 30)/135$
$= 15.56$

Expected number of drivers under 40 in superminis $= (65 \times 30)/135$
$= 14.44$

Expected number of drivers 40 or over in family cars $= (70 \times 48)/135$
$= 24.88$

Expected number of drivers under 40 in family cars $= (65 \times 48)/135$
$= 23.12$

These can now be included in the contingency table.

	Performance/Sports	Superminis	Family cars	Total
Drivers 40 or over	30 (29.56)	12 (15.56)	28 (24.89)	70
Drivers under 40	27 (27.44)	18 (14.44)	20 (23.11)	65
Total	57	30	48	135

The test statistic:

$$\chi^2 = [(30 - 29.56)^2/29.56] + [(12 - 15.56)^2/15.56] + [(28 - 24.89)^2/24.89]$$

$$+ [(27 - 27.44)^2/27.44] + [(18 - 14.44)^2/14.44] + [(20 - 23.11)^2/23.11]$$

$$= 0.007 + 0.814 + 0.389 + 0.007 + 0.878 + 0.419 = 2.514$$

The degrees of freedom $= (\text{rows} - 1) \times (\text{columns} - 1) = (2 - 1) \times (3 - 1) = 2.$

According to Table 5 on page 337 the value of χ^2 that cuts off a 5 per cent area in the right-hand side of the χ^2 distribution that has two degrees of freedom is 5.991. This is the critical value of χ^2. Since the test statistic, 2.514, is less than the critical value we cannot reject the null hypothesis. The evidence suggests there is no significant association between driver age category and type of vehicle driven. However, it is worth noting that the largest two of the six components of the test statistic, 0.814 and 0.878, both relate to superminis. Fewer drivers 40 or over and more drivers under 40 drive this type of car than we would expect.

Alternatively you can use MINITAB to find the probability that χ^2 with 2 degrees of freedom is more than 2.514, which is 0.2845 or 28.45 per cent. This is clearly greater than 5 per cent, the level of significance, so again the conclusion is that we cannot reject the null hypothesis.

9.2 Testing and estimating using quantitative bivariate data

The analysis of quantitative bivariate that we looked at in Chapter 4 consisted of two related techniques, correlation and regression. Correlation analysis, which is about the calculation and evaluation of the correlation coefficient, enables us to tell whether there is a connection between the observed values of two variables. Regression analysis, which is about fitting lines of best fit, enables us to find the equation of the line that is most appropriate for the data, the regression model.

In this section we will consider how the results from applying correlation and regression to sample data can be used to test hypotheses and make estimates for the populations the sets of sample data belong to.

9.2.1 Testing correlation coefficients

The correlation coefficient, represented by the letter r, measures the extent of the linear association between two variables, X and Y. You can find the correlation coefficient of a set of bivariate data using computer software, or the formula:

$$r = \frac{\text{Cov}_{XY}}{(s_x \times s_y)}$$

where

$$\text{Cov}_{XY} = \frac{\Sigma \ (x - \bar{x})(y - \bar{y})}{(n - 1)}$$

and s_x and s_y are the standard deviations of the x and y values respectively.

If we select a random sample from populations of X and Y that are *both* Normal in shape, the correlation coefficient calculated from the sample data will be a legitimate estimate of the population coefficient, represented by the Greek r, the letter rho, ρ. In fact the main reason for calculating the sample correlation coefficient is to find out if there is any linear association between the X and Y populations.

The value of the sample correlation coefficient alone is some help in assessing correlation between the populations, but a more thorough approach is to test the null hypothesis that the population correlation coefficient is zero,

$$H_0: \rho = 0$$

The alternative hypothesis we use depends on what we would like to prove. If we are interested in demonstrating that there is significant correlation in the population, then we should use:

$$H_1: \rho \neq 0$$

If we want to show that there is significant positive correlation in the population then:

$$H_1: \rho > 0$$

If we want to show that there is significant negative correlation in the population then:

$$H_1: \rho < 0$$

If we adopt the first of these versions of the alternative hypothesis, $H_1: \rho \neq 0$, we need to use a two-tail test, if we use one of the other forms we need to conduct a one-tail test. In practice it is more usual to test for either positive or negative correlation rather than for both.

Once we have established the nature of our alternative hypothesis we need to calculate the test statistic from our sample data.

The test statistic: $\quad t = \dfrac{r \ \sqrt{n - 2}}{\sqrt{1 - r^2}}$

where r is the sample correlation coefficient and n is the number of pairs of observations in the sample.

As long as the populations of X and Y are Normal the test statistic will belong to a t distribution with $n - 2$ degrees of freedom and a mean of zero, *if* there is no linear association between the populations of X and Y.

Example 9.6

The proprietor of a garage believes that the temperature outside and the number of cans of soft drinks sold are connected. She noted the maximum daytime temperature (in degrees Celsius) and the soft drinks sales on 10 working days chosen at random.

Temperature	Cans sold
14	19
11	29
17	47
8	12
20	45
13	41
24	67
3	10
16	28
5	21

The correlation coefficient for this sample is 0.871 to three decimal places. Test the hypothesis that there is no correlation between temperature and sales against the alternative that there is positive correlation. Use a 5 per cent level of significance.

The test statistic,

$$t = \frac{r\sqrt{n-2}}{\sqrt{1-r^2}} = \frac{0.871 \times \sqrt{10-2}}{\sqrt{1-0.871^2}}$$

$$= \frac{0.871 \times \sqrt{8}}{\sqrt{0.24}} = \frac{0.871 \times 2.83}{0.49} = 5.02$$

We need to compare this test statistic to the t distribution that has $n - 2$, which in this case is 8, degrees of freedom. According to Table 4 on page 336 the value of t with 8 degrees of freedom that cuts off the 5 per cent tail on the right-hand side of the distribution, $t_{0.05,8}$, is 1.860. Since the test statistic is clearly larger than 1.860 we can reject the null hypothesis at the 5 per cent level of significance. The sample evidence strongly suggests that there is positive correlation between temperature and sales in the population.

MINITAB enables you to test hypotheses about population correlation coefficients without having to calculate a test statistic by providing a *P*-value alongside the sample correlation coefficient. This is the probability of getting the sample correlation coefficient if there is no correlation in the population. You can look at this if you put the data from Example 9.6 in two columns of the worksheet and select **Basic Statistics** from the **Stat** menu. Pick **Correlation** from the **Basic Statistics** sub-menu and specify the column locations of your data in the command window, checking that there is a cross in the box next to **Display p-values**. You should see the following:

$$\text{Correlation of Temperature and Sales} = 0.871$$
$$\text{P-Value} = 0.001$$

The *P*-value, or *population value*, is the probability that the null hypothesis of no population correlation is true. If it is below the level of significance in our decision rule, as it is in this case, we can reject the null hypothesis and conclude that there is significant population correlation.

The *P*-value that MINITAB gives us is based on the assumption that the alternative hypothesis is H_1: $\rho \neq 0$ and therefore the test is a two-tail test. The *P*-value in this case is therefore the probability that *r* is 0.871 or more, or *−0.871 or less*. If we want to use another form of alternative hypothesis, one that requires a one tail-test, we would have to divide the *P*-value by two.

9.2.2 Testing bivariate models

The second technique used to analyse quantitative bivariate data is simple linear regression analysis, the method we used in Chapter 4 to find the equation of the line of best fit between two variables, *X* and *Y*. Such a line has two distinguishing features, its intercept and its slope. In the standard formula we used for the line the intercept was represented by the letter *a* and the slope by the letter *b*:

$$Y = a + bX$$

The line that this equation describes is the best way of representing the connection between the dependent variable, *Y*, and the independent variable, *X*. In practice it is almost always the result of a sample investigation that is intended to shed light on the connection between the populations of *X* and *Y*. That is why we have used ordinary rather than Greek letters in the equation.

The results of such a sample investigation can provide an understanding of the relationship between the populations. The intercept and slope of the line of best fit for the sample are point or single-figure estimates for the intercept and slope of the line of best fit for the populations, which are represented by the Greek equivalents of *a* and *b*, α and β:

$$Y = \alpha + \beta X$$

The intercept and slope from the analysis of the sample can be used to test hypotheses about the equivalent figures for the populations. Typically we use null hypotheses that suggest that the population values are zero:

$$H_0: \alpha = 0 \quad \text{for the intercept}$$

and
$$H_0: \beta = 0 \quad \text{for the slope.}$$

If the population intercept is zero, the population line of best fit will be represented by the equation $Y = 0 + \beta X$, and the line will begin at the origin of the graph, that is where both X and Y are zero. You can see this type of line in Figure 9.2.

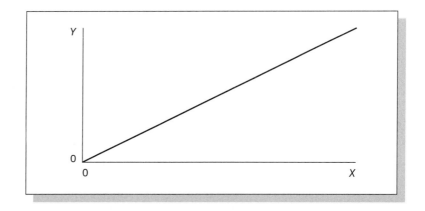

Figure 9.2
Line with zero intercept,
$Y = 0 + \beta X$

If we wanted to see whether the population intercept is likely to be zero, we would test the null hypothesis $H_0: \alpha = 0$ against the alternative hypothesis:

$$H_1: \alpha \neq 0$$

When you use regression analysis you will find that investigating the value of the intercept is rarely important. Occasionally it is of interest, for instance if we are looking at the connection between an organization's levels of operational activity and its total costs at different periods of time the intercept of the line of best fit represents the organization's fixed costs.

Typically we are much more interested in evaluating the slope of the line of best fit. The slope is pivotal; it tells us how the dependent variable responds to changes in the independent variable. For this reason you will find that the slope is also known as the *coefficient* of the independent variable.

If the population slope turns out to be zero, it would tell us that the dependent variable does not respond to the independent variable. The implication of this is that our independent variable is of no use in explaining how our dependent variable behaves and there would be no point in using it to make predictions of our dependent variable.

If the slope of the line of best fit is zero, the equation of the line would be $Y = \alpha + 0X$, and the line would be perfectly horizontal. You can see this illustrated in Figure 9.3.

Figure 9.3
Line with zero slope,
$Y = \alpha + 0X$

The line in Figure 9.3 shows that whatever the value of X, whether it is a small one to the left of the horizontal axis or a large one to the right of the horizontal axis, the value of Y remains the same. The size of the x value has no impact whatsoever on Y, and the regression model is useless.

We usually want to use regression analysis to find useful rather than useless models, that is, regression models that do help us to understand and anticipate the behaviour of dependent variables. Therefore, in order to demonstrate that a model is valid, it is important that we test the null hypothesis that the slope is zero. Hopefully the sample evidence will enable us to reject the null hypothesis in favour of the alternative, that the slope is not zero, and we can proceed to use our model.

The test statistic we shall use to test the hypothesis is:

$$t = \frac{b - 0}{S_b}$$

where b is the sample slope, 0 is the population slope suggested by the null hypothesis, and s_b is the estimated standard error of the sampling distribution of the sample slopes.

To calculate the estimated standard error, s_b, divide s^2, the variance of the sample residuals, the parts of the y values that the line of best fit does not explain, by the sum of the squared deviations between the x values and their mean, $\bar{x}$. Then take the square root. That is:

$$s_b = \sqrt{\frac{s^2}{\Sigma\,(x - \bar{x})^2}}$$

Once we have the test statistic we can assess it by comparing it to the t distribution with $n - 2$ degrees of freedom, two fewer than the number of pairs of x and y values in our sample data.

Example 9.7

The equation of the line of best fit for the sample data in Example 9.6 is:

Sales = 0.74 + 2.38 Temperature

Test the hypothesis that the population slope is zero using a 5 per cent level of significance.

$$H_0: \beta = 0 \qquad H_1: \beta \neq 0$$

To find the test statistic we first need to calculate the standard deviation of the residuals. We can identify the residuals by taking each x value, putting it into the equation of the line of best fit and then working out what Y 'should' be, according to the model. The difference between the y value that the equation says should be associated with the x value and the y value that is actually associated with the x value is the residual.

To illustrate this, we will look at the first pair of values in our sample data, a day when the temperature was 14° Celsius and 19 cans of soft drink were sold. If we insert the temperature into the equation of the line of best fit we can use the equation to estimate the number of cans that 'should' have been sold on that day:

Sales = 0.74 + (2.38 × 14) = 34.06

The residual is the difference between the actual sales level, 19, and this estimate, that is:

Residual = 19 − 34.06 = −15.06

The standard deviation of the residuals is based on the squared residuals. The residuals and their squares are given in the table below.

Temperature	Sales	Residuals	Squared residuals
14	19	−15.06	226.80
11	29	2.10	4.39
17	47	5.82	33.91
8	12	−7.77	60.35
20	45	−3.31	10.98
13	41	9.34	87.20
24	67	9.17	84.12
3	10	2.13	4.52
16	28	−10.80	116.61
5	21	8.37	70.02
			698.90

We find the standard deviation of the residuals by taking the square root of the sum of the squared residuals divided by n, the number of residuals, minus two. (We have to subtract two because we have 'lost' two degrees of freedom in using the intercept and slope to calculate the residuals.)

$$s = \sqrt{698.90/n - 2} = \sqrt{698.90/8} = 9.347 \text{ to three decimal places}$$

To get the estimated standard error we divide the square of this by the sum of squared differences between the temperature figures and their mean then take the square root.

Temperature (x)	$\bar{x}$	$x - \bar{x}$	$(x - \bar{x})^2$
14	13.1	0.9	0.81
11	13.1	−2.1	4.41
17	13.1	3.9	15.21
8	13.1	−5.1	26.01
20	13.1	6.9	47.61
13	13.1	−0.1	0.01
24	13.1	10.9	118.81
3	13.1	−10.1	102.01
16	13.1	2.9	8.41
5	13.1	−8.1	65.61
			388.90

The estimated standard error is:

$$s_b = \sqrt{s^2/\Sigma \, (x - \bar{x})^2,} = \sqrt{9.347^2/388.90} = 0.4738$$

and the test statistic $t = (b - 0)/s_b = 2.38/0.4738 = 5.02$ to two decimal places

From Table 4 on page 336 the t value with 8 degrees of freedom that cuts off a tail area of $2\frac{1}{2}$ per cent, $t_{8,0.025}$ is 2.306. If the null hypothesis is true and the population slope is zero only $2\frac{1}{2}$ per cent of test statistics will be more than 2.306 and only $2\frac{1}{2}$ per cent will be less than −2.306. The level of significance is 5 per cent so our decision rule is therefore to reject the null hypothesis if the test statistic is outside ± 2.306. Since the test statistic in this case is 5.02 we should reject H_0 and conclude that the evidence suggests that the population slope is not zero.

The implication of the sort of result we arrived at in Example 9.7 is that the model, represented by the equation, is sufficiently sound to enable the temperature variable to be used to predict sales.

If you compare the test statistic for the sample slope in Example 9.7 with the test statistic for the sample correlation coefficient in Example 9.6, you will see that they are both 5.02. This is no coincidence; the two tests are equivalent. The slope represents the form of the association between the variables whereas the correlation coefficient measures its strength. We use the same data in the same sort of way to test the rigour of each of them.

9.2.3 Testing bivariate models using computer software

The calculations we had to employ in Example 9.7 are quite laborious, but they should enable you to see how the data is used to produce the conclusion. However, you should seldom, if ever, have to work through this sort of calculation yourself. Regression analysis is a statistical technique that is very widely used which means that just about every spreadsheet and statistical package will be able to do this sort of work for you.

MINITAB will produce a regression analysis that includes p-values for both the sample intercept and slope. You can obtain it by selecting **Regression** from the **Stat** menu and **Regression** from the **Regression** sub-menu. Try putting the data from Example 9.6 into two columns in the worksheet then specify in the command window the column location of the sales figures in the **Response** box and the column location of the temperature figures in the **Predictor** box. You should see in the session window an analysis that includes:

The regression equation is
Sales = 0.74 + 2.38 Temperature

Predictor	Coef	StDev	T	P
Constant	0.738	6.874	0.11	0.917
Temperature	2.3788	0.4738	5.02	0.001

S = 9.343

You may recognize some of these figures from Example 9.7. At the top there is the equation of the line of best fit derived from the sample data.

In the next block of output the column headed 'Predictor' contains the two components of the model that we would like to use to predict the sales on the basis of the temperature, the 'Constant' (the intercept) and the temperature variable. The 'Coef' (coefficient) column lists the numerical values of the sample intercept and the sample slope. Under the next heading, 'SECoeff' (standard errors of the coefficients), we have the estimated standard errors of first the sample intercepts then the sample slopes. The 'T' column contains the test statistics based on the sample intercept (the upper figure) and the sample slope (the lower figure). Finally the 'P' column contains the 'p-values' for the sample intercept and the sample slope.

The value labelled S at the bottom is the standard deviation of the residuals. You should recognize this figure as well as the figures in the 'Temperature' row of output.

We can use the figures listed in the 'P' column to assess the hypotheses that the population intercept and slope are zero. The first 'P' value is the probability that we obtain a sample intercept of 0.738 if the population intercept is zero, often described as the probability that the null hypothesis (a population intercept of zero) is true. The 'P' value 0.917 indicates that there is a strong possibility that the population intercept is zero.

The second 'P' value, 0.001, is of more interest. This is the probability that the sample slope is 2.3788 or more if the population slope is zero, or we could say that it is the probability that the null hypothesis (a population slope of zero) is true. Since the figure is well below the level of significance, 5 per cent or 0.05 we would emphatically reject the null hypothesis.

If there are any outliers in your data, in other words points that lay a long way from the line of best fit, MINITAB will list them under 'Unusual Observations' at the end of the output. There is a row of information about each unusual observation including both the x and y values so they are quite easy to identify on a fitted line plot. As well as outlying points MINITAB also lists any points that are a long way from the rest of the data but not significantly distant from the line of best fit. To distinguish between the two types of unusual observation, MINITAB codes outliers with the letter R and the others with the letter X. If your data does include unusual observations you should first check that they have been recorded correctly and if so, investigate what might explain their unusual nature. It is well worth spending time studying outliers. For one thing they make the model a less effective way of representing the data, but they can also help you to think of ways of improving the model, perhaps by measuring the variables in different ways.

You can use EXCEL to produce the same analysis, although it will appear in a different sequence, by selecting **Data Analysis** from the **Tools** menu. Pick the **Regression** option from the sub-menu and then provide the cell locations of the values of X and Y. The output will include the following:

	Coefficients	Standard Error	t Stat	P-value
Intercept	0.738236	6.873624	0.107401	0.917115
X Variable	2.378761	0.473761	5.021009	0.001026

The figures here are the same as the ones we have derived by calculation and using MINITAB. It is the second row that contains the information that we need to assess the null hypothesis that the slope, the coefficient on the X variable, is zero.

9.2.4 Constructing interval predictions

When we use a regression model to make a prediction, as we had to do in Example 9.7 to obtain the residuals, we have a single figure that is the value of Y that the model suggests should be associated with the value of X that we specify.

Example 9.8

Use the regression model in Example 9.7 to predict the level of sales that will be achieved on a day when the temperature is 22° Celsius.

If temperature = 22, according to the regression equation:

$$\text{Sales} = 0.74 + 2.38\,(22) = 53.1.$$

Since the number of cans sold is a discrete variable, in practice we would round this to 53 cans.

The problem with all single-figure predictions is that we simply have no idea of how likely they are to be accurate. It is far better to have an interval that we know, with a certain amount of confidence, will be accurate.

Before we look at how we can produce such intervals, we need to clarify exactly what we want to find. The figure we produced in Example 9.8 we described as a *prediction* of sales on a day when the temperature is 22° Celsius. In fact it can also be used as an *estimate* of the mean level of sales that occur on days when the temperature is 22° Celsius. Because it is a single figure it is a point estimate of the sales levels on such days.

We can construct an interval estimate, or confidence interval of the mean level of sales on days when the temperature is at a particular level by taking the point estimate and adding and subtracting an error. The error is the product of the standard error of the sampling distribution of the point estimates and a figure from the appropriate t distribution. The t distribution we use should have $n - 2$ degrees of freedom, n being the number of pairs of data in our sample, and the t value we select from it is based on the level of confidence we want to have that our interval estimate will be accurate.

We can express this procedure using the formula:

$$\text{Confidence interval} = \hat{y} \pm t_{\alpha/2,\ n-2} \times s \sqrt{\frac{1}{n} + \frac{(x_0 - \bar{x})^2}{\Sigma(x - \bar{x})^2}}$$

where $\hat{y}$ is the point estimate of the mean of the y values associated with x_0 and s is the standard deviation of the sample residuals.

Example 9.9

Construct a 95 per cent confidence interval for the mean sales of soft drinks that the proprietor of the garage in Example 9.6 can expect on days when the temperature is 22° Celsius.

From Example 9.8 we know that the point estimate for the mean, $\hat{y}$, is 53.1 cans. We will use the original, unrounded figure because the mean, unlike sales on a particular day, does not have to be discrete. We also know from Example 9.8 that s, the standard deviation of the sample residuals, is 9.347, $\bar{x}$ is 13.1, and $\Sigma(x - \bar{x})^2$ is 388.90.

The t value we need is 2.306, the value that cuts off a tail of $2\frac{1}{2}$ per cent in the t distribution that has $10 - 2$, 8, degrees of freedom. The value of x_0, the temperature on the days whose mean sales figure we want to estimate, is 22.

$$\text{Confidence interval} = \hat{y} \pm t_{\alpha/2,\ n-2} \times s \sqrt{\frac{1}{n} + \frac{(x_0 - \bar{x})^2}{\Sigma(x - \bar{x})^2}}$$

$$= 53.1 \pm 2.306 \times 9.347 \sqrt{[(1/10 + (22 - 13.1)^2/388.90)]}$$

$$= 53.1 \pm 2.306 \times 9.347 \sqrt{0.304}$$

$$= 53.1 \pm 2.306 \times 5.15$$

$$= 53.1 \pm 11.87 = 41.23 \text{ to } 64.97 \text{ to two decimal places}$$

The confidence interval we produced in Example 9.9 is a reliable guide to what the mean sales are on days when the temperature is 22° Celsius. This is because, although this level of temperature is not among the temperature values in our sample data, it is within the range of the temperatures in our sample data, which is from a minimum of 3° Celsius to a maximum of 24° Celsius.

If we produce a confidence interval for the mean of the y values associated with an x value outside the range of x values in the sample it will be both wide and unreliable.

Example 9.10

Construct a 95 per cent confidence interval for the mean sales of cans of soft drinks in the garage in Example 9.6 on days when the temperature is 35° Celsius.

The point estimate for the mean, $\hat{y} = 0.74 + 2.38 (35) = 84.04$

$$\text{Confidence interval} = \hat{y} \pm t_{\alpha/2, n-2} \times s \sqrt{\frac{1}{n} + \frac{(x_0 - \bar{x})^2}{\Sigma(x - \bar{x})^2}}$$

$$= 84.04 \pm 2.306 \times 9.347 \sqrt{[(1/10 + (35 - 13.1)^2/388.90)}$$

$$= 84.04 \pm 2.306 \times 9.347 \sqrt{1.33}$$

$$= 84.04 \pm 2.306 \times 10.79$$

$$= 84.04 \pm 24.88 = 59.16 \text{ to } 108.92 \text{ to two decimal places}$$

The confidence interval we produced in Example 9.10 is of no real use to us because the temperature on which it is based, 35° Celsius, is beyond the range of temperatures in our sample. Confidence intervals produced from regression lines will be wider when they are based on x values further away from the mean of the x values. You can see this in Figure 9.4.

If we want to produce a prediction of an individual value rather than an estimate of a mean of a set of values, with a given level of confidence, we can do so by producing what is called a *prediction interval*. This is to distinguish this type of forecast from a confidence interval, which is a term reserved for estimates of population measures.

The procedure we use to produce prediction intervals is very similar to the one we have used to produce confidence intervals

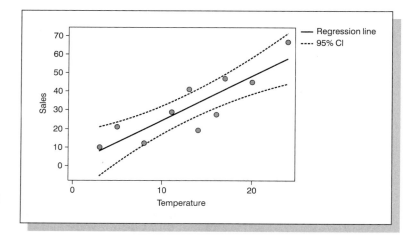

Figure 9.4
Ninety-five per cent confidence intervals for the data in Example 9.6

for means of values of dependent variables. It is represented by the formula:

$$\text{Prediction interval} = \hat{y} \pm t_{\alpha/2,\, n-2} \times s \sqrt{1 + \frac{1}{n} + \frac{(x_0 - \bar{x})^2}{\Sigma\, (x - \bar{x})^2}}$$

If you look carefully you can see that the difference between this and the formula for a confidence interval is that we have added one to the expression under the square root sign. The effect of this will be to widen the interval considerably. This is to reflect the fact that individual values vary more than statistical measures like means, which are based on sets of values.

Example 9.11

Construct a 95 per cent prediction interval for the sales of cans of soft drinks in the garage in Example 9.6 on a day when the temperature is 22° Celsius.

$$\text{Prediction interval} = \hat{y} \pm t_{\alpha/2,\, n-2} \times s \sqrt{1 + \frac{1}{n} + \frac{(x_0 - \bar{x})^2}{\Sigma\, (x - \bar{x})^2}}$$

$$= 53.1 \pm 2.306 \times 9.347 \sqrt{[1 + (1/10 + (22 - 13.1)^2/388.90)}$$

$$= 53.1 \pm 2.306 \times 9.347 \sqrt{1.304}$$

$$= 53.1 \pm 2.306 \times 10.67$$

$$= 53.1 \pm 24.60 = 28.50 \text{ to } 77.70 \text{ to two decimal places}$$

If you compare the prediction interval in Example 9.11 to the confidence interval in Example 9.9 you will see that the prediction interval is much wider, although the level of confidence involved, 95 per cent, is the same.

Just like confidence intervals produced using regression models, prediction intervals are more dependable if they are based on x values nearer the mean of the x values. Prediction intervals based on x values that are well outside the range that we have in our sample are of no use.

Producing interval estimates from regression models is rather laborious when we have to use a formula and carry out the calculations ourselves. MINITAB will produce both confidence intervals and prediction intervals for you. Select **Regression** from the **Stat** menu then **Regression** from the sub-menu. Specify the column locations of the **Response** and **Predictor** variables, that is, Y and X respectively, in the command window then click the **Options** button. In the **Options** window there is a box labelled

Prediction intervals for new observations. Type the x value that you want the package to use to produce the intervals in the box, then **OK**. If you want intervals based on several different x values, put them in a column in the worksheet and type the column location in the **Prediction intervals for new observations** box. The confidence and prediction intervals, labelled 'CI' and 'PI' respectively, will appear at the end of the regression analysis.

The usefulness of the estimates that you produce from a regression model depends to a large extent on the size of the sample that you have. The larger the sample on which your regression model is based, the more precise and confident your predictions and estimates will be.

As we have seen, the width of the intervals increases the further the x value is away from the mean of the x values, and estimates and predictions based on x values outside the range of x values in our sample are useless. So, if you want to construct intervals based on specific values of x, try to ensure that these values are within the range of x values in your sample.

9.2.5 When simple linear models won't do the job

So far we have concentrated on the simple linear regression model. Although it is used extensively and is the appropriate model in very many cases, some sets of bivariate data show patterns that cannot be represented adequately by a simple linear model. If you use such data to test hypotheses about the slopes of linear models you will probably find that the slopes are not significant. This may be because the relationship between the variables is non-linear and therefore the best-fit model will be some form of curve.

Example 9.12

A retail analyst wants to investigate the efficiency of the operations of a large supermarket chain. She has taken a random sample of 22 of their stores and produced the following plot of the weekly sales per square foot of selling area (in pounds) against the sales area of the store (in 000s ft^2).

It is clear from Figure 9.5 that the relationship between the two variables does not appear to take the form of a straight line. In these circumstances to fit a line you would have to look to the methods of non-linear regression. The variety of non-linear models means that it is not possible to discuss them here, but they are covered in Bates and Watts (1988) and Seber and Wild (1989). Non-linear models themselves can look daunting but in

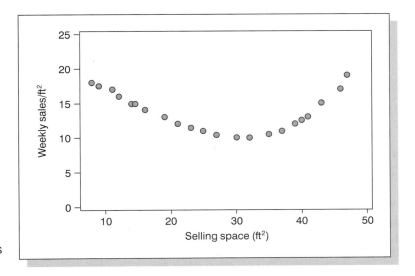

Figure 9.5
Sales per square foot and sales area

essence using them typically involves transforming the data so that the simple linear regression technique can be applied; in effect you 'straighten' the data to use the straight-line model.

The simple linear regression model you produce for a set of data may not be effective because the true relationship is non-linear. But it might be that the two variables that you are trying to relate are not the whole story; perhaps there are other factors that should be taken into account. One way of looking into this is to use the residual plots available in MINITAB. Select **Regression** from the **Regression** sub-menu of the **Stat** menu. Once you have specified the column locations of the **Response** and **Predictor** variables in the command window, click **Graphs.** Click next to **Residuals versus fits** then click **OK** and **OK** on the **Regression** command window. The graph that appears is the plot of the residuals against the fits (the values of the Y variable that should, according to the line, have occurred). This shows whether there is some systematic variation not explained by the model.

Example 9.13

Produce a plot of the residuals against fits for the best-fit simple linear regression model for the temperature and sales data in Example 9.6.

There is no apparent systematic pattern to the scatter in Figure 9.6 so we would conclude that there is no case for looking for another variable to include in the model; the simple linear model appears to be suitable.

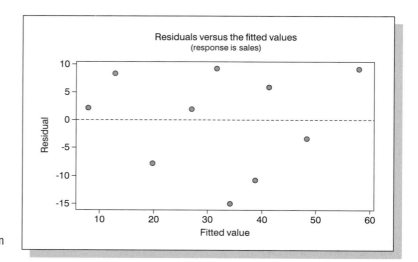

Figure 9.6
A residual plot for the model in
Example 9.6

Example 9.14

Produce a plot of the residuals against fits for the best-fit simple linear regression model
for the supermarket data in Example 9.12.

In Figure 9.7 there is clearly a pattern of variation in the residuals.
It appears that the stores with smaller sales areas and the stores
with larger sales areas seem to have higher sales rates than
medium-sized stores. If this company has modern smaller stores
in prime city-centre locations that perform well and modern large

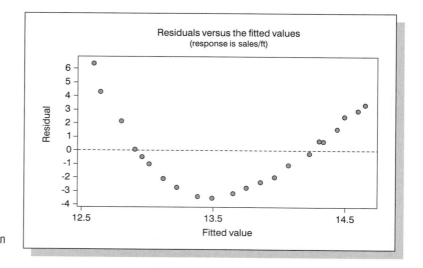

Figure 9.7
A residual plot for the model in
Example 9.12

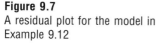

stores on new retail parks that also perform well, yet also had stores that were constructed in the 1970s in locations where the income of the local population has fallen, then it is clear that other factors such as the age of the store should be included. We should consider regressing the sales variable not just against one variable, the sales area, but another variable as well. The appropriate technique for this is multiple regression, a technique that is outside the scope of this book, but covered in Dielman (1996), Draper and Smith (1998) and Mendenhall and Sincich (1989).

Review questions

Answers to these questions, including fully worked solutions to those questions marked with an asterisk (*), are on pages 356–358.

9.1 As part of a survey of commuting patterns a random sample of 120 employees at a large administrative complex were asked how they travelled to work and whether they considered there were enough car parking spaces at the complex

	Mode of travel:	
	Car	Other
Enough parking spaces	27	23
Not enough parking spaces	53	17

Test the hypothesis that there is no association between mode of travel and opinion on parking places:

(a) At the 5 per cent level of significance.
(b) At the 1 per cent level of significance.

9.2* A mail-order company has commissioned market research in an attempt to find whether there is a connection between the type of area that people live in and if they buy from mail-order companies. The following table gives the results from a random sample of 150 people:

	Area:		
	Urban	Suburban	Rural
Use mail-order	14	33	31
Don't use mail-order	26	37	9

Test the hypothesis that there is no association between the area people live in and their use of mail-order companies using a 1 per cent level of significance.

9.3 A leak of a hazardous substance at a factory threatens the health of the workforce. A random sample of 80 employees had their contamination levels checked. The results were:

Level of contamination	Department: Production	Administration
High	11	4
Medium	24	10
Low	15	16

Test the hypothesis that there is no association between department and contamination level. Use a 5 per cent level of significance.

9.4 A clothing retailer operates a 'no-questions' returns policy that enables customers to return goods and get their money back as long as they have proof of purchase. A random sample of 500 transactions were tracked in order to find out whether there is a connection between type of garment and the likelihood of returns.

	Garment type: Ladies'	Men's	Children's
Returned	37	14	19
Not returned	163	106	161

Test for association between garment type and whether or not a garment is returned using a 5 per cent level of significance.

9.5 In a survey a random sample of 200 adults were each asked whether they preferred talk or music radio. The results, broken down by socio-economic class were:

	Talk	Music
AB	16	24
C1C2	27	43
DE	41	49

Does this set of data suggest there is significant association between socio-economic class and listening preference at the 10 per cent level of significance?

9.6 A multinational company owns four plants in Europe. The International HR Director has produced the following table, based on data about a random sample of 250 employees, as part of an analysis of union membership patterns:

| | Plant location: | | | |
	Belgium	Germany	Spain	UK
Members of a union	26	62	41	37
Not members of a union	14	18	29	23

Is there evidence of association

(a) At the 10 per cent level of significance?
(b) At the 5 per cent level of significance?

9.7 A survey of a random sample of 320 pet owners undertaken by a petfood manufacturer yielded the following data about type of pet and size of household:

| | Type of household: | | |
Pet	Single person	Couple	Family
Dog	31	40	55
Cat	67	17	12
Other	52	13	33

(a) Using a 1 per cent level of significance test for association between type of pet and type of household.
(b) Examine the components of the test statistic and comment on the patterns they reveal.

9.8 In a survey a random sample of 140 male teenagers from different regions of the UK were each asked to name their favourite sport. The responses are given in the following table:

| | | Region: | |
Favourite sport	North	Midlands	South
Cricket	12	7	16
Football	19	25	27
Rugby	9	8	17

Test for association between region and sport preference using a 10 per cent level of significance, and comment on any prominent component of the test statistic.

9.9 A survey of the cinema-going habits of a random sample of 500 children, adults of working age, and retirees produced the follow responses to the question 'How often do you go to the cinema?'

	Never	Rarely	Sometimes	Frequently
Children	8	15	56	21
Adults	19	83	111	37
Retirees	47	39	30	34

Test the hypothesis that there is no association at the 1 per cent level of significance and interpret any particularly large components of the test statistic.

9.10* In an investigation into household expenditure on home entertainment products researchers studied a random sample of 28 households. They found that there was a correlation coefficient of +0.683 between the amount spent on home entertainment products and household income. Test the hypothesis that there is no positive correlation between household income and expenditure on home entertainment products using a 5 per cent level of significance.

9.11 The correlation coefficient between the percentage increase in profits and the percentage increase in share price on the day the profits were announced for a random sample of 19 publicly quoted companies was +0.490. Test the hypothesis of no positive correlation at the 5 per cent level of significance.

9.12 An HR consultant undertook a survey of a random sample of 52 employees of a large bank. She found a correlation coefficient of −0.377 between the satisfaction level reported by employees and the length of service they had achieved. Test the hypothesis that there is significant negative correlation at the 1 per cent level.

9.13* A promoter stages 'disco classics' on an occasional basis at a large city-centre venue. Teams of casual employees hand out 'discount' ticket cards at colleges and music venues to advertise these events. The number of cards handed out before each of the ten events staged so far, and the audience they attracted are given below.

Number of cards:	3750	4100	4500	4750	4800	5250	4600	4800	4320
Audience:	925	1000	1150	1200	1100	1680	1480	1370	860

(a) Find the least squares regression equation and test the hypothesis, at the 5 per cent level of significance, that the population slope is zero.

(b) Construct a 95 per cent confidence interval for the mean number of people attracted to an event when 4400 cards have been distributed.

9.14 The number of cash machines in a random sample of eight towns, and the population of the towns are:

Cash machines	20	23	28	41	53	46	82	126
Population (000s)	37	51	69	72	90	105	163	227

(a) Regress the number of cash machines against population and test the hypothesis that the population slope is zero at the 5 per cent level of significance.

(b) Produce a 95 per cent confidence interval for the mean number of cash machines in towns with a population of 80 000 people.

9.15 An auctioneer has recorded the profit made at a random sample of eight auctions and the number of people attending each of them.

Attendance	100	120	140	250	420	470	580	650
Profit (£)	275	192	380	372	518	611	546	973

(a) Find the regression equation and test the hypothesis that the population slope is zero at the 5 per cent level of significance.

(b) Produce a 95 per cent confidence interval for the mean profit from auctions that attract 300 people.

(c) Produce a 95 per cent prediction interval for the profit that can be expected from a single auction that attracts 300 people.

9.16 A new office block is being built fifteen miles from the location of an international financial centre. A study of the number of inquiries from prospective tenants received by a random sample of nine recently let office blocks in the area showed that the number of inquiries and the distances, in miles, between the office blocks and the financial centre were:

Inquiries	35	61	74	92	113	159	188	217	328
Distance	28	20	17	12	16	8	2	3	1

(a) Find the regression equation and test the hypothesis, at the 5 per cent level of significance, that the population slope is zero.

(b) Produce a 95 per cent confidence interval for the mean number of inquiries from prospective tenants for office blocks 15 miles from the financial centre could expect.

(c) Produce a 95 per cent prediction interval for the number of inquiries that could be expected for one office block 15 miles from the financial centre.

9.17   The engine capacity (in litres) and the fuel efficiency (in miles per gallon) of a random sample of 10 petrol-driven cars are:

Capacity   1.0 1.2 1.4 1.6 2.0 2.4 2.5 2.8 3.2 4.0
Fuel efficiency 44   47   41   37   33   30   25   26   23   21

(a) Determine the regression equation and test the hypothesis that the population slope is zero using a 1 per cent level of significance.

(b) Construct a 99 per cent confidence interval for the mean fuel efficiency of cars with an engine capacity of 1.8 litres.

(c) Construct a 99 per cent prediction interval for the fuel efficiency of a car with an engine capacity of 1.8 litres.

9.18   The ages and annual expenditure on traditional suits by a random sample of eight males belonging to the AB socio-economic class were:

Age   27   29   33   34   39   42   49   56
Expenditure (£) 280 400 650 800 1200 1100 1250 1800

(a) Regress expenditure against age and test the hypothesis of a zero population slope at the 10 per cent level of significance.

(b) Produce a 90 per cent confidence interval for 35-year-old AB class males' mean annual expenditure on suits.

(c) Produce a 90 per cent confidence interval for 75-year-old AB class males' mean annual expenditure on suits.

(d) Compare your answers to (b) and (c). Which is the more valid, and why?

9.19   A college canteen has a selection of pre-packed sandwiches on sale. The prices of each of the 10 types of sandwich on sale and the number sold on a single day selected at random were:

Price (£)	1.20	1.30	1.35	1.40	1.55	1.60	1.75	1.90	2.05	2.10
Sales	27	23	20	24	17	14	7	12	3	6

(a) Find the best-fit regression model and test the null hypothesis that the slope of the population line of best fit is zero using a 1 per cent level of significance.

(b) Obtain 99 per cent confidence intervals for the mean sales of sandwiches that cost (i) £1.80, and (ii) £2.75. Which of these estimates is likely to be the more reliable, and why?

9.20   Select the appropriate definition from the list on the right-hand side for the terms and symbols listed on the left-hand side.

(a) ρ

(b) contingency test

(c) χ^2

(d) α

(e) β

(f) p-value

(g) confidence interval

(h) prediction interval

(i)   the intercept of the population regression line

(ii) an interval estimate of a population measure

(iii) the probability that a null hypothesis is true

(iv) the slope of the population regression line

(v)   the population correlation coefficient

(vi) an interval estimate of an individual value

(vii) a test of association between characteristics

(viii) a test statistic used in tests of association

'Going solo . . .'

CHAPTER **10**

Managing statistical research

Chapter Objectives

This chapter will help you:

- To plan statistical work for a project.
- To consider different means of obtaining data.
- To undertake sample surveys.
- To present your results effectively.

In this chapter you will find:

- Suggestions on managing time for statistical research.
- Advice on using secondary data.
- Approaches to sample selection.
- Guidance on questionnaire design.

When you reach the final stage of your course, or possibly earlier, you will probably be told that one of the course requirements is that you produce a final-year project or dissertation. This typically means that you have to identify a project idea, write a project proposal, undertake research to investigate your project idea, and then produce a substantial written document that delivers your findings.

You may see this as a daunting task, particularly when you are trying to think of ideas for a project, but if you approach it positively and manage the task well you can get a great deal out of it. A good final-year project could improve the grade of the qualification that you receive. It could also be a useful document to show potential employers as an example of your work.

Your project is probably the first, if not the only time during you course when your tutors offer you the opportunity to study what you like. The parts of your course that you have done so far have probably consisted of studying things that somebody else has decided you should do. Your project is different; it is 'your baby'.

It is very hard to produce a good project if you are not committed to it, so it is worth putting time and effort into thinking up three or four possible ideas at a very early stage. But how can you generate project ideas? It may help if you ask yourself a series of questions:

- Which parts of the course have I enjoyed most?

- Were there any particularly interesting aspects of my experience of work?

- What interests do I have outside my studies?

- What are my academic strengths?

- Do I have any special contacts and resources at my disposal?

Make a list of your responses to these questions. Look at the responses in relation to one another; perhaps there are some interesting combinations? You may have enjoyed Marketing as a subject, you may have worked at a football ground on a part-time basis, and you may have a strong interest in football. If all this is true then perhaps a project that looks into how football clubs market season tickets is a possibility?

If you have thought about your responses and no project ideas come to mind, try talking through your responses with somebody else, perhaps a friend or a tutor. It doesn't matter too much if that person is not involved with your course, simply explaining your thinking to somebody else may prompt some excellent project ideas.

Once you have established at least one viable project idea you will probably have to shape your outline ideas into a formal proposal and carry out some sort of literature survey. A good proposal will identify specific propositions and hypotheses that your project is intended to investigate. A good literature survey will find what published material is available through your college library or electronically on the subject you have chosen. This is important because it will influence the nature and scope of the research you will have to undertake.

At this stage you need to consider the data that you will need for your investigation. Perhaps the data is available from published or electronic sources, if not, you will have to consider how you can obtain it yourself. In fact you will probably find that some of the data you need is already available but other data will need to be collected.

Data that is already available, perhaps in a publication in a library or on the Internet, is there because somebody else collected and analysed it. As far as you are concerned it is secondary data, in other words 'second-hand'. Whoever has produced it did so to fulfil their requirements rather than yours, so be careful.

As we shall see later on in this chapter when you collect data yourself, that is, when you gather primary or first-hand data, you will have to decide what to ask, who to ask, and so on. These are issues that require careful thought.

Whether the data you analyse in your work is primary or secondary, you will have to consider how to present the analysis in your final document. This is something we will consider in the last section of the chapter.

10.1 Secondary data

If you use secondary data it is the person or agency that collected the data that has decided how the data was collected. You have had no say in the matter. You also have had no say in the way in which the data is presented to you. It may be that the secondary data that you have found is exactly what you require for your investigation, and it could be already presented in a form that will suit your purposes. But you need to look into both of these issues carefully.

There are a number of questions you should consider about the collection of secondary data. First, exactly when was it collected? Published results are by definition historic, they relate to the past. This is inevitable because publication takes time. The data may be fairly recent if it is in a journal or on a web site, but may be much older if it is in a book.

If you are researching a field that has changed relatively little since the publication of the secondary data that you have found then data published some time ago may still be useful.

However, if your field of research is rapidly changing then ageing secondary data is likely to be of limited value to you. If you decide to use it you will have to caution your readers about its validity as a reflection of the current situation and explain how what has happened since the data was collected has reduced its usefulness.

If you want to use the data as the basis of a comparison between then and now, the age of the data is what makes it useful. You will of course need to make sure that if you collect data as part of your investigation of the current situation, you generate data that can be compared to the secondary data. This means you will have to ask or measure the same sort of things about the same sort of sample.

A second issue that you need to look at is how the secondary data was collected. Unless the results are about a small population, it is sample data. So, how large was the sample? How were the people or items in the sample selected? Was it a random or at least representative sample of the population it came from?

If the population consisted of things, how were the items in the sample measured or counted? If the population consisted of people, how were they asked for the data they provided?

You will probably have to study the source in which you found the secondary data very carefully to find the answers to these questions. Look for a section called 'Methodology', which should explain the methods used to gather the data. Look through any footnotes or notes at the end of the source for information about how the data was collected, any difficulties the researchers had, and any warnings they give about the validity of their results.

You may be fortunate in finding secondary data that is sufficiently up to date and collected properly. If this is the case the next thing you have to think about is the way in which the secondary data is presented in the secondary source.

The author or authors who prepared the secondary source may have included their original data in their publication, perhaps in an appendix, so check the source carefully. If the original data is included you will be able to consider various ways in which you can present their data in your report. You can decide which form of presentation will be most appropriate for your discussion of the data.

However, it is more likely that the researchers who collected the original data have not included it in their published results. This is almost inevitable if the study they undertook was a large one. The data will probably be presented in the form of statistical measures and diagrams. You may find that although the forms of presentation that have been used in the secondary source may not be the ones that you would have chosen, they are ones that will be appropriate for your discussion.

If the form of presentation used in the published source will not be appropriate for your report the first thing to consider is alternative ways of presenting the data that can be based on the form in which it is published. If the secondary source contains a grouped frequency distribution, you can produce a histogram or an approximation of the mean from it. If they have used a contingency table, you can produce a bar chart, and so on.

But you may not be able to present the data in the form you would like using the forms that appear in the secondary source. This may be a problem if you are trying to compare two or more studies from different points in time or locations.

If you really would like to present the data in forms that cannot be based on the data as it is published, then it is worth contacting the authors of the study directly to ask whether you can get access to the original data. If this seems rude remember that the secondary source you have found has been produced by people who have probably spent considerable time and effort in carrying out their research and are quite justifiably proud of it. They would probably welcome any inquiry about their work, particularly from somebody like you, who is undertaking their own research and may well introduce their work to a new audience. Authors of published articles often provide details of the place they work or an e-mail address so that interested readers can contact them. At the very worst they can only turn down your request or ignore it.

It is also worth contacting authors of secondary sources if you have any questions about their research, or if they know of any follow-up work that has been done on it. However, you must give them time to respond to your request. Perhaps they have changed jobs, or are simply too busy to reply to you right away. Try to contact them at least a month or two before the latest time you would need to have their response in order to make use of it.

When you prepare your project report for submission you must make sure that you acknowledge the sources of all secondary data that you use, even if the form in which it is presented in your report is your own work. There is nothing at all wrong with quoting data or text from other publications in your report as long as you cite the reference, in other words indicate clearly using a recognized style such as the Harvard system where it came from.

10.2 Primary data

Often the main difficulty in using secondary data for a project is that it may not fit your requirements. It may not be the data that you would like to have to support the arguments and discussion that you want to develop in your work. You can get around this by collecting primary data. The advantage of doing this is that the data will be up to date and it should be exactly what you want for your project. The disadvantage is that collecting primary data requires careful thought, detailed planning, and plenty of time.

You will have to decide if you are going to collect primary data as early as possible. You should try to identify your data requirements at the same stage as you produce your literature survey. Successful primary data collection is very difficult to do successfully in a short period of time.

After you have identified your data requirements you will need to address two questions: first, from whom can you get the data and second, how will you be able to get it?

If you require data that you yourself can collect by undertaking experiments in a particular place such as a laboratory, or by making direct observations then the first of these questions is answered. You will next need to consider the second question. This means you will have to identify the method of investigation or the means of observation, define the population, decide how large the sample you will study needs to be and how you will select it.

However, much research in the business sphere involves getting data from individuals or organizations. If this is true in your case then define the types of people or organizations carefully. If the number of people or organizations that fit your definition is quite small then you might carry out a survey of the whole population. This situation is rare, so you will probably have to take a sample from the population.

10.2.1 Selecting your sample

The approach you take to selecting a sample depends on whether you can list all the things, people or organizations that make up the population you want to investigate. Such a list is called a *sampling frame*. If you can do this, which is possible if you are looking, for instance, at quoted companies in the UK, then there are a number of ways in which you can select your sample.

If you want to select a random sample, number each item listed on your sampling frame. One way of picking your random sample is called the lottery method. Put one numbered ticket for each entry on the list into some sort of receptacle, traditionally a hat, and blindly pick the same number of tickets from the hat as the number of items that you want in your sample. You could write numbers on pieces of paper but it is much easier to buy a set of raffle tickets.

An alternative way of getting a random sample is to use random numbers. These are not, as the name may suggest, numbers that just come into your head (which would not be random), but sequences of numbers generated at random using computer software. You can get such a sequence from EXCEL by selecting the **Data Analysis** option from the **Tools** menu. Choose the **Random Number Generation** option from the list in the command window.

The way you use the random number depends on how many elements there are in your sampling frame. If there are less than ten, take a sequence of random numbers and use them one at a time to pick your sample. If there are up to a hundred in your sampling frame, use the random numbers two at a time. If you have up to a thousand, use them three at a time and so on.

Example 10.1

A sampling frame identifies 68 companies that have offices in a former Soviet republic. We want to study a random sample of 10 of these companies. The following sequence of random numbers has been produced to help us select a sample:

15030   61249   01802   91561   93175   1

The sampling frame consists of less than 100 entries so we take the random numbers two at a time:

15   03   06   12   49   01   80   29   15   61   93   17   51

The first pair is 15, so the first company in our sample will be the one that appears 15th in the sampling frame. The second pair is 03, so we pick the third company on the list. As we continue we find that the seventh pair of numbers is 80, which means that the seventh company we should select is the one that appears 80th on the list. As we only have 68 companies on the list we ignore the 80 and use the next pair, 29, to select our seventh company. This means the next pair, 15, should be used to select the eighth company. But we have already picked the 15th company, so again we take the next pair of numbers instead, 61.

MINITAB offers a more direct approach to making a random selection. List the number of each of the entries on your sampling frame in a worksheet column. If you have a lengthy sampling frame it will be easier to use the **Make Patterned Data** option on the **Calc** menu, then choose **Simple Set of Numbers** from the sub-menu and you can ask it to generate the list of numbers for you. Once the list is in a column, choose **Random Data** from the **Calc** menu, then **Sample from Columns** from the sub-menu. In the command window you will have to specify the size of the sample, the column where you have located the numbers, and the column where you would like the package to store the random selection it makes.

In general, random sampling is the best way of selecting your sample because it means you will be able to use statistical decision-making techniques to generalize from your results. However, you may need to modify the approach in order to make sure that a balanced sample is produced. This is important when the population is composed of clearly divided categories and you want to ensure that each category is represented in your sample. Such categories are called strata and the method we use to take a sample from such a population is called stratified sampling.

To use stratified sampling you need to identify how many elements in the population belong to each category. You have to work out the proportion of the population that you want to have in your sample and apply this proportion to the number of elements in each category to find out how many need to be selected from each category. You can then use random sampling to make the selection from each category.

Example 10.2

An organization has 500 employees. Of these, 200 are based at Aberdeen, 180 at Barnet and 120 at Canterbury. We want to select a sample of 100 of the organization's employees.

The sample will consist of 20 per cent of the organization's employees so we will select a random sample of 20 per cent of the employees at each site. To make up our sample we will select a random sample of 20 per cent of the employees at Aberdeen, 20 per cent from Barnet and 20 per cent from Canterbury. The 40 we choose from Aberdeen, with the 36 from Barnet and the 24 from Canterbury will give us the sample of 100.

Using stratified sampling is particularly useful if you want to perform contingency analysis on your data. It should enable you to avoid having too few data in some categories and not being able to get valid test results.

The methods of sampling that we have looked at so far assume that it is possible to compile a list of elements in the population, a sampling frame. But what if this is not possible? Perhaps the population is very large or it is not possible to identify all of the elements in it.

If you can't produce a sampling frame you could use cluster sampling to select a sample. This is a good approach to take if the population is finite. For instance, you may want to study a sample of 'Do-It-Yourself' shops in the UK. There are many of these, but not so many that we could describe the number of them as infinite. Constructing a sampling frame may be difficult if they are not all listed in a readily available source.

To apply cluster sampling to produce a sample in such circumstances would mean dividing the UK into areas and selecting a small random sample of areas. Sub-divide these areas into smaller areas and select a small random sample of each of them. Keep going until you have a suitable number of small areas. You then study every element in each of the small areas you have selected.

Using cluster sampling is easier if you use existing ways in which the areas are divided to make your selections. The way in which the UK is divided up on maps and between different telephone directories and postcodes can provide useful frameworks for cluster sampling.

You should be wary of using cluster sampling if your method of data collection entails visiting each person or organization or location in your sample. The expense of making visits to a selection of far-flung areas may be prohibitive. You can reduce the prospect of this somewhat by excluding areas that you could not feasibly visit.

If you need to select a sample from a very large population, such as the general public, then the construction of a sampling frame is just not feasible. For instance, suppose you want to interview a sample of 100 people in the UK to find out about their attitude to computer games. You could find the most recent electoral roll of the UK population, use it as a sampling frame and select from it a random sample of 100 people, but this would be a huge task.

It would be much more feasible to take a clipboard and ask 100 people that you approach on the street. However, if you do this you should try to ensure that the sample you select is balanced. If you want to research the relationship between gender and attitudes to computer games then you will not be able to do so effectively if your sample consists of 99 men and 1 woman. If you want to contrast the opinions of school students with those of others you won't be able to do so if you conduct your interviews on a working day during a school term.

To make sure that you get a balanced sample from this sort of investigation use quota sampling. Suppose you want to make sure that a sample of 100 people is balanced by gender and whether or not the respondents are school students. You might decide to interview a quota of 25 male school students, a quota of 25 female school students, a quota of 25 adult males, and a quota of 25 adult females. This would mean that once you have interviewed the 25th male school student you don't bother interviewing any more male school students and so on.

10.2.2 Choosing the size of your sample

As well as deciding how you will select your sample you need to decide how large it should be. Basically the larger the sample, the better, but also the larger the sample, the more time and resources will be required to collect the data. There are two issues that you have to consider. The first is how large a data set you will need in order to use the techniques you would like to use to analyse it.

The second issue is the proportion of inquiries that will be successful, the response rate.

Although we can say that the larger the sample, the better, we should add that the larger the sample, the less the marginal advantage of a large sample tends to be. For instance, a sample that consists of 30 elements means we will be able to use the Standard Normal Distribution in any statistical decision making based on the sample data and the sample doesn't have to come from a Normal population. So having a sample that consists of at least 30 elements is to our advantage. The extra advantage of having a sample much larger than 30, for instance 100, is not so great, in fact so little that it may be difficult to justify the extra time involved.

If you need to produce inference results to a particular degree of precision and level of confidence then you must calculate the minimum sample size you should use. Sections 8.1.1 and 8.2.1 in Chapter 8 illustrate how this is done.

If you plan to carry out contingency analysis on your sample data to test for association between characteristics, then you have to take into account the number of categories in each of the characteristics. Suppose you want to ask a sample of respondents from five different geographical regions their opinion of five different types of leisure activity, then the contingency table you will be using for your results will have five rows and five columns, making 25 cells in all. If your sample consists of 100 respondents then the sample data will be spread around these cells far too thinly. If you cannot reduce the number of categories you will have to increase the sample size as well as use cluster sampling to ensure that your results are substantial enough to make your conclusions reasonably sound.

You should also consider that the sample size is not necessarily the same as the number of people or organizations that you will need to approach for data. The reason is that some of them will be disinclined or unable to respond to your request. The proportion of responses that are successful is the *response rate*.

The response rate you achieve will depend partly on the method you use to collect your data and there are a number of things that you can do to make the response rate higher. We will look at these in the next section. However, when you are planning your data collection you need to build a figure for the response rate into your calculations.

Response rates vary widely, but in most investigations like the one you are undertaking a response rate of more than 40 per cent, which means that more than 40 per cent of requests made are successful, would be considered very good. A response rate of less than 20 per cent, on the other hand, would be considered poor.

To make sure that you get enough responses to satisfy your sample size requirements multiply the sample size you need by a factor of three, or even four if your requests will be difficult for your respondents to fulfil. This means that if, for the purposes of your analysis you need a sample of 30, then you should approach a sample of 90, or even 120.

10.2.3 Methods of collecting primary data

If the primary data that you require will be collected as a result of experiments you will be carrying out in laboratory-style conditions, planning the process of collection involves allocating your time and making sure you have access to the appropriate facilities when you need to use them. The process of collection is under your control. You should allow sufficient time for conducting the experiments and, if you are wise some extra margin of time in case something goes wrong. Even if things go badly wrong there is every chance that you will be able to reschedule your other work in order to complete your research in time to be able to use the data.

Although there are areas of research in the field of business that do involve this sort of work, for instance research into workplace ergonomics, it is much more likely that your project will involve seeking information from other people or organizations. If your project involves collecting data from others, your planning needs to take into account that you do not control their actions. You will have to consider how and when to make your requests very carefully and allow time in your schedule for the organizations or people who will be asked for data to make their response.

You must start by being absolutely clear about the information you want from them. If you do not understand this, how can you expect them to understand your request? Probably the least effective approach that you could make is to write to them, tell them what your project is about and ask them if they can supply you with any relevant information. At the very best they will send you a leaflet about their business that will probably be of little value to you. Most likely they will not respond to your request at all. After all, if you don't take the trouble to be clear about your information needs why should they take the trouble to help you?

So, you have to be absolutely clear about what you want to know, who will be able to give you the information you need, and how you plan to ask them for it. You will have to be precise about your requirements, make sure you are approaching the right people and ask them for what you need in such a way that they will find it as easy as possible to help you.

If your respondents are individuals, make sure that you have the correct name and address for every one of them. If your respondents are people who hold certain types of posts within organizations, make sure you have the correct name, job title, and business address for every one of them. Getting these details right will improve your response rate. The fastest way that anything you send gets binned is if it isn't directed to a named individual.

Your request for information should be made in the form of a business letter. It must be word-processed and you should use appropriate opening and closing formalities, after all you are not writing to a friend. The letter should explain clearly to the recipient who you are, what research you are undertaking, and how they can help you. The final paragraph should thank them in anticipation of their help.

You may prefer to send out your questionnaire electronically. The advantage is that it is usually quicker and cheaper. The disadvantage is that the recipient can dismiss it as yet another piece of junk email and delete it. To reduce the risk of this happening it is even more important to express the request in a suitably polite and formal style, and to ensure that your questionnaire is as concise as possible.

On balance, unless you have a particular reason for using e-mail to send your questionnaire, for instance you may want to survey respondents abroad, it is probably better to use the postal service. The amount of postal junk mail that your recipients receive is probably less than the amount of junk e-mail they receive. In addition many older respondents will treat a request by letter much more seriously than they will an e-mail message.

What you ask your respondents to do depends on the depth and breadth of the information that you are seeking. If you only want one or two pieces of data, then simply ask for this in your letter, making sure that you are as precise as possible about your requirements. For instance, if you want a figure relating to a particular year or location, then say so.

If you need information in depth, such as opinion and comment on particular issues, then consider requesting an interview with each of your respondents. If you decide to do this, ask for an interview in your letter and explain in the letter what sort of issues you would like to ask them about. To make it easy to compare the results from the different respondents, conduct *structured interviews*, interviews that consist of the same framework of primary and supplementary questions.

If you need a broad range of information, then you will probably have to design and use a questionnaire. This is a standard document that consists of a series of questions and spaces for the respondent to provide written responses.

Before you start compiling a questionnaire, make sure that it is the most appropriate method of collecting the data you need. Good questionnaire research is not easy to conduct, so explore all other ways of assembling the data you need first.

Unfortunately, there are many final-year students who have launched themselves straight into collecting data using questionnaires without thinking things through. One student studying the effectiveness of special hospitality events in boosting sales sent a questionnaire to every member of the Marketing Department of a multinational IT company. She asked each respondent to say how many new sales leads had come from special events over the previous year. The Administrative Officer in the Marketing Department had this information at her fingertips. In that case one well-directed letter would have produced better results more quickly than the 50 or so questionnaires the student sent out.

However, if you want responses to many precise questions from many respondents, then a questionnaire is probably the best way of getting them. If you do it properly, questionnaire research will give you the data you need at relatively little expense. But done badly, questionnaire research can result in poor response rates and inappropriate data.

So, how can we undertake questionnaire research to maximize the chances of good results? The key is to design the questionnaire carefully and to test it before sending it out to all the respondents in your sample. If you make the effort to produce a questionnaire that is straightforward for your respondents to complete, you will get a higher response rate.

You should send the questionnaire out with the letter requesting help from your respondents. If you do not send it out with an accompanying letter, perhaps because you will be distributing it personally, insert a message thanking your respondents for their help at the top of the questionnaire. If you want your respondents to return the completed questionnaires by post, you can improve the chances of them doing so by enclosing a self-addressed envelope with the questionnaire.

You may also be able to improve the chances of getting a good response rate if you offer 'lures' for respondents who return completed questionnaires such as entry into a raffle for a prize, or a copy of your results when they are available. The effectiveness of these depends largely on the respondents you are targeting. The raffle prize is probably a better bet if you are contacting individuals, whereas your results may be more useful when your respondents have a specific type of role within organizations and may well have a specialist interest in your field of research.

Aim to restrict the length of the questionnaire to two sides. This will make the task of completing it feel less onerous for your respondents and make it easier for you to collate the results at a later stage.

The sequence in which you pose the questions needs careful thought. You may want to know some details about the respondents, such as the time they have worked in their current post, or their qualifications. It is probably best to ask these sorts of questions first, because they will be easy for your respondents to answer, and once they have started filling in your questionnaire they are likely to finish it.

Sometimes researchers will put questions that seek personal information at the very end of the questionnaire. They do this because they are concerned that putting requests for personal information first makes the questionnaire seem too intrusive and respondents will be wary about completing it. This is a matter of judgement. Unless the questions you use to request personal information are invasive, it is probably better to put them first.

Arrange the questions that you want to put in your questionnaire in a logical sequence. Avoid jumping from one topic to another. You may find it useful to arrange the questionnaire in sections, with each section containing a set of questions about a particular topic or theme.

Design the questions so that they will be easy for your respondents to answer and so that the answers will be easy for you to collate. Avoid open-ended questions like 'What do you think about Internet marketing?' Many respondents will be deterred from answering questions like this because they feel they have to write a sentence or a paragraph to respond to them. You will find the responses difficult to analyse because there will probably be no obvious way of segregating and arranging them. At best you will be able to put them into broad categories of response.

You will find the results far easier to analyse if you build the categories into the questions. In some cases these categories are obvious, such as female and male for gender. In other cases you may need to establish the categories yourself, for instance types of qualification.

If you want to find what opinions your respondents have, you might use rating scales. One way of doing this is to make a statement and invite your respondents to express the strength of their agreement or disagreement with the statement using a numerical scale. For instance, we might ask respondents to give their assessment of the statement,

> 'Internet marketing is vital for the future of our business.'

We could ask them to indicate their opinion by giving us a rating on a scale of 1 to 5, where 1 is strong agreement with the statement and 5 is strong disagreement with the statement.

The data we get from questions that use rating scales is often described as 'soft', to suggest that is likely to be a little vague or erratic. The adjectives 'firm' or 'hard', on the other hand, describe data that is clear and consistent.

The reason that data collected by means of rating scales is probably soft is that the scales are subject to the interpretation of the respondents. Different respondents will have different perceptions of concepts like 'strong agreement'. Two people may have identical viewpoints but one may consider it to be 'strong agreement' and put a '1' whereas the other may consider it 'general agreement' and put a '2'. We would not have the same difficulty with a question like 'how many children do you have?' which would generate hard data.

It is better to ask questions that will provide hard data if you can. For instance, instead of the request for an opinion on a statement about Internet marketing, it would be better to ask if the organization uses the Internet in its marketing activities, how much business has been generated through it, and so on.

There are a number of specialist texts on questionnaire design. For more guidance on the subject, try Converse and Presser (1986), Hague (1993), or Oppenheim (1997).

When you have designed your questionnaire it is absolutely vital that you try it out before you send it out to your respondents. You need to make sure that somebody who is reading it for the first time will understand it completely and be able to respond to the questions asked. This is something you simply cannot do yourself. You have written and designed it, so of course it makes sense to you, but the key question is, will it make sense to the people that you want to complete it?

Try to test or 'pilot' your questionnaire by asking a number of people to complete it. Ideally these people should be the same sort of people as the respondents in your sample, the same sort of age, occupation etc. If you can't find such people then ask friends.

Whoever you get to test the questionnaire for you, talk to them about it after they have completed it. You need to know which questions were difficult to understand, which ones difficult to answer, was the sequence right, and so on. If necessary, modify the questionnaire in the light of their criticisms. Then test it again, preferably on different people. Keep testing it until it is as easy for respondents to use as possible, yet will still enable you to get the information you need.

Testing a questionnaire can be a tedious and annoying process, not least because you are convinced that your questionnaire is something that even a compete idiot can understand. The point is that it is not your assessment of the questionnaire that matters. It is whether the respondents who can provide you with the information you want will understand it. If they can't then the whole exercise will turn into a waste of time. So, be patient and learn from the people who test your questionnaire. Their advice can improve your response rate and the quality of information you get.

10.3 Presenting your analysis

When you have completed you investigations and analysed your results you will need to think about how you will incorporate your analysis into your report. The key editorial questions that you have to address are what to include, how to present it, and where to put it. You will have to think about these issues when you plan the structure of your final document.

If you have collected primary data you will need to explain how you collected it. You should do this in a section called 'Methodology' that ought to be located among the early sections of the report, probably after the introductory sections. Your reader should be able to find out from your methodology section how you selected your sample, and what process you used to gather your data.

You shouldn't need to include the raw data in your report. Your reader is unlikely to want to comb through letters, completed questionnaires, or record sheets. However, it may be wise to put a single example in an appendix, and make reference to that appendix in the methodology section, to help your reader understand how the data was collected.

Unless you have a very modest amount of data use a suitable computer package to produce your analysis. If you have a set of completed questionnaires make sure you number each one of them before you store data from them in the package. Put the data from questionnaire number one into row one of the worksheet or spreadsheet and so on. If you do this you will find it much easier to rectify any mistakes that you make when you enter your data. You will also find it convenient if you need to check specific responses when you come to examine the analysis.

The package you use to analyse your data may provide ways of saving you time when you enter your data. For instance, you may have data about business locations in the UK that consists of replies that are 'England', 'Scotland', or 'Wales'. Typing these words repeatedly is laborious. If you use MINITAB you can use the coding facility to change labels like 'E' for England and 'S' for Scotland, which are much easier to enter, to the full country name. Select **Code** from the **Manip** menu then **Text to Text** from the submenu (or **Numeric to Text** if you use numeric labels). In the command window you will have to specify the location of the data you want to change, where you want the changed data stored, and exactly how you want the data changed.

The results that you do eventually include in your report should be those that have proved useful. There may be data that you tried to collect, but were unable to. Perhaps your respondents simply didn't have the information; perhaps they supplied the wrong data. For a variety of reasons collecting primary data can produce disappointment.

If part of your data collection activity has not borne fruit, there's not a lot you can do about it. Don't be tempted to include inappropriate data purely because you have collected it. The results you include in the report should be the ones that have a part to play within your report, not ones for which you have to create an artificial role.

You may well need to discuss the reasons for the failure of part of your quest for information in your report, particularly if it relates to an important aspect of your project. Others could use your work and you will be making a valid contribution to knowledge if your unfortunate experience is something they can learn from.

The structural plan of your final report should help you decide what results you will need to include, but you will also have to decide how to present them. You need to remember that your reader will be looking at your final report without experiencing the process of carrying out the project. You will have to introduce the results to them gradually, starting with the more basic forms of presentation before showing them more elaborate types of analysis.

In the early parts of the discussion of your results you should explain the composition of your sample. You can do this effectively by using simple tables and diagrams. Further on you may want to show what your respondents said in response to the questions you asked them. Again there is scope here for using simple tables and diagrams. If the results you are reporting consist of quantitative data, use summary measures to give your reader an overview of them.

Later on in your report you will probably want to explore connections between the characteristics of your respondents, or the organizations they work for, and the facts or opinions they have provided. Here you can make use of bivariate techniques: contingency tables for qualitative data, and scatter diagrams, regression and correlation for quantitative data.

The techniques we have referred to so far in this section are descriptive methods, techniques we can use to show or describe data. Look back at the first few chapters of this book for more information about them.

At the heart of most good projects is at least one proposition or hypothesis that the project is designed to evaluate. You should be able to put your hypothesis to the test by using statistical decision-making techniques, the methods of statistical inference that feature in the later chapters of this book. These techniques will enable you to make judgements about the population from which your sample is drawn using your sample results.

For instance, suppose the proposition that your project is intended to assess is that successful clothing retailers use Internet marketing. You could use a contingency test to test for association between whether or not clothing retailers use Internet marketing and whether or not they recorded an increase in turnover in their most recent accounts. If your proposition is that hours worked in the road haulage industry exceed those specified in working time regulations you could test the hypothesis using data from a random sample of haulage contractors.

If you want to produce estimates or test hypotheses and your sample results come from a small population you may have to make a small adjustment when you calculate the estimated standard error. You need to multiply it by the *finite population correction factor*. If we use n to represent the size of the sample and N to represent the size of the population, we can express the correction factor as:

$$\frac{(N - n)}{N}$$

Example 10.3

A random sample of 40 car dealers is taken from the 160 dealers franchised to a particular manufacturer. The standard deviation of the number of cars sold per month by these 40 dealers is 25. Calculate the estimated standard error using the appropriate finite population correction factor.

$$\text{Estimated standard error} = \frac{s}{\sqrt{n}} \times \frac{(N - n)}{N}$$

$$= \frac{25}{\sqrt{40}} \times \frac{(160 - 40)}{160}$$

$$= 3.953 \times 0.75 = 2.965 \quad \text{to three decimal places}$$

The adjustment is important if the sample constitutes a large proportion of a population as in Example 10.3. However, if the sample constitutes less than 5 per cent of the population it is not necessary to make the adjustment.

Once you have decided which analysis to include in your final report and the form in which you will present it, you must consider exactly where the various tables, diagrams and numerical results will be located within your report. You will have gone to a lot of trouble to collect your data and analyse it so it is worth making sure that you use it in the most effective way.

Your guiding principle should be to make it as easy as possible for your readers to find the pieces of your analysis that you want them to consult. If the piece of analysis is a diagram or a table you have two options: you can insert it within the text of your report or you can put it in an appendix. If the piece of analysis is a numerical result you have a third option; you can weave it into the text itself.

In order to decide where to put a piece of analysis, consider how important it is that your readers look at it. If it is something that readers must see in order to follow your discussion, then it really should be inserted within the text. Avoid full-page inserts and make sure that the analysis is positioned as closely as possible to the section of the text that first refers to it. It will be very frustrating for your readers if they have to comb through the whole report to look for something that you refer to pages away from it. Every insert you place within the text must be labelled, for instance 'Figure 1' or 'Table 3', and you should always refer to it using the label, e.g. '. . .. is shown in Figure 1'.

If you have some analysis that you consider your readers may want to refer to, but don't need to look at, put it in an appendix. Make sure that the appendix is numbered, and that you use the appendix number whenever you refer to the analysis in it. Arrange your appendices so that the first one that readers find referred to in your text is Appendix 1, and so on. Don't be tempted to use appendices as a 'dustbin' for every piece of analysis that you have produced, whether you refer to it or not. Any analysis that you do not refer to directly will be superfluous as far as your readers are concerned and may distract them from what you want them to concentrate on.

Single numerical results such as means and standard deviations can be reported directly as part of your text. However, you may want to draw your readers' attention to the way in which it has been produced. If so, you can put the derivation of the result in an appendix and refer your readers to it. This is a particularly good idea if you have had to adjust the procedure that your readers would expect you to use to produce such a result, for instance if you have to use the finite population correction factor that we looked at in Example 10.3.

Allow yourself time in your schedule to read through your final report carefully before submitting it. Make sure that all your inserts are labelled, all your appendices numbered, and all your sources acknowledged. If you have time ask a friend to read through in case there are any mistakes that you have overlooked. Ask them how easy it was to find the inserts and appendices when they were referred to them.

Checking the draft and the final version can be tedious and time-consuming, but it is time and effort well spent. When your tutors read it in order to assess it you want to make sure that the version they read is as polished and professional as possible.

Statistical tables

Table 1 Binomial probabilities and cumulative binomial probabilities

You can use this table to solve problems involving a series of n trials each of which can result in 'success' or 'failure'. Begin by finding the section of the table for the appropriate values of n (the number of trials) and p (the probability of success in any one trial). You can then use the table in three ways:

1 To find the probability that there are exactly x 'successes' in n trials look for the entry in the $P(x)$ column and the row for x.

2 To find the probability that there are x or fewer 'successes' in n trials look for the entry in the $P(X \leq x)$ column and the row for x.

3 To find the probability that there are more than x 'successes' in n trials, $P(X > x)$, look for the entry in the $P(X \leq x)$ column and the row for x. Subtract the figure you find from one. The result, $1 - P(X \leq x)$ is $P(X > x)$.

Example

The probability of success in a trial is 0.4 and there are 5 trials. The probability that there are exactly 2 successes, $P(2)$, is 0.346. The probability that there are two or fewer successes, $P(X \leq 2)$ is 0.683. The probability that there are more than two successes, $P(X > 2)$, is $1 - 0.683$, 0.317.

FOR 5 TRIALS ($n = 5$)

	$p = 0.1$		$p = 0.2$		$p = 0.3$		$p = 0.4$		$p = 0.5$	
	$P(x)$	$P(X \leq x)$	$P(x)$	$P(X \leq x)$	$P(x)$	$P(X \leq x)$	$P(x)$	$P(X \leq x)$	$P(x)$	$P(X \leq x)$
x:0	0.590	0.590	0.328	0.328	0.168	0.168	0.078	0.078	0.031	0.031
x:1	0.328	0.919	0.410	0.737	0.360	0.528	0.259	0.337	0.156	0.187
x:2	0.073	0.991	0.205	0.942	0.309	0.837	0.346	0.683	0.313	0.500
x:3	0.008	1.000	0.051	0.993	0.132	0.969	0.230	0.913	0.313	0.813
x:4	0.000	1.000	0.006	1.000	0.028	0.998	0.077	0.990	0.156	0.969
x:5	0.000	1.000	0.000	1.000	0.002	1.000	0.010	1.000	0.031	1.000

FOR 10 TRIALS ($n = 10$)

	$p = 0.1$		$p = 0.2$		$p = 0.3$		$p = 0.4$		$p = 0.5$	
	$P(x)$	$P(X \leq x)$	$P(x)$	$P(X \leq x)$	$P(x)$	$P(X \leq x)$	$P(x)$	$P(X \leq x)$	$P(x)$	$P(X \leq x)$
x: 0	0.349	0.349	0.107	0.107	0.028	0.028	0.006	0.006	0.001	0.001
x: 1	0.387	0.736	0.268	0.376	0.121	0.149	0.040	0.046	0.010	0.011
x: 2	0.194	0.930	0.302	0.678	0.233	0.383	0.121	0.167	0.044	0.055
x: 3	0.057	0.987	0.201	0.879	0.267	0.650	0.215	0.382	0.117	0.172
x: 4	0.011	0.998	0.088	0.967	0.200	0.850	0.251	0.633	0.205	0.377
x: 5	0.001	1.000	0.026	0.994	0.103	0.953	0.201	0.834	0.246	0.623
x: 6	0.000	1.000	0.006	0.999	0.037	0.989	0.111	0.945	0.205	0.828
x: 7	0.000	1.000	0.001	1.000	0.009	0.998	0.042	0.988	0.117	0.945
x: 8	0.000	1.000	0.000	1.000	0.001	1.000	0.011	0.998	0.044	0.989
x: 9	0.000	1.000	0.000	1.000	0.000	1.000	0.002	1.000	0.010	0.999
x:10	0.000	1.000	0.000	1.000	0.000	1.000	0.000	1.000	0.001	1.000

Table 2 Poisson probabilities and cumulative Poisson-probabilities

You can use this table to solve problems involving the number of incidents, x, that occurs during a period of time or over an area. Begin by finding the section of the table for the mean number of incidents per unit of time or space, μ. You can then use the table in three ways:

1 To find the probability that there are exactly x incidents occur look for the entry in the $P(x)$ column and the row for x.

2 To find the probability that there are x or fewer incidents look for the entry in the $P(X \leq x)$ column and the row for x.

3 To find the probability that there are more than x incidents, $P(X > x)$, look for the entry in the $P(X \leq x)$ column and the row for x. Subtract the figure you find from one. The result, $1 - P(X \leq x)$ is $P(X > x)$.

Example

The mean number of incidents is 5. The probability that there are exactly 3 incidents, $P(3)$, is 0.140. The probability that there are three or fewer incidents, $P(X \leq 3)$, is 0.265. The probability that there are more than three incidents, $P(X > 3)$, is $1 - 0.265$, 0.735.

	$\mu = 1.0$		$\mu = 2.0$		$\mu = 3.0$		$\mu = 4.0$		$\mu = 5.0$	
	$P(x)$	$P(X \leq x)$	$P(x)$	$P(X \leq x)$	$P(x)$	$P(X \leq x)$	$P(x)$	$P(X \leq x)$	$P(x)$	$P(X \leq x)$
x: 0	0.368	0.368	0.135	0.135	0.050	0.050	0.018	0.018	0.007	0.007
x: 1	0.368	0.736	0.271	0.406	0.149	0.199	0.073	0.092	0.034	0.040
x: 2	0.184	0.920	0.271	0.677	0.224	0.423	0.147	0.238	0.084	0.125
x: 3	0.061	0.981	0.180	0.857	0.224	0.647	0.195	0.433	0.140	0.265
x: 4	0.015	0.996	0.090	0.947	0.168	0.815	0.195	0.629	0.175	0.440
x: 5	0.003	0.999	0.036	0.983	0.101	0.916	0.156	0.785	0.175	0.616
x: 6	0.001	1.000	0.012	0.995	0.050	0.966	0.104	0.889	0.146	0.762
x: 7	0.000	1.000	0.003	0.999	0.022	0.988	0.060	0.949	0.104	0.867
x: 8	0.000	1.000	0.001	1.000	0.008	0.996	0.030	0.979	0.065	0.932
x: 9	0.000	1.000	0.000	1.000	0.003	0.999	0.013	0.992	0.036	0.968
x:10	0.000	1.000	0.000	1.000	0.001	1.000	0.005	0.997	0.018	0.986
x:11	0.000	1.000	0.000	1.000	0.000	1.000	0.002	0.999	0.008	0.995
x:12	0.000	1.000	0.000	1.000	0.000	1.000	0.001	1.000	0.003	0.998
x:13	0.000	1.000	0.000	1.000	0.000	1.000	0.000	1.000	0.001	0.999
x:14	0.000	1.000	0.000	1.000	0.000	1.000	0.000	1.000	0.000	1.000
x:15	0.000	1.000	0.000	1.000	0.000	1.000	0.000	1.000	0.000	1.000

Table 3 Cumulative probabilities of the standard normal distribution

This table describes the pattern of variation of the Standard Normal Variable, Z, which has a mean μ, of 0 and a standard deviation, σ, of 1. You can use this table to find proportions of the area of the distribution that lie either to the right or to the left of a particular value of Z, z.

To find the proportion of the area to the right of z, which represents the probability that Z is greater than z, $P(Z > z)$, find the row for the value of z to the first decimal place and then look across the columns until you reach the column associated with the second figure after the decimal place.

Example 1

The probability that Z is greater than -1.62 is in the row for -1.6 and in the column labelled 0.02. $P(Z > -1.62) = 0.9474$.

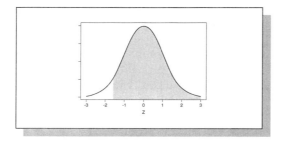

Example 2

The probability that Z is greater than 0.57 is in the row for 0.5 and in the column labelled 0.07. $P(Z > 0.57) = 0.2843$.

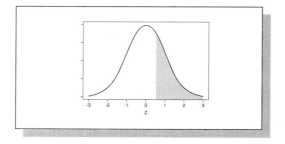

To find the proportion of the area to the left of z, which represents the probability that Z is less than z, $P(Z < z)$, find the row for the value of z to the first decimal place and then look across the columns until you reach the column associated with the second figure after the decimal place. Subtract the figure from 1.

Example 3

To obtain the probability that Z is less than -0.85, first find the figure in the row for -0.8 and in the column labelled 0.05. This is $P(Z > -0.85)$, 0.8023. $P(Z < -0.85) = 1 - 0.8023 = 0.1977$.

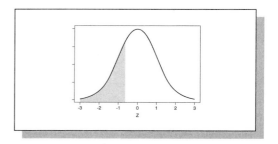

Example 4

To obtain the probability that Z is less than 2.10, first find the figure in the row for 2.1 and in the column labelled 0.00. This is $P(Z > 2.1)$, 0.0179. $P(Z < 2.1) = 1 - 0.0179 = 0.9821$.

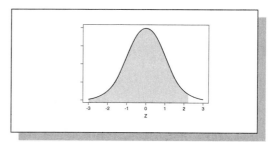

Note that the probability that Z is greater than a z value is -3.0 or less is 0.999 or more, and the probability that Z is greater than a z value is 3.0 or more is 0.001 or less.

z	0.00	0.01	0.02	0.03	0.04	0.05	0.06	0.07	0.08	0.09
−2.9	0.9981	0.9982	0.9982	0.9983	0.9984	0.9984	0.9985	0.9985	0.9986	0.9986
−2.8	0.9974	0.9975	0.9976	0.9977	0.9977	0.9978	0.9979	0.9979	0.9980	0.9981
−2.7	0.9965	0.9966	0.9967	0.9968	0.9969	0.9970	0.9971	0.9972	0.9973	0.9974
−2.6	0.9953	0.9955	0.9956	0.9957	0.9959	0.9960	0.9961	0.9962	0.9963	0.9964
−2.5	0.9938	0.9940	0.9941	0.9943	0.9945	0.9946	0.9948	0.9949	0.9951	0.9952
−2.4	0.9918	0.9920	0.9922	0.9925	0.9927	0.9929	0.9931	0.9932	0.9934	0.9936
−2.3	0.9893	0.9896	0.9898	0.9901	0.9904	0.9906	0.9909	0.9911	0.9913	0.9916
−2.2	0.9861	0.9864	0.9868	0.9871	0.9875	0.9878	0.9881	0.9884	0.9887	0.9890
−2.1	0.9821	0.9826	0.9830	0.9834	0.9838	0.9842	0.9846	0.9850	0.9854	0.9857
−2.0	0.9772	0.9778	0.9783	0.9788	0.9793	0.9798	0.9803	0.9808	0.9812	0.9817
−1.9	0.9713	0.9719	0.9726	0.9732	0.9738	0.9744	0.9750	0.9756	0.9761	0.9767
−1.8	0.9641	0.9649	0.9656	0.9664	0.9671	0.9678	0.9686	0.9693	0.9699	0.9706
−1.7	0.9554	0.9564	0.9573	0.9582	0.9591	0.9599	0.9608	0.9616	0.9625	0.9633
−1.6	0.9452	0.9463	0.9474	0.9484	0.9495	0.9505	0.9515	0.9525	0.9535	0.9545
−1.5	0.9332	0.9345	0.9357	0.9370	0.9382	0.9394	0.9406	0.9418	0.9429	0.9441
−1.4	0.9192	0.9207	0.9222	0.9236	0.9251	0.9265	0.9279	0.9292	0.9306	0.9319
−1.3	0.9032	0.9049	0.9066	0.9082	0.9099	0.9115	0.9131	0.9147	0.9162	0.9177
−1.2	0.8849	0.8869	0.8888	0.8907	0.8925	0.8944	0.8962	0.8980	0.8997	0.9015
−1.1	0.8643	0.8665	0.8686	0.8708	0.8729	0.8749	0.8770	0.8790	0.8810	0.8830
−1.0	0.8413	0.8438	0.8461	0.8485	0.8508	0.8531	0.8554	0.8577	0.8599	0.8621
−0.9	0.8159	0.8186	0.8212	0.8238	0.8264	0.8289	0.8315	0.8340	0.8365	0.8389
−0.8	0.7881	0.7910	0.7939	0.7967	0.7995	0.8023	0.8051	0.8078	0.8106	0.8133
−0.7	0.7580	0.7611	0.7642	0.7673	0.7703	0.7734	0.7764	0.7794	0.7823	0.7852
−0.6	0.7257	0.7291	0.7324	0.7357	0.7389	0.7422	0.7454	0.7486	0.7517	0.7549
−0.5	0.6915	0.6950	0.6985	0.7019	0.7054	0.7088	0.7123	0.7157	0.7190	0.7224
−0.4	0.6554	0.6591	0.6628	0.6664	0.6700	0.6736	0.6772	0.6808	0.6844	0.6879
−0.3	0.6179	0.6217	0.6255	0.6293	0.6331	0.6368	0.6406	0.6443	0.6480	0.6517
−0.2	0.5793	0.5832	0.5871	0.5910	0.5948	0.5987	0.6026	0.6064	0.6103	0.6141
−0.1	0.5398	0.5438	0.5478	0.5517	0.5557	0.5596	0.5636	0.5675	0.5714	0.5753
−0.0	0.5000	0.5040	0.5080	0.5120	0.5160	0.5199	0.5239	0.5279	0.5319	0.5359
0.0	0.5000	0.4960	0.4920	0.4880	0.4840	0.4801	0.4761	0.4721	0.4681	0.4641
0.1	0.4602	0.4562	0.4522	0.4483	0.4443	0.4404	0.4364	0.4325	0.4286	0.4247
0.2	0.4207	0.4168	0.4129	0.4090	0.4052	0.4013	0.3974	0.3936	0.3897	0.3859
0.3	0.3821	0.3783	0.3745	0.3707	0.3669	0.3632	0.3594	0.3557	0.3520	0.3483
0.4	0.3446	0.3409	0.3372	0.3336	0.3300	0.3264	0.3228	0.3192	0.3156	0.3121
0.5	0.3085	0.3050	0.3015	0.2981	0.2946	0.2912	0.2877	0.2843	0.2810	0.2776
0.6	0.2743	0.2709	0.2676	0.2643	0.2611	0.2578	0.2546	0.2514	0.2483	0.2451
0.7	0.2420	0.2389	0.2358	0.2327	0.2297	0.2266	0.2236	0.2206	0.2177	0.2148
0.8	0.2119	0.2090	0.2061	0.2033	0.2005	0.1977	0.1949	0.1922	0.1894	0.1867
0.9	0.1841	0.1814	0.1788	0.1762	0.1736	0.1711	0.1685	0.1660	0.1635	0.1611
1.0	0.1587	0.1562	0.1539	0.1515	0.1492	0.1469	0.1446	0.1423	0.1401	0.1379
1.1	0.1357	0.1335	0.1314	0.1292	0.1271	0.1251	0.1230	0.1210	0.1190	0.1170
1.2	0.1151	0.1131	0.1112	0.1093	0.1075	0.1056	0.1038	0.1020	0.1003	0.0985
1.3	0.0968	0.0951	0.0934	0.0918	0.0901	0.0885	0.0869	0.0853	0.0838	0.0823
1.4	0.0808	0.0793	0.0778	0.0764	0.0749	0.0735	0.0721	0.0708	0.0694	0.0681
1.5	0.0668	0.0655	0.0643	0.0630	0.0618	0.0606	0.0594	0.0582	0.0571	0.0559
1.6	0.0548	0.0537	0.0526	0.0516	0.0505	0.0495	0.0485	0.0475	0.0465	0.0455
1.7	0.0446	0.0436	0.0427	0.0418	0.0409	0.0401	0.0392	0.0384	0.0375	0.0367
1.8	0.0359	0.0351	0.0344	0.0336	0.0329	0.0322	0.0314	0.0307	0.0301	0.0294
1.9	0.0287	0.0281	0.0274	0.0268	0.0262	0.0256	0.0250	0.0244	0.0239	0.0233
2.0	0.0228	0.0222	0.0217	0.0212	0.0207	0.0202	0.0197	0.0192	0.0188	0.0183
2.1	0.0179	0.0174	0.0170	0.0166	0.0162	0.0158	0.0154	0.0150	0.0146	0.0143
2.2	0.0139	0.0136	0.0132	0.0129	0.0125	0.0122	0.0119	0.0116	0.0113	0.0110
2.3	0.0107	0.0104	0.0102	0.0099	0.0096	0.0094	0.0091	0.0089	0.0087	0.0084
2.4	0.0082	0.0080	0.0078	0.0075	0.0073	0.0071	0.0069	0.0068	0.0066	0.0064
2.5	0.0062	0.0060	0.0059	0.0057	0.0055	0.0054	0.0052	0.0051	0.0049	0.0048
2.6	0.0047	0.0045	0.0044	0.0043	0.0041	0.0040	0.0039	0.0038	0.0037	0.0036
2.7	0.0035	0.0034	0.0033	0.0032	0.0031	0.0030	0.0029	0.0028	0.0027	0.0026
2.8	0.0026	0.0025	0.0024	0.0023	0.0023	0.0022	0.0021	0.0021	0.0020	0.0019
2.9	0.0019	0.0018	0.0018	0.0017	0.0016	0.0016	0.0015	0.0015	0.0014	0.0014

Table 4 Selected points of the *t* distribution

This table provides values of the *t* distribution, with different numbers of degrees of freedom, which cut off certain tail areas to the right of the distribution, $t_{\alpha,\nu}$. To use it you will need to know the number of degrees of freedom, ν, and the size of the tail area, α. Find the row for the number of degrees of freedom and then look to the right along the row until you come to the figure in the column for the appropriate tail area.

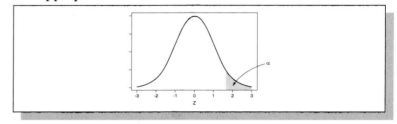

Example

The value in the *t* distribution with 7 degrees of freedom that cuts off a tail area of 0.05, $t_{0.05,7}$, is in the row for 7 degrees of freedom and the column headed 0.05, 1.895.

Note that as the number of degrees of freedom increases, the *t* distribution becomes more like the Standard Normal Distribution. Look at the bottom row of this table and you will see a row of *t* values that are from the *t* distribution that has an infinite (∞) number of degrees of freedom. This 'extreme' *t* distribution is the Standard Normal Distribution, and the figures along the bottom row here can also be found in Table 3, e.g. look up the z value 1.96 in Table 3 and you will see the probability that Z is more than 1.96 is 0.025. In this table, 1.96 is listed as the value of *t* with infinite degrees of freedom that cuts off a tail area of 0.025.

ν	0.10	0.05	0.025	0.01	0.005
1	3.078	6.314	12.706	31.821	63.657
2	1.886	2.920	4.303	6.965	9.925
3	1.638	2.353	3.182	4.541	5.841
4	1.533	2.132	2.776	3.747	4.604
5	1.476	2.015	2.571	3.365	4.032
6	1.440	1.943	2.447	3.143	3.707
7	1.415	1.895	2.365	2.998	3.499
8	1.397	1.860	2.306	2.896	3.355
9	1.383	1.833	2.262	2.821	3.250
10	1.372	1.812	2.228	2.764	3.169
11	1.363	1.796	2.201	2.718	3.106
12	1.356	1.782	2.179	2.681	3.055
13	1.350	1.771	2.160	2.650	3.012
14	1.345	1.761	2.145	2.624	2.977
15	1.341	1.753	2.131	2.602	2.947
16	1.337	1.746	2.120	2.583	2.921
17	1.333	1.740	2.110	2.567	2.898
18	1.330	1.734	2.101	2.552	2.878
19	1.328	1.729	2.093	2.539	2.861
20	1.325	1.725	2.086	2.528	2.845
21	1.323	1.721	2.080	2.518	2.831
22	1.321	1.717	2.074	2.508	2.819
23	1.319	1.714	2.069	2.500	2.807
24	1.318	1.711	2.064	2.492	2.797
25	1.316	1.708	2.060	2.485	2.787
26	1.315	1.706	2.056	2.479	2.779
27	1.314	1.703	2.052	2.473	2.771
28	1.313	1.701	2.048	2.467	2.763
29	1.311	1.699	2.045	2.462	2.756
30	1.310	1.697	2.042	2.457	2.750
50	1.299	1.676	2.009	2.403	2.678
100	1.290	1.660	1.984	2.364	2.626
∞	1.282	1.645	1.960	2.326	2.576

Table 5 Selected points of the χ^2 distribution

This table provides values of the χ^2 distribution, with different numbers of degrees of freedom, which cut off certain tail areas to the right of the distribution, $\chi^2_{\alpha,\nu}$. To use it you will need to know the number of degrees of freedom, ν, and the size of the tail area, α. Find the row for the number of degrees of freedom and then look to the right along the row until you come to the figure in the column for the appropriate tail area.

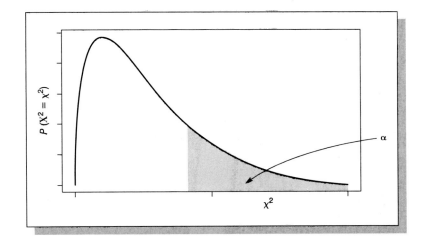

Example

The value in the χ^2 distribution with 3 degrees of freedom that cuts off a tail area of 0.05, $\chi^2_{0.05,3}$ is in the row for 3 degrees of freedom and the column headed 0.05, 7.815.

ν	0.10	0.05	0.01
1	2.706	3.841	6.635
2	4.605	5.991	9.210
3	6.251	7.815	11.345
4	7.779	9.488	13.277
5	9.236	11.070	15.086
6	10.645	12.592	16.812
7	12.017	14.067	18.475
8	13.362	15.507	20.090
9	14.684	16.919	21.666
10	15.987	18.307	23.209

Answers and selected worked solutions to review questions

The solutions to some review questions are given in full, and the numerical and verbal answers to the rest are provided. Unless the full solution is given, you will find the Example(s) in the chapter that most closely resemble the question in square brackets to the right of the question number.

All numerical answers are precise or accurate to at least three decimal places unless stated otherwise.

Chapter 1

1.1	(a) (v), (b) (vi), (c) (i), (d) (ii), (e) (iii), (f) (iv)	
1.2	(a) (iii), (b) (v), (c) (iv), (d) (i), (e) (ii)	
1.3	(a) £25.60 (b) £18.39	[1.2]
1.4	(a) 1740 hours (b) 1015 hours	[1.7]
1.5	38.704	[1.11]
1.6	(a) 196 (b) 13 m × 13 m	[1.12, 1.13]

1.7 Total charge = (8.50 + 829 × 0.0608) × 1.05
    = (8.50 + 50.4032) × 1.05
    = (58.9032) × 1.05 = £61.85
      to the nearest penny

1.8	£97.85 to the nearest penny	[1.9, 1.14]
1.9	405	[1.15]

1.10　Taxable pay = 18 000 − 4600 = 13 400
15% of 4200 = 0.15 × 4200 = 630
23% of 13 400 less 4200 = (13 400 − 4200) × 0.23
= (9200) × 0.23 = 2116
National Insurance = 10% of 18 000 = 1800
Annual take-home pay = 4600 + (4200 − 630)
+ (9200 − 2116) − 1800
= 4600 + 3570 + 7084 − 1800
= 13 454
Monthly take-home pay = 13 454/12 = £1121.17 to the nearest penny

1.11　(a) £225.77 to the nearest penny　　　　　　　　[1.8]
　　　(b) £11.29 to the nearest penny　　　　　　　　　[1.9]

1.12　(a) Cost in dollars = 500 000/120 = $4167.67
　　　　　Cost in pounds = 4167.67 × 0.65 = £2708.33 to the nearest penny
　　　(b) Cost in dollars = 500 000/180 = $2777.78
　　　　　Cost in pounds = 2777.78 × 0.65 = £1805.56 to the nearest penny

1.13　Vodka (1.125 l) and lemonade (0.5 l)　　　　　　[1.15]

1.14　6.13% (warning), 4.82%, 20.15% (fine), 4.94%,
6.08% (warning). All to two decimal places.　　　[1.10]

1.15　(a) (i)　6 602 000 (V), 5 192 000 (A), 4 052 000 (L)
　　　　　(ii)　6 600 000 (V), 5 200 000 (A), 4 100 000 (L)　[1.17]
　　　(b) 11.24% (V), 8.84% (A), 6.90% (L)　　　　　　[1.18]

Chapter 2

2.1 (i) (b), (e) (ii) (d), (f) (iii) (a), (c)

2.2　(a)
Area	Pass	Cash	Total
East	35 000	43 000	78 000
North	43 000	81 000	124 000
South	29 000	34 000	63 000
West	51 000	114 000	165 000
Total	158 000	272 000	430 000

(b)

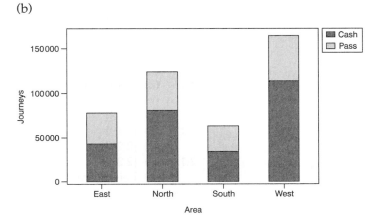

2.3 (a) [2.9]
    (b) [2.8]
2.4 (a) [2.10]
    (b) [2.7]
2.5 (a) [2.10]
    (b) [2.7]
2.6 (a)

Speed	Frequency
20 and under 25	4
25 and under 30	6
30 and under 35	6
35 and under 40	7
40 and under 45	1

    (b)

2.7 (a) [2.11]
    (b) [2.13]
2.8 (a) [2.12]
    (b) [2.13]
2.9 (a) [2.13]
    (b) [2.15]
    (c) [2.16]
2.10 (a) [2.13]
    (b) [2.18]
    (c) [2.18]
2.11 (a) [2.14]
    (b) [2.18]
    (c) [2.18]
2.12 (a) [2.19]
    (b) [2.20]
2.13 (a) [2.21]
    (b) Leisure centre fees lower and less varied [2.21]
2.14 (a) [2.23]
    (b) [2.22]

2.15 (a) [2.23]
    (b) [2.22]
    (c) [2.24]
2.16 (a)

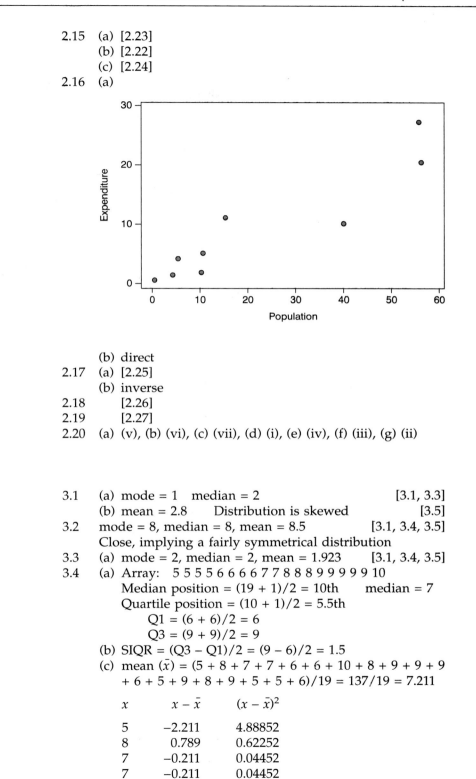

    (b) direct
2.17 (a) [2.25]
    (b) inverse
2.18   [2.26]
2.19   [2.27]
2.20 (a) (v), (b) (vi), (c) (vii), (d) (i), (e) (iv), (f) (iii), (g) (ii)

Chapter 3

3.1 (a) mode = 1   median = 2   [3.1, 3.3]
    (b) mean = 2.8   Distribution is skewed   [3.5]
3.2   mode = 8, median = 8, mean = 8.5   [3.1, 3.4, 3.5]
    Close, implying a fairly symmetrical distribution
3.3 (a) mode = 2, median = 2, mean = 1.923   [3.1, 3.4, 3.5]
3.4 (a) Array: 5 5 5 5 6 6 6 6 7 7 8 8 8 9 9 9 9 9 10
       Median position = (19 + 1)/2 = 10th   median = 7
       Quartile position = (10 + 1)/2 = 5.5th
           Q1 = (6 + 6)/2 = 6
           Q3 = (9 + 9)/2 = 9
    (b) SIQR = (Q3 − Q1)/2 = (9 − 6)/2 = 1.5
    (c) mean ($\bar{x}$) = (5 + 8 + 7 + 7 + 6 + 6 + 10 + 8 + 9 + 9 + 9
       + 6 + 5 + 9 + 8 + 9 + 5 + 5 + 6)/19 = 137/19 = 7.211

x	$x - \bar{x}$	$(x - \bar{x})^2$
5	−2.211	4.88852
8	0.789	0.62252
7	−0.211	0.04452
7	−0.211	0.04452

6	−1.211	1.46652
6	−1.211	1.46652
10	2.789	7.77852
8	0.789	0.62252
9	1.789	3.20052
9	1.789	3.20052
9	1.789	3.20052
6	−1.211	1.46652
5	−2.211	4.88852
9	1.789	3.20052
8	0.789	0.62252
9	1.789	3.20052
5	−2.211	4.88852
5	−2.211	4.88852
6	−1.211	1.46652

$$\Sigma(x - \bar{x})^2 = 51.158$$

$$\text{Standard deviation} = \sqrt{\Sigma\,(x - \bar{x})^2/(n - 1)}$$
$$= \sqrt{51.158/18} = 1.686$$

3.5 (a) AA: median = 1781.5, Q1 = 1564, Q3 = 1976,
SIQR = 206
RSR: median = 1992, Q1 = 1879,
Q3 = 2098, SIQR = 109.5   [3.4, 3.15, 3.16]
(b) AA has lower central tendency and more spread

3.6 Bus: mean = 35.75, s.d.= 5.148
Cycle: mean = 28.75, s.d. = 3.012   [3.5, 3.22, 3.23]

3.7 (a) False (b) False (c) True (d) False (e) False (f) True

3.8 Yes. Less variation in ages at Bistry

3.9

Class	Midpoint	Frequency	fx
80 a.u. 120	100	3	300
120 a.u. 160	140	11	1540
160 a.u. 200	180	9	1620
200 a.u. 240	220	7	1540
240 a.u. 280	260	2	520

$\Sigma fx = 5520$ approximate mean = 5520/32 = 172.5
median position = (32 + 1)/2 = 16.5th
median class is 160 a.u. 200
approximate median = 160 + (2.5/9 × 40) = 171.111
Approximate mean and median are close. Distribution is
fairly symmetrical.

3.10 (a) Contemporary: median = 47.045   mean = 46.974
Reissue: median = 43.382   mean = 42.917   [3.12]
(b) Contemporary s.d. = 5.801   Reissue s.d = 5.242 [3.25]
(c) Contemporary albums have higher central tendency
and more spread.

3.11 (a) Before: mean = 29.937   median = 30
After: mean = 20.410   median = 21.613   [3.12]
(b) Before s.d. = 11.753   After s.d. = 8.281   [3.25]

3.12 (a) Peeshar: mean = 48.182   s.d. = 23.702
       Peevar: mean = 32.031   s.d = 19.088   [3.12, 3.25]
       Average spend higher in Peeshar with larger spread.
   (b) Weekly shopping at Peeshar.

3.13 median = £12   SIQR = £4   [3.10, 3.15, 3.16]

3.14 median = £289   Q1 = £230   Q3 = 408   [3.3, 3.15, 3.18]

3.15 median = 10.215   Q1 = 8.52   Q3 = 12.92   [3.4, 3.15, 3.18]

3.16

Balance	Relative frequency	Cumulative relative frequency
0 a.u. 500	0.12	0.12
500 a.u. 1000	0.29	0.41
1000 a.u. 1500	0.26	0.67
1500 a.u. 2000	0.19	0.86
2000 a.u. 2500	0.09	0.95
2500 a.u. 3000	0.05	1.00

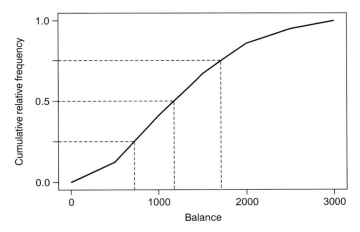

Approximate values: median = 1175 Q1 = 725 Q3 = 1710
                          SIQR = 492.5

3.17 (a) [3.13]
   (b) Approximate values: median = 720 Q1 = 425
                              Q3 = 1060 SIQR = 317.5

3.18 (a) False (b) True   (c) True   (d) False   (e) True
   (f) False (g) True   (h) False

3.19 Times are higher. The 1st, 8th and 10th times are
   out of control.   [3.27]

3.20 (a) (v)   (b) (iv)   (c) (i)   (d) (ii)   (e) (vi)   (f) (iii)

Chapter 4

4.1   Positive: (a) (e) (f)   Negative: (b) (c) (d)
4.2   (a) Cost
       (b)

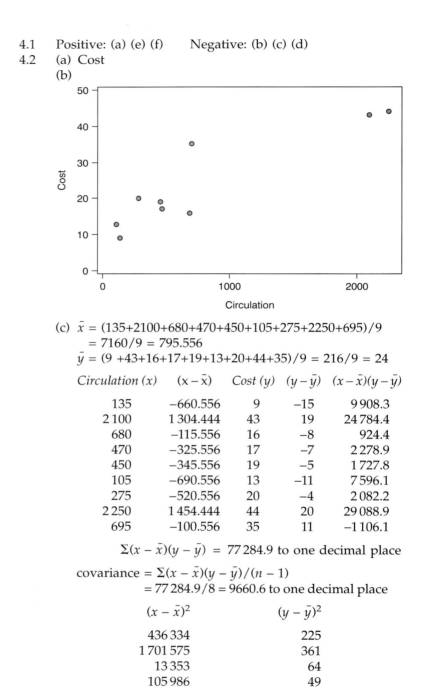

(c) $\bar{x}$ = (135+2100+680+470+450+105+275+2250+695)/9
       = 7160/9 = 795.556
    $\bar{y}$ = (9 +43+16+17+19+13+20+44+35)/9 = 216/9 = 24

Circulation (x)	(x − x̄)	Cost (y)	(y − ȳ)	(x − x̄)(y − ȳ)
135	−660.556	9	−15	9 908.3
2 100	1 304.444	43	19	24 784.4
680	−115.556	16	−8	924.4
470	−325.556	17	−7	2 278.9
450	−345.556	19	−5	1 727.8
105	−690.556	13	−11	7 596.1
275	−520.556	20	−4	2 082.2
2 250	1 454.444	44	20	29 088.9
695	−100.556	35	11	−1 106.1

$\Sigma(x - \bar{x})(y - \bar{y})$ = 77 284.9 to one decimal place

covariance = $\Sigma(x - \bar{x})(y - \bar{y})/(n - 1)$
          = 77 284.9/8 = 9660.6 to one decimal place

$(x - \bar{x})^2$	$(y - \bar{y})^2$
436 334	225
1 701 575	361
13 353	64
105 986	49
119 409	25
476 867	121
270 978	16
2 115 409	400
10 111	121
$\Sigma (x - \bar{x})^2$ = 5 250 022	$\Sigma (y - \bar{y})^2$ = 1382

$S_x = \sqrt{5250022/8} = 810.1$

$S_y = \sqrt{1382/8} = 13.1$ each to one decimal place

$r =$ covariance$/(S_x \times S_y) = 9660.6/(810.1 \times 13.1) = 0.91$

to two decimal places

High positive correlation.

4.3 $r = -0.493$ Modest negative correlation   [4.1, 4.2]

4.4 $r = -0.964$ Very high negative correlation   [4.1, 4.2]

4.5   (a) Turnover

      (c) $r = 0.943$ Very high positive correlation   [4.1, 4.2]

4.6   (b) Score = 16.722 + 0.607 Price   [4.5]

      (d) 41 to the nearest whole number   [4.7]

4.7   (b) Position = 31.264 − 0.381 Goals   [4.5]

      (c) 12th to the nearest whole number   [4.7]

4.8   (b) Time = 1.204 + 4.781 Distance   [4.5]

      (c) 44.233 minutes   [4.7]

4.9   (b) Price = 7.049 − 0.089 Mileage   [4.5]

      (c) 4.8 to 1 decimal place   [4.7]

4.10 (a) 143.9 (1999), 173.9 (2001) to 1 decimal place   [4.9]

      (b) Consumption data

4.11 (a) $\dfrac{(0.76 \times 4100) + (115 \times 4) + (750 \times 1)}{(0.48 \times 4100) + (83 \times 4) + (500 \times 1)} \times 100 = \dfrac{4326}{2800} \times 100$

      = 154.5

      (b) $\dfrac{(0.76 \times 4000) + (115 \times 4) + (750 \times 1)}{(0.48 \times 4000) + (83 \times 4) + (500 \times 1)} \times 100 = \dfrac{4250}{2752} \times 100$

      = 154.4 to one decimal place

      (c) Little change in consumption so historic figures are adequate.

4.12 (a) 109.8 (1999), 118.5 (2000) to one decimal place [4.10]

      (b) 109.8 (1999), 119.6 (2000) to one decimal place [4.11]

      (c) Price of Outer is increasing most, and more of
          it is used in 2000.

4.13 (a) 118.6 (1997), 132.1 (2000) to one decimal place [4.10]

      (b) 117.8 (1997), 127.7 (2000) to one decimal place [4.11]

      (c) More milk solids used in 1997, less cocoa
          butter in 2000

4.14 £7022 (1995), £6933.589 (1996), £6958 (1997),
      £7179.499 (1998), £7436.070 (1999), £7527.668 (2000) [4.12]

4.15 £5280.722 (1992), £4550.451 (1994), £4541.912 (1996)
      £4799.386 (1998), £4442.748 (2000)   [4.12]

4.16 (b) 531 550 553 592 610 631 650   [4.14]

      (c) −303.833 (am), −113.833 (pm), 417.667 (eve)   [4.18]

      (d) 690.996 711.567 732.138   [4.20]

      (e) 387.163 597.734 1149.805   [4.20]

4.17 (b) 14.8 14.6 14.6 15 15.8 16.8 17.4 17.6 18.2 18 18.6 [4.14]

      (c) −11 (Tue), −8.3 (Wed), −5.3 (Thu),
          4.1 (Fri), 20.5 (Sat)   [4.18]

      (d) 20.142 20.598 21.055 21.511 21.967   [4.20]

      (e) 9.142 12.298 15.755 25.611 42.467   [4.20]

4.18

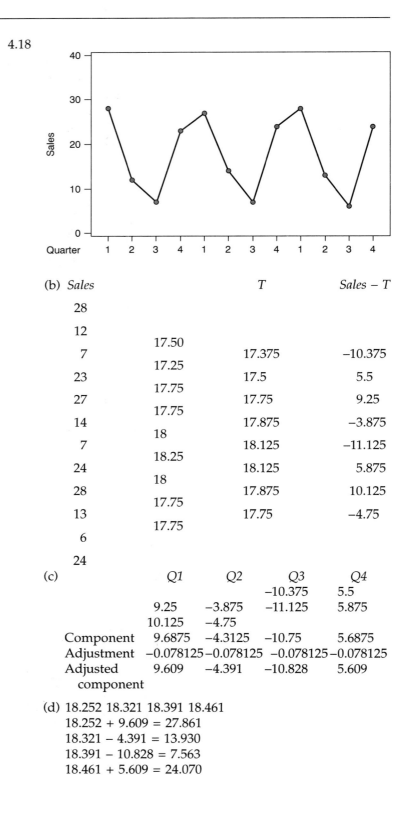

(b)

Sales	T	Sales – T
28		
12		
	17.50	
7		
		17.375	–10.375
	17.25	
23	17.5	5.5
	17.75	
27	17.75	9.25
	17.75	
14	17.875	–3.875
	18	
7	18.125	–11.125
	18.25	
24	18.125	5.875
	18	
28	17.875	10.125
	17.75	
13	17.75	–4.75
	17.75	
6		
24		

(c)

	Q1	Q2	Q3	Q4
			–10.375	5.5
	9.25	–3.875	–11.125	5.875
	10.125	–4.75		
Component	9.6875	–4.3125	–10.75	5.6875
Adjustment	–0.078125	–0.078125	–0.078125	–0.078125
Adjusted component	9.609	–4.391	–10.828	5.609

(d) 18.252 18.321 18.391 18.461
18.252 + 9.609 = 27.861
18.321 – 4.391 = 13.930
18.391 – 10.828 = 7.563
18.461 + 5.609 = 24.070

4.19　(b) 32 33.75 34.875 34.25 34.375 35.25 36.75 38　　[4.16]
　　　(c) −21.906 14.281 25.719 −18.094　　　　　　　　　[4.18]
　　　(d) 17.508 54.388 66.520 23.400　　　　　　　　　　[4.20]

4.20　(a) (viii)　(b) (vi)　(c) (v)　(d) (vii)　(e) (iv)
　　　(f) (i)　(g) (ii) (h)　(iii)

Chapter 5

5.1　(a) 0.427　　　　　　　　　　　　　　　　　　　　　[5.1]
　　　(b) 0.573　　　　　　　　　　　　　　　　　　　　　[5.1]
5.2　(a) 0.915　　　　　　　　　　　　　　　　　　　　　[5.1]
　　　(b) 0.085　　　　　　　　　　　　　　　　　　　　　[5.1]
5.3　(a) 0.054　　　　　　　　　　　　　　　　　　　　　[5.1]
　　　(b) 0.027　　　　　　　　　　　　　　　　　　　　　[5.1]
5.4　(a) total days = 68 + 103 + 145 + 37 + 12 = 365
　　　　2 call-outs on 145 days
　　　　P (2 call-outs) = 145/365 = 0.397
　　　(b) P (2 or fewer) = P (2 or 1 or 0) = P (2) + P (1) + P (0)
　　　　　= 145/365 + 103/365 + 68/365 = 0.866
　　　(c) P (1 or more) = P (1 or 2 or 3 or 4) = P (1) + P (2)
　　　　　+ P (3) + P (4)
　　　　　= 103/365 + 145/365 + 37/365 + 12/365
　　　　　= 0.814
　　　(d) P (less than 4) = P (0 or 1 or 2 or 3) = P (0) + P (1)
　　　　　　　　　　　　　　　　+ P (2) + P (3)
　　　　　　　　　　　　　　= 68/365 + 103/365 + 145/365
　　　　　　　　　　　　　　+ 37/365
　　　　　　　　　　　　　= 0.967
　　　(e) P (more than 2) = P (3 or 4) = P (3) + P (4)
　　　　　　　　　　　　　= 37/365 + 12/365 = 0.134

5.5　(a) 0.313　　　　　　　　　　　　　　　　　　　　　[5.1]
　　　(b) 0.277　　　　　　　　　　　　　　　　　　　　　[5.1]
　　　(c) 0.723　　　　　　　　　　　　　　　　　　　　　[5.5]
5.6　(a) P (more respect) = P (manual and more respect)
　　　　　　　　　　　　　+ P (clerical and more respect)
　　　　　　　　　　　　　+ P (managerial and more respect)
　　　　　　　　　　　　　= 7/120 + 6/120 + 6/120
　　　　　　　　　　　　　= (7 + 6 + 6)/120 = 19/120 = 0.158
　　　(b) P (clerical or better promotion)
　　　　　　= P (clerical) + P (better promotion)
　　　　　　　− P (clerical and better promotion)
　　　　　　= (12 + 19 + 6)/120 + (12 + 12 + 3)/120 − 12/120
　　　　　　= 37/120 + 27/120 − 12/120 = 52/120 = 0.433
　　　(c) P (higher pay/manual)
　　　　　　= P (higher pay and manual)/P (manual)
　　　　　　= 53/120 ÷ (12 + 53 + 7)120 = 53/120 ÷ 72/120
　　　　　　= 53/120 × 120/72 = 53/72 = 0.736
　　　(d) P (more respect and managerial) = 6/120 = 0.05

(e) P (higher pay/managerial)

$\quad = P$ (higher pay and managerial)$/P$ (managerial)

$\quad = 2/120 \div (3 + 2 + 6)/120 = 2/120 \div 11/120$

$\quad = 2/120 \times 120/11 = 2/11 = 0.182$

5.7   (a) 0.129   [5.3]

      (b) 0.1   [5.3]

      (c) 0.686   [5.5]

      (d) 0.181   [5.4]

      (e) 0.190 Higher than (a) so not independent.   [5.6, 5.12]

5.8   (a) 0.216   [5.3]

      (b) 0.256   [5.3]

      (c) 0.464   [5.5]

      (d) 0.572   [5.5]

      (e) 0.1   [5.4]

      (f) 0.116   [5.4]

      (g) 0.093   [5.6]

      (h) 0.481   [5.6]

      (i) 0.256 ≠ 0.481 Class and destination not independent.

           [5.12]

5.9   0.008   [5.11]

5.10 (a) 0.795   [5.11]

      (b) 0.205   [5.10]

      (c) 0.060   [5.11]

5.11 Let D represent Declan succeeds and D' represent Declan fails.

      Let E represent Emily succeeds and E' represent Emily fails.

      Let F represent Farid succeeds and F' represent Farid fails.

      (a) P (D and E and F) $= P$ (D) $\times$ P (E) $\times$ P (F)

                 (independent outcomes)

         P (D) $= 1 - P$ (D') $= 1 - 0.6 = 0.4$

         P (E) $= 1 - P$ (E') $= 1 - 0.75 = 0.25$

         P (F) $= 1 - P$ (F') $= 1 - 0.8 = 0.2$

         P (D and E and F) $= 0.4 \times 0.25 \times 0.2 = 0.02$

      (b) P (two succeed) $= P$ (D and E and F') $+ P$ (D and E' and F) $+ P$ (D' and E and F)

           $= (0.4 \times 0.25 \times 0.8) + (0.4 \times 0.75 \times 0.2) + (0.6 \times 0.25 \times 0.2)$

           $= 0.08 + 0.06 + 0.03 = 0.17$

      (c) P (D' and E' and F') $= P$ (D') and P (E') and P (F') $= 0.6 \times 0.75 \times 0.8 = 0.36$

5.12 (a) 0.042   [5.11]

      (b) 0.167   [5.11]

5.13 (a) 0.074   [5.11]

      (b) 0.601   [5.16]

      (c) 0.681   [5.16]

5.14   (a) 0.333   [5.11]

5.14	(a) 0.333	[5.11]
	(b) 0.333	[5.11]
	(c) 0.333	[5.11]
5.15	(a) 0.857	[5.11]
	(b) 0.064	[5.11]
	(c) 0.422	[5.11]
	(d) 0.189	[5.11]
	(e) 0.2685	[5.11]
5.16	(a) 0.36176	[5.17]
	(b) 0.11424	[5.17]
	(c) 0.43952	[5.17]
	(d) 0.07296	[5.17]
	(e) 0.17568	[5.17]
5.17	(a) 0.050	[5.17]
	(b) 0.265	[5.17]
	(c) 0.686	[5.17]
5.18	0.417	[5.15]
5.19	0.597 Agency should pay 59.7% of costs.	[5.15]
5.20	(a)(ix) (b) (iii) (c) (vi) (d) (viii) (e) (i)	
	(f) (iv) (g) (ii) (h) (x) (i) (vii) (j) (v)	

Chapter 6

6.1   Binomial distribution: $n = 5$, p = 0.4. Use Table 1 on page 332.

(a) P (0 females) = P $(X = 0)$ = 0.078

(b) P (3 females) = P $(X = 3)$ = 0.230

(c) P (3 or fewer females) = P $(X \leq 3)$ = 0.913

(d) P (majority female) = P $(X > 2)$ = $1 - P$ $(X \leq 2)$

$$= 1 - 0.683 = 0.317$$

6.2	(a) 0.107	[6.5]
	(b) 0.879	[6.5]
	(c) 0.624	[6.5]
	(d) 0.967	[6.5]
	(e) 0.006	[6.5]
6.3	(a) 0.590	[6.5]
	(b) 0.991	[6.5]
	(c) 0.081	[6.5]
	(d) 0.009	[6.5]
6.4	(a) 0.028	[6.5]
	(b) 0.121	[6.5]
	(c) 0.650	[6.5]
	(d) 0.150	[6.5]
	(e) 0.047	[6.5]
6.5	(a) 0.349	[6.5]
	(b) 0.170	[6.5]
	(c) 0.001	[6.5]
	(d) 0.736	[6.5]

6.6	(a) 0.328	[6.5]
	(b) 0.672	[6.5]
	(c) 0.006	[6.5]
6.7	(a) 0.368	[6.7]
	(b) 0.184	[6.7]
	(c) 0.996	[6.7]
	(d) 0.019	[6.7]
6.8	(a) 0.050	[6.7]
	(b) 0.149	[6.7]
	(c) 0.423	[6.7]
	(d) 0.185	[6.7]
6.9	(a) 0.135	[6.7]
	(b) 0.406	[6.7]
	(c) 0.018	[6.7]
	(d) 0.908	[6.7]
6.10	(a) 0.050	[6.7]
	(b) 0.224	[6.7]
	(c) 0.647	[6.7]
	(d) 0.950	[6.7]
6.11	(a) 0.368	[6.7]
	(b) 0.920	[6.7]
	(c) 0.264	[6.7]

6.12 P (no side effect) = 0.85,
P (minor side effect) = 0.11,
P (major side effect) = 0.04
Expected value of compensation = $(0.85 \times £0)$
  $+ (0.11 \times £2500) + (0.04 \times £20\,000)$
  $= 0 + £275 + £800 = £1075$

6.13	£30 824	[6.10]
6.14	£415	[6.10]
6.15	Profit of $200 000	[6.10]

6.16 (a)

EMV (Complete deal) = $(0.6 \times £27m) + (0.4 \times £7m)$
  $= £16.2m + £2.8m = £19m$
This is higher than the return from cancelling the deal, £17m, so complete.

(b) EMV (Complete deal) = $(0.4 \times £27m) + (0.6 \times £7m)$
  $= £10.8m + £4.2m = £15m$
This is lower than the return from cancelling the deal, £17m, so cancel.

6.17 EMV (Stay) = £1.26m, EMV (Leave) = £1m so stay. [6.11]

6.18 (a) EMV (Modified crop) = £58 000, EMV (Unmodified crop) = £50 000 Sow modified crop. [6.11]

(b) EMV (Modified crop) = £49 500. Sow unmodified crop. [6.11]

6.19 EMV (Large order) = £1250, EMV (Small order) = £200 [6.11]

6.20 (a) (iii)　(b) (vi)　(c) (iv)　(d) (i)　(e) (ii)　(f) (v)

Chapter 7

7.1 (a) 0.0749 [7.4]
(b) 0.6141 [7.4]
(c) 0.9803 [7.4]
(d) 0.0418 [7.4]
(e) 0.2782 [7.4]
(f) 0.1297 [7.4]
(g) 0.5762 [7.4]

7.2 μ = 70 grams σ = 0.8 grams. Use Table 3 on page 335.

(a) $P(X > 71) = P\left(Z > \dfrac{71 - 70)}{0.8}\right) = P(Z > 1.25) = 0.1056$

(b) $P(X > 68) = P\left(Z > \dfrac{68 - 70)}{0.8}\right) = P(Z > -2.5) = 0.9938$

(c) $P(X < 70) = P\left(Z < \dfrac{70 - 70)}{0.8}\right) = P(Z < 0) = 0.5$

(d) $P(69 < X < 72) = P\left(\dfrac{69 - 70}{0.8} < Z < \dfrac{72 - 70)}{0.8}\right)$

$= P(-1.25 < Z < 2.5)$
$= 0.8944 - 0.0062 = 0.8882$

7.3 (a) 0.2843 [7.4, 7.6]
(b) 0.1949 [7.4, 7.6]
(c) 0.4572 [7.4, 7.6]

7.4 (a) 0.2946 [7.4, 7.6]
(b) 0.0838 [7.4, 7.6]
(c) 0.9931 [7.4, 7.6]
(d) 0.8054 [7.4, 7.6]
(e) 38.152 [7.5, 7.7]
(f) 36.475 [7.5, 7.7]

7.5 (a) 0.1056 [7.4, 7.6]
(b) 0.0018 [7.4, 7.6]
(c) 0.6493 [7.4, 7.6]
(d) 67.048 [7.5, 7.7]
(e) 49.192 [7.5, 7.7]

7.6	(a) 0.0027	[7.4, 7.6]
	(b) 0.8665	[7.4, 7.6]
	(c) 0.7123	[7.4, 7.6]
	(d) 0.0132	[7.4, 7.6]
	(e) 0.2402	[7.4, 7.6]
	(f) 0.4868	[7.4, 7.6]
7.7	(a) 0.4761	[7.4, 7.6]
	(b) 0.8159	[7.4, 7.6]
	(c) 0.9761	[7.4, 7.6]
	(d) 0.0307	[7.4, 7.6]
	(e) 0.8388	[7.4, 7.6]
	(f) 23.4	[7.5, 7.7]
	(g) 27.404	[7.5, 7.7]
7.8	(a) 0.9015	[7.4, 7.6]
	(b) 0.0495	[7.4, 7.6]
	(c) 0.3067	[7.4, 7.6]
	(d) 0.3108	[7.4, 7.6]
	(e) 0.6165	[7.4, 7.6]
7.9	(a) 0.4013	[7.4, 7.6]
	(b) 0.9664	[7.4, 7.6]
	(c) 0.0778	[7.4, 7.6]
	(d) 0.9726	[7.4, 7.6]
	(e) 0.7091	[7.4, 7.6]
	(f) 147.732	[7.5, 7.7]
	(g) 150.504	[7.5, 7.7]
7.10	(a) 0.1131	[7.4, 7.6]
	(b) 0.3446	[7.4, 7.6]
	(c) 0.9783	[7.4, 7.6]
	(d) 0.2555	[7.4, 7.6]
	(e) 0.2991	[7.4, 7.6]
	(f) 0.4479	[7.4, 7.6]

7.11 $\mu = 23450$ miles, $\sigma = 1260$ miles, $n = 4$.
Use Table 3 on page 335.

(a) $P(\overline{X} > 25\,000) = P\left(Z > \dfrac{25\,000 - 23\,450)}{1260/\sqrt{4}}\right.$

$$= P\left(Z > \dfrac{1550)}{630}\right.$$

$$= P(Z > 2.46) = 0.0069$$

(b) $P(\overline{X} > 22\,000) = P\left(Z > \dfrac{22\,000 - 23\,450)}{1260/\sqrt{4}}\right.$

$$= P\left(Z > \dfrac{-1450)}{630}\right.$$

$$= P(Z > -2.30) = 0.9893$$

(c) $P\,(\overline{X} < 24\,000) = P\,(Z < \dfrac{24\,000 - 23\,450)}{1260/\sqrt{4}}$

$= P\,(Z < \dfrac{550)}{630}$

$= P\,(Z < 0.87) = 1 - P\,(Z > 0.87)$
$= 1 - 0.1922 = 0.8078$

(d) $P\,(\overline{X} < 23\,000) = P\,(Z < \dfrac{23\,000 - 23\,450)}{1260/\sqrt{4}}$

$= P\,(Z < \dfrac{-450)}{630}$

$= P\,(Z < -0.71) = 1 - P\,(Z > -0.71)$
$= 1 - 0.7611 = 0.2389$

(e) $P\,(22\,500 < \overline{X} < 24\,500)$

$= P\left(\dfrac{22\,500 - 23\,450}{1260/\sqrt{4}} < Z < \dfrac{24\,500 - 23\,450}{1260/\sqrt{4})}\right)$

$= P\left(\dfrac{-950}{630} < Z < \dfrac{1050}{630}\right) = P\,(-1.51 < Z < 1.67)$

$P\,(Z > -1.51) = 0.9345$
$P\,(Z > 1.67) = 0.0475$
$P\,(-1.51 < Z < 1.67) = 0.9345 - 0.0475 = 0.8870$

(f) $P\,(23\,400 < \overline{X} < 24\,200)$

$= P\left(\dfrac{23\,400 - 23\,450}{1260/\sqrt{4}} < Z < \dfrac{24\,200 - 23\,450}{1260/\sqrt{4})}\right)$

$= P\left(\dfrac{-50}{630} < Z < \dfrac{750}{630}\right) = P\,(-0.08 < Z < 1.19)$

$P\,(Z > -0.08) = 0.5319$
$P\,(Z > 1.19) = 0.1170$
$P\,(-0.08 < Z < 1.19) = 0.5319 - 0.1170 = 0.4149$

7.12	(a)	0.1515	[7.8]
	(b)	0.7549	[7.8]
	(c)	0.9970	[7.8]
	(d)	0.0080	[7.8]
	(e)	0.5069	[7.8]
	(f)	0.4031	[7.8]
7.13	(a)	0.7673	[7.8]
	(b)	0.0630	[7.8]
	(c)	0.0455	[7.8]
	(d)	0.6576	[7.8]
	(e)	0.1867	[7.8]
7.14	(a)	0.1251	[7.8]
	(b)	0.0104	[7.8]

7.15   0.1469   [7.8]

7.16   (a) 0.1841   [7.9]
       (b) 0.8159   [7.9]
       (c) 0.0034   [7.9]
       (d) 0.5   [7.9]
       (e) 0.2913   [7.9]
       (f) 0.2395   [7.9]
       (g) 0.9097   [7.9]

7.17   (a) 0.9960   [7.10]
       (b) 0.0384   [7.10]
       (c) 0.8106   [7.10]
       (d) 0.1894   [7.10]
       (e) 0.9576   [7.10]

7.18 $\mu = 101.4$ grams, $s = 3.1$ grams, $n = 4$, $v = 3$.
       Use Table 4 on page 336.
       (a) $t_{0.10,3} = 1.638$

$$\text{heaviest 10\% will weigh} > 101.4 + \left(1.638 \times \frac{3.1}{\sqrt{4}}\right)$$

$$= 101.4 + (1.638 \times 1.55)$$
$$= 101.4 + 2.539 = 103.939$$

       (b) $t_{0.05,3} = 2.353$

$$\text{heaviest 5\% will weigh} > 101.4 + \left(2.353 \times \frac{3.1}{\sqrt{4}}\right)$$

$$= 101.4 + (2.353 \times 1.55)$$
$$= 101.4 + 3.647 = 105.047$$

       (c) $t_{0.01,3} = 4.541$

$$\text{heaviest 1\% will weigh} > 101.4 + \left(4.541 \times \frac{3.1}{\sqrt{4}}\right)$$

$$= 101.4 + (4.541 \times 1.55)$$
$$= 101.4 + 7.039 = 108.439$$

7.19   (a) 14.885   [7.12]
       (b) 15.116   [7.12]
       (c) 14.643   [7.12]

7.20   (a) (iv)   (b) (vii)   (c) (vi)   (d) (i)   (e) (viii)
       (f) (v)   (g) (ii)   (h) (iii)

Chapter 8

8.1 $\sigma = 0.8$, $\overline{X} = 24.7$, $n = 33$
       (a) $\alpha = 5\%$, $z_{\alpha/2} = z_{0.025} = 1.96$

$$95\% \text{ CI} = 24.7 \pm 1.96 \times \frac{0.8}{\sqrt{33}} = 24.7 \pm 1.96 \times 0.139$$

$$= 24.7 \pm 0.273$$
$$= 24.427 \text{ to } 24.973 \text{ grams}$$

       (b) $\alpha = 1\%$, $z_{\alpha/2} = z_{0.005} = 2.58$

$$99\% \text{ CI} = 24.7 \pm 2.58 \times \frac{0.8}{\sqrt{33}} = 24.7 \pm 2.58 \times 0.139$$

$$= 24.7 \pm 0.359$$
$$= 24.341 \text{ to } 25.059 \text{ grams}$$

8.2   (a) 228.674 minutes to 233.326 minutes   [8.2]
     (b) 227.357 minutes to 234.643 minutes   [8.3]

8.3   (a) 22.644 miles to 25.556 miles   [8.2]
     (b) 153   [8.5]

8.4   (a) £387.567 to £418.433   [8.2]
     (b) 95   [8.5]

8.5   (a) 0.999 lb to 1.121 lb   [8.2]
     (b) 0.975 lb to 1.145 lb   [8.3]

8.6   (a) 20.712 kg to 46.954 kg   [8.7]
     (b) No. Confidence interval includes 40 kg.

8.7   (a) $p = 175/281 = 0.623$ $\alpha = 5\%$ $z_{\alpha/2} = z_{0.025} = 1.96$

$$95\% \text{ CI} = 0.623 \pm 1.96 \times \sqrt{\frac{0.623 \times (1 - 0.623)}{281}}$$

$$= 0.623 \pm 1.96 \times \sqrt{\frac{0.235}{281}}$$

$$= 0.623 \pm 1.96 \times 0.029$$
$$= 0.623 \pm 0.057$$
$$= 0.566 \text{ to } 0.680 \quad 56.6\% \text{ to } 68.0\%$$

     (b) $p = 65/138 = 0.471$ $\alpha = 5\%$ $z_{\alpha/2} = z_{0.025} = 1.96$

$$95\% \text{ CI} = 0.471 \pm 1.96 \times \sqrt{\frac{0.471 \times (1 - 0.471)}{138}}$$

$$= 0.471 \pm 1.96 \times \sqrt{\frac{0.249}{138}} = 0.471 \pm 1.96 \times 0.0425$$

$$= 0.471 \pm 0.083 = 0.388 \text{ to } 0.554 \quad 38.8\% \text{ to } 55.4\%$$

     (c) UK proportion significantly higher.

8.8   (a) 0.694 to 0.828   [8.8]
     (b) 0.779 to 0.893   [8.8]
     (c) Some overlap. Business students seem more
        appreciative.

8.9   2401   [8.9]

8.10 $\sigma = 1.3$, $\bar{x} = 12.9$, $n = 40$
     $H_0: \mu = 12$ $H_1: \mu \neq 12$ $\alpha = 5$ per cent   two-sided test

$$\text{Test statistic} = \frac{12.9 - 12}{1.3/\sqrt{40}} = \frac{0.9}{0.2055}$$
$$= 4.379$$

     Critical values $= \pm z_{0.025} = \pm 1.96$
     Reject H_0 because the test statistic, 4.379, > 1.96

8.11 Test statistic $= -1.669$. Reject H_0 at the 5% level.
                                [8.12, 8.14]

8.12 Test statistic $= 4.393$. Reject H_0 at the 1% level.   [8.16]

8.13 (a) Test statistic $= -1.052$. Can't reject H_0 at the 5% level.
                                    [8.17]
     (b) Lifetimes of air fresheners are Normally distributed.

8.14 (a) Test statistic = −0.696. Can't reject H_0 at the 10% level. [8.16]
(b) Test statistic = −1.625. Can't reject H_0 at the 10% level. [8.17]

Assume number of hits is Normally distributed

8.15 (a) Test statistic = 5.144. Reject H_0 at the 5% level. [8.16]
(b) Test statistic = 3.290. Reject H_0 at the 5% level. [8.17]
(c) Journey times are Normally distributed.

8.16 Test statistic = −4.384. Reject H_0 at the 1% level. [8.18]
8.17 Test statistic = −2.130. Reject H_0 at the 5% level. [8.19]
8.18 Test statistic = −4.134. Reject H_0 at the 1% level. [8.20]
8.19 Test statistic = −1.793. Reject H_0 at the 10% level. [8.21]
8.20 Test statistic = −1.044. Can't reject H_0 at the 5% level. [8.21]

8.21 $6 + s$ and $4 − s$. Can't reject H_0 at the 5% level. [8.22]
8.22 (a) (v) (b) (vi) (c) (vii) (d) (i) (e) (iv)
(f) (iii) (g) (viii) (h) (ii)

Chapter 9

9.1 (a) Test statistic = 6.189. Reject H_0 at the 5% level. [9.1–9.5]
(b) Can't reject H_0 at the 1% level. [9.1–9.5]

9.2 H_0: No association H_1: Association
Expected frequencies:

$$\frac{78 \times 40}{150} = 20.8 \qquad \frac{78 \times 70}{150} = 36.4 \qquad \frac{78 \times 40}{150} = 20.8$$

$$\frac{72 \times 40}{150} = 19.2 \qquad \frac{72 \times 70}{150} = 33.6 \qquad \frac{72 \times 40}{150} = 19.2$$

$$\text{Test statistic} = \frac{(14 − 20.8)^2}{20.8} + \frac{(33 − 36.4)^2}{36.4} + \frac{(31 − 20.8)^2}{20.8}$$

$$+ \frac{(26 − 19.2)^2}{19.2} + \frac{(37 − 33.6)^2}{33.6} + \frac{(9 − 19.2)^2}{19.2}$$

$$= 2.223 + 0.318 + 5.002$$
$$+ 2.408 + 0.344 + 5.419 = 15.714$$

Degrees of freedom, $\nu = (2 − 1) \times (3 − 1) = 2$ $\alpha = 0.01$
Critical value, $\chi^2_{0.01,2} = 9.210$
Test statistic > critical value, so reject H_0.

9.3 Test statistic = 4.335. Can't reject H_0 at the 5% level. [9.5]
9.4 Test statistic = 5.680. Can't reject H_0 at the 5% level. [9.5]
9.5 Test statistic = 0.871. Can't reject H_0 at the 10% level. [9.5]
9.6 (a) Test statistic = 6.979. Reject H_0 at the 10% level. [9.5]
(b) Can't reject H_0 at the 5% level. [9.5]

9.7 (a) Test statistic = 51.769. Reject H_0 at the 1% level. [9.5]
   (b) Large components for Single/Dog, Single/Cat, and Family/Cat

9.8 Test statistic = 3.690. Can't reject H_0 at the 10% level. [9.5]
   Largest components are Midlands/Cricket and Midlands/Football.

9.9 Test statistic = 74.895. Reject H_0 at the 1% level. [9.5]
   Largest components are Retirees/Never and Retirees/Sometimes.

9.10 $H_0: \rho = 0$ $H_1: \rho > 0$ $\alpha = 0.05$ one-sided test
   $r = 0.683$ $n = 28$ degrees of freedom, $\nu = n - 2 = 26$

$$\text{Test statistic } = \frac{0.683 \times \sqrt{28 - 2}}{\sqrt{1 - 0.683^2}} = \frac{0.683 \times \sqrt{26}}{\sqrt{0.534}}$$

$$= \frac{0.683 \times 5.099}{0.7304} = 4.768$$

Critical value, $t_{-0.05,26} = 1.706$
Reject H_0 because the test statistic, 4.768, > 1.706

9.11 Test statistic = 2.318. Reject H_0 at the 5% level. [9.6]
9.12 Test statistic = −2.878. Reject H_0 at the 1% level. [9.6]
9.13 The regression equation is
   Audience = −1018 + 0.487 Cards
   $H_0: \beta = 0$ Alternative hypothesis, $H_1: \beta \neq 0$

Cards (x)	Audience (y)	Residuals	Squared residuals
3750	925	114.544	13120
4100	1000	18.924	358
4500	1150	−26.070	680
4750	1200	−97.941	9593
4800	1100	−222.316	49424
5250	1680	138.316	19131
4600	1480	255.181	65118
4800	1370	47.684	2274
4320	860	−228.323	52131
			211829

Standard deviation of the residuals, $s = \sqrt{211829/7}$
$= 173.958$

(a)

Cards (x)	$\bar{x}$	$(x - \bar{x})$	$(x - \bar{x})^2$
3750	4541.1	−791.1	625839
4100	4541.1	−441.1	194569
4500	4541.1	−41.1	1689
4750	4541.1	208.9	43639
4800	4541.1	258.9	67029
5250	4541.1	708.9	502539
4800	4541.1	258.9	67029
4320	4541.1	−221.1	48885
			1554689

$$\text{Estimated standard error, } s_b = \sqrt{173.958^2/1554689}$$

$$= 0.140$$

$$\text{Test statistic, } t = \frac{0.487 - 0}{0.140} = 3.479$$

This is higher than $t_{0.025,\,7}$, 2.365, so reject H_0.

(b) $\hat{y} = -1018 + 0.487\,(4400) = 1124.8$

$$95\% \text{ CI} = 1124.8 \pm 2.365 \times 173.958$$
$$\times \sqrt{[1/9 + (4400 - 4541.111)^2/1554689]}$$
$$= 1124.8 \pm 2.365 \times 173.958 \times \sqrt{[1/9 + (0.0128)]}$$
$$= 1124.8 \pm 2.365 \times 173.958 \times \sqrt{0.124}$$
$$= 1124.8 \pm 2.365 \times 173.958 \times 0.352$$
$$= 1124.8 \pm 2.365 \times 61.237$$
$$= 1124.8 \pm 144.825 = 979.975 \text{ to } 1269.625$$

9.14 (a) Test statistic = 15.005. Reject H_0 at the 5% level.   [9.7]
    (b) 34.55 to 46.03 to two decimal places.   [9.9]

9.15 (a) Test statistic = 4.929. Reject H_0 at the 5% level.   [9.7]
    (b) 339.1 to 545.2 to one decimal place.   [9.9]
    (c) 138.6 to 745.7 to one decimal place.   [9.11]

9.16 (a) Test statistic = −5.136. Reject H_0 at the 5% level.   [9.7]
    (b) 75.0 to 151.0 to one decimal place.   [9.9]
    (c) −0.8 to 226.8 to one decimal place.   [9.11]

9.17 (a) Test statistic = −8.198. Reject H_0 at the 1% level.   [9.7]
    (b) 32.73 to 40.14 to two decimal places.   [9.9]
    (c) 25.13 to 47.74 to two decimal places.   [9.11]

9.18 (a) Test statistic = 9.141. Reject H_0 at the 10% level.   [9.7]
    (b) £656.4 to £863.0 to one decimal place.   [9.9]
    (c) £2308.0 to £3080.4 to one decimal place.   [9.10]
    (d) 75 is beyond the range of the data.
       Answer (c) not valid.

9.19 (a) Test statistic = −8.040. Reject H_0 at the 1% level.   [9.7]
    (b) (i)   7.301 to 14.492   [9.9]
        (ii) −24.290 to −0.401
    Unreliable − 2.75 beyond the data range.   [9.10]

9.20 (a) (v)   (b) (vii)   (c) (viii)   (d) (i)   (e) (iv)   (f) (iii)
    (g) (ii)   (h) (vi)

REFERENCES

Bates, D. M. and Watts, D. G. 1988. *Nonlinear Regression Analysis and its Applications*. New York: Wiley.

Chatfield, C. 1996. *The Analysis of Time Series* (5th edn). London: Chapman and Hall.

Converse, J. M. and Presser, S. 1986. *Survey Questions: Handcrafting the Standardised Questionnaire*. London: Sage.

Cryer, J. D. 1986. *Time Series Analysis*. Boston: Duxbury Press.

Dielman, T. E. 1996. *Applied Regression Analysis for Business and Economics* (2nd edn). Belmont, California: Duxbury Press.

Draper, N. R. and Smith, H. 1998. *Applied Regression Analysis* (3rd edn). New York: Wiley.

Hague, P. N. 1993. *Questionnaire Design*. London: Kogan Page.

Mendenhall, W. and Sincich, T. 1988. *A Second Course in Business Statistics: Regression Analysis* (3rd edn). San Francisco: Dellen.

Montgomery, D. C. 2000. *Introduction to Statistical Quality Control* (4th edn). Chichester: Wiley.

Oppenheim, A. N. 1997. *Questionnaire Design and Attitude Measurement* (2nd edn). London: Heinemann.

Seber, G. A. F. and Wild, C. J. 1989. *Nonlinear Regression*. New York: Wiley.

Sprent, P. 1989. *Applied Nonparametric Statistical Methods*. London: Chapman and Hall.

Tukey, J. W. 1977. *Exploratory Data Analysis*. London: Addison-Wesley.

Velleman, P. F. and Hoaglin, D. C. 1981. *Applications, Basics and Computing of Exploratory Data Analysis*. Boston: Duxbury Press.

Index